Ending the Era

of

Ideology

Spiritualizing the World, vol 13

Ending the Era

of

Ideology

KIM MICHAELS

MORE TO LIFE PUBLISHING

www.morepublish.com

For foreign and translation rights,

contact: info@ morepublish.com

ISBN: 978-87-93297-82-1

Cover art by Sandra Singer

For more information: *www.ascendedmasterlight.com and*
www.transcendencetoolbox.com

Content

INTRODUCTION

This book belongs to the series *Spiritualizing the World*. The books in this series are given by the ascended masters as workbooks that provide the knowledge and practical tools we need in order to make a contribution to solving concrete world problems. This book contains the knowledge and the tools we need in order to end the era where ideology and various power elite groups have such a dominant influence on earth. These books do not contain foundational knowledge about ascended masters and their teachings. In order to make the most efficient use of this book, you need to have a general knowledge of the following topics:

- You need to know who the ascended masters are, how they give their teachings and how you can make the best use of them on a personal and planetary level. You can find extensive teachings on this in the books: *How You Can Help Change the World* and *The Power of Self*.

- You need to know how the earth functions as a cosmic schoolroom. You need to know your own role and the authority you have as a spiritual being in embodiment. You need to know the role of the ascended masters and how only we who are in embodiment can give them the authority to use their unlimited power to affect change on earth. You can find more on these topics in the first book in this series: *How You Can Help Change the World.*

- You need to know how to use the practical tools given by the ascended masters. You can find more on this topic in: *How You Can Help Change the World* and on the website: *www.transcendencetoolbox.com.*

- You need to know about the existence and methods of the dark forces who are ultimately responsible for creating problems on earth. You can find foundational teachings on this in: *Cosmology of Evil.*

How to use this book

There is no one way of using the teachings and tools in this book. However, if you want to make a significant contribution to solving world problems, it is suggested that you start by following this program:

- You read one of the chapters in the book completely in order to increase your understanding of the topic.

- You give the invocation associated with that chapter once a day for nine days while studying the same chapter again.

The reasoning behind this program is that the chapters in the book form a progression. As you give an invocation for one chapter, you are also clearing your own consciousness from certain energies and illusions. This makes it easier for you to absorb and apply the teachings from the next chapter.

You can of course also read the book all the way through and then select one or more invocation(s) that you give several times. It is always more powerful to give an invocation once a day for nine or 33 days.

Because some of the invocations in this book are quite long, they have been divided into two or more parts. It takes about 15-20 minutes to give each part. If you prefer, you can give all of the parts for one invocation in succession. In that case, you do not need to give the sealing after the first invocation or the preamble to the next. You give a preamble in the beginning, continue through the parts and give a sealing in the end.

1 IDEOLOGY AND THE RATIONAL MIND

I AM the Ascended Master Gautama Buddha. I know that traditionally I am the one who gives the last dictation at these events. There is of course no natural or cosmic law that says I cannot give the first dictation.

I want you to realize that the reason we can give this conference on *Ending the Era of Ideology* is because so many of you have been willing to set the groundwork by participating in our previous conferences on *Dictatorships*, *Fanaticism* and *Elitism*. Also, so many of you have used the books and the invocations that have been created based on these previous conferences. By making the calls you have set the stage whereby there is now an opening in the collective consciousness, so that the more creative people (the more constructive people, the ones in the top 10%) are now more open to this underlying topic of ideology.

Ideology is connected to dictatorships, fanaticism and elitism

Naturally, there is a connection between ideology and dictatorships, fanaticism and elitism. There will be some overlap between what we have said before and what we will say now, so that we can complete this very intricate, very complex and very subtle picture of how the fallen beings have used all means available to them to manipulate the people on earth.

Truly, we might say that behind most dictatorships there is some form of ideology. As we have said before, a dictator cannot suppress an entire population through physical means alone. There must be some psychological component, some belief that causes people to submit to the dictator. Likewise, what is it that causes fanaticism? It is in most cases some form of idea, some form of ideology. Of course, what is it that allows an elite to exist and to either control the population in an obvious way, or to control them in a subtle, hidden way? It is again some form of ideology, some form of thought system, some form of belief system.

Now, what then is ideology? Well, the broadest use of the word ideology of course means the study of ideas. However, most people, when they hear the word "ideology," they think about specific ideologies, specific thought systems, specific belief systems.

There has for quite some time (several centuries in the western world) been a certain debate among philosophers and thinkers about what ideology is and what it means. There is a certain irony here in the sense that when many people hear the word ideology, the first ideology that comes to mind is communism or Marxism. This is ironic because Karl Marx himself used the word ideology in a derogatory way to refer to a set of ideas that the ruling class used to suppress the masses. The irony of course being that his ideas, the ideas that he brought forth, were very quickly turned into an ideology where the ruling class of the party elite used the ideas of Karl Marx to suppress the population. He might, in his outer mind, have believed that these ideas were given to liberate the population from an elite, but they of course were very quickly used by a new elite, an aspiring power elite, to control the population even more strictly than previous power elites had done.

You see here that in many cases there is a benevolent intent behind creating an ideology, or even spreading an ideology. It is clear that many of the people who have brought forth a new ideology and many of the people who have believed in it and promoted it, they have not been fallen beings. They have not had an evil, selfish or self-centered intent of controlling, dominating, suppressing or even destroying other people. Nevertheless, you will see from history that in many cases, regardless of the good intentions, ideologies have been used to suppress and control people.

The five elements of an ideology

Now, if you look at various definitions of ideology, you can find some that say that there are five elements to an ideology:

- The first element is a theory or system that seeks to explain certain things about how life works.

- The second element is that there is a program of social change or political change that needs to happen.

- The third element is that the fulfillment of this program is portrayed as a struggle.

- The fourth element is that there is a call for people who have commitment to the cause, to join this cause and to support the cause.

- Then finally, there is an appeal, a broad appeal, to the general population but there is also a portrayal that there is a certain group of people who are the only ones who can really implement the program. This can often be intellectuals, but it can be other types of elites.

Now, I would like to comment here on the first of these elements. There is a theory that seeks to explain something. What is it that it seeks to explain? What is it on earth that needs to be explained? You may look at various ideologies and you might say that Christianity can be considered an ideology because it did, and does, seek to explain how life works, how life was created. You may look at Marxism and say that it also seeks to explain how life works, at least life on earth. There is a certain distinction made by many philosophers between ideologies that are strictly materialistic or political, and that deal only with how the physical, material life works. Then, there are ideologies that have a religious element, and that also seek to explain what is beyond the material world and how the material world was created. Nevertheless, both of these have an element in common that they seek to explain, they seek to explain how something works that relates to people's lives.

Ideologies seek to explain the cause of dissatisfaction

You may say that many of these ideologies take different approaches, they focus on different things, different elements. Karl Marx focused on the class struggle, Christianity focuses on God and how God created the universe. Regardless of this, there is an attempt to explain something about people's everyday lives. What is that something? Well, one way to explain it is to reach back to the teaching I gave 2,500 years ago about the Four Noble Truths.

What is the first Noble Truth? Well, it is normally translated as "life is suffering." The original word that was used was actually "duhkha." Duhkha can be translated as suffering but it actually has a much broader meaning. If you take it to the broadest meaning and translate that into a modern English word, you can say that life is "dissatisfaction." Life is not satisfying.

You can look at the vast majority of people on earth and you will see that they are not satisfied with their lives. There is something in their lives that causes a certain dissatisfaction. They are not at peace. They feel perhaps that something is missing. They feel perhaps that something is wrong, something is preventing them from living the life they would like to live, something is obstructing them, something is restricting them and perhaps even controlling and suppressing them. Really, the most broad, the most basic, element that any ideology seeks to explain is why life is dissatisfaction, why the vast majority of people are dissatisfied. This is what an ideology addresses and attempts to explain.

The claim to have absolute authority

Now, this means we can look at how this is explained. I would like to start by going to a more universal, a more broad, consideration. What does it actually mean when something is being attempted to be explained? What is an explanation? Where does it come from? What is the aim of an explanation? Here is the crucial distinction. The simple fact of life on earth is that an explanation will do no good if a majority of the population cannot grasp it. In other words, if you bring forth an ideology with the intention to create change in society, then you need an explanation that most people can grasp in their present state of consciousness. This of course – right there – is the crux of the matter, as they say. This is the real turning point, the real key understanding when it comes to ideology.

There are many of the thought systems you see on earth that will claim that their explanation has a supernatural origin. Most religions claim this. Some philosophers even claim the same. It may not necessarily be a revelation directly from God as some religions claim. It can also be that there is, as some philosophers claim, some universal principles or natural laws that their explanation is based on. These are invariable. Whether they were created by God or whether they just arose spontaneously when the universe arose (however that is explained to have happened), there is this claim that there is some infallible authority behind the explanation given by this particular ideology. This is the first thing that people need to begin to question.

Naturally, you could say that this sounds like a contradiction because I am claiming to be an ascended master speaking through a human messenger. I am claiming that I am a spiritual being living in a higher energetic realm than the material world on earth. I am claiming that I have risen beyond all human ego, all human subjectivity and idiosyncrasy, and therefore I have a distinctly higher grasp of how the world works than human beings on earth. I am claiming that I am speaking these words through a human messenger and therefore it would seem that I am claiming that these words have absolute authority. As we have attempted to explain through this messenger (which is the first time we have been able to do this through any messenger) over the last couple of years, this is not the case. We are not attempting to set forth an absolute teaching that can never change.

We are in a state of consciousness that is beyond the state of consciousness of anyone in embodiment. We are able to speak fairly directly through this messenger because his consciousness does not color or obstruct our message, or at least it does so very little. Nevertheless, we are not able to say absolutely anything we want because what is our purpose for speaking? It is to reach out to at least the most constructive, the most creative, the most self-aware people and give them something that they can grasp at their present level of consciousness.

The purpose of progressive revelation

If we were to give a message that no one in embodiment could grasp, what would be the point of giving the message? There would be no point, would there? We are not seeking to bring forth a teaching (as indeed some false hierarchy imposters do through various channelers) that basically nobody can understand. We are not seeking to project that even though people cannot understand the message, those who at least are willing to study it and follow it are clearly more advanced than those who are not. This is not our goal. This is not our aim. We have, for a very long time now, been trying to discourage this form of spiritual pride in our students, which we have seen in many spiritual movements, past and present.

What we do is a very carefully calculated release based on our studies of the collective consciousness, our studies of the individual consciousness of most of the people who are the more creative, the more open-minded people. Then, we release something that is measured for this particular level of consciousness, this particular configuration that is there right now. Our aim is to raise that consciousness up so that we can in the future release a higher teaching. As you see, this teaching on ideology is a higher teaching than the teachings on dictatorships, fanaticism and elitism.

This is the entire idea behind progressive revelation. When you understand this, you can of course look back at previous times. You can look back for example at the Christian claim that the Bible, the *New Testament*, is some ultimate, absolute revelation from God, the "Word of God." You can see that even if the *New Testament* had been directly dictated by Jesus or another ascended being, which of course it was not, then it would still not be the ultimate revelation because it could only have been given based on the level of the collective consciousness at the time and the level of the consciousness of those who were able to receive something about Jesus and his teachings.

You can go back 2,500 years to the time of the Buddha, and there are many Buddhists who believe that what I gave was the ultimate spiritual teaching that could ever be given on this planet. This of course is not the case. I gave a teaching based on not only the collective consciousness of the planet, but the collective consciousness in the area where I was in physical embodiment. It was based on how many people there were that were ahead of the collective consciousness and therefore able to grasp a teaching that could stand for a long time.

Now, you understand that when we give a teaching at a certain time, we give that teaching for the most evolved people of that time. Of course, that means that there are many, many people (the vast majority of people at a lower level of consciousness) that cannot grasp the teaching at the time. As time moves on, more and more people will be able to grasp it. A teaching that was given 2,500 years ago or 2,000 years ago has not become obsolete because there are still people who need that teaching. This is why you see there are still people who follow the Buddhist teaching and the Christian teaching and other teachings. They are at the level of consciousness where they need it.

There is of course always the danger that a teaching given can be interpreted in various ways and therefore take on an entire culture that is beyond what was originally given. This is not progressive revelation and therefore is in fact a dead end that can keep people trapped for a longer period of time than is desirable, but that is another matter. The reality here is that there never has been, there is not now and there never will be any ideology, any system of thought and belief that would be an ultimate truth, an ultimate form of revelation.

The false claim of ideologies

This means that an ideology that claims to have some ultimate truth or some ultimate authority, that particular claim is false. It may be that the ideology has certain ideas that have a specific validity, in the sense that they address certain issues, they provide a certain understanding of those issues and they might even point to a way to improve society. It is not that I am saying here that if an ideology makes the claim that it has an absolute authority, that means the ideology is completely false and all of its ideas are completely false. But that particular claim, to have the absolute truth, the absolute understanding, is false. It always has been, it always will be.

Of course, you as ascended master students who have followed our teachings can understand why. You understand that there are 144 levels of consciousness, you understand that it is possible for people to gradually rise from lower levels to higher levels of consciousness. You understand, if you have grasped the truth behind our teaching, that there are certain levels of consciousness. There is a distinction made between below the 48th level of consciousness and between the 48th and the 96th level of consciousness and above the 96th level of consciousness. You understand that when you are below the 48th level of consciousness, there are certain ideas, a certain understanding, that you simply cannot grasp.

Then, as you rise above the 48th level, you begin to see beyond this veil, this energy veil, this evil. You begin to see beyond duality, see the shortcomings of duality. Finally, as you go beyond the 96th level, you then become truly able to see the dualistic lies, see the lies that spring from the mind of anti-christ and begin to free yourself from them so that you are no longer fooled by even the most subtle lies.

The important distinction here is that when you are below the 48th level of consciousness there are certain ideas you simply cannot grasp. We might say that when you look at our situation as ascended masters today, we recognize that when we have a sponsored messenger who has a mantle as messenger, there is no point in using that messenger to seek to address people who are below the 48th level of consciousness. There is very little we can give through a sponsored messenger for those people. We can, as we have done, seek to give certain teachings that help them anchor themselves on the path that leads from the 48th to the 96th level. Then of course we have given many teachings (*The Course in Self-Mastery* and others) to help people systematically walk that path from the 48th to the 96th level and then of course go beyond.

We have attempted to reach those who are closer to the 48th level and help them realize that there is a path that you can follow to higher levels of consciousness, but there are many teachings that we know these people cannot grasp. There are for that matter also teachings that we know that people who are walking the path between the 48th and 96th level cannot grasp. Many of the teachings on non-duality, these people are not able to grasp, at least until they come closer to the 96th level.

When you are looking at the equation that we are applying, when we consider what teachings to give on the topic of ideology, we are realizing here that we have a messenger who is capable of taking dictations for the levels of consciousness beyond the 96th level. We have a certain critical mass of students who are able to grasp these teachings. There is a certain amount of people in the world who, even though they have not heard of our teachings or this messenger, are able to grasp at least some of these ideas.

That is why we have set a certain level where we are giving these teachings for the higher levels of consciousness closer to the 96th level and beyond the 96th level. This is simply necessary in order for us to give what the planet is ready to receive at this moment, at this critical juncture in time where we are beginning to move into the golden age and where many people are beginning to see some of the shortcomings of the duality consciousness, even though they do not know that terminology.

How the rational mind influences ideologies

Based on this long explanation, I now want to look at again the topic of what is it people seek to explain? Well, there is often the claim as I said to some absolute authority, some absolute truth, but this we have dismissed. Now we come to an even more subtle point, and that is: How are people seeking to explain something? I have said that even we of the ascended masters—there is a certain limitation to what we can bring forth because it has to be something that people can grasp. Of course there are many ideologies that do not originate from the spiritual realm. Some originate from the identity realm, some from the mental realm and a few even from the emotional realm. Most of them actually originate from the mental realm.

You may say that there is a certain amount of ideologies, of philosophies, even spiritual teachings that do not originate from the human level, from the minds of human beings in embodiment. It is not so that a human being sat down and came up with all of these ideas based on his or her outer mind. There are of course many philosophers who have been able to tune in to the beings, the non-material beings, who exist in the mental realm. A few can even reach the lower identity realm. These philosophers, spiritual teachers, prophets, or whatever you call them, have received a teaching that came from a higher level than the material realm.

This is in a way ironic because some of these philosophies claim that there is nothing beyond the material realm, even though they were actually given by beings that are beyond the material realm. Of course, it is not understood where the teaching comes from. Many of these philosophers have been aware that they have a certain inspiration from above, but some of them have not been aware of this. Karl Marx was inspired by certain beings in the mental realm. He was not consciously aware of this but actually thought that he was so brilliant, so intelligent, that he came up with these ideas on his own. The same of course holds true for many other philosophers.

What have these philosophers used to come up with their ideas? Well, the vast majority of them have been inspired, but they have believed themselves that they have used their rational minds. Of course, some of the beings in the mental realm (who are inspiring these philosophers or spiritual leaders) they are also believing that they are using their rational minds. What we arrive at here is the realization that behind most of the ideologies found on earth, the rational mind is a very big factor. Even ascended master teachings, we take into consideration the rational mind. What can people grasp with their rational minds?

You can say of course that we are also attempting to give a teaching that explains how life works and explains why people are dissatisfied in their everyday lives. That is just what I did as the Buddha 2,500 years ago. It is what Jesus did 2,000 years ago, and it is what we are doing today. We are attempting to give an explanation that appeals to the rational mind. We have also given many teachings that explained that there is a limitation to what the rational mind can grasp. This is what is missing from the majority of ideologies found on earth.

Ignoring the limitations of the rational mind

Both the people who brought forth these ideologies and the people who follow the ideologies have believed that there is no limitation to the rational mind. There is no limitation to what the rational mind can grasp, there is no limitation to what can be explained through the rational mind. This idea goes far back into the mists of time.

In recorded history, it was very much solidified and codified by Aristotle, who believed that the rational mind could explain and grasp everything about how life works and that in order to explain how life works, you only needed to look at the material realm. These two claims of course are somewhat related because as the rational mind works currently on earth, people who use the rational mind cannot use it to grasp something beyond the material realm. You may say: "But the teachings that you of the ascended masters are giving are very rational, and I can certainly use my rational mind to understand how the spiritual realm works or the four levels of the material universe." You *can*, but this is not actually how these philosophers use the rational mind. You who are spiritual students are not spiritual students exclusively because of the rational mind. You have a certain intuition, intuitional awareness. It is this intuition that makes you see that there is something beyond the material world. In other words, when we explain that there are four levels of the material universe, it is your intuition that makes you see that there is validity to this explanation. You may say that you can also come up with a rational explanation and a rational argument, but it is not the rational argument that convinces you. It is your intuitive insight that convinces you.

This is why you often find it difficult to convince other people of the validity of our teachings. You tend to use your rational understanding of the teachings to create a rational argument and then you give this rational argument to other people. You cannot understand why they cannot grasp and accept this argument that seems so logical to you. The reason it seems rational to you is that your intuitive insight gives validity to it. If people do not have that intuitive insight, they will only use their rational minds to evaluate your argument and their rational minds cannot come up with a definitive argument for something that is beyond the material realm. Why is this so? It is because the collective consciousness is at a certain level where it is not possible to come up with a rational argument for the existence of something beyond the material realm.

In fact, we might as well say that it is a product of a specific ideology. It is an ideology that was founded by Aristotle but it has been built upon by many other scientists, thinkers, philosophers and it is what we have called the ideology of Materialism—that there is nothing beyond the material universe. This particular ideology (even though it is not normally called an ideology, but it *is* an ideology) has had such an influence, especially on the western world, that so many people are still trapped in Materialism and the rational mind. They cannot see, with the rational mind, an absolute proof that there must be something beyond the material universe. Some of you can see this, but you see it because you have an intuitive connection. Therefore, you know there is something beyond the material world. You *know* this. You might even in your mind construct an argument that seems very rational to you, but as I said, for people who do not have that intuitive connection, your argument will not seem as valid to them as it seems to you.

The reality that is found on earth right now (the equation found on earth right now) is that humankind at large is trapped in seeking to explain how life works based on the rational mindset, the rational mind, the rational reasoning process. Furthermore, they are limited, they are boxed in, to a certain mental box that cannot grasp any rational argument for the existence of something beyond what is currently defined as the material universe.

The ideology of rational materialism and emotions

We might very well say that the material universe is not just the physical octave, the physical realm, but that the material universe could be construed as being both the emotional, mental and identity realms as well. This is the totality of the material universe beyond which there is the spiritual realm. Humankind at large, the collective consciousness at large, is not able to grasp this, precisely because the most widespread (the most subtle, the most successful, the most dominant, the most mind-controlling, the most brainwashing) ideology found on earth right now is that of rational Materialism.

This is precisely why humankind cannot explain that life is not satisfying. They cannot come up with a rational explanation for why life is not satisfying because of these limitations defined by the rational mind and Materialism. You cannot explain why life is dissatisfying based on the rational mind alone because the rational mind cannot deal with fully (cannot explain) emotions. It can name emotions, it can label emotions, it can suppress emotions but it cannot deal with emotions. You cannot rationally explain emotions.

What you see in the world today as the dominant dichotomy that puts people in a bind is precisely this. People have an emotional experience of being dissatisfied with life and they are attempting to come up with a mental level, rational explanation for this—and it cannot be done. Furthermore, they are attempting to explain this emotional dissatisfaction based on a completely materialistic explanation. In other words, they are only looking at what is found in what is currently defined as the material universe (the physical realm) and they are attempting to explain this.

Materialism cannot explain people's dissatisfaction

You cannot explain the dissatisfaction based only on the material realm because as we have said human beings are not material beings. They are not even *physical* beings. They are first of all *psychological* beings and therefore, even beyond this, spiritual beings. If you are to explain the dissatisfaction, you cannot simply look at human beings as material beings. If you think that everything that goes on in the human mind is the product of chemical processes in the brain and that those chemical processes are a product of your genetic makeup, you cannot explain the general dissatisfaction experienced by virtually everybody on earth. How can you then come to explain this? Well that of course will be the topic for another discourse because I have gone as far as I want to go in this one. What I want to point out here is simply this. Since the beginning of what we would call modern time (in other words since humanity on earth, the original inhabitants of the earth, stepped into duality and became trapped in duality) there has been dissatisfaction. Dissatisfaction has been the dominant experience that people have had on earth ever since then, which is a very long time ago. Ever since then, numerous ideologies, the vast majority of which have been forgotten by history, have sprung up, have been developed, have been given, attempting to explain this general dissatisfaction.

It cannot be done by looking only at the earth. It cannot be done through the rational mind and therefore all of these ideologies are doomed to fail. They cannot provide an ultimate explanation. They cannot even provide a *useful* explanation that helps people overcome the dissatisfaction.

What does this mean? This means that any ideology is not developed, is not given, is not spread, for the purpose of setting people free from dissatisfaction. It is in fact given, developed, spread for the purpose of keeping people trapped in dissatisfaction but giving them – listen carefully – giving them the impression that there is a way out of their dissatisfaction by bringing certain changes to society. Or perhaps (as some religions say) that there is no way out of their dissatisfaction on earth, but by obeying their religion in this lifetime, there is a way out of the dissatisfaction beyond earth in a higher realm after this lifetime.

In either case, whether deliverance comes through changes here on earth or whether deliverance comes after earthly existence, the key to deliverance is portrayed as the general population following the ideology and the small elite of people who are defining, interpreting, promoting or enforcing the ideology. In other words, the conclusion we reach here is there has always (since the step into duality) been an elite that attempted to use ideology to control the population.

With this thought I seal this release and I thank you for setting the foundation for the possibility of releasing these teachings on ideology by using our previous teachings on fanaticism, dictatorships and elitism and by using all of our teachings on duality so that you are able to receive this. Your minds can therefore become the open doors for projecting this into the collective consciousness. To the extent that *you* can grasp these ideas, that is what determines how powerful of an impulse I can release through you personally while this dictation is given through the messenger.

You all play an important role when you listen to, when you read, when you take in these dictations in broadcasting it into the collective consciousness. The degree of power that can be put into this broadcast depends on your minds' ability to grasp it, your willingness to be open to these ideas and let a dictation take you beyond the level of consciousness you have when it starts, to a higher level that you have when it ends. This of course goes through the entire conference and how far you are willing to let this conference raise your consciousness during these next few days so that you end up at a higher level of consciousness than you had when you started. For this, I seal you in my gratitude for being willing to be the open doors.

Gautama I AM. The Buddha I AM. Beyond ideology I AM.

2 INVOKING AWARENESS OF THE LIMITATIONS OF THE RATIONAL MIND

In the name of the I AM THAT I AM, Jesus Christ, I use the authority that I have as a being in embodiment on earth to call upon Gautama Buddha to reinforce my calls and use my chakras to project the statements in this invocation into the collective consciousness and awaken people to the need to free ourselves from the ideological mindset. Awaken people to the reality that we are spiritual beings and that we can co-create a new future by working with the ascended masters. I especially call for …

[Make your own calls here.]

Part 1

1. Gautama Buddha, awaken the most creative people to see the connection between dictatorships, fanaticism, elitism and ideology.

> Archangel Michael, light so blue,
> my heart has room for only you.

My mind is one, no longer two,
your love for me is ever true.

**Archangel Michael, you are here,
consuming now all doubt and fear.
Your Presence is forever near,
you are to me so very dear.**

2. Gautama Buddha, awaken the most creative people to see the intricate, complex and subtle picture of how the power elite beings have used all means available to them to manipulate the people on earth.

Archangel Michael, I will be,
all one with your reality.
No fear can hold me as I see,
this world no power has o'er me.

**Archangel Michael, you are here,
consuming now all doubt and fear.
Your Presence is forever near,
you are to me so very dear.**

3. Gautama Buddha, awaken the most creative people to see that behind most dictatorships there is some form of ideology. A dictator cannot suppress a population through physical means alone. There must be a psychological component, some belief that causes people to submit to the dictator.

Archangel Michael, hold me tight,
shatter now the darkest night.
Clear my chakras with your light,
restore to me my inner sight.

**Archangel Michael, you are here,
consuming now all doubt and fear.
Your Presence is forever near,
you are to me so very dear.**

4. Gautama Buddha, awaken the most creative people to see that the deeper cause of fanaticism is some form of idea, some form of ideology.

Archangel Michael, now I stand,
with you the light I do command.
My heart I ever will expand,
till highest truth I understand.

Archangel Michael, you are here,
consuming now all doubt and fear.
Your Presence is forever near,
you are to me so very dear.

5. Gautama Buddha, awaken the most creative people to see that what allows an elite to exist and to either control the population in an obvious way, or to control in a subtle way, is some form of ideology.

Archangel Michael, in my heart,
from me you never will depart.
Of hierarchy I am a part,
I now accept a fresh new start.

Archangel Michael, you are here,
consuming now all doubt and fear.
Your Presence is forever near,
you are to me so very dear.

6. Gautama Buddha, awaken the most creative people to see that in many cases there is a benevolent intent behind creating or spreading an ideology.

Archangel Michael, sword of blue,
all darkness you are cutting through.
My Christhood I do now pursue,
discernment shows me what is true.

Archangel Michael, you are here,
consuming now all doubt and fear.
Your Presence is forever near,
you are to me so very dear.

7. Gautama Buddha, awaken the most creative people to see that many of the people who have brought forth a new ideology and many of the people who have promoted it, have not had an evil, selfish or self-centered intent of controlling, dominating, suppressing or destroying other people.

Archangel Michael, in your wings,
I now let go of lesser things.
God's homing call in my heart rings,
my heart with yours forever sings.

**Archangel Michael, you are here,
consuming now all doubt and fear.
Your Presence is forever near,
you are to me so very dear.**

8. Gautama Buddha, awaken the most creative people to look at history and see that in many cases, regardless of the good intentions, ideologies have been used to suppress and control people.

Archangel Michael, take me home,
in higher spheres I want to roam.
I am reborn from cosmic foam,
my life is now a sacred poem.

**Archangel Michael, you are here,
consuming now all doubt and fear.
Your Presence is forever near,
you are to me so very dear.**

9. Gautama Buddha, awaken the most creative people to see that the first element of any ideology is a theory or system that seeks to explain certain things about how life works.

Archangel Michael, light you are,
shining like the bluest star.
You are a cosmic avatar,
with you I will go very far.

Archangel Michael, you are here,
consuming now all doubt and fear.
Your Presence is forever near,
you are to me so very dear.

Part 2

1. Gautama Buddha, awaken the most creative people to see that although some ideologies are materialistic or political and some have a religious element, they all seek to explain something that relates to people's lives.

Archangel Michael, light so blue,
my heart has room for only you.
My mind is one, no longer two,
your love for me is ever true.

Archangel Michael, you are here,
consuming now all doubt and fear.
Your Presence is forever near,
you are to me so very dear.

2. Gautama Buddha, awaken the most creative people to see that the first Noble Truth says that "life is suffering," life is dissatisfaction, life is not satisfying.

Archangel Michael, I will be,
all one with your reality.
No fear can hold me as I see,
this world no power has o'er me.

Archangel Michael, you are here,
consuming now all doubt and fear.
Your Presence is forever near,
you are to me so very dear.

3. Gautama Buddha, awaken the most creative people to see that the vast majority of people on earth are not satisfied with their lives. There is something in their lives that causes dissatisfaction.

Archangel Michael, hold me tight,
shatter now the darkest night.
Clear my chakras with your light,
restore to me my inner sight.

**Archangel Michael, you are here,
consuming now all doubt and fear.
Your Presence is forever near,
you are to me so very dear.**

4. Gautama Buddha, awaken the most creative people to see that the most basic, element that any ideology seeks to explain is why life is dissatisfaction, why the vast majority of people are dissatisfied.

Archangel Michael, now I stand,
with you the light I do command.
My heart I ever will expand,
till highest truth I understand.

**Archangel Michael, you are here,
consuming now all doubt and fear.
Your Presence is forever near,
you are to me so very dear.**

5. Gautama Buddha, awaken the most creative people to see that if we bring forth an ideology with the intention to create change in society, then we need an explanation that most people can grasp *in their present state of consciousness.* This is the central understanding when it comes to ideology.

Archangel Michael, in my heart,
from me you never will depart.
Of hierarchy I am a part,
I now accept a fresh new start.

Archangel Michael, you are here,
consuming now all doubt and fear.
Your Presence is forever near,
you are to me so very dear.

6. Gautama Buddha, awaken the most creative people to question the claim that there is some infallible authority behind the explanation given by a particular ideology.

Archangel Michael, sword of blue,
all darkness you are cutting through.
My Christhood I do now pursue,
discernment shows me what is true.

Archangel Michael, you are here,
consuming now all doubt and fear.
Your Presence is forever near,
you are to me so very dear.

7. Gautama Buddha, awaken the most creative people to see that there is a progression in the collective consciousness of humankind and over time this allows the most creative people to grasp progressively higher knowledge.

Archangel Michael, in your wings,
I now let go of lesser things.
God's homing call in my heart rings,
my heart with yours forever sings.

Archangel Michael, you are here,
consuming now all doubt and fear.
Your Presence is forever near,
you are to me so very dear.

8. Gautama Buddha, awaken the most creative people to see that the Bible is not some ultimate, absolute revelation from God. Even if the *New Testament* had been directly dictated by Jesus, it would still not be the ultimate revelation because it could only have been given based on the level of the collective consciousness at the time.

Archangel Michael, take me home,
in higher spheres I want to roam.
I am reborn from cosmic foam,
my life is now a sacred poem.

**Archangel Michael, you are here,
consuming now all doubt and fear.
Your Presence is forever near,
you are to me so very dear.**

9. Gautama Buddha, awaken the most creative people to see that you did not give the ultimate spiritual teaching that could ever be given on this planet. You gave a teaching based on not only the collective consciousness of the planet, but the collective consciousness in the area where you were in physical embodiment.

Archangel Michael, light you are,
shining like the bluest star.
You are a cosmic avatar,
with you I will go very far.

**Archangel Michael, you are here,
consuming now all doubt and fear.
Your Presence is forever near,
you are to me so very dear.**

Part 3

1. Gautama Buddha, awaken the most creative people to see that a teaching that was given 2,500 or 2,000 years ago has not become obsolete because there are still people who need that teaching.

O Jesus, blessed brother mine,
I walk the path that you outline,
a great example to us all,
I follow now your inner call.

**O Jesus, let the Fire of Joy,
consume the devil's subtle ploy,
transfigured is our planet earth,
the golden age is given birth.**

2. Gautama Buddha, awaken the most creative people to see that there is always the danger that a teaching can be interpreted in various ways and therefore take on a culture that is beyond what was originally given. This is a dead end that can keep people trapped for a long time.

O Jesus, open inner sight,
the ego wants to prove it's right,
but this I will no longer do,
I want to be all one with you.

**O Jesus, let the Fire of Joy,
consume the devil's subtle ploy,
transfigured is our planet earth,
the golden age is given birth.**

3. Gautama Buddha, awaken the most creative people to see the reality that there never has been, there is not now and there never will be any ideology, any system of thought and belief that would be an ultimate truth, an ultimate form of revelation.

O Jesus, I now clearly see,
the Key of Knowledge given me,
my Christ self I hereby embrace,
as you fill up my inner space.

**O Jesus, let the Fire of Joy,
consume the devil's subtle ploy,
transfigured is our planet earth,
the golden age is given birth.**

4. Gautama Buddha, awaken the most creative people to see that if an ideology claims to have some ultimate truth or some ultimate authority, that particular claim is false.

O Jesus, show me serpent's lie,
expose the beam in my own eye,
as Christ discernment you me give,
in oneness I forever live.

**O Jesus, let the Fire of Joy,
consume the devil's subtle ploy,
transfigured is our planet earth,
the golden age is given birth.**

5. Gautama Buddha, awaken the most creative people to see that an ideology may provide an understanding of certain issues and point to a way to improve society. If an ideology makes the claim that it has an absolute authority, this doesn't mean the ideology is completely false. But the claim to have the absolute truth is false. It always has been, it always will be.

O Jesus, I am truly meek,
and thus I turn the other cheek,
when the accuser attacks me,
I go within and merge with thee.

**O Jesus, let the Fire of Joy,
consume the devil's subtle ploy,
transfigured is our planet earth,
the golden age is given birth.**

6. Gautama Buddha, awaken the most creative people to see that there are different levels of consciousness, and it is possible for people to gradually rise from lower to higher levels of consciousness.

O Jesus, ego I let die,
surrender ev'ry earthly tie,
the dead can bury what is dead,
I choose to walk with you instead.

**O Jesus, let the Fire of Joy,
consume the devil's subtle ploy,
transfigured is our planet earth,
the golden age is given birth.**

7. Gautama Buddha, awaken the most creative people to see that when people are below a certain level of consciousness, there are certain ideas they cannot grasp.

O Jesus, help me rise above,
the devil's test through higher love,
show me separate self unreal,
my formless self you do reveal.

**O Jesus, let the Fire of Joy,
consume the devil's subtle ploy,
transfigured is our planet earth,
the golden age is given birth.**

8. Gautama Buddha, awaken the most creative people to see some of the shortcomings of the duality consciousness even though they do not know that terminology.

O Jesus, what is that to me,
I just let go and follow thee,
with this I do pass ev'ry test,
to find with you eternal rest.

**O Jesus, let the Fire of Joy,
consume the devil's subtle ploy,
transfigured is our planet earth,
the golden age is given birth.**

9. Gautama Buddha, awaken the most creative people to consider the process whereby people are seeking to explain something, seeing that most ideologies originate from the rational, intellectual, mental realm.

O Jesus, fiery master mine,
my heart now melting into thine,
I love with heart and mind and soul,
the God who is my highest goal.

**O Jesus, let the Fire of Joy,
consume the devil's subtle ploy,**

**transfigured is our planet earth,
the golden age is given birth.**

Part 4

1. Gautama Buddha, awaken the most creative people to see that some ideologies, philosophies and spiritual teachings do not originate from the minds of human beings in embodiment. Many philosophers have been able to tune in to the non-material beings who exist in the mental realm and receive a teaching from beyond the material realm.

> Maitreya, I am truly meek,
> your counsel wise I humbly seek,
> your vision I so want to see,
> with you in Eden I will be.

> **Maitreya, kindness is the cure,
> in fires of kindness I am pure.
> Maitreya, now release the fire,
> that raises me forever higher.**

2. Gautama Buddha, awaken the most creative people to see that this is ironic because some of these philosophies claim that there is nothing beyond the material realm, even though they were actually given by beings that are beyond the material realm.

> Maitreya, help me to return,
> to learn from you, I truly yearn,
> as oneness is all I desire
> I feel initiation's fire.

> **Maitreya, kindness is the cure,
> in fires of kindness I am pure.
> Maitreya, now release the fire,
> that raises me forever higher.**

3. Gautama Buddha, awaken the most creative people to see that some philosophers have been aware that they have inspiration from above, but some of them have not been aware of this. Karl Marx was inspired by beings in the mental realm but thought that he was so intelligent that he came up with these ideas on his own.

Maitreya, I hereby decide,
from you I will no longer hide,
expose to me the very lie
that caused edenic self to die.

**Maitreya, kindness is the cure,
in fires of kindness I am pure.
Maitreya, now release the fire,
that raises me forever higher.**

4. Gautama Buddha, awaken the most creative people to see that most philosophers have been inspired by beings in a different realm, but they believed they used their rational minds.

Maitreya, blessed Guru mine,
my heart of hearts forever thine,
I vow that I will listen well,
so we can break the serpent's spell.

**Maitreya, kindness is the cure,
in fires of kindness I am pure.
Maitreya, now release the fire,
that raises me forever higher.**

5. Gautama Buddha, awaken the most creative people to see that behind most of the ideologies found on earth, the rational mind is a very big factor.

Maitreya, help me see the lie
whereby the serpent broke the tie,
the serpent now has naught in me,
in oneness I am truly free.

**Maitreya, kindness is the cure,
in fires of kindness I am pure.
Maitreya, now release the fire,
that raises me forever higher.**

6. Gautama Buddha, awaken the most creative people to see that ascended master teachings take into consideration what people can grasp with their rational minds. The masters also explain that there is a limitation to what the rational mind can grasp. This is what is missing from the majority of ideologies found on earth.

Maitreya, truth does set me free
from falsehoods of duality,
the fruit of knowledge I let go,
so your true spirit I do know.

**Maitreya, kindness is the cure,
in fires of kindness I am pure.
Maitreya, now release the fire,
that raises me forever higher.**

7. Gautama Buddha, awaken the most creative people to see that both the people who brought forth ideologies and the people who follow them have believed that there is no limitation to the rational mind. There is no limitation to what the rational mind can grasp or what can be explained through the rational mind.

Maitreya, I submit to you,
intentions pure, my heart is true,
from ego I am truly free,
as I am now all one with thee.

**Maitreya, kindness is the cure,
in fires of kindness I am pure.
Maitreya, now release the fire,
that raises me forever higher.**

8. Gautama Buddha, awaken the most creative people to see that in recorded history, the belief in the rational mind was solidified and codified

by Aristotle, who believed that the rational mind could explain and grasp everything about how life works, and that in order to explain how life works, we only need to look at the material realm.

> Maitreya, kindness is the key,
> all shades of kindness teach to me,
> for I am now the open door,
> the Art of Kindness to restore.

> **Maitreya, kindness is the cure,**
> **in fires of kindness I am pure.**
> **Maitreya, now release the fire,**
> **that raises me forever higher.**

9. Gautama Buddha, awaken the most creative people to see that these two claims are related because as the rational mind works currently on earth, people who use the rational mind cannot grasp something beyond the material realm.

> Maitreya, oh sweet mystery,
> immersed in your reality,
> the myst'ry school will now return,
> for this, my heart does truly burn.

> **Maitreya, kindness is the cure,**
> **in fires of kindness I am pure.**
> **Maitreya, now release the fire,**
> **that raises me forever higher.**

Part 5

1. Gautama Buddha, awaken the most creative people to see that we are not exclusively using the rational mind. We have a certain intuitional awareness.

Gautama, show my mental state
that does give rise to love and hate,
your exposé I do endure,
so my perception will be pure.

Gautama, Flame of Cosmic Peace,
unruly thoughts do hereby cease,
we radiate from you and me
the peace to still Samsara's Sea.

2. Gautama Buddha, awaken the most creative people to see that the rational mind can come up with a rational explanation and a rational argument for the existence of something beyond the material world, but it is not the rational argument that convinces us. It is our intuitive insight that convinces us.

Gautama, in your Flame of Peace,
the struggling self I now release,
the Buddha Nature I now see,
it is the core of you and me.

Gautama, Flame of Cosmic Peace,
unruly thoughts do hereby cease,
we radiate from you and me
the peace to still Samsara's Sea.

3. Gautama Buddha, awaken the most creative people to see that this explains why it is so difficult to convince other people. If people do not have intuitive insight, they will use their rational minds to evaluate an argument, and their rational minds cannot come up with a definitive argument for something that is beyond the material realm.

Gautama, I am one with thee,
Mara's demons do now flee,
your Presence like a soothing balm,
my mind and senses ever calm.

Gautama, Flame of Cosmic Peace,
unruly thoughts do hereby cease,

we radiate from you and me
the peace to still Samsara's Sea.

4. Gautama Buddha, awaken the most creative people to see that this is a product of a specific ideology. It is an ideology that was founded by Aristotle but it has been built upon by many other scientists, thinkers and philosophers. It is the ideology of Materialism, claiming there is nothing beyond the material universe.

Gautama, I now take the vow,
to live in the eternal now,
with you I do transcend all time,
to live in present so sublime.

Gautama, Flame of Cosmic Peace,
unruly thoughts do hereby cease,
we radiate from you and me
the peace to still Samsara's Sea.

5. Gautama Buddha, awaken the most creative people to see that Material-ism *is* an ideology, and it has had such an influence on the western world that many people are still trapped in Materialism and the rational mind. People cannot see, with the rational mind, an absolute proof that there must be something beyond the material universe.

Gautama, I have no desire,
to nothing earthly I aspire,
in non-attachment I now rest,
passing Mara's subtle test.

Gautama, Flame of Cosmic Peace,
unruly thoughts do hereby cease,
we radiate from you and me
the peace to still Samsara's Sea.

6. Gautama Buddha, awaken the most creative people to see that we *know* there is something beyond the material world. We might even in our minds construct an argument that seems rational to us, but for people who do not have an intuitive connection, our argument will not seem valid to them.

Gautama, I melt into you,
my mind is one, no longer two,
immersed in your resplendent glow,
Nirvana is all that I know.

Gautama, Flame of Cosmic Peace,
unruly thoughts do hereby cease,
we radiate from you and me
the peace to still Samsara's Sea.

7. Gautama Buddha, awaken the most creative people to see that the equation found on earth right now is that humankind is trapped in seeking to explain how life works based on the rational mindset, the rational reasoning process. People are boxed in by a certain mental box that cannot grasp any rational argument for the existence of something beyond what is currently defined as the material universe.

Gautama, in your timeless space,
I am immersed in Cosmic Grace,
I know the God beyond all form,
to world I will no more conform.

Gautama, Flame of Cosmic Peace,
unruly thoughts do hereby cease,
we radiate from you and me
the peace to still Samsara's Sea.

8. Gautama Buddha, awaken the most creative people to see that the material universe is not just the physical realm, but also the emotional, mental and identity realms. This is the totality of the material universe beyond which there is the spiritual realm.

Gautama, I am now awake,
I clearly see what is at stake,
and thus I claim my sacred right
to be on earth the Buddhic Light.

Gautama, Flame of Cosmic Peace,
unruly thoughts do hereby cease,

**we radiate from you and me
the peace to still Samsara's Sea.**

9. Gautama Buddha, awaken the most creative people to see that the collective consciousness is not able to grasp this, precisely because the most dominant ideology on earth right now is that of rational Materialism.

Gautama, with your thunderbolt,
we give the earth a mighty jolt,
I know that some will understand,
and join the Buddha's timeless band.

**Gautama, Flame of Cosmic Peace,
unruly thoughts do hereby cease,
we radiate from you and me
the peace to still Samsara's Sea.**

Part 6

1. Gautama Buddha, awaken the most creative people to see that this is precisely why humankind cannot explain that life is not satisfying. We cannot come up with a rational explanation for why life is not satisfying because of the limitations defined by the rational mind and Materialism.

Sanat Kumara, Ruby Fire,
I seek my place in love's own choir,
with open hearts we sing your praise,
together we the earth do raise.

**Sanat Kumara, Ruby Ray,
bring to earth a higher way,
light this planet with your fire,
clothe her in a new attire.**

2. Gautama Buddha, awaken the most creative people to see that we cannot explain why life is dissatisfying based on the rational mind alone because

the rational mind cannot deal with emotions. It can name emotions, it can label emotions, it can suppress emotions but it cannot deal with emotions. We cannot rationally explain emotions.

> Sanat Kumara, Ruby Fire,
> initiations I desire,
> I am for you an electrode,
> Shamballa is my true abode.

> **Sanat Kumara, Ruby Ray,**
> **bring to earth a higher way,**
> **light this planet with your fire,**
> **clothe her in a new attire.**

3. Gautama Buddha, awaken the most creative people to see that the world today has a dominant dichotomy that puts people in a bind. People have an emotional experience of being dissatisfied with life and they are attempting to come up with a mental level, rational explanation for this—and it cannot be done.

> Sanat Kumara, Ruby Fire,
> I follow path that you require,
> initiate me with your love,
> the open door for Holy Dove.

> **Sanat Kumara, Ruby Ray,**
> **bring to earth a higher way,**
> **light this planet with your fire,**
> **clothe her in a new attire.**

4. Gautama Buddha, awaken the most creative people to see that we are attempting to explain this emotional dissatisfaction based on a completely materialistic explanation. We are only looking at what is found in what is currently defined as the material universe and we are attempting to explain this.

> Sanat Kumara, Ruby Fire,
> your great example all inspire,

with non-attachment and great mirth,
we give the earth a true rebirth.

Sanat Kumara, Ruby Ray,
bring to earth a higher way,
light this planet with your fire,
clothe her in a new attire.

5. Gautama Buddha, awaken the most creative people to see that we cannot explain the dissatisfaction based only on the material realm because human beings are not material beings. We are not even *physical* beings. We are first of all *psychological* beings.

Sanat Kumara, Ruby Fire,
you are this planet's purifier,
consume on earth all spirits dark,
reveal the inner Spirit Spark.

Sanat Kumara, Ruby Ray,
bring to earth a higher way,
light this planet with your fire,
clothe her in a new attire.

6. Gautama Buddha, awaken the most creative people to see that if we are to explain the dissatisfaction, we cannot look at human beings as material beings. If we think that everything that goes on in the human mind is the product of chemical processes in the brain and that those chemical processes are a product of our genetic makeup, we cannot explain the general dissatisfaction experienced by virtually everybody on earth.

Sanat Kumara, Ruby Fire,
you are a cosmic amplifier,
the lower forces can't withstand,
vibrations from Venusian band.

Sanat Kumara, Ruby Ray,
bring to earth a higher way,
light this planet with your fire,
clothe her in a new attire.

7. Gautama Buddha, awaken the most creative people to see that since the beginning of modern time, dissatisfaction has been the dominant experience on earth. Numerous ideologies have been developed, attempting to explain this general dissatisfaction. It cannot be done through the rational mind and therefore all of these ideologies are doomed to fail. They cannot provide a *useful* explanation that helps people overcome the dissatisfaction.

Sanat Kumara, Ruby Fire,
I am on earth your magnifier,
the flow of love I do restore,
my chakras are your open door.

Sanat Kumara, Ruby Ray,
bring to earth a higher way,
light this planet with your fire,
clothe her in a new attire.

8. Gautama Buddha, awaken the most creative people to see that any ideology is not developed for the purpose of setting people free from dissatisfaction. It is given for the purpose of keeping people trapped in dissatisfaction but giving them the impression that there is a way out of their dissatisfaction by bringing certain changes to society.

Sanat Kumara, Ruby Fire,
Venusian song the multiplier,
as we your love reverberate,
the densest minds we penetrate.

Sanat Kumara, Ruby Ray,
bring to earth a higher way,
light this planet with your fire,
clothe her in a new attire.

9. Gautama Buddha, awaken the most creative people to see that the key to deliverance is portrayed as the general population following the ideology and the small elite of people who are defining and enforcing the ideology. There has always been an elite that attempted to use duality to control the population.

Sanat Kumara, Ruby Fire,
you are for all the sanctifier,
the earth is now a holy place,
purified by cosmic grace.

Sanat Kumara, Ruby Ray,
bring to earth a higher way,
light this planet with your fire,
clothe her in a new attire.

Sealing

In the name of the I AM THAT I AM, I accept that Archangel Michael, Astrea and Shiva form an impenetrable shield around myself and all constructive people, sealing us from all fear-based energies in all four octaves. I accept that the Light of God is consuming and transforming all fear-based energies that make up the dark forces working against ending the era of ideology on earth!

3 WHY PEOPLE BELIEVE IN IDEOLOGIES

I AM the Ascended Master Gautama Buddha. I have said that the rational mind has limitations for what can be explained, what can be grasped. This means that an ideology always seeks to explain why people are dissatisfied but it can never give a full and complete explanation. Now, you will of course be able to look at history and see any number of incidents where people have become what we might say "pulled" into a certain ideology. They have been pulled into the forcefield, the energetic matrix, of a certain ideology and they have been absolutely convinced that this ideology did give a full, complete, accurate and ultimate explanation for life as they saw it. They might even have felt it gave the full explanation of why people are dissatisfied and how to get over their dissatisfaction.

What I want to consider here is how it is possible that human beings have an explanation that is not absolute, that is not even fully true, that might not be completely true at all (might not have any truth to it), but they are fully convinced that it *is* the truth. In order to understand this, we need to incorporate the knowledge that we have given you as ascended master students, that there are certain beings who are doing everything possible to deceive human beings for the purpose of controlling them.

History proves the existence of a power elite

We have called them fallen beings (you can call them a power elite to use a more neutral term) but it is not difficult to see, when you look at history, that there has always been a certain elite in any society. There is a tendency for an elite to form. They seek to gain a certain position where they have an ultimate position, a position that they think cannot be challenged, that cannot be overthrown. They are the ruling elite and no one can challenge their power, no one can speak out against them—or so they think. You can also see in history how there have been many times where a ruling elite has sat (an *established* power elite has sat) on this position for a long time, sometimes even centuries, but eventually there came a point where that elite was overturned. In many cases this happened because there was an aspiring power elite that managed to overthrow the ruling elite and they then took the position that the ruling elite had. In many cases the aspiring power elite claimed that they were aiming to free the people from the tyranny of the established elite, but their real goal was to set themselves up in the position of the established elite. Only, they wanted to make their position even more secure so that they could think that even though they overthrew the previous elite, they themselves cannot be overthrown. You see many examples of this dynamic, as we have explained before.

What is it that happens in this process? You can see that in many cases the established elite took power because they had a certain ideology that supported their power. They maintained that power because they managed to keep that ideology active, and that kept the people believing in the ideology. Then, when an aspiring power elite overthrew the established elite, they used a different ideology that challenged the previous one. The previous one claimed to have the ultimate truth but then a new ideology came up that claimed the old ideology was an error, but *now* they had the final one, the ultimate one that was the truth.

The inescapable tension of duality

Why is it that people can become convinced that an ideology really does explain life in a way they feel is complete, believable, satisfactory, logical, rational, appealing—whatever you want to call this? Well, in order to fully understand this, you need to step back, *we* need to step back and again realize that the moment you step into the duality consciousness, you are stepping into a very specific state of mind. Once you are in that state of mind, you have no idea what you have stepped into because once you are trapped in duality, blinded by duality, you think there is nothing else except duality, there is nothing outside of duality, there is no alternative. There simply is not a different state of consciousness, duality is the only state of consciousness that is possible for a human being on earth. This is what people think when they become trapped in duality. Therefore, of course they do not realize that duality has a built-in, an inherent, an inescapable tension. There is this tension that causes the dissatisfaction.

Now, why then is it that hardly anyone realizes they are trapped in a certain state of mind, that it is the state of mind that causes the dissatisfaction and that the only way out is to transcend the duality consciousness? Well, they do not realize this because, as we have explained before in greater detail, going into duality is part of what is allowed by the Law of Free Will on a planet like earth. For that matter, it is theoretically allowed on all planets in an unascended sphere. This duality is simply an experience one can have in the full spectrum of free will. There are many different experiences you can have through free will. Duality is one of them.

Now, duality is of course a very specific experience that you can have. We have described it in many different ways and there are many different ways to describe it. What you *can* say is that in duality, you have a state where everything is relative. There is in a sense nothing absolute in duality. This will make little sense to most people on earth because they do not remember the alternative to duality. When you can begin to glimpse non-duality, as compared to duality, you realize that when you are not in duality, there is always an absolute guiding rod, there is always an absolute frame of reference. It is again, various words can be put on it. We can say that you know that all life is one, therefore there is no separation and you know that there is no need to compare yourself to other people because you are following an individual path that leads you towards higher and higher states of consciousness. You are not setting yourself up as being better or more important than others. *That* is not part of the experience you are having when you are not in duality.

However, when you *do* step into duality, part of the experience that you want to have is that everything is relative, meaning you can now see yourself relative to other people. You can see your state of mind as relative to an opposite state of mind, which is what gives rise to the many dualistic polarities, such as happiness and unhappiness. We have explained before that when you are not in duality, it is not that you are dissatisfied or unhappy but neither would you say that you are happy, as happiness is defined on earth. The happiness, which is what I called "bliss" 2,500 years ago (for want of a better word), is not defined in relation to an opposite. You are in a state of mind that is what you might call positive and uplifting, but it has no opposite. You see, even the words as they are used on earth cannot describe what is beyond duality because they have been so affected by duality. You are in a state of mind that has no opposite, you are at peace, you are content, you are not dissatisfied in that state of mind.

When you step into duality, you step into a state of mind where there must be an opposite to any state of mind. It is possible to have an experience of happiness in duality but it is in contrast to unhappiness. This means that your happiness can never be absolute, it is a relative happiness, it is defined in relation to an opposite. This means there is always the tension because you might be in a position where you feel happy but you know in the back of your mind there is always the possibility that you could lose your happiness and go into unhappiness. It is always there. Just as an example, you know that your physical body will eventually die. You always have that tension and this means that you can never be fully and completely satisfied. It is not possible because you cannot relate to anything absolute. You can only relate to something relative. You always have the contrasts.

How the quest for happiness creates unhappiness

Now there is a, we might call it an "advantage," to going into duality. You can have experiences that you cannot have when you are not in duality. The experience you can have in duality is that you can have tremendous contrast. In duality, you can, in a certain sense, feel much more happy than you ever feel when you are not in duality because you have the contrast between what you call happiness and what you call unhappiness. What you see here is that you are defining two states of consciousness in duality. You are defining happiness and unhappiness.

Naturally, most people will experience (once they are in duality) that unhappiness is unpleasant and happiness is pleasant. What does that mean? It means they want to always have happiness and avoid unhappiness. This is the mindset you go into in duality. You want to avoid the unpleasant, you want to always have the pleasant. This is an *inevitable* reaction but it is also an *impossible* reaction. You cannot have happiness without unhappiness because if you did, there would be no contrast and then there would be no duality. What is it that people do? Well, they go into a mindset of striving for something different than what they have now.

Now, you may say, but are not we saying that even before you have ever gone into duality, you start out with a point-like sense of identity and you are meant to continue to expand your sense of identity until you reach the full God consciousness. Are you not in a sense always wanting something more than what you have because there is always a higher state of consciousness? This is true but it is not dualistic, it is not relative. There is not the contrast between unhappiness and happiness because when you start out as a new spiritual being with a point-like sense of identity, you are not unhappy. You are not feeling lack. You are feeling fulfilled in what you are and then you are feeling more fulfilled when you become more. You continue to feel more and more fulfilled without having the opposite. The opposite is only possible in duality. You can go into duality, you forget who you really are as a spiritual being, but as we have said before there is still that striving for something more. You want to have more than what you have in duality.

What does this mean? It means that when you are now trapped in the contrast of seeing unhappiness contrasted with happiness, you inevitably determine in your mind (not necessarily consciously, you simply go into this reaction) that you want *more* happiness, you want to be more happy. You want to have an experience of being more happy than you have ever been before.

What did I just say? In duality, happiness can only exist relative to unhappiness. Now you have a planet where all people have gone into duality. They are all striving for a greater and greater experience of happiness but how can they have this greater experience of happiness? Only when happiness is contrasted with unhappiness. What does this mean? How can you have a greater experience of *happiness?* Well, only if there is also a greater experience of *unhappiness.* You see, when the earth first went into duality, there was a certain spectrum, a certain difference between the deepest unhappiness that was possible on earth and the highest happiness that was possible on earth. There was that distance, that spectrum. What has happened since is that people have expanded that spectrum. How have you done this? By making it possible to become more and more unhappy. This gives you the sense that you are more and more happy in contrast to the unhappiness. Or rather, you are more happy than those people who are in unhappiness.

Do you see what this means, my beloved? It means that when an entire planet has gone into duality, it is inevitable that large groups of people must be unhappy so that other people can feel happy compared to them. It cannot be any other way in duality. What does this mean? It means that in reality the majority of the population are condemned to be unhappy. You look at any period in history, there has been what we might call an elite, or people who felt they had some happiness, and then there has been a majority of the population who felt they did not have happiness compared to the elite. Now, what has been the measure for determining whether you are happy or unhappy? Has it been your state of mind? Not really, because what also happens in duality is that you have no absolute frame of reference so you cannot see that the ultimate way to be fulfilled, whole, at peace is through oneness with your Higher Self, with your I AM Presence.

How outer conditions determine happiness

Only by being complete within yourself can you be ultimately at peace and fulfilled. In duality you have lost the connection to your I AM Presence, you cannot even conceive that you have such a connection or that this could satisfy you. You are in duality focused on outer conditions, outer conditions on earth. That is what your focus is. What determines your happiness when you are in duality? It is the outer conditions that you have. What determines your unhappiness? It is the outer conditions that you do *not* have. So you see here that what has happened, going back into history, is that in every society, whatever the situation was in that society, there was a certain outer definition of what it meant to be well to do, well off, to be one of the elite. The assumption based on this was that if you had the outer conditions of the elite, you should be happy.

You will see in many time periods where the majority of the people felt unhappy because they did not have the physical conditions that they saw the elite having. The majority of the people assumed that the elite must be happy because they have these wonderful conditions. They do not need to work, they have plenty of food, they have luxurious living conditions, they have servants to do all the work and whatever criteria was there in the actual society. When you look at the reality of the situation, you see that the elite, most of them, were not happy after all even though they had these conditions. They felt they *should* be happy but they were not. Why were they not? Because of their psychology, their psychological conditions.

Many among the elite were fallen beings who had set themselves up as an elite, and fallen beings can never be happy, at least not until they undo the decision that caused them to fall. You also saw some among the elite who felt they were happy, who forced themselves to feel they were happy (at least for a time), *felt* happy and acted as if they *were* happy.

You see the same thing today where there are people who feel that: We have such good conditions today, compared to what was there a generation or two ago—we *should* be happy. There are, even in some of the richer nations in the world, large parts of the population who look back at their parents and grandparents and the conditions they had back in the 1930's, 20's whatever you have. They realize they are so much better off materially and therefore they decide with their outer minds: "I should be happy, I must be happy, I think I am happy." There is a certain feeling of happiness based on these outer conditions but it is not an inner feeling of happiness, it is relative.

You of course have many people around the world also who live in poor conditions, in appalling conditions and violent conditions, chaotic conditions and who feel very unhappy because of their outer conditions. This leads to this belief (that has been perpetrated by the fallen beings for a very long time but has really been solidified with materialism) that your state of mind depends on physical, material conditions, either conditions outside yourself or conditions in your own brain and body. (For many people the brain and body still seems to be outside themselves because even though they have been brought up in a materialistic society, they have some knowledge that they are not the body, they are more than the body.)

Anyway, they see that their state of mind depends on outer conditions. This is what they have been brainwashed to believe for many lifetimes. This is of course exactly the engineering of the fallen beings who want people to believe this. They want you to believe that your state of mind depends on external conditions, which means you have no control over your state of mind. The only way to change your state of mind is to change the external conditions. Why do the fallen beings want people to believe this? Well, partly because they can control people. Other fallen beings want it because it allows them to get people into conflicts with other groups of people so they can steal their energy. Some simply want to create chaos.

Why ideologies define a needed change

What I want to discourse on here is how this ties in with ideology. Now, I said earlier that there were five common elements of an ideology. These are what are defined in the world, they are not the full explanation of course but one of them was that you have a system of thought, ideas, that seeks to give an explanation. The second element is that an ideology defines certain changes that should happen. Often, in society it can be political, it can be specific physical changes, but there is always a definition by the ideology that there is a change that should happen.

Why should this change happen? Well, this is often not even stated in the ideology, or at least the real reason is not stated, but the real reason is that if this change happens, supposedly people will feel better, they will be happy. This ties in with what I just said: Your state of mind depends on external conditions. Here is an ideology that defines that there are certain changes in the external conditions in your society that need to happen and the implicit promise is that if these changes do happen, those who are unhappy today are going to be happy when the changes have taken place. This is what has been used in many, many ideologies, obviously so in Marxism where it was stated that you have the bourgeoisie, you have the factory owners who are exploiting the population, therefore the population is unhappy. When you get rid of the bourgeoisie and create a society based on Marxist principles, supposedly, the workers will be happy because now their outer conditions have changed and therefore their inner conditions, their state of mind, must change accordingly.

You see variants of this in religions where for example you might say that Christianity defines that happiness really cannot be attained on earth. It can only be attained after the earthly existence in a higher realm. Still, if you look at the history of Christianity, you will see that after the formation of the Roman Catholic church, Christianity became an ideology that was used to control the population. It was actually used to justify certain changes, which in this case were not really changes that benefitted the broad population but that cemented the formation of an elite. The elite not only owned the land and the means of production, but actually owned the people who lived on their land, namely the feudal societies in medieval Europe. This was a state of social change, political change that could not have happened without the backing of the Catholic church and how they made certain people believe that it was not possible to have ideal conditions on earth so therefore they should accept the current conditions and the bidding of the church, so they could have ideal conditions in heaven after this lifetime.

Just two variations of the same thing but still, the promise that in some future time you will be happy, the people will be happy, if they follow an elite. In Marxism of course you will see that after the bourgeoisie and the noble class were overthrown, there emerged a new elite, namely the party elite. Again, the promise was: If the people follow the party elite, they will one day have these conditions and be happy. This is a very subtle element of ideology, which often is not fully explained. Often, there is some outer explanation focusing on people's material situations, such as the workers working very hard, dirty, dangerous jobs for very little pay where they could barely survive and feed their children and families and there was a promise that this would change.

Why people are attracted to an ideology

If you go even deeper behind this implicit unspoken promise, you see of course that there is the deeper promise that if people follow the elite, if they obey the elite that has defined and is administering the current ideology, then they will be happy. Why is this appealing to many people? Well, it is appealing because people have for many lifetimes experienced that they have tried to make their own decisions to make themselves feel better but nothing has worked. There are people who have come to a point where they are reluctant to make decisions because they realize it just leads to unhappiness. They become susceptible to the promise that if you follow this elite, that has this superior ideology, then you will be happy without you having to make your own decisions. This is another manipulation of the fallen beings. Your unhappiness is caused by the decisions you have made personally. Make the decision to follow us and do what we tell you, then you will escape this unhappiness.

Now, we see that there is a certain group of people for whom an ideology appeals to them at what we might call the physical level. In other words, you have people who are very poor, living in appalling conditions and thinking that if their physical conditions changed, they would feel better. They are likely to believe in an ideology (or follow an ideology or at least submit to an ideology) out of the promise of better physical conditions. What does this lead to? It leads to a consideration that there are different groups of people and there are different things that appeal to them.

We have talked about the four levels of a material universe, the physical, emotional, mental and identity level. There is a large group of the population on earth whose consciousness is still focused at the physical level. This means they are primarily concerned about their physical conditions. You can somewhat compare this to Maslow's pyramid of needs where you have the physiological needs, the safety needs and these are primarily physical. There are people who are at that level, they are focused on these needs, they are focusing on physical conditions and therefore the promise of better physical conditions, whether here on earth or in a world to come, is what appeals to them. It does not really mean that these people understand the ideas behind the ideology, they lock in to the promise of better physical conditions.

Then you have another group of people, also a fairly large group of people, who are at the level where they are primarily focused on the emotional body. These are the people who are partly affected by safety needs but also the love and belonging needs. They need to have a certain feeling, often a feeling that they belong to a special group of people. They have a very strong need to feel that they are special somehow. This is what you see in many, many ideologies. You can even go back to the Old Testament times and look at the Jews and you can say: Did they have what you would normally call an ideology? Well, it has not been identified as such, but if you look at what they believed and their thought system, you can certainly see it as a form of ideology. Part of that ideology, a very important part for them, was that they were God's chosen people. Of all the people on earth, they were the chosen ones, they were special. They were chosen not only by some tribal God, but by the ultimate God.

You see how many Christians even today (and certainly since the formation of the Catholic church) have felt special because they are belonging to the only true religion and they are the only ones who will be saved and all the others will be condemned to an eternity of suffering in hell. Muslims feel the same, even some Buddhists, certainly many Hindus. Many other religions have felt this way. This is why you see that there are people for whom the emotions are very important. They respond to the emotions.

You will see for example if you look at the situation in the United States, as we have talked about, that there was a large group of people who were pulled into a certain emotional reaction to the election and many of them were fundamentalist, evangelical Christians. Many of these Christians go to church every Sunday to get a certain feeling, a certain emotion. Some of the pastors who attract the biggest congregations, they have realized that you need to give people a certain emotional experience in order to get them to come back to your church. This is what they do and this is what they extended into the political realm, that here is finally a movement, finally a president, that will satisfy our need to feel that we belong to this select group of people. You see of course many other examples of this. You see how some people were pulled into Marxism because it gave them a certain feeling. You see how in the Soviet Union many, many events and rituals and songs and parades and all of these things, much ideology that people were brought up with from childhood, was aimed at giving them a certain feeling that they were so special because they were Russians, they belonged to the Soviet Union, they were communists and so forth and so on. This is the emotional level.

Then you have a smaller group of people, but still in the modern democracies a fairly large group of people (at least a large percentage of the population) who are focused at the mental level. For these people what is very, very important is what I talked about in my previous discourse: the rational mind. They may have a certain desire to see physical changes. They may have a certain emotional reaction to feeling special but what primarily attracts them to an ideology is the logical, rational arguments. You also have a smaller group of people who are focused at the identity level. Many of these people are intuitive. They are spiritual people and therefore they are not very easily pulled into an ideology but there are some that have been and still are. It is because for them, the ideology gives them a sense of identity as being special. As it was said in the five elements of an ideology, it appealed to certain intellectuals as being the driving force behind world changes so for them this is very important. It is also because they are in the lower levels of the identity realm and the rational arguments are still very important for these people.

How people become convinced by an ideology

What I want to discourse on here is this: How do people become so absolutely convinced that their ideology explains everything that needs to be explained? Even though people are focused at the various levels, you will see that as you go higher into the mental and identity realm, all four elements are important. People who are primarily focused at the physical level, the rational thought is not important to them because they cannot grasp the rational thought behind the ideology. They do not actually see that the ideology does not explain everything. They hardly even see what the ideology explains, they are focused on the promise of better physical conditions.

Then there are people at the emotional level, they also cannot really grasp the rational thought behind the ideology because they respond to the feelings that it gives them. But when you go to people at the mental and identity level, all four come into play. What happens here is this: At the identity level these people feel they are special. However it is defined by the thought system, ideology, they feel special. Some Christians feel special by being Christians, but even in the Christian religion you saw a certain group of clergy, priests, that felt that they were really special compared to the congregation. You saw in Marxism how the higher ups in the Communist Party felt really special. They were the special people, the driving force behind the changes. It was only because of them that physical changes could happen. Physical changes do not just happen, they need someone to make them happen and they were the people who could do it. Then, you saw people who are focused in the mental realm and they also had a sense that they were the driving force but they were mainly the driving force, not because of who they were, but because of what they could understand. They could grasp the ideology.

Here is the question I want to pose. You have certain people who are focused at the physical level, who are incapable of grasping the ideas behind a certain ideology. You have people at the emotional level who cannot grasp it. Then you have people who are focused at the mental and identity level and they are capable of grasping the ideas behind a certain ideology. What does this mean? This means they are actually capable of looking at the ideology and saying: "Okay, I can see that the ideology can explain this condition and that condition and that condition. But over here is another condition and another condition and another condition and I cannot see how the ideology can explain those." In other words, these people are capable of seeing the limitations of the ideology, the contradictions in the ideology and the fact that the ideology cannot explain everything. Given that their minds are capable of grasping this, why are they not grasping it? Why are they not seeing it? Why are they pulled into this state of mental, spiritual blindness where they think (they are convinced) that the ideology is perfect, it is complete, it explains everything?

Well, it is because, as we have said before, the intellect, the rational mind, can prove and disprove *anything.* When you use the intellect, the rational mind, it is a *relative* faculty but you are always striving to come up with something that is *absolute,* something that is a foundation. It has been called a paradigm by philosophers. It is something that does not need to be questioned. Here is something that you do not need to question.

This is what basically all philosophers have done throughout history. If you read philosophy, you will see that philosopher after philosopher has started by establishing a basis, a firm foundation that says: "Here is something I cannot doubt. Therefore, this is the starting point for my philosophy and upon this set of ideas that I do not doubt, I build my philosophy." This is how the rational mind works. The rational mind could actually create a philosophy that did not have an absolute or firm starting point, but how would that appeal to people when people have the needs I have talked about: the need to feel that one day they can be happy and avoid unhappiness, one day they can overcome dissatisfaction.

The purpose of an ideology is not to explain, but to give people the impression that they can overcome the dissatisfaction. How can they do that if it does not have a firm foundation? How could the promise seem believable if everything can be questioned and nothing is really firm? You see that even the intellectuals who are capable of seeing the limitations of, for example Marxism, they do not see them. They are not looking because they have such a desire to see physical changes in society. They have for example (as many intellectuals have) a desire that nobody should be poor, that everybody should have a decent standard of living, the entire population should have a decent standard of living. They see that this was not fulfilled in the capitalist societies that followed the industrial revolution. Nor was it of course fulfilled in the feudal societies. They become convinced that something new is needed, here is something new, Marxism, so they convince themselves that Marxism will produce the changes because it is so different from what has come before. This is the physical level.

Then you have the emotional level where they also have a need to feel secure, to feel that if they follow this ideology, everything will be all right. This gives them this sense that: "Yes, I trust that we are going in the right direction. I am convinced that everything will work out and that everything will be good—when these changes are made that the ideology specifies." Once these two decisions have been made, people have decided that an ideology can produce the physical changes that I desire, and therefore it can give me the feeling that I desire (that of having the kind of society I desire and the kind of physical, personal conditions that I desire). Once they have decided that the ideology can fulfill this, they are using their intellectual, rational minds very selectively. They begin to look only for what confirms the ideology, what seems to validate it, and they discount, ignore or seek to argue against whatever questions the ideology.

The religious conversion to an ideology

You see many, many people who in their teenage years went through this state of rebelling against authority, rebelling against the established order of society (feeling that this was not right, that something needed to change). Then, as they become a little older, perhaps go to university, all of a sudden they go through this shift. They would deny it, many of them would not describe it this way, but it is the same kind of shift that people go through when they are converted into a particular religion. They are literally converted into this ideology and now they believe, they have faith. They believe that this is the ultimate ideology. It will produce the physical changes they desire. It will give them the feeling they desire and it will explain to their satisfaction how the world works so they can feel that they are understanding how the world works, they are in control of their lives because they understand how the world works. For some, it will give them the sense that they belong to a special group, a special class, of people who are the only ones who can bring these changes.

When you look at people, when you look at their state of consciousness, you can literally see that they go through a period where they have started to have some genuine insights that the old belief system, the old thought system, the old ideology has limitations. In other words, they start seeing the limitations in the old ideology. Many people in previous decades grew up in a largely Christian society in the West. They started seeing the shortcomings of the Christian religion. They started seeing how many things that church doctrine could not explain and they became dissatisfied and gave up on this ideology. Then, they were looking for something else and they went through a period where they were actively thinking, they were very actively thinking about how to explain the world. Then, many of them went to college. They were exposed to teachers who were Marxists, flaming, convinced Marxists, and suddenly these young people also became pulled into the Marxist energetic spiral. Now their critical minds, that could see all the shortcomings of the old religion, were not applied to Marxism, and therefore they could not see any of the contradictions and shortcomings in that ideology. You can literally see, if you could see the auric force fields of these people, the shift that happens. You can see how their emotional bodies are open to a certain feeling and all of a sudden it affects their mental bodies. Something clicks, something turns, something shifts and now they are literally aligning themselves with this energetic matrix of ideas and energies created by this ideology—Marxism or something else. They are literally surrendering themselves to the collective beast that has been created by this ideology. They are suspending their critical thinking when it comes to Marxism but they are maintaining it when it comes to Christianity and capitalism and any other ideology. It is like they are constantly projecting their critical minds outside of themselves and the ideology that has now become part of themselves, part of their sense of identity, part of the way they think about the world, part of what they feel about the world and part of how they act. It is a fundamental shift. There is a certain religious conversion aura over it, and it is not necessarily dissimilar to what some people have gone through when they have found a spiritual teaching, including an ascended master teaching.

You can go back to previous ascended master teachings and you will see that when people entered a teaching, became convinced about this, they had all the same elements. They felt there were certain changes that *should* happen and that the teachings could bring about. This gave them a certain feeling because they were in this teaching. Intellectually they felt that the teaching could explain something and they felt it gave them a special sense of identity as the lightbearers who were saving the world for Saint Germain. I am not mocking this in any way. I am simply pointing out the similarities, because what happened to some of these ascended master students is that after they entered that ascended master organization, their growth came to a halt because they stopped being open. They stopped asking questions, they stopped seeking for higher and higher explanations.

I am not saying that it cannot be done in this dispensation either, as some people have certainly done so, but we have given many teachings to help you overcome this mindset. We have constantly talked about growing towards a higher and higher state of consciousness. We have given levels of teachings that you can see go back to where we, in the early years, gave teachings that were fairly similar to what was given in the last dispensation. They could serve as a bridge for people but then we started giving teachings on the ego, nonduality, duality, the epic mindset. Now we are giving teachings on the separate selves and we have stepped up the teachings, as was said in the Christhood seminar and in other answers, way beyond what we have previously been able to do in one dispensation. You have the tools to avoid this reaction where you can continue to grow for the rest of this lifetime, using this teaching, using other teachings as you see fit, but you are first of all loyal to your growth not to an outer teaching, not to an outer messenger, not to an ideology.

An ideology is more than a collection of ideas

What is an ideology? Is it just any collection of ideas? No, it is not the ideas that make an ideology. It is the reaction I have just described where you go into a specific state of mind, where you become converted to this ideology and you are only using your critical mind to look outside of the ideology. Any collection of ideas is not an ideology in itself. The teachings of Karl Marx were not an ideology in itself. The teachings of Jesus were not an ideology. The teachings of the ascended masters were not an ideology in themselves. When people become converted, when they become convinced that this is the ultimate understanding, then a collection of ideas becomes an ideology because now people think they do not need to go higher. *This* is the primary function of an ideology: To make you believe that you now have the ultimate definition of life. To make you feel that way, act that way and identify yourself as a being who is defined by this teaching and therefore you do not need to transcend the outer teaching and go within and have experiences that are beyond any outer teaching. We might say that the purpose of an ideology, from the mindset of the most advanced fallen beings, is precisely this: to fool the most advanced and most creative people into stopping their growth because they are focused on the ideology instead of going within.

Now, you will see, as I talked about those who are focused in the mental and identity realm, that many of these are spiritual people. All of you are primarily focused in the mental or the identity realm or you would not be open to an ascended master teaching. When you look at history, you can see that many spiritual people who had greater intuition have still been pulled into an ideology. As Sanat Kumara has talked about, there are even avatars who have been pulled into supporting various ideologies including Nazism and communism, Christianity, Buddhism, whatever you have.

This is what you who are ascended master students can benefit from looking at honestly. Looking at yourselves, taking these teachings I have given, evaluating them very carefully by questioning: "Have I been pulled into this? Can I see these tendencies in myself, that there are certain things I so would like to have happen at the physical, there is a certain feeling I really would like to have, there is a certain sense of understanding everything that I really want, and there is even a certain sense of wanting to be a special kind of person?" If you see this in yourself, then you can use our teachings, these teachings that we are giving at this, at the Christ discernment seminar and many other teachings in the three previous books on dictatorships, fanaticism, elitism, to free yourself from this. You can literally free yourself from it.

Why is this important? Well, it is important for your own growth but it is important also because as long as you have this in your mind, you are tied to the collective consciousness, to the collective beast. That collective beast has a pull on your emotional body, your mental body, your identity body and it is constantly pulling you back to earth, back to earth, back to earth. Therefore, there is a limit to what you can transcend because as we have said many times, the key to the ascension is not what you *hold on to* from earth, but that what you *let go of* from earth, meaning you have to let go of *everything* from earth in order to ascend. Otherwise, how can you make the completely free choice to leave the earth behind forever? If you have any attachments, unfulfilled desires. If you have any change that you think must happen on earth before you can leave, if you have a certain feeling you have not had enough of, if you have a certain understanding that you feel you must have on earth, or if you have that need to feel special and be in a special group of people—if you have that, how can you leave?

When you stand there in front of that gate where one step takes you through the ascension gate, it has to be a completely free choice. You might say that a person at the lowest level of consciousness possible on earth, has hardly any ability to make free choices. As you raise your consciousness towards the 144th level, your free will becomes increasingly free because there is less and less ties to the collective consciousness, less and less reactionary patterns, separate selves and so on. You can make freer and freer choices. Until you are at the 144th level, you cannot make the ultimate free choice that can be made on earth. It is the choice to look back at earth, look at everything that is happening here, look at everything you have gone through in your many lifetimes since you came, look at it all and say: "There is nothing here for me anymore. I am ready to move on." Then, you can turn around, look into the ascended realm and you can make this absolutely, completely free decision to forever leave the earth behind and step into a new identity as an ascended master.

No ideology will take you to the ascended state. Only letting go of all ideologies will take you to the ascended state. How do I know? Because I had to let go of all ideologies in order to ascend, even what one might call the ideology of Buddhism. Even though I spent the last many years of my last embodiment teaching, I still had to let go of that teaching in order to ascend and that is why I am now Gautama Buddha, the Ascended Master.

4 INVOKING AWARENESS OF WHY PEOPLE BELIEVE IN IDEOLOGIES (PART 1)

In the name of the I AM THAT I AM, Jesus Christ, I use the authority that I have as a being in embodiment on earth to call upon Gautama Buddha to reinforce my calls and use my chakras to project the statements in this invocation into the collective consciousness and awaken people to the need to free ourselves from the ideological mindset. Awaken people to the reality that we are spiritual beings and that we can co-create a new future by working with the ascended masters. I especially call for …

[Make your own calls here.]

Part 1

1. Gautama Buddha, awaken the most creative people to see that throughout history, many people have been pulled into the energetic matrix of a certain ideology and they have been absolutely convinced that this ideology did give a full explanation for life, even for why people are dissatisfied and how to get over their dissatisfaction.

Archangel Michael, light so blue,
my heart has room for only you.
My mind is one, no longer two,
your love for me is ever true.

Archangel Michael, you are here,
consuming now all doubt and fear.
Your Presence is forever near,
you are to me so very dear.

2. Gautama Buddha, awaken the most creative people to consider how it is possible that human beings have an explanation that is not absolute, that might not be true, but they are fully convinced that it *is* the truth.

Archangel Michael, I will be,
all one with your reality.
No fear can hold me as I see,
this world no power has o'er me.

Archangel Michael, you are here,
consuming now all doubt and fear.
Your Presence is forever near,
you are to me so very dear.

3. Gautama Buddha, awaken the most creative people to see that there are certain beings who form a power elite and who are doing everything possible to deceive human beings for the purpose of controlling us.

Archangel Michael, hold me tight,
shatter now the darkest night.
Clear my chakras with your light,
restore to me my inner sight.

Archangel Michael, you are here,
consuming now all doubt and fear.
Your Presence is forever near,
you are to me so very dear.

4. Gautama Buddha, awaken the most creative people to look at history and see that there has always been a certain elite in any society. There is a tendency for an elite to form. They seek to gain a position that they think cannot be challenged, that cannot be overthrown.

> Archangel Michael, now I stand,
> with you the light I do command.
> My heart I ever will expand,
> till highest truth I understand.

> **Archangel Michael, you are here,**
> **consuming now all doubt and fear.**
> **Your Presence is forever near,**
> **you are to me so very dear.**

5. Gautama Buddha, awaken the most creative people to see that many times an *established* power elite has sat on this position for a long time, but eventually the elite was overturned.

> Archangel Michael, in my heart,
> from me you never will depart.
> Of hierarchy I am a part,
> I now accept a fresh new start.

> **Archangel Michael, you are here,**
> **consuming now all doubt and fear.**
> **Your Presence is forever near,**
> **you are to me so very dear.**

6. Gautama Buddha, awaken the most creative people to see that in many cases this happened because there was an aspiring power elite that managed to overthrow the ruling elite and they then took the position of the ruling elite.

> Archangel Michael, sword of blue,
> all darkness you are cutting through.
> My Christhood I do now pursue,
> discernment shows me what is true.

Archangel Michael, you are here,
consuming now all doubt and fear.
Your Presence is forever near,
you are to me so very dear.

7. Gautama Buddha, awaken the most creative people to see that in many cases the aspiring power elite claimed that they were aiming to free the people from the tyranny of the established elite, but their real goal was to set themselves up in the position of the established elite.

Archangel Michael, in your wings,
I now let go of lesser things.
God's homing call in my heart rings,
my heart with yours forever sings.

Archangel Michael, you are here,
consuming now all doubt and fear.
Your Presence is forever near,
you are to me so very dear.

8. Gautama Buddha, awaken the most creative people to see that in many cases the established elite took power because they had a certain ideology that supported their power. They maintained that power because they managed to keep the people believing in that ideology.

Archangel Michael, take me home,
in higher spheres I want to roam.
I am reborn from cosmic foam,
my life is now a sacred poem.

Archangel Michael, you are here,
consuming now all doubt and fear.
Your Presence is forever near,
you are to me so very dear.

9. Gautama Buddha, awaken the most creative people to see that when an aspiring power elite overthrew the established elite, they used a different ideology that challenged the previous one. The previous one claimed to

have the ultimate truth, but then a new ideology came up that claimed the old ideology was in error and now they had the final truth.

Archangel Michael, light you are,
shining like the bluest star.
You are a cosmic avatar,
with you I will go very far.

Archangel Michael, you are here,
consuming now all doubt and fear.
Your Presence is forever near,
you are to me so very dear.

Part 2

1. Gautama Buddha, awaken the most creative people to consider why people can become convinced that an ideology really does explain life in a way they feel is complete, logical and rational.

O Jesus, blessed brother mine,
I walk the path that you outline,
a great example to us all,
I follow now your inner call.

O Jesus, let the Fire of Joy,
consume the devil's subtle ploy,
transfigured is our planet earth,
the golden age is given birth.

2. Gautama Buddha, awaken the most creative people to see that the moment we step into the duality consciousness, we are stepping into a very specific state of mind. Once we are in that state of mind, we think there is nothing else except duality, there is nothing outside of duality, there is no alternative.

O Jesus, open inner sight,
the ego wants to prove it's right,
but this I will no longer do,
I want to be all one with you.

O Jesus, let the Fire of Joy,
consume the devil's subtle ploy,
transfigured is our planet earth,
the golden age is given birth.

3. Gautama Buddha, awaken the most creative people to see that when we are trapped in duality, we think there is not a different state of consciousness, duality is the only state of consciousness that is possible for a human being on earth.

O Jesus, I now clearly see,
the Key of Knowledge given me,
my Christ self I hereby embrace,
as you fill up my inner space.

O Jesus, let the Fire of Joy,
consume the devil's subtle ploy,
transfigured is our planet earth,
the golden age is given birth.

4. Gautama Buddha, awaken the most creative people to see that once we become trapped in duality, we do not realize that duality has a built-in, an inherent, an inescapable tension. There is this tension that causes the dissatisfaction.

O Jesus, show me serpent's lie,
expose the beam in my own eye,
as Christ discernment you me give,
in oneness I forever live.

O Jesus, let the Fire of Joy,
consume the devil's subtle ploy,
transfigured is our planet earth,
the golden age is given birth.

5. Gautama Buddha, awaken the most creative people to consider why hardly anyone realizes they are trapped in a certain state of mind, that it is the state of mind that causes the dissatisfaction and that the only way out is to transcend the duality consciousness.

O Jesus, I am truly meek,
and thus I turn the other cheek,
when the accuser attacks me,
I go within and merge with thee.

**O Jesus, let the Fire of Joy,
consume the devil's subtle ploy,
transfigured is our planet earth,
the golden age is given birth.**

6. Gautama Buddha, awaken the most creative people to see that we do not realize this because going into duality is part of what is allowed by the Law of Free Will on a planet like earth. Duality is simply an experience one can have in the full spectrum of free will.

O Jesus, ego I let die,
surrender ev'ry earthly tie,
the dead can bury what is dead,
I choose to walk with you instead.

**O Jesus, let the Fire of Joy,
consume the devil's subtle ploy,
transfigured is our planet earth,
the golden age is given birth.**

7. Gautama Buddha, awaken the most creative people to see that in duality, we have a state where everything is relative. Nothing is absolute in duality.

O Jesus, help me rise above,
the devil's test through higher love,
show me separate self unreal,
my formless self you do reveal.

O Jesus, let the Fire of Joy,
consume the devil's subtle ploy,
transfigured is our planet earth,
the golden age is given birth.

8. Gautama Buddha, awaken the most creative people to see that when we begin to glimpse non-duality, as compared to duality, we realize that when we are not in duality, there is always an absolute frame of reference.

O Jesus, what is that to me,
I just let go and follow thee,
with this I do pass ev'ry test,
to find with you eternal rest.

O Jesus, let the Fire of Joy,
consume the devil's subtle ploy,
transfigured is our planet earth,
the golden age is given birth.

9. Gautama Buddha, awaken the most creative people to see that when we are not in duality, we know that all life is one, therefore there is no separation and we know that there is no need to compare ourselves to other people because we are following an individual path that leads towards higher states of consciousness. We are not setting ourselves up as being better or more important than others.

O Jesus, fiery master mine,
my heart now melting into thine,
I love with heart and mind and soul,
the God who is my highest goal.

O Jesus, let the Fire of Joy,
consume the devil's subtle ploy,
transfigured is our planet earth,
the golden age is given birth.

Part 3

1. Gautama Buddha, awaken the most creative people to see that when we *do* step into duality, part of the experience that we want to have is that everything is relative, meaning we can now see ourselves relative to other people.

> Maitreya, I am truly meek,
> your counsel wise I humbly seek,
> your vision I so want to see,
> with you in Eden I will be.

> **Maitreya, kindness is the cure,**
> **in fires of kindness I am pure.**
> **Maitreya, now release the fire,**
> **that raises me forever higher.**

2. Gautama Buddha, awaken the most creative people to see that in duality we can see our state of mind as relative to an opposite state of mind, which is what gives rise to the many dualistic polarities, such as happiness and unhappiness.

> Maitreya, help me to return,
> to learn from you, I truly yearn,
> as oneness is all I desire
> I feel initiation's fire.

> **Maitreya, kindness is the cure,**
> **in fires of kindness I am pure.**
> **Maitreya, now release the fire,**
> **that raises me forever higher.**

3. Gautama Buddha, awaken the most creative people to see that when we are not in duality, it is not that we are dissatisfied or unhappy but neither are we happy, as happiness is defined on earth.

Maitreya, I hereby decide,
from you I will no longer hide,
expose to me the very lie
that caused edenic self to die.

Maitreya, kindness is the cure,
in fires of kindness I am pure.
Maitreya, now release the fire,
that raises me forever higher.

4. Gautama Buddha, awaken the most creative people to see that the happiness is not defined in relation to an opposite. We are in a state of mind that is positive and uplifting, but it has no opposite.

Maitreya, blessed Guru mine,
my heart of hearts forever thine,
I vow that I will listen well,
so we can break the serpent's spell.

Maitreya, kindness is the cure,
in fires of kindness I am pure.
Maitreya, now release the fire,
that raises me forever higher.

5. Gautama Buddha, awaken the most creative people to see that words as they are used on earth cannot describe what is beyond duality because they have been so affected by duality. In nonduality we are in a state of mind that has no opposite, we are at peace, we are content, we are not dissatisfied.

Maitreya, help me see the lie
whereby the serpent broke the tie,
the serpent now has naught in me,
in oneness I am truly free.

Maitreya, kindness is the cure,
in fires of kindness I am pure.
Maitreya, now release the fire,
that raises me forever higher.

6. Gautama Buddha, awaken the most creative people to see that when we step into duality, we step into a state of mind where there must be an opposite to any state of mind. It is possible to have an experience of happiness in duality but it is in contrast to unhappiness.

> Maitreya, truth does set me free
> from falsehoods of duality,
> the fruit of knowledge I let go,
> so your true spirit I do know.

> **Maitreya, kindness is the cure,**
> **in fires of kindness I am pure.**
> **Maitreya, now release the fire,**
> **that raises me forever higher.**

7. Gautama Buddha, awaken the most creative people to see that in duality, our happiness can never be absolute, it is a relative happiness, it is defined in relation to an opposite. There is always the tension because we might feel happy, but we know there is the possibility that we could lose our happiness and go into unhappiness.

> Maitreya, I submit to you,
> intentions pure, my heart is true,
> from ego I am truly free,
> as I am now all one with thee.

> **Maitreya, kindness is the cure,**
> **in fires of kindness I am pure.**
> **Maitreya, now release the fire,**
> **that raises me forever higher.**

8. Gautama Buddha, awaken the most creative people to see that because we know that our physical bodies will eventually die, we always have that tension and this means that we can never be fully and completely satisfied. It is not possible because we cannot relate to anything absolute, we can only relate to something relative, we always have the contrasts.

> Maitreya, kindness is the key,
> all shades of kindness teach to me,

for I am now the open door,
the Art of Kindness to restore.

Maitreya, kindness is the cure,
in fires of kindness I am pure.
Maitreya, now release the fire,
that raises me forever higher.

9. Gautama Buddha, awaken the most creative people to see that in duality we can have experiences that we cannot have when we are not in duality. The experience we can have in duality is that we can have tremendous contrast.

Maitreya, oh sweet mystery,
immersed in your reality,
the myst'ry school will now return,
for this, my heart does truly burn.

Maitreya, kindness is the cure,
in fires of kindness I am pure.
Maitreya, now release the fire,
that raises me forever higher.

Part 4

1. Gautama Buddha, awaken the most creative people to see that in duality, we can feel much more happy than we ever feel when we are not in duality because we have the contrast between what we call happiness and what we call unhappiness. We are defining two states of consciousness in duality: happiness and unhappiness.

Gautama, show my mental state
that does give rise to love and hate,
your exposé I do endure,
so my perception will be pure.

**Gautama, Flame of Cosmic Peace,
unruly thoughts do hereby cease,
we radiate from you and me
the peace to still Samsara's Sea.**

2. Gautama Buddha, awaken the most creative people to see that once we are in duality, we experience that unhappiness is unpleasant and happiness is pleasant. We want to always have happiness and avoid unhappiness.

Gautama, in your Flame of Peace,
the struggling self I now release,
the Buddha Nature I now see,
it is the core of you and me.

**Gautama, Flame of Cosmic Peace,
unruly thoughts do hereby cease,
we radiate from you and me
the peace to still Samsara's Sea.**

3. Gautama Buddha, awaken the most creative people to see that this is the mindset we go into in duality. We want to avoid the unpleasant, we want to always have the pleasant.

Gautama, I am one with thee,
Mara's demons do now flee,
your Presence like a soothing balm,
my mind and senses ever calm.

**Gautama, Flame of Cosmic Peace,
unruly thoughts do hereby cease,
we radiate from you and me
the peace to still Samsara's Sea.**

4. Gautama Buddha, awaken the most creative people to see that this is an *inevitable* reaction but it is also an *impossible* reaction. We cannot have happiness without unhappiness because if we did, there would be no contrast and then there would be no duality. Therefore, we go into a mindset of striving for something different than what we have now.

Gautama, I now take the vow,
to live in the eternal now,
with you I do transcend all time,
to live in present so sublime.

**Gautama, Flame of Cosmic Peace,
unruly thoughts do hereby cease,
we radiate from you and me
the peace to still Samsara's Sea.**

5. Gautama Buddha, awaken the most creative people to see that when we go into duality, we forget we are spiritual beings, but there is still a striving for something more. We want to have more than what we have in duality.

Gautama, I have no desire,
to nothing earthly I aspire,
in non-attachment I now rest,
passing Mara's subtle test.

**Gautama, Flame of Cosmic Peace,
unruly thoughts do hereby cease,
we radiate from you and me
the peace to still Samsara's Sea.**

6. Gautama Buddha, awaken the most creative people to see that when we are trapped in seeing unhappiness contrasted with happiness, we inevitably determine that we want *more* happiness, we want to be more happy, we want to have an experience of being more happy than we have ever been before.

Gautama, I melt into you,
my mind is one, no longer two,
immersed in your resplendent glow,
Nirvana is all that I know.

**Gautama, Flame of Cosmic Peace,
unruly thoughts do hereby cease,
we radiate from you and me
the peace to still Samsara's Sea.**

7. Gautama Buddha, awaken the most creative people to see that in duality, happiness can only exist relative to unhappiness. Now we have a planet where all people have gone into duality. We are all striving for a greater and greater experience of happiness, but we can have this greater experience of happiness only when happiness is contrasted with unhappiness.

Gautama, in your timeless space,
I am immersed in Cosmic Grace,
I know the God beyond all form,
to world I will no more conform.

Gautama, Flame of Cosmic Peace,
unruly thoughts do hereby cease,
we radiate from you and me
the peace to still Samsara's Sea.

8. Gautama Buddha, awaken the most creative people to see that we can have a greater experience of *happiness* only if there is also a greater experience of *unhappiness*. When the earth first went into duality, there was a certain spectrum between the deepest unhappiness that was possible on earth and the highest happiness that was possible on earth.

Gautama, I am now awake,
I clearly see what is at stake,
and thus I claim my sacred right
to be on earth the Buddhic Light.

Gautama, Flame of Cosmic Peace,
unruly thoughts do hereby cease,
we radiate from you and me
the peace to still Samsara's Sea.

9. Gautama Buddha, awaken the most creative people to see that people have expanded that spectrum by making it possible to become more and more unhappy. This gives some people the sense that they are more and more happy in contrast to those people who are in unhappiness.

Gautama, with your thunderbolt,
we give the earth a mighty jolt,

I know that some will understand,
and join the Buddha's timeless band.

Gautama, Flame of Cosmic Peace,
unruly thoughts do hereby cease,
we radiate from you and me
the peace to still Samsara's Sea.

Part 5

1. Gautama Buddha, awaken the most creative people to see that when an entire planet has gone into duality, it is inevitable that large groups of people must be unhappy so that other people can feel happy compared to them. It cannot be any other way in duality.

Sanat Kumara, Ruby Fire,
I seek my place in love's own choir,
with open hearts we sing your praise,
together we the earth do raise.

Sanat Kumara, Ruby Ray,
bring to earth a higher way,
light this planet with your fire,
clothe her in a new attire.

2. Gautama Buddha, awaken the most creative people to see that in reality, the majority of the population are condemned to be unhappy. In any period in history, there has been an elite who felt they had some happiness, and then there has been a majority of the population who felt they did not have happiness compared to the elite.

Sanat Kumara, Ruby Fire,
initiations I desire,
I am for you an electrode,
Shamballa is my true abode.

**Sanat Kumara, Ruby Ray,
bring to earth a higher way,
light this planet with your fire,
clothe her in a new attire.**

3. Gautama Buddha, awaken the most creative people to see that the measure for determining whether we are happy or unhappy has not been our state of mind. In duality we have no absolute frame of reference so we cannot see that the ultimate way to be fulfilled is through oneness with our Higher Self.

Sanat Kumara, Ruby Fire,
I follow path that you require,
initiate me with your love,
the open door for Holy Dove.

**Sanat Kumara, Ruby Ray,
bring to earth a higher way,
light this planet with your fire,
clothe her in a new attire.**

4. Gautama Buddha, awaken the most creative people to see that only by being complete within ourselves, can we be ultimately at peace and fulfilled. In duality we have lost the connection to the I AM Presence, we cannot even conceive that we have such a connection or that this could satisfy us.

Sanat Kumara, Ruby Fire,
your great example all inspire,
with non-attachment and great mirth,
we give the earth a true rebirth.

**Sanat Kumara, Ruby Ray,
bring to earth a higher way,
light this planet with your fire,
clothe her in a new attire.**

5. Gautama Buddha, awaken the most creative people to see that in duality we are focused on outer conditions on earth. What determines our

happiness is the outer conditions we have. What determines our unhappiness is the outer conditions that we do *not* have.

> Sanat Kumara, Ruby Fire,
> you are this planet's purifier,
> consume on earth all spirits dark,
> reveal the inner Spirit Spark.

> **Sanat Kumara, Ruby Ray,**
> **bring to earth a higher way,**
> **light this planet with your fire,**
> **clothe her in a new attire.**

6. Gautama Buddha, awaken the most creative people to see that in every society, there has been an outer definition of what it means to be well to do, to be one of the elite. The assumption was that if you had the outer conditions of the elite, you should be happy.

> Sanat Kumara, Ruby Fire,
> you are a cosmic amplifier,
> the lower forces can't withstand,
> vibrations from Venusian band.

> **Sanat Kumara, Ruby Ray,**
> **bring to earth a higher way,**
> **light this planet with your fire,**
> **clothe her in a new attire.**

7. Gautama Buddha, awaken the most creative people to see that in many time periods the majority of the people felt unhappy because they did not have the physical conditions of the elite. The majority of the people assumed that the elite must be happy because they have these wonderful conditions.

> Sanat Kumara, Ruby Fire,
> I am on earth your magnifier,
> the flow of love I do restore,
> my chakras are your open door.

**Sanat Kumara, Ruby Ray,
bring to earth a higher way,
light this planet with your fire,
clothe her in a new attire.**

8. Gautama Buddha, awaken the most creative people to see that most among the elite were not happy after all even though they had these conditions. They felt they *should* be happy but they were not, and the reason was their psychological conditions.

Sanat Kumara, Ruby Fire,
Venusian song the multiplier,
as we your love reverberate,
the densest minds we penetrate.

**Sanat Kumara, Ruby Ray,
bring to earth a higher way,
light this planet with your fire,
clothe her in a new attire.**

9. Gautama Buddha, awaken the most creative people to see that today there are people who feel that, we have such good conditions today, compared to the past—we *should* be happy. Many decide with their outer minds: "I should be happy, I must be happy, I think I am happy." There is a certain feeling of happiness based on these outer conditions but it is not an inner feeling of happiness, it is relative.

Sanat Kumara, Ruby Fire,
you are for all the sanctifier,
the earth is now a holy place,
purified by cosmic grace.

**Sanat Kumara, Ruby Ray,
bring to earth a higher way,
light this planet with your fire,
clothe her in a new attire.**

Sealing

In the name of the I AM THAT I AM, I accept that Archangel Michael, Astrea and Shiva form an impenetrable shield around myself and all constructive people, sealing us from all fear-based energies in all four octaves. I accept that the Light of God is consuming and transforming all fear-based energies that make up the dark forces working against ending the era of ideology on earth!

5 INVOKING AWARENESS OF WHY PEOPLE BELIEVE IN IDEOLOGIES (PART 2)

In the name of the I AM THAT I AM, Jesus Christ, I use the authority that I have as a being in embodiment on earth to call upon Gautama Buddha to reinforce my calls and use my chakras to project the statements in this invocation into the collective consciousness and awaken people to the need to free ourselves from the ideological mindset. Awaken people to the reality that we are spiritual beings and that we can co-create a new future by working with the ascended masters. I especially call for …

[Make your own calls here.]

Part 1

1. Gautama Buddha, awaken the most creative people to see that there is a very old belief that our state of mind depends on physical, material conditions, either conditions outside ourselves or conditions in our own brains and bodies.

Archangel Michael, light so blue,
my heart has room for only you.
My mind is one, no longer two,
your love for me is ever true.

**Archangel Michael, you are here,
consuming now all doubt and fear.
Your Presence is forever near,
you are to me so very dear.**

2. Gautama Buddha, awaken the most creative people to see that people have been brainwashed for many lifetimes to believe that their state of mind depends on outer conditions. This is the engineering of the power elite who wants people to believe this.

Archangel Michael, I will be,
all one with your reality.
No fear can hold me as I see,
this world no power has o'er me.

**Archangel Michael, you are here,
consuming now all doubt and fear.
Your Presence is forever near,
you are to me so very dear.**

3. Gautama Buddha, awaken the most creative people to see that when we believe that our state of mind depends on external conditions, we have no control over our state of mind. The only way to change our state of mind is to change the external conditions.

Archangel Michael, hold me tight,
shatter now the darkest night.
Clear my chakras with your light,
restore to me my inner sight.

**Archangel Michael, you are here,
consuming now all doubt and fear.
Your Presence is forever near,
you are to me so very dear.**

4. Gautama Buddha, awaken the most creative people to see that the power elite wants us to believe this partly because they can control people. Other power elite beings want it because it allows them to get people into conflicts with other groups of people so they can steal their energy. Some simply want to create chaos.

Archangel Michael, now I stand,
with you the light I do command.
My heart I ever will expand,
till highest truth I understand.

**Archangel Michael, you are here,
consuming now all doubt and fear.
Your Presence is forever near,
you are to me so very dear.**

5. Gautama Buddha, awaken the most creative people to see that there is always a definition by an ideology that there is a change that should happen.

Archangel Michael, in my heart,
from me you never will depart.
Of hierarchy I am a part,
I now accept a fresh new start.

**Archangel Michael, you are here,
consuming now all doubt and fear.
Your Presence is forever near,
you are to me so very dear.**

6. Gautama Buddha, awaken the most creative people to see that the reason this change should happen is to supposedly make people feel better, to make them happy.

Archangel Michael, sword of blue,
all darkness you are cutting through.
My Christhood I do now pursue,
discernment shows me what is true.

**Archangel Michael, you are here,
consuming now all doubt and fear.
Your Presence is forever near,
you are to me so very dear.**

7. Gautama Buddha, awaken the most creative people to see that an ideology defines that there are certain changes in the external conditions in our society that need to happen, and the implicit promise is that if these changes do happen, those who are unhappy today are going to be happy when the changes have taken place.

Archangel Michael, in your wings,
I now let go of lesser things.
God's homing call in my heart rings,
my heart with yours forever sings.

**Archangel Michael, you are here,
consuming now all doubt and fear.
Your Presence is forever near,
you are to me so very dear.**

8. Gautama Buddha, awaken the most creative people to see that this scheme has been used in many ideologies, for example in Marxism where it was stated that when we get rid of the bourgeoisie and create a society based on Marxist principles, supposedly the workers will be happy because now their outer conditions have changed and therefore their inner conditions, their state of mind, must change accordingly.

Archangel Michael, take me home,
in higher spheres I want to roam.
I am reborn from cosmic foam,
my life is now a sacred poem.

**Archangel Michael, you are here,
consuming now all doubt and fear.
Your Presence is forever near,
you are to me so very dear.**

9. Gautama Buddha, awaken the most creative people to see that this is also found in religions, for example Christianity defines that happiness cannot be attained on earth. It can only be attained after the earthly existence in a higher realm.

Archangel Michael, light you are,
shining like the bluest star.
You are a cosmic avatar,
with you I will go very far.

**Archangel Michael, you are here,
consuming now all doubt and fear.
Your Presence is forever near,
you are to me so very dear.**

Part 2

1. Gautama Buddha, awaken the most creative people to see that after the formation of the Roman Catholic church, Christianity became an ideology that was used to control the population. It was used to justify changes, which did not benefit the broad population but cemented the formation of an elite.

O Jesus, blessed brother mine,
I walk the path that you outline,
a great example to us all,
I follow now your inner call.

**O Jesus, let the Fire of Joy,
consume the devil's subtle ploy,
transfigured is our planet earth,
the golden age is given birth.**

2. Gautama Buddha, awaken the most creative people to see that in the feudal societies in medieval Europe the elite not only owned the land but

even the people who lived on their land. This was a change that could not
have happened without the backing of the Catholic church.

> O Jesus, open inner sight,
> the ego wants to prove it's right,
> but this I will no longer do,
> I want to be all one with you.

> **O Jesus, let the Fire of Joy,**
> **consume the devil's subtle ploy,**
> **transfigured is our planet earth,**
> **the golden age is given birth.**

3. Gautama Buddha, awaken the most creative people to see that the Catholic church made people believe that it was not possible to have ideal conditions on earth so therefore they should accept the current conditions and
the bidding of the church, so they could have ideal conditions in heaven
after this lifetime.

> O Jesus, I now clearly see,
> the Key of Knowledge given me,
> my Christ self I hereby embrace,
> as you fill up my inner space.

> **O Jesus, let the Fire of Joy,**
> **consume the devil's subtle ploy,**
> **transfigured is our planet earth,**
> **the golden age is given birth.**

4. Gautama Buddha, awaken the most creative people to see that there
are many variations, but the common element is the promise that in some
future time, the people will be happy if they follow an elite.

> O Jesus, show me serpent's lie,
> expose the beam in my own eye,
> as Christ discernment you me give,
> in oneness I forever live.

**O Jesus, let the Fire of Joy,
consume the devil's subtle ploy,
transfigured is our planet earth,
the golden age is given birth.**

5. Gautama Buddha, awaken the most creative people to see that this is a very subtle element of ideology, which is not fully explained. Often, there is some outer explanation focusing on people's material situations, and there is a promise that this will change.

O Jesus, I am truly meek,
and thus I turn the other cheek,
when the accuser attacks me,
I go within and merge with thee.

**O Jesus, let the Fire of Joy,
consume the devil's subtle ploy,
transfigured is our planet earth,
the golden age is given birth.**

6. Gautama Buddha, awaken the most creative people to see that behind this implicit unspoken promise, there is the deeper promise that if people follow the elite, if they obey the elite that has defined and is administering the current ideology, then they will be happy.

O Jesus, ego I let die,
surrender ev'ry earthly tie,
the dead can bury what is dead,
I choose to walk with you instead.

**O Jesus, let the Fire of Joy,
consume the devil's subtle ploy,
transfigured is our planet earth,
the golden age is given birth.**

7. Gautama Buddha, awaken the most creative people to see that this is appealing to many people because they have for many lifetimes experienced that they have tried to make their own decisions to make themselves feel better but nothing has worked.

O Jesus, help me rise above,
the devil's test through higher love,
show me separate self unreal,
my formless self you do reveal.

**O Jesus, let the Fire of Joy,
consume the devil's subtle ploy,
transfigured is our planet earth,
the golden age is given birth.**

8. Gautama Buddha, awaken the most creative people to see that many people have come to a point where they are reluctant to make decisions because they realize it just leads to unhappiness. They become susceptible to the promise that if they follow an elite that has a superior ideology, they will be happy without having to make their own decisions.

O Jesus, what is that to me,
I just let go and follow thee,
with this I do pass ev'ry test,
to find with you eternal rest.

**O Jesus, let the Fire of Joy,
consume the devil's subtle ploy,
transfigured is our planet earth,
the golden age is given birth.**

9. Gautama Buddha, awaken the most creative people to see that this is another manipulation of the elite. Our unhappiness is caused by the decisions we have made personally. Make the decision to follow the elite and do what they tell us, then we will escape unhappiness.

O Jesus, fiery master mine,
my heart now melting into thine,
I love with heart and mind and soul,
the God who is my highest goal.

**O Jesus, let the Fire of Joy,
consume the devil's subtle ploy,**

**transfigured is our planet earth,
the golden age is given birth.**

Part 3

1. Gautama Buddha, awaken the most creative people to see that there is a certain group of people for whom an ideology appeals at the physical level. People who are very poor are likely to submit to an ideology that promises better physical conditions.

Maitreya, I am truly meek,
your counsel wise I humbly seek,
your vision I so want to see,
with you in Eden I will be.

**Maitreya, kindness is the cure,
in fires of kindness I am pure.
Maitreya, now release the fire,
that raises me forever higher.**

2. Gautama Buddha, awaken the most creative people to see that there is another group of people who are primarily focused on the emotional body. They have a strong need to feel that they are special, and many ideologies give them this feeling.

Maitreya, help me to return,
to learn from you, I truly yearn,
as oneness is all I desire
I feel initiation's fire.

**Maitreya, kindness is the cure,
in fires of kindness I am pure.
Maitreya, now release the fire,
that raises me forever higher.**

3. Gautama Buddha, awaken the most creative people to see that another group of people are focused at the mental level. For these people the

rational mind is very important. What primarily attracts them to an ideology is the logical, rational arguments.

> Maitreya, I hereby decide,
> from you I will no longer hide,
> expose to me the very lie
> that caused edenic self to die.

> **Maitreya, kindness is the cure,**
> **in fires of kindness I am pure.**
> **Maitreya, now release the fire,**
> **that raises me forever higher.**

4. Gautama Buddha, awaken the most creative people to see that a smaller group of people are focused at the identity level. Many of these people are intuitive and are not easily pulled into an ideology but for some, the ideology gives them a sense of identity as being the driving force behind world changes.

> Maitreya, blessed Guru mine,
> my heart of hearts forever thine,
> I vow that I will listen well,
> so we can break the serpent's spell.

> **Maitreya, kindness is the cure,**
> **in fires of kindness I am pure.**
> **Maitreya, now release the fire,**
> **that raises me forever higher.**

5. Gautama Buddha, awaken the most creative people to see that for those who are primarily focused at the physical level, the rational thought is not important to them because they cannot grasp the ideas behind the ideology. Those at the emotional level also cannot grasp the rational thought behind the ideology because they respond to the feelings that it gives them.

> Maitreya, help me see the lie
> whereby the serpent broke the tie,
> the serpent now has naught in me,
> in oneness I am truly free.

**Maitreya, kindness is the cure,
in fires of kindness I am pure.
Maitreya, now release the fire,
that raises me forever higher.**

6. Gautama Buddha, awaken the most creative people to see that for those at the mental and identity level, all four come into play. At the identity level these people feel they are special, however it is defined by the ideology.

Maitreya, truth does set me free
from falsehoods of duality,
the fruit of knowledge I let go,
so your true spirit I do know.

**Maitreya, kindness is the cure,
in fires of kindness I am pure.
Maitreya, now release the fire,
that raises me forever higher.**

7. Gautama Buddha, awaken the most creative people to see that such people know that physical changes do not just happen, they need someone to make them happen and they are the people who can do it.

Maitreya, I submit to you,
intentions pure, my heart is true,
from ego I am truly free,
as I am now all one with thee.

**Maitreya, kindness is the cure,
in fires of kindness I am pure.
Maitreya, now release the fire,
that raises me forever higher.**

8. Gautama Buddha, awaken the most creative people to see that those who are focused in the mental realm also have a sense that they are the driving force, but they are mainly the driving force because of what they can understand. They can grasp the ideology.

Maitreya, kindness is the key,
all shades of kindness teach to me,
for I am now the open door,
the Art of Kindness to restore.

Maitreya, kindness is the cure,
in fires of kindness I am pure.
Maitreya, now release the fire,
that raises me forever higher.

9. Gautama Buddha, awaken the most creative people to see that these people are capable of seeing the limitations of the ideology, the contradictions in the ideology and the fact that the ideology cannot explain everything. Given that their minds are capable of grasping this, why are they not grasping it? They are pulled into a state of mental, spiritual blindness where they are convinced that the ideology is perfect and explains everything.

Maitreya, oh sweet mystery,
immersed in your reality,
the myst'ry school will now return,
for this, my heart does truly burn.

Maitreya, kindness is the cure,
in fires of kindness I am pure.
Maitreya, now release the fire,
that raises me forever higher.

Part 4

1. Gautama Buddha, awaken the most creative people to see that this is because the intellect, the rational mind, can prove and disprove *anything*. The intellect is a *relative* faculty but we are always striving to come up with something that is *absolute*. It has been called a paradigm, something that does not need to be questioned.

Gautama, show my mental state
that does give rise to love and hate,
your exposé I do endure,
so my perception will be pure.

Gautama, Flame of Cosmic Peace,
unruly thoughts do hereby cease,
we radiate from you and me
the peace to still Samsara's Sea.

2. Gautama Buddha, awaken the most creative people to see that some people are capable of grasping the ideas behind a certain ideology. They are capable of looking at the ideology and saying: "Okay, I can see that the ideology can explain certain conditions, but some conditions the ideology cannot explain."

Gautama, in your Flame of Peace,
the struggling self I now release,
the Buddha Nature I now see,
it is the core of you and me.

Gautama, Flame of Cosmic Peace,
unruly thoughts do hereby cease,
we radiate from you and me
the peace to still Samsara's Sea.

3. Gautama Buddha, awaken the most creative people to see that basically all philosophers have started by establishing a basis, a firm foundation that says: "Here is something I cannot doubt. Therefore, this is the starting point and upon this set of ideas, I build my philosophy."

Gautama, I am one with thee,
Mara's demons do now flee,
your Presence like a soothing balm,
my mind and senses ever calm.

Gautama, Flame of Cosmic Peace,
unruly thoughts do hereby cease,

we radiate from you and me
the peace to still Samsara's Sea.

4. Gautama Buddha, awaken the most creative people to see that this is how the rational mind works. The rational mind could create a philosophy that did not have an absolute or firm starting point, but how would that appeal to people, when people have the need to feel that one day they can be happy and avoid unhappiness, one day they can overcome dissatisfaction.

Gautama, I now take the vow,
to live in the eternal now,
with you I do transcend all time,
to live in present so sublime.

Gautama, Flame of Cosmic Peace,
unruly thoughts do hereby cease,
we radiate from you and me
the peace to still Samsara's Sea.

5. Gautama Buddha, awaken the most creative people to see that the purpose of an ideology is not to explain, but to give people the impression that they can overcome the dissatisfaction. How can they do that if it does not have a firm foundation? How could the promise seem believable if everything can be questioned and nothing is really firm?

Gautama, I have no desire,
to nothing earthly I aspire,
in non-attachment I now rest,
passing Mara's subtle test.

Gautama, Flame of Cosmic Peace,
unruly thoughts do hereby cease,
we radiate from you and me
the peace to still Samsara's Sea.

6. Gautama Buddha, awaken the most creative people to see that even the intellectuals who are capable of seeing the limitations of an ideology do not see them. Some are not looking because they have a desire to see physical

changes. They become convinced that something new is needed, here is an ideology that promises it can do what has not been done before.

Gautama, I melt into you,
my mind is one, no longer two,
immersed in your resplendent glow,
Nirvana is all that I know.

**Gautama, Flame of Cosmic Peace,
unruly thoughts do hereby cease,
we radiate from you and me
the peace to still Samsara's Sea.**

7. Gautama Buddha, awaken the most creative people to see that at the emotional level people have a need to feel secure, to feel that if they follow this ideology everything will be all right. This gives them a sense that: "Yes, I trust that we are going in the right direction. I am convinced that everything will work out and that everything will be good, when the changes are made that the ideology specifies."

Gautama, in your timeless space,
I am immersed in Cosmic Grace,
I know the God beyond all form,
to world I will no more conform.

**Gautama, Flame of Cosmic Peace,
unruly thoughts do hereby cease,
we radiate from you and me
the peace to still Samsara's Sea.**

8. Gautama Buddha, awaken the most creative people to see that once people have decided that an ideology can produce the physical changes, and therefore give them the feeling they desire, they are using their intellectual, rational minds selectively. They begin to look only for what confirms the ideology and they discount whatever questions the ideology.

Gautama, I am now awake,
I clearly see what is at stake,

and thus I claim my sacred right
to be on earth the Buddhic Light.

Gautama, Flame of Cosmic Peace,
unruly thoughts do hereby cease,
we radiate from you and me
the peace to still Samsara's Sea.

9. Gautama Buddha, awaken the most creative people to see that in their teenage years many people went through a state of rebelling against the established order of society. Then, as they became a little older, they went through the same kind of shift that people go through when they are converted into a particular religion.

Gautama, with your thunderbolt,
we give the earth a mighty jolt,
I know that some will understand,
and join the Buddha's timeless band.

Gautama, Flame of Cosmic Peace,
unruly thoughts do hereby cease,
we radiate from you and me
the peace to still Samsara's Sea.

Part 5

1. Gautama Buddha, awaken the most creative people to see that many are literally converted into an ideology and now they believe, they have faith. They believe that this is the ultimate ideology. It will produce the physical changes they desire and give them the feeling they desire.

Sanat Kumara, Ruby Fire,
I seek my place in love's own choir,
with open hearts we sing your praise,
together we the earth do raise.

Sanat Kumara, Ruby Ray,
bring to earth a higher way,
light this planet with your fire,
clothe her in a new attire.

2. Gautama Buddha, awaken the most creative people to see that many believe an ideology will explain to their satisfaction how the world works. They think that when they understand how the world works, they are in control of their lives.

Sanat Kumara, Ruby Fire,
initiations I desire,
I am for you an electrode,
Shamballa is my true abode.

Sanat Kumara, Ruby Ray,
bring to earth a higher way,
light this planet with your fire,
clothe her in a new attire.

3. Gautama Buddha, awaken the most creative people to see that for some, an ideology gives them the sense that they belong to a special class of people who are the only ones who can bring the needed changes.

Sanat Kumara, Ruby Fire,
I follow path that you require,
initiate me with your love,
the open door for Holy Dove.

Sanat Kumara, Ruby Ray,
bring to earth a higher way,
light this planet with your fire,
clothe her in a new attire.

4. Gautama Buddha, awaken the most creative people to see that some go through a period where they have started to have some genuine insights that the old thought system, the old ideology has limitations. Many people have started seeing the shortcomings of the Christian religion.

Sanat Kumara, Ruby Fire,
your great example all inspire,
with non-attachment and great mirth,
we give the earth a true rebirth.

**Sanat Kumara, Ruby Ray,
bring to earth a higher way,
light this planet with your fire,
clothe her in a new attire.**

5. Gautama Buddha, awaken the most creative people to see that many have given up on the ideology of Christianity. Then, they were looking for something else and they went through a period where they were actively thinking about how to explain the world.

Sanat Kumara, Ruby Fire,
you are this planet's purifier,
consume on earth all spirits dark,
reveal the inner Spirit Spark.

**Sanat Kumara, Ruby Ray,
bring to earth a higher way,
light this planet with your fire,
clothe her in a new attire.**

6. Gautama Buddha, awaken the most creative people to see that many people in the West were exposed to teachers who were materialists and these young people became pulled into the materialist energetic spiral. Now their critical minds, that could see all the shortcomings of the old religion, were not applied to Materialism, and therefore they could not see any of the contradictions and shortcomings in that ideology.

Sanat Kumara, Ruby Fire,
you are a cosmic amplifier,
the lower forces can't withstand,
vibrations from Venusian band.

**Sanat Kumara, Ruby Ray,
bring to earth a higher way,**

light this planet with your fire,
clothe her in a new attire.

7. Gautama Buddha, awaken the most creative people to see that people's emotional bodies are open to a certain feeling and this affects their mental bodies. Something shifts and now they are aligning themselves with this energetic matrix of ideas and energies created by the ideology.

Sanat Kumara, Ruby Fire,
I am on earth your magnifier,
the flow of love I do restore,
my chakras are your open door.

Sanat Kumara, Ruby Ray,
bring to earth a higher way,
light this planet with your fire,
clothe her in a new attire.

8. Gautama Buddha, awaken the most creative people to see that they are literally surrendering themselves to the collective beast that has been created by this ideology. They are suspending their critical thinking when it comes to the new but they are maintaining it when it comes to the old ideology.

Sanat Kumara, Ruby Fire,
Venusian song the multiplier,
as we your love reverberate,
the densest minds we penetrate.

Sanat Kumara, Ruby Ray,
bring to earth a higher way,
light this planet with your fire,
clothe her in a new attire.

9. Gautama Buddha, awaken the most creative people to see that they are constantly projecting their critical minds outside of themselves and the ideology that has now become part of themselves. There is a certain religious conversion aura over it.

Sanat Kumara, Ruby Fire,
you are for all the sanctifier,
the earth is now a holy place,
purified by cosmic grace.

**Sanat Kumara, Ruby Ray,
bring to earth a higher way,
light this planet with your fire,
clothe her in a new attire.**

Part 6

1. Gautama Buddha, awaken the most creative people to see that after some ascended master students entered an organization, their growth came to a halt because they stopped being open. They stopped asking questions, they stopped seeking for higher and higher explanations.

Surya, cosmic being bright,
your balance is my pure delight,
I am in orbit round God Star,
in perfect unity we are.

**Surya, banish all extremes,
Surya, shatter Serpent's schemes,
Surya, balance to me bring,
Surya, making my heart sing.**

2. Gautama Buddha, awaken the most creative people to see that we need to continue to grow for the rest of this lifetime, using various teachings, being loyal to our growth not to an outer teaching, messenger or ideology.

Surya, there is more to life,
than human conflict, war and strife,
your balance gives me inner peace,
all outer conflicts do now cease.

Surya, banish all extremes,
Surya, shatter Serpent's schemes,
Surya, balance to me bring,
Surya, making my heart sing.

3. Gautama Buddha, awaken the most creative people to see that an ideology is more than a collection of ideas. It is not the ideas that make an ideology. It is the reaction where people go into a specific state of mind, where we become converted to this ideology and we are only using our critical minds to look outside of the ideology.

Surya, what a wondrous sight,
from Sirius you send the light,
of one mind, I now call to thee,
for your apprentice I would be.

Surya, banish all extremes,
Surya, shatter Serpent's schemes,
Surya, balance to me bring,
Surya, making my heart sing.

4. Gautama Buddha, awaken the most creative people to see that any collection of ideas is not an ideology in itself. When people become converted, when we become convinced that this is the ultimate understanding, then a collection of ideas becomes an ideology because now we think we do not need to go higher.

Surya, radiate your light,
with balance you set all things right,
consuming energetic dross,
my letting go is not a loss.

Surya, banish all extremes,
Surya, shatter Serpent's schemes,
Surya, balance to me bring,
Surya, making my heart sing.

5. Gautama Buddha, awaken the most creative people to see that the primary function of an ideology is to make people believe that we now have

the ultimate definition of life. This makes us feel a certain way, act a certain way and identify ourselves as beings who are defined by this teaching. Therefore, we do not need to transcend the outer teaching and go within and have experiences that are beyond any outer teaching.

Surya, your light is alive,
for inner balance I do strive,
the alchemy is now begun,
my heart transformed into a sun.

**Surya, banish all extremes,
Surya, shatter Serpent's schemes,
Surya, balance to me bring,
Surya, making my heart sing.**

6. Gautama Buddha, awaken the most creative people to see that the purpose of an ideology, from the mindset of the power elite, is to fool the most advanced and most creative people into stopping our growth because we are focused on the ideology instead of going within.

Surya, come enlighten me,
duality you help me see,
extremes they cannot pull me in,
on Middle Way I always win.

**Surya, banish all extremes,
Surya, shatter Serpent's schemes,
Surya, balance to me bring,
Surya, making my heart sing.**

7. Gautama Buddha, awaken the most creative people to see that many spiritual people who had greater intuition have still been pulled into an ideology.

Surya, in your cosmic sphere,
with Cuzco I your light revere,
from your perspective o so grand,
life finally I understand.

Surya, banish all extremes,
Surya, shatter Serpent's schemes,
Surya, balance to me bring,
Surya, making my heart sing.

8. Gautama Buddha, awaken the most creative people to question: "Have I been pulled into this? Can I see these tendencies in myself, that there are certain things I so would like to have happen at the physical, there is a certain feeling I really would like to have, there is a certain sense of understanding everything that I really want, and there is a sense of wanting to be a special kind of person."

Surya, show me God's design,
I see that God is all benign,
you calm my feeling body's storm,
I know the God beyond all form.

Surya, banish all extremes,
Surya, shatter Serpent's schemes,
Surya, balance to me bring,
Surya, making my heart sing.

9. Gautama Buddha, awaken the most creative people to overcome this and instead attain the Christ discernment that helps us fulfill the highest potential of our Divine plans, so we can truly bring changes to earth.

Surya, I come from afar,
and as you show me my home star,
I see now my internal light,
a star I am in my own right.

Surya, banish all extremes,
Surya, shatter Serpent's schemes,
Surya, balance to me bring,
Surya, making my heart sing.

Sealing

In the name of the I AM THAT I AM, I accept that Archangel Michael, Astrea and Shiva form an impenetrable shield around myself and all constructive people, sealing us from all fear-based energies in all four octaves. I accept that the Light of God is consuming and transforming all fear-based energies that make up the dark forces working against ending the era of ideology on earth!

6 HOW SCIENCE WAS PERVERTED BY IDEOLOGY

I AM the Ascended Master Gautama Buddha. I have talked about the different elements that, according to a worldly definition, are contained in the concept of ideology. The first element being that there is a set of ideas that attempts to explain how the world works, or at least how certain aspects of the world work. The next element is that there is a program for social and political or economic change that needs to happen. Now, the third element normally defined here is that this element of change that needs to happen is presented as a struggle. This is a correct observation because most ideologies contain the idea that there will be a struggle to implement the program defined by the ideology. What the worldly philosophers and theorists have not fully grasped is why there is this struggle—and there are a number of elements behind it.

One is that, as I have already talked about, when you go into duality, there is no ultimate truth that can be defined. Of course, you have a need to find an ultimate truth, and that is why, in order to appeal to people, most ideologies define some ultimate or absolute truth or understanding. Because this, regardless of the claim of absoluteness, is not an absolute truth but a relative truth, it is inevitable that some people on earth will not accept it. They will not accept the claim that this is an ultimate truth because they have another relative truth that they believe is the ultimate truth.

You now have at least two groups of people and the members of each group believe they have the ultimate truth, meaning the other group must be wrong in claiming that they have the ultimate truth. This is an inescapable aspect of duality, however, it is only an inescapable element of duality taken beyond a certain level. During the Christ Discernment Webinar that was given last year (see *www.ascendedmasterlight.com*), Maitreya explained that it is possible to go into duality without going into the more aggressive forms of duality. In other words, when the original inhabitants of the earth went into duality, they started seeing themselves as separate beings. This did create a division or segmentation into various groups of people, but this did not necessarily lead to conflict because these groups did not claim to have the ultimate truth in their understanding. They simply saw themselves as a particular group of people who wanted to have a particular experience of the many experiences possible on earth. There was a certain understanding that there are many different ways to live on earth and that it is acceptable that there are many different ways to live on earth. This created a certain tolerance where, even though these groups of people saw themselves as distinctly different, they did not have that epic value judgment that those who were not like them were wrong in some ultimate way. There was a certain tolerance for differences, for different ideas, beliefs and different experiences.

It is sort of a "live and let live" attitude, which you can also see in some of the democratic nations on earth who have a certain tolerance for the fact that they have slightly different versions of democracy. There may be some that believe they have the ultimate version of democracy, but it does not really lead to a massive armed conflict where one democratic nation is attempting to conquer another democratic nation because they think they do not have the ultimate version of democracy. It is possible to be in duality and have a certain tolerance.

When tolerance for differences is lost

The tolerance was lost on earth only after the fallen beings started embodying here, and that is why, if you really want to understand this, you have to understand about fallen beings. You have to understand that there are some beings who have gone against the design principles of the universe and who want to prove God wrong and who will do absolutely anything to pull people into these spirals that they have created.

Now, the fallen beings, from their very inception (as we have explained several times) created the epic mindset because they would not admit that they could be wrong. Therefore, even God himself had to be wrong—if the fallen beings could not be wrong. The ascended masters had to be wrong, and so forth. This creates that epic mindset where there is an absolute truth and therefore anything that deviates from it must be wrong in an absolute way. On top of that comes this sense that the fallen beings cannot tolerate anything that challenges their view, their absolute truth. They find it extremely difficult to tolerate other people with different beliefs. This is what sets up this epic clash where the fallen beings believe that it is absolutely necessary that one thought system, one ideology, becomes the dominant or even the *only* one on earth.

In order for the fallen beings to feel secure on earth, whether they are in physical embodiment or in the emotional, mental, or identity realm, they must (they think) eradicate all conflicting viewpoints. They must come to a point where there is only one ideology. This is their sense. Of course, it can never be fulfilled, not only because it is difficult to make people accept one ideology, but also because the fallen beings cannot descend onto a planet as only one or as a coherent group. There will always be at least two polarities among the fallen beings who are allowed to embody on a planet. It would never be possible that the fallen beings associated with earth could agree to support the same ideology. They will always be divided into at least two groups, each claiming to have the ultimate ideology, each feeling the epic need to eradicate the other ideology and establish their ideology as the only one.

After the earth was "infested," we might say, with the fallen beings, the epic mindset has had a very dominant influence on history, on the mindset and the thinking of earth, on the collective consciousness. You can see this if you look at, not even religions, but just look at philosophers. If you study the philosophers from modern times going back to the ancient Greeks, you will see that most philosophers were striving to come up with the ultimate thought system. This of course is inspired by the fallen beings, or at least by the mindset that the fallen beings have created on earth, the epic mindset. Many, many philosophers had started out their efforts to define a new philosophy based on this desire to come up with some ultimate truth, some ultimate understanding, that all the previous philosophers had failed to come up with.

There is of course a certain element of spiritual pride behind this, but the philosophers failed to see this. They believed firmly that it had to be possible to come up with an ultimate truth. You will of course see that many people today believe the same, whether they are philosophers, whether they are scientists, whether they are religious people, whether they are in the field of politics or economics or any of the particular sciences. They all believe, or at least many of them believe, that it is possible to come up with some ultimate understanding, a theory of everything, the theory that explains every aspect of life as it is known to human beings.

The first point I want to make here is simply to build on what we have said many times before, namely that this is an impossible quest. It is impossible partly because in duality, as I said, every viewpoint is relative and so it will always have an opposite. It is also impossible because there are certain things that the rational mind cannot grasp, cannot fathom.

What the rational mind cannot grasp

You can see this very simply. What are human beings? We have said you are really spiritual beings in human bodies, but you have forgotten this. We have said you are psychological beings, but beyond that, what are you? You are *experiential* beings. You are having an experience of what it is like to be on earth. What is it that the rational mind does? It seeks to create an *understanding* of life on earth. Now, why do you need an understanding when you have the direct experience?

Think about this seemingly simple sentence and what a world of thought can open up from it. You are all *experiencing* life on earth. You are having a direct experience of living on earth. Why isn't that enough? Well, for many people it actually *is*. But for some it is not, and of course this goes back to the fallen beings.

It is not enough for them to have an experience of what it is like because they fell. After they fell, they had to explain why they had fallen, and they could not explain this of course through experience because how do you explain an experience? They had to come up with an explanation for why they had fallen, and that explanation had to point the finger at someone else so it was not their "fault" that they fell. This mindset has then enveloped the earth to such a degree that many people, in fact most people on earth, cannot be satisfied with just experiencing life. They need to have some kind of explanation. Again, think about this. You have a direct experience, but now someone comes and they want to use the ratio- nal mind to create a theory, an explanation, and then they want to project that, to superimpose that, upon your direct experience. Now, first of all, it is impossible to come up with a complete explanation for all of the experiences human beings have on earth. You can see this through a simple example. Try to come up with a rational explanation for the taste of an orange. You all know what an orange tastes like, but how do you know it? Because you have experienced the taste with your senses. Imagine meeting a person who has not tasted an orange and now you have to use the rational mind to explain the taste to that person. Could you do it? Could you even come up with words that would describe the taste so that the person would experience the taste and not have to actually eat an orange?

You will see that this is simply not possible. You will not truly have the experience of what an orange tastes like until you eat it. There is no amount of explanation that can substitute the actual experience. It is an impossible quest to start with. What is more, what happens when you try to explain something with the rational mind? You distance yourself from it.

While your mouth is full with the soft, juicy fruit of an orange, and you are chewing that orange and the sap of the orange is running down your cheeks, how can you even begin to explain this? You are immersed in the experience. Then you finish, you swallow the orange, and after some time has passed, you get the idea: "You know, I should explain what an orange tastes like." How can you do this? Well, you cannot do it by taking another bite of the orange because then you are again immersed in the experience. What must you do? You must step back. You must distance yourself from the direct experience, and now you must seek to explain the experience. How can you explain it? You cannot explain it by referring to the taste, the feeling of holding the orange, the smell of the orange, the softness of the flesh and the juice, because these are experiences.

What must you do? You must create *concepts,* ideas in the rational mind. Then, you must seek to define these ideas in such a way that, in your mind, they describe the taste of an orange. As I said, this is doomed to failure, unless you no longer have the direct experience as a frame of reference. If you have never tasted an orange, or if it was so long ago that you can barely remember it, then perhaps you can be susceptible to believing that the concepts and ideas you have defined with the rational mind actually describe the experience. You can even come to believe that perhaps they describe the experience to such an extent, to such a degree, that you do not need the experience because the explanation is enough. You can refrain from having the experience.

Why explanations become a closed box

What is the result of *not* having the experience, of choosing not to have the experience? It is that you will never have a frame of reference for challenging your ideas, your explanation. Your explanation exists in the mind. There is nothing in the physical world that challenges your explanation so in your mind you can convince yourself that the explanation of the taste of an orange is complete and that you have the full understanding of what an orange tastes like, to the point where you do not need to eat an orange.

This is what the fallen beings did after they fell. After they fell, they lost the connection to their I AM Presences, to the ascended masters, to the spiritual realm. What did they have to do because they felt a sense of loss? Well, they had to come up with an explanation for why they did not need this connection. They did not need the direct experience of their I AM Presence or the flow of the Holy Spirit because their explanation was enough. The explanation they had created in their own minds was enough.

That is how they have justified (some of them falling through several spheres) not turning around and seeking the direct experience, which we would have helped them to have as soon as they were open to it. They have continued to walk further and further away from that experience by creating ever more elaborate layers of explanation for why it either is not real, why God does not exist, why it is not necessary, why it is not beneficial, and so on.

Of course, they are threatened when they come to a planet like earth where people are having so many different experiences. Of course, they are primarily threatened by those who say: "But I have a spiritual experience. I intuitively experience that there is a higher realm beyond the material, that I have a higher self, that there are beings in that higher realm that I can connect to." This is the ultimate threat, but they are even threatened by ordinary people who have physical experiences because the fallen beings live in their minds. They are still experiential beings but instead of having a *direct* experience, they are having a *substitute* experience in their minds. The fallen beings who came to earth, from the very start looked at this and felt that they were condemned to go to earth. They were punished by being sent to earth, and the earth was a primitive and low planet, compared to what they had known before. Therefore, they had no desire to experience life on this earth, at least not most aspects of it. They desired to have a certain privileged, easy lifestyle but the purpose for that was really that they could live in this ivory tower where they could stay within this aerial castle they had created in their minds and not have it challenged.

The fallen beings are narcissists

The fallen beings do not want a *physical* experience, they want a *psychic, mental, emotional* experience of earth, and therefore they are threatened by people who are immersing themselves in physical life, enjoying physical life. That is why they have come up with so many ideologies that are telling people how to live life on earth, what they should or should not do. For the fallen beings, an experience is not enough. There needs to be a mental construct that puts the experience into some broader context, which ultimately is their own attempt to explain the workings of the universe so that they have never been at fault in anything. They live in this world. They live in their own minds, which is the definition of a narcissist who cannot see beyond his own belly button, which he is constantly gazing at. This of course is the symbol behind the old Greek myth of Narcissus who was in love with his own mirror image. It is not the mirror image that the fallen beings are so in love with, it is their own mental image that they are in love with.

Now, as an example of what they have done, look at the fact that one of the things you can do with the physical body on earth is to have sex. It is not that some fallen beings have not enjoyed having sex, but they could not just enjoy the experience, as many people on earth are able to do. They had to explain it somehow, there had to be some kind of meaning behind it. That is why they were jealous of the people who just had an experience and enjoyed the experience without having to explain it. They could see that these people were happy and content and enjoying the experience in a way that they could not enjoy it.

You have some concept in some spiritual teachings, including the Bible, that there were angels (as they were called) in heaven who lusted after the daughters of men, and fell because they wanted to have sex with them. This is not actually the full explanation. First of all, they were not angels, they were beings in an unascended sphere, otherwise they could not have fallen, and they did not actually lust after the physical sex, they were jealous of the fact that the people on earth were just enjoying physical life in a way that the fallen beings could not do. You look at how they have used various religions, including most prominently the Christian religion, to create an entire explanation around sex and why sex is not spiritual, and why it is something that spiritual people should restrict themselves from doing. Or if they *are* doing it, they at least should not enjoy it, or they should not enjoy it too much, and so forth, and so on. Just an example of how the fallen beings have tried to create explanations, superimposed upon the physical experience.

Explanations create endless blind alleys

This is something that can be taken into almost endless blind alleys. There is almost no end to how far you can take this creation of explanations to superimpose upon the experiences that are possible when you are in a physical body on earth. It is not restricted to sex, it can be any aspect of physical life that the fallen beings have attempted to superimpose an explanation upon. What is that explanation? It is an ideology. An ideology, in most cases, projects that people cannot just have a simple experience of enjoying physical life. Because, while they are engaged in physical life, they always have to have in their minds some mental construct that they have to apply to whatever situation they encounter. Every experience they are having, instead of just being immersed in the experience, they have to be a little bit separated from the experience. They have to be evaluating and analyzing it with their rational, analytical minds, otherwise, they are not really sophisticated people, they are not really the way people should be—according to this ideology.

Now, who are the people who are most susceptible to this? Well, I talked about people who are focused on the physical, and they obviously are the ones who are most likely to just enjoy a physical experience without reflecting on it. You have people who are focused on the emotional and they can also enjoy a physical experience, but there has to be a certain emotional component to it. Then you have people who are focused on enjoying the mental and of course, they are the ones who in most cases are pulled right into the fallen beings' deception and thinking that they have to always apply some mental evaluation upon every experience they are having. They can be having sex, but a part of their mind has to stand outside the bed, looking in and evaluating whether this is really the way sex should be, or whether this is the right position, or whether this is the right sound to make, or this is the right experience to have or the right feeling to have. Then, of course, you have people who are focused in the identity level, and those who are at the lower levels are susceptible to the fallen beings because they think that in order to be a sophisticated person, you have to apply this evaluation.

As people rise higher and begin to become more intuitive, well, then you can begin to transcend this mindset. There is an example that is often used by Zen Buddhists: A Buddhist teacher was living in a monastery where he was often teaching students but still he had to participate in some of the mundane tasks that had to be done in the monastery, including drawing water from the well. One day, as he was drawing a bucket of water up from the well, he suddenly snapped out of the analytical mind and he was fully present in the moment, and a realization came to him: "I am drawing water." He was completely fulfilled, completely immersed in the experience of drawing that bucket of water up from the well. There was nothing else that he needed, there was no explanation that he needed, the experience was enough in itself.

Now, this Buddhist teacher was not focused at the physical level, at the emotional level or the mental level, he was focused in the identity level. Even though he was fully immersed in the experience – the physical experience – it was not the same immersion as those who are focused in the physical because he was not trapped in or attached to the physical. He had risen above the physical, but he was able to go back down, so to speak, and again be fully immersed in the experience without being identified with it. Those who are focused on the physical, identify themselves as physical beings. He identified himself as a spiritual being but he was still able to fully be present and immerse himself in the physical experience. Now, he was of course a Buddhist scholar so he still had a mental construct that said that he should live the life of a recluse and not have sex. If he had not had this construct, he would have been able to have sex and be immersed in the experience and fully enjoy it without any explanation necessary.

How ideologies set the stage for conflict

You see here the central point: An ideology seeks to come up with an explanation, but in doing so, it distances itself from the experience. It is precisely this distancing from the experience that sets the stage for conflict between different groups of people. If everybody on earth was having their own experience and being fully immersed in it, without being concerned about other people having a different experience, what would be the basis of conflict? You look at the world today and you see that there are some people who live on the island of Manhattan where they are surrounded by skyscrapers. They hardly ever see a tree, they hardly ever go out in nature, they are living their whole lives in this concrete jungle and they are having a very specific experience. I am not judging it or saying there is anything wrong with it: They are having a particular experience. Then, there are people that live in a different kind of jungle, on a different island in the Pacific. They are living what some would consider a primitive lifestyle, but they have everything they need. If the roof on their hut starts leaking, they pick some leaves off the coconut palms and thatch the roof. If they are hungry, they go and get coconuts, they go and catch a fish. Otherwise, they just enjoy life. They sit there and do various mundane tasks or they talk or they enjoy the sun or whatever, but they are having a different experience.

Now, these people living on this remote island are not likely to suddenly decide that they are going to go on a crusade and travel to Manhattan and try to convince those who live in Manhattan that they should not live like they are doing in the city, but they should come and live on their little island in the jungle. It is not likely to happen. They are just enjoying their lifestyle. There may indeed be some of the people who live in Manhattan, who form the mental construct that it is wrong for these people to live on these remote islands, that they should be connected to society, to the world and they should come into the 21st century and be part of the modern world and live like they do in the modern world. There certainly have been many examples throughout history where one group of people did go on a crusade to either convince other people to change their lifestyle according to these people's ideology, or to force them to do so, or even to eradicate the people who would not be forced.

What has been the basis for this attempt to force other people? It has always been an ideology that defined something that *should* happen, defined it as having epic importance, defined it as requiring a struggle against those people who did not accept the ideology. Here comes the real coup de gras of the fallen beings: The ideology defined that it was justified to force other people to come into conformity with the ideology, the ultimate ideology. If those people did not want to be forced, it was justified to kill them. It was justified (as we have said before several times) to override your natural instinct not to kill.

Well, what is your natural instinct not to kill based on? It is actually based on an experience, not necessarily an experience you have consciously had in this lifetime, but an experience that has accumulated in the collective consciousness over a very long period of time. This simply is an experience that killing other human beings is not constructive for yourself. It does (as we have said before, because all people are connected) affect yourself when you kill other people. It may not seem so in the short run, but it will in the long run. That is an experience that has built up over a very long time in the collective consciousness. We have called it instinctual, but it is actually experience-based. In order to override that experience-based knowledge, you have to create a mental construct that replaces it, that makes people doubt it, that makes people feel that under certain circumstances of epic importance, it is not only necessary but justifiable, perhaps even desirable to kill other human beings.

How ideologies justify doing what people want to do

What is it you see here? Well, what have we said is the case on earth? Free will reigns supreme. The earth is a reality simulator, an experience-machine designed to give people the experiences they want for as long as they want. Is it not just possible that there are some people that want to have the experience of what it is like to kill other human beings? And it *is*. You have seen various warrior cultures throughout history (you see some even today) where these people desire to have the experience of what it is like to battle against and ultimately kill other human beings. They simply desire that experience. Again, within free will, this is still allowed on earth, even though the collective consciousness is being raised and therefore it is becoming less and less common, but it is still allowed.

However, what I am pointing out is that because you have this long, instinctual experience that killing affects yourself, the warriors always need an ideology in order to justify their killing. Yes, you can point to certain psychopaths that seemingly have no ideology, but be careful. If you study this phenomenon of serial killers for example you will see that they always have some explanation in their minds that justifies what they are doing. It may not be something that would be considered some official ideology, but it is actually the same as an ideology. They have an explanation that justifies them doing what they want to do.

You can step even further back and say that we have always talked about free will, but on a natural planet you exercise your free will in a way that does not harm other people. This is of course possible on earth as well but when you step into duality, then you cannot exercise your free will in a way that does not harm or force other people and therefore you need the explanation. You need the ideology that justifies you doing what you at some level of your awareness, you know it harms other people—and you know that by harming other people, you will harm yourself.

We could say: What is the purpose of ideology? Well, one purpose is to give people the temporary feeling that they can do whatever they want, including killing other people, and they can feel at peace about it, they can set aside on a temporary basis the instinctual knowledge that it actually hurts themselves. They can believe that it does not hurt themselves, that they can get away with it. In order to do this, to have that experience, you need to have an ideology that explains why it is justified or necessary. It is very simple. That is the way it is.

Why is it possible to set aside for a time your instinctual knowing, your intuitive knowing? It is because you have that sense of distance between the direct experience and some mental construct in the mind. You are superimposing that mental construct on the mind, you are using the ideology to explain why it is necessary to do this. You can go to the Nazi concentration camps during the Second World War, and you could easily find examples of prison guards who were completely sadistic in the way they treated the prisoners. You take those same people and put them in a context where they did not have the Nazi ideology, and most of them, the majority of them, would not behave in a sadistic way. It was the ideology that enabled them to do this. I am not saying they did not have the desire to do this, but it was only because of the ideology that they could set aside their inner knowing that this not only was wrong, but that it would hurt themselves.

How ideologies use right and wrong

You see what I just did there, introducing the word "wrong." It was actually the "wrong" context in which to use the word "wrong" because when you are talking about an instinctual experience, or experience-based knowledge, there is no evaluation of right and wrong. When you are tasting an orange, would you say this is wrong, a wrong taste, that the orange should not taste that way? You may say: "I do not like it, so I will not eat it again." There is no point in saying that this was *wrong*, the taste is wrong, and the taste of apples is right. It just isn't there. When you have this very, very ancient, instinctual experience that killing other people affects yourself negatively, this is also beyond right and wrong. It is not that killing other people is wrong. It is just that it affects yourself negatively. Therefore, why would you do it, if you know that? If you are standing in front of a hot stove, and you put your hand on the stove and it burns you, it was not really right and wrong. It just had a consequence that was unpleasant. When you have experienced that once, why would you do it again when you know what the consequence will be?

You see again: An ideology not only defines a mental construct of what *should* or *should not* happen, but it also introduces the value judgment between right and wrong, good and evil. Now, the rational mind can take any statement made with words, and it can begin to do what the rational mind does. It can begin to compare, to analyze, to look for contradictions, to look at this and look at that. You can take with the rational mind what I just said (as some people have done throughout the ages with similar ideas) and say: "But are you not the ascended masters, telling us that the fallen beings are wrong?" Well, you might think we are. I would not say that there has never been any of us who have used the word "wrong" in connection with fallen beings. The deeper reality is that we are beyond duality, we are beyond the value judgment, it is not a matter of right and wrong, it is a matter of looking at the consequence, the consequence of what the fallen beings are doing.

What we can observe is that the fallen beings are causing tremendous harm to the people on earth. They are causing tremendous harm to themselves and they have done so for a very, very long time. It is not a matter of even saying that Marxism is wrong and capitalism is right. It is a matter of saying: What are the consequences of Marxism? What are the consequences of capitalism? Is this the experience we want in our modern societies?

Science is meant to take us beyond ideologies

You see, what we are saying (and have been saying for a long time) is that when you transcend the dualistic mindset, you transcend this value judgment between right and wrong. This is what Saint Germain attempted to introduce into modern civilization by sponsoring science as Roger Bacon, as Francis Bacon, setting the stage (not him alone, but in connection with others) for the scientific revolution. His desire was to help people get beyond ideology. He did not necessarily use that word, but certainly he looked at the superstition and the superstitious self-contradictory doctrines of the Catholic church of the Middle Ages. He realized that society could not progress beyond a certain point before people got beyond this attempt to define how the world *should* work.

That is why he attempted to set the stage for the development of certain processes that could evaluate: How does the world actually work. What could be observed based on experiment, how does the world work, not how somebody thinks it *should* work, according to a theory, a mental construct. In a sense, you could say that when Galileo walked up to the top of the tower and allowed things of different weight to fall to earth, he was attempting to go beyond theory, beyond mental construct, and have a direct experience of how gravity affects falling bodies. The same when the first scientists built telescopes and observed how the heavenly bodies worked, in a closer way than could be done by the naked eye. Therefore, they could compare observations to the theory of epicycles and they could see that something did not add up. Even though this was Catholic doctrine, it could not be the full explanation.

Why every ideology has an opposite

What does the struggle come from? Well, it comes from this: You are distancing yourself from the experience. You are creating a mental construct and by the very fact that the planet is trapped in duality, you can never create an ultimate theory, there will always be an opposing viewpoint. Why is this? Because when you create a theory, you must (as I already said) take certain things for granted. Here is a foundation that I build my theory upon, these are self-evident, absolute truths that I do not need to question. They are so valid, so absolute, that I can build an entire worldview upon these basic truths.

This is of course just a choice you are making. What you choose is not some absolute truth, it is just one relative viewpoint. It is inevitable that in duality, there will always be pairs, there will always be opposing polarities. Someone else is bound to take the opposite viewpoint or a different viewpoint and say: "No, this is the self-evident truth that I will build my philosophy on." If you build two philosophies on different foundations, of course they will reach different forms, different conclusions, different "ultimate" truths. When you then add the value judgment, well, the one philosophy will say: "I am right, so the other is wrong." And the other will say: "Well, I am right, so the other is wrong." Now, you have two groups of people who are pulled into this, each of them are trying to convince the other group that they are right. How can this not end in a struggle? Well, you can avoid the struggle, or you can transcend the struggle, by transcending both of the previous viewpoints, realizing there is more to understand than what they had defined.

The hope of a science free from ideology

This is what Saint Germain was hoping to see as a result of the development of science. You had, throughout the Middle Ages, two opposing ideologies, Christianity and Islam, and they had created much conflict between them. Saint Germain hoped that it would be possible to come up with a way to make observations and draw conclusions that was neutral, that was not polarized towards either of the known ideologies. Beyond this, he even hoped that it was possible for the scientific method to avoid being pulled into the field of ideology because it was strictly focused on observation, and making conclusions only based on the observations.

Of course, this hope was not fulfilled because the fallen beings will use any new development to try and pervert it, to prevent it from setting people free, or even try to use it for controlling people even more. The fallen beings took the scientific method and they said: "We do not need to experiment with everything because there are some things that cannot be demonstrated through experience or experiment. And therefore there must be some theory that we take for granted as a truth that does not need to be questioned."

They then elevated this materialistic viewpoint that there is nothing beyond the material universe and that we can explain the workings of the material universe by only looking at the material universe. In doing this, in taking these simple viewpoints that started with Aristotle and reintroducing them in the modern world, they created a new ideology. They pulled the scientific method into the realm of ideology and superimposed an ideology on what was meant to be purely an investigative tool that was not dependent on ideology. It was aimed at setting people free from mental constructs, but now it was pulled into the world of mental constructs.

Mental constructs were superimposed upon it to the point where today, scientists do not feel free to investigate anything they want. Because if they investigate something that points beyond the materialistic ideology, they will lose funding, they will lose their reputations, they will be opposed at every turn by the scientific establishment, the ideological establishment, the thought police.

You see very clearly that even science has been pulled into the realm of ideology. Again, what is the result? Well, there is an endless conflict between science and religion. Originally, Saint Germain's vision was that science would be beyond religion, that it could actually be embraced by all religions. Because how could you really object to making an observation of how the world works? How could this be a religious matter? How could it be a political matter? How could it, to use a recent example, become an ideological matter whether you wear a face mask? Is it not simply a matter of making a scientific observation that a virus is carried not by the air, but by respiratory droplets. If you put a cloth of a certain density in front of your mouth and nose, you will not expel as many respiratory droplets and therefore you are not likely to infect other people. If all people wear this cloth in front of their mouth and nose, you can either stop or at least dramatically slow down an epidemic. How did this become an ideological issue?

You see, if you say that: "This is taking away my freedom," then you are making it an ideological issue. It is because you have separated yourself in your mind from a neutral observation of how the world actually works. You think that the world works or *should* work according to your mental construct, your ideology. You might not officially call it an ideology, but it *is* an ideology. It is a mental construct.

When people take an ideological approach

You see how people, even in a democratic nation, can allow themselves to be pulled into an ideological approach to everything, to where they cannot cooperate on anything. You can have a nation (the oldest modern democracy) that has two political parties that today cannot cooperate about anything. There is no bipartisanship. Even if everybody knows that something is the right thing to do, well, then the opposite party has to object and obstruct, just because they have to be opposite. Another example of how ideology creates conflict after conflict after conflict.

We would much prefer that at least all ascended master students understood this mechanism, freed themselves from it, and simply said: "Let's observe how the world works. Let us not superimpose some ideological belief about how it *should* work. And let us do what is practically necessary in every facet of life, whether it be a disease, whether it be the economy, whether it be any other aspect of life."

Yet, as I said in my last release, some ascended master students have taken an ascended master teaching and effectively turned it into an ideology. Would you not *please* consider if you have done this, and then consider that it is not a matter of right and wrong, it is a matter of saying: What are the consequences for you? How does this affect your spiritual growth? Does it slow down or speed up your spiritual growth?

I have now attempted to explain to you that it slows down your spiritual growth. If this is the experience you want, I have no problem with this. Then, of course you do not need me, you do not need any other ascended master, you do not need an ascended master teaching. You do not need a messenger who can say what we of the ascended masters want to say, and not what a group of students want the ascended masters to say.

If this is the experience you desire to have, leave in peace. Or do not leave in peace, if that is the experience you desire to have. Of course, for those who are open, just take a look, see if you have any selves that have this tendency to be pulled into this ideological approach. Naturally, many avatars have been pulled into it simply because you came to earth with a desire to improve conditions on earth, to make a positive difference. You have all had your own motivation for doing so and that motivation was based on a certain viewpoint, on certain beliefs, certain decisions you had made.

This messenger has spent the better part of the last three years investigating his motivation for coming to earth, the beliefs that he had, and giving them up one at a time. He realized that as long as he did not give them up, he would be bound to earth. Therefore, he would be bound to reincarnate and could not make his ascension. In fact, he realized that you cannot rise beyond a certain level of consciousness until you start looking at this very deepest motivation for why you are on earth. Even if you are an original inhabitant, you need to look at: Why are you on earth. What can you learn from it, and what will take you beyond earth instead of keeping you here?

These were the remarks that I wanted to give you in this installment. I have, and we have in unison, decided that I would be the main speaker for this conference, for a variety of complex reasons. First of all, because I am the Lord of the World, and this means that (as I have explained before) nothing can occur on earth unless I allow space for it. Not necessarily only physical space, but emotional space, mental space and identity level space. I decide ultimately what there is space for on earth.

We are approaching a turning point where it is possible for me, based on the growth in the collective consciousness, to begin to consider deciding that I will no longer allow space for ideology on earth. We are not there yet and that is why you who are willing to take these teachings can play a vital role, a decisive role, in shifting the collective consciousness above that critical limit where it becomes possible for me to say: "No more will there be space for the mindset behind ideology."

This does not mean that the outer ideologies will disappear, but they will be seen in a different light when people are not blinded by the mindset that sucks people into the collective beast behind a particular ideology, or even the collective beast behind all ideologies. This is of course the goal that we have: That this conference will be the trigger for a development that will ultimately lead to ideology not being allowed space on earth. Thereby, really, people can free themselves from this ideological baggage that is only obstructing the manifestation of Saint Germain's Golden Age. Because as Saint Germain set the foundation for science, you can see that this is also the foundation for his golden age. Looking at how things actually work by freeing your mind from the mental constructs of how they *should* work.

So with this, I seal you in the gratitude of the Buddha, for your willingness to broadcast this message into the collective consciousness where it has already had profound effects that will only continue to spread as rings in the water as you make use of these teachings. Be sealed then in the heart of the Buddha that I AM.

7 INVOKING AWARENESS OF HOW SCIENCE WAS PERVERTED BY IDEOLOGY (PART 1)

In the name of the I AM THAT I AM, Jesus Christ, I use the authority that I have as a being in embodiment on earth to call upon Gautama Buddha to reinforce my calls and use my chakras to project the statements in this invocation into the collective consciousness and awaken people to the need to free ourselves from the ideological mindset. Awaken people to the reality that we are spiritual beings and that we can co-create a new future by working with the ascended masters. I especially call for …

[Make your own calls here.]

Part 1

1. Gautama Buddha, awaken the most creative people to see that most ideologies contain the idea that there will be a struggle to implement the program defined by the ideology—and we need to understand why.

Archangel Michael, light so blue,
my heart has room for only you.
My mind is one, no longer two,
your love for me is ever true.

**Archangel Michael, you are here,
consuming now all doubt and fear.
Your Presence is forever near,
you are to me so very dear.**

2. Gautama Buddha, awaken the most creative people to see that many people have a need to find an ultimate understanding, and that is why most ideologies define some ultimate or absolute truth.

Archangel Michael, I will be,
all one with your reality.
No fear can hold me as I see,
this world no power has o'er me.

**Archangel Michael, you are here,
consuming now all doubt and fear.
Your Presence is forever near,
you are to me so very dear.**

3. Gautama Buddha, awaken the most creative people to see that, regardless of the claim of absoluteness, this is not an absolute truth but a relative truth, it is inevitable that some people on earth will not accept it—and this sets up a struggle.

Archangel Michael, hold me tight,
shatter now the darkest night.
Clear my chakras with your light,
restore to me my inner sight.

**Archangel Michael, you are here,
consuming now all doubt and fear.
Your Presence is forever near,
you are to me so very dear.**

4. Gautama Buddha, awaken the most creative people to see that there are often two groups of people and each group believes they have the ultimate truth, meaning the other group must be wrong in claiming that they have the ultimate truth. This is an inescapable aspect of duality.

Archangel Michael, now I stand,
with you the light I do command.
My heart I ever will expand,
till highest truth I understand.

**Archangel Michael, you are here,
consuming now all doubt and fear.
Your Presence is forever near,
you are to me so very dear.**

5. Gautama Buddha, awaken the most creative people to see that it is possible to go into duality without going into the more aggressive forms of duality. If we understand that there are many different ways to live on earth, this creates a certain tolerance so groups can "live and let live."

Archangel Michael, in my heart,
from me you never will depart.
Of hierarchy I am a part,
I now accept a fresh new start.

**Archangel Michael, you are here,
consuming now all doubt and fear.
Your Presence is forever near,
you are to me so very dear.**

6. Gautama Buddha, awaken the most creative people to see that in some of the democratic nations there is tolerance for the fact that they have different versions of democracy. There is no armed conflict where one democratic nation is attempting to conquer another democratic nation because they think they do not have the ultimate version of democracy.

Archangel Michael, sword of blue,
all darkness you are cutting through.

My Christhood I do now pursue,
discernment shows me what is true.

**Archangel Michael, you are here,
consuming now all doubt and fear.
Your Presence is forever near,
you are to me so very dear.**

7. Gautama Buddha, awaken the most creative people to see that the tolerance was lost on earth because of the power elite, namely beings who have gone against the design principles of the universe and who want to prove God wrong and who will do anything to pull people into their spirals.

Archangel Michael, in your wings,
I now let go of lesser things.
God's homing call in my heart rings,
my heart with yours forever sings.

**Archangel Michael, you are here,
consuming now all doubt and fear.
Your Presence is forever near,
you are to me so very dear.**

8. Gautama Buddha, awaken the most creative people to see that the power elite created the epic mindset because they would not admit that they could be wrong. Therefore, even God himself had to be wrong.

Archangel Michael, take me home,
in higher spheres I want to roam.
I am reborn from cosmic foam,
my life is now a sacred poem.

**Archangel Michael, you are here,
consuming now all doubt and fear.
Your Presence is forever near,
you are to me so very dear.**

9. Gautama Buddha, awaken the most creative people to see that the power elite finds it difficult to tolerate other people with different beliefs.

This is what sets up the epic clash where the elite people believe that it is absolutely necessary that one thought system, one ideology, becomes the dominant or even the *only* one on earth.

> Archangel Michael, light you are,
> shining like the bluest star.
> You are a cosmic avatar,
> with you I will go very far.
>
> **Archangel Michael, you are here,**
> **consuming now all doubt and fear.**
> **Your Presence is forever near,**
> **you are to me so very dear.**

Part 2

1. Gautama Buddha, awaken the most creative people to see that in order for the power elite people to feel secure, they think they must eradicate all conflicting viewpoints. They must come to a point where there is only one ideology.

> O Jesus, blessed brother mine,
> I walk the path that you outline,
> a great example to us all,
> I follow now your inner call.
>
> **O Jesus, let the Fire of Joy,**
> **consume the devil's subtle ploy,**
> **transfigured is our planet earth,**
> **the golden age is given birth.**

2. Gautama Buddha, awaken the most creative people to see that this can never be fulfilled, not only because it is difficult to make people accept one ideology, but also because the power elite is not a coherent group.

O Jesus, open inner sight,
the ego wants to prove it's right,
but this I will no longer do,
I want to be all one with you.

**O Jesus, let the Fire of Joy,
consume the devil's subtle ploy,
transfigured is our planet earth,
the golden age is given birth.**

3. Gautama Buddha, awaken the most creative people to see that there will always be at least two polarities among the power elite. It would never be possible that the power elite associated with earth could agree to support the same ideology.

O Jesus, I now clearly see,
the Key of Knowledge given me,
my Christ self I hereby embrace,
as you fill up my inner space.

**O Jesus, let the Fire of Joy,
consume the devil's subtle ploy,
transfigured is our planet earth,
the golden age is given birth.**

4. Gautama Buddha, awaken the most creative people to see that the power elite will always be divided into at least two groups, each claiming to have the ultimate ideology, each feeling the epic need to eradicate the other ideology and establish their ideology as the only one.

O Jesus, show me serpent's lie,
expose the beam in my own eye,
as Christ discernment you me give,
in oneness I forever live.

**O Jesus, let the Fire of Joy,
consume the devil's subtle ploy,
transfigured is our planet earth,
the golden age is given birth.**

5. Gautama Buddha, awaken the most creative people to see that the epic mindset has had a very dominant influence on history, on the mindset and thinking of the collective consciousness.

O Jesus, I am truly meek,
and thus I turn the other cheek,
when the accuser attacks me,
I go within and merge with thee.

**O Jesus, let the Fire of Joy,
consume the devil's subtle ploy,
transfigured is our planet earth,
the golden age is given birth.**

6. Gautama Buddha, awaken the most creative people to see that most philosophers were striving to come up with the ultimate thought system. This is inspired by the power elite, or at least by the mindset that they have created on earth, the epic mindset.

O Jesus, ego I let die,
surrender ev'ry earthly tie,
the dead can bury what is dead,
I choose to walk with you instead.

**O Jesus, let the Fire of Joy,
consume the devil's subtle ploy,
transfigured is our planet earth,
the golden age is given birth.**

7. Gautama Buddha, awaken the most creative people to see that many philosophers started out their efforts to define a new philosophy based on the desire to come up with some ultimate truth, some ultimate understanding, that all the previous philosophers had failed to see.

O Jesus, help me rise above,
the devil's test through higher love,
show me separate self unreal,
my formless self you do reveal.

**O Jesus, let the Fire of Joy,
consume the devil's subtle ploy,
transfigured is our planet earth,
the golden age is given birth.**

8. Gautama Buddha, awaken the most creative people to see that many philosophers believed it had to be possible to come up with an ultimate truth. Many people today believe it is possible to come up with some ultimate understanding, a theory of everything, the theory that explains every aspect of life.

O Jesus, what is that to me,
I just let go and follow thee,
with this I do pass ev'ry test,
to find with you eternal rest.

**O Jesus, let the Fire of Joy,
consume the devil's subtle ploy,
transfigured is our planet earth,
the golden age is given birth.**

9. Gautama Buddha, awaken the most creative people to see that this is an impossible quest. It is impossible partly because in duality, every viewpoint is relative so it will always have an opposite. It is also impossible because there are certain things that the rational mind cannot grasp.

O Jesus, fiery master mine,
my heart now melting into thine,
I love with heart and mind and soul,
the God who is my highest goal.

**O Jesus, let the Fire of Joy,
consume the devil's subtle ploy,
transfigured is our planet earth,
the golden age is given birth.**

Part 3

1. Gautama Buddha, awaken the most creative people to see that human beings are psychological beings, but beyond that we are *experiential* beings. We are having an experience of what it is like to be on earth.

Maitreya, I am truly meek,
your counsel wise I humbly seek,
your vision I so want to see,
with you in Eden I will be.

Maitreya, kindness is the cure,
in fires of kindness I am pure.
Maitreya, now release the fire,
that raises me forever higher.

2. Gautama Buddha, awaken the most creative people to see that the rational mind seeks to create an *understanding* of life on earth. Why do we need an understanding when we have the direct experience?

Maitreya, help me to return,
to learn from you, I truly yearn,
as oneness is all I desire
I feel initiation's fire.

Maitreya, kindness is the cure,
in fires of kindness I am pure.
Maitreya, now release the fire,
that raises me forever higher.

3. Gautama Buddha, awaken the most creative people to see that we are all *experiencing* life on earth. We are having a direct experience of living on earth. Why isn't that enough? For many people it actually *is*, but for some it is not, and this goes back to the power elite.

Maitreya, I hereby decide,
from you I will no longer hide,

expose to me the very lie
that caused edenic self to die.

Maitreya, kindness is the cure,
in fires of kindness I am pure.
Maitreya, now release the fire,
that raises me forever higher.

4. Gautama Buddha, awaken the most creative people to see that the power elite beings had to explain why they had gone against the design principles of the universe, and they did so in a way that points the finger at someone else so it was not their "fault" that they made a mistake.

Maitreya, blessed Guru mine,
my heart of hearts forever thine,
I vow that I will listen well,
so we can break the serpent's spell.

Maitreya, kindness is the cure,
in fires of kindness I am pure.
Maitreya, now release the fire,
that raises me forever higher.

5. Gautama Buddha, awaken the most creative people to see that this mindset has enveloped the earth to such a degree that most people cannot be satisfied with just experiencing life. They need to have some kind of explanation.

Maitreya, help me see the lie
whereby the serpent broke the tie,
the serpent now has naught in me,
in oneness I am truly free.

Maitreya, kindness is the cure,
in fires of kindness I am pure.
Maitreya, now release the fire,
that raises me forever higher.

6. Gautama Buddha, awaken the most creative people to see that we have a direct experience, but now someone uses the rational mind to create a theory, an explanation, and then they want to superimpose that upon our direct experience.

Maitreya, truth does set me free
from falsehoods of duality,
the fruit of knowledge I let go,
so your true spirit I do know.

Maitreya, kindness is the cure,
in fires of kindness I am pure.
Maitreya, now release the fire,
that raises me forever higher.

7. Gautama Buddha, awaken the most creative people to see that it is impossible to come up with a complete explanation for all of the experiences human beings have on earth.

Maitreya, I submit to you,
intentions pure, my heart is true,
from ego I am truly free,
as I am now all one with thee.

Maitreya, kindness is the cure,
in fires of kindness I am pure.
Maitreya, now release the fire,
that raises me forever higher.

8. Gautama Buddha, awaken the most creative people to see that it is impossible to use the rational mind to explain the taste of an orange to a person. We cannot come up with words that would describe the taste so that the person would experience the taste and not have to eat an orange.

Maitreya, kindness is the key,
all shades of kindness teach to me,
for I am now the open door,
the Art of Kindness to restore.

Maitreya, kindness is the cure,
in fires of kindness I am pure.
Maitreya, now release the fire,
that raises me forever higher.

9. Gautama Buddha, awaken the most creative people to see that we will not truly have the experience of what an orange tastes like until we eat it. There is no amount of explanation that can substitute the actual experience. It is an impossible quest to begin with.

Maitreya, oh sweet mystery,
immersed in your reality,
the myst'ry school will now return,
for this, my heart does truly burn.

Maitreya, kindness is the cure,
in fires of kindness I am pure.
Maitreya, now release the fire,
that raises me forever higher.

Part 4

1. Gautama Buddha, awaken the most creative people to see that when we try to explain something with the rational mind, we distance ourselves from it.

Gautama, show my mental state
that does give rise to love and hate,
your exposé I do endure,
so my perception will be pure.

Gautama, Flame of Cosmic Peace,
unruly thoughts do hereby cease,
we radiate from you and me
the peace to still Samsara's Sea.

2. Gautama Buddha, awaken the most creative people to see that in order to explain experience, we must distance ourselves from the direct experience, and now we must seek to explain the experience.

> Gautama, in your Flame of Peace,
> the struggling self I now release,
> the Buddha Nature I now see,
> it is the core of you and me.

> **Gautama, Flame of Cosmic Peace,**
> **unruly thoughts do hereby cease,**
> **we radiate from you and me**
> **the peace to still Samsara's Sea.**

3. Gautama Buddha, awaken the most creative people to see that in order to explain experience, we must create *concepts,* ideas in the rational mind. Then, we must seek to define these ideas in such a way that, in our minds, they describe the experience.

> Gautama, I am one with thee,
> Mara's demons do now flee,
> your Presence like a soothing balm,
> my mind and senses ever calm.

> **Gautama, Flame of Cosmic Peace,**
> **unruly thoughts do hereby cease,**
> **we radiate from you and me**
> **the peace to still Samsara's Sea.**

4. Gautama Buddha, awaken the most creative people to see that this is doomed to failure, unless we no longer have the direct experience as a frame of reference. If we have never tasted an orange, then we might be susceptible to believing that the concepts and ideas defined with the rational mind actually describe the experience.

> Gautama, I now take the vow,
> to live in the eternal now,
> with you I do transcend all time,
> to live in present so sublime.

Gautama, Flame of Cosmic Peace,
unruly thoughts do hereby cease,
we radiate from you and me
the peace to still Samsara's Sea.

5. Gautama Buddha, awaken the most creative people to see that we might even come to believe that perhaps they describe the experience to such an extent that we do not need the experience because the explanation is enough. We can refrain from seeking the experience.

Gautama, I have no desire,
to nothing earthly I aspire,
in non-attachment I now rest,
passing Mara's subtle test.

Gautama, Flame of Cosmic Peace,
unruly thoughts do hereby cease,
we radiate from you and me
the peace to still Samsara's Sea.

6. Gautama Buddha, awaken the most creative people to see that the result of *not* having the experience, of choosing not to have the experience, is that we will never have a frame of reference for challenging our ideas, our explanation.

Gautama, I melt into you,
my mind is one, no longer two,
immersed in your resplendent glow,
Nirvana is all that I know.

Gautama, Flame of Cosmic Peace,
unruly thoughts do hereby cease,
we radiate from you and me
the peace to still Samsara's Sea.

7. Gautama Buddha, awaken the most creative people to see that the explanation exists in the mind. There is nothing in the physical world that challenges our explanation, so in our minds we can convince ourselves

that the explanation is complete and that we have the full understanding of what life is like.

> Gautama, in your timeless space,
> I am immersed in Cosmic Grace,
> I know the God beyond all form,
> to world I will no more conform.

> **Gautama, Flame of Cosmic Peace,**
> **unruly thoughts do hereby cease,**
> **we radiate from you and me**
> **the peace to still Samsara's Sea.**

8. Gautama Buddha, awaken the most creative people to see that this is what the power elite beings did after they went into separation. They lost the connection to the spiritual realm and they felt a sense of loss. They had to come up with an explanation for why they did not need this connection.

> Gautama, I am now awake,
> I clearly see what is at stake,
> and thus I claim my sacred right
> to be on earth the Buddhic Light.

> **Gautama, Flame of Cosmic Peace,**
> **unruly thoughts do hereby cease,**
> **we radiate from you and me**
> **the peace to still Samsara's Sea.**

9. Gautama Buddha, awaken the most creative people to see that this is how they have justified not turning around and seeking the direct experience. They have continued to walk further and further away from that experience by creating ever more elaborate layers of explanation for why it is not real, why there is no reality beyond their explanation, their ideology.

> Gautama, with your thunderbolt,
> we give the earth a mighty jolt,
> I know that some will understand,
> and join the Buddha's timeless band.

Gautama, Flame of Cosmic Peace,
unruly thoughts do hereby cease,
we radiate from you and me
the peace to still Samsara's Sea.

Part 5

1. Gautama Buddha, awaken the most creative people to see that the power elite is primarily threatened by those who say: "But I have a spiritual experience. I intuitively experience that there is a higher realm beyond the material, that I have a higher self, that there are beings in the higher realm that I can connect to."

Sanat Kumara, Ruby Fire,
I seek my place in love's own choir,
with open hearts we sing your praise,
together we the earth do raise.

Sanat Kumara, Ruby Ray,
bring to earth a higher way,
light this planet with your fire,
clothe her in a new attire.

2. Gautama Buddha, awaken the most creative people to see that this is the ultimate threat to the power elite beings, but they are even threatened by ordinary people who have physical experiences because they live in their minds. They are still experiential beings but instead of having a *direct* experience, they are having a *substitute* experience in their minds.

Sanat Kumara, Ruby Fire,
initiations I desire,
I am for you an electrode,
Shamballa is my true abode.

Sanat Kumara, Ruby Ray,
bring to earth a higher way,

**light this planet with your fire,
clothe her in a new attire.**

3. Gautama Buddha, awaken the most creative people to see that the power elite beings look at earth as a primitive and low planet, and they have no desire to experience life on earth. They want to have a privileged, easy lifestyle so they can live in an ivory tower where they can stay within this aerial castle they have created in their minds and not have it challenged.

Sanat Kumara, Ruby Fire,
I follow path that you require,
initiate me with your love,
the open door for Holy Dove.

**Sanat Kumara, Ruby Ray,
bring to earth a higher way,
light this planet with your fire,
clothe her in a new attire.**

4. Gautama Buddha, awaken the most creative people to see that members of the power elite do not want a *physical* experience, they want a *psychic, mental, emotional* experience of earth, and therefore they are threatened by people who are immersing themselves in physical life.

Sanat Kumara, Ruby Fire,
your great example all inspire,
with non-attachment and great mirth,
we give the earth a true rebirth.

**Sanat Kumara, Ruby Ray,
bring to earth a higher way,
light this planet with your fire,
clothe her in a new attire.**

5. Gautama Buddha, awaken the most creative people to see that this is why the members of the power elite have come up with so many ideologies that are telling people how to live life on earth, what they should or should not do.

Sanat Kumara, Ruby Fire,
you are this planet's purifier,
consume on earth all spirits dark,
reveal the inner Spirit Spark.

**Sanat Kumara, Ruby Ray,
bring to earth a higher way,
light this planet with your fire,
clothe her in a new attire.**

6. Gautama Buddha, awaken the most creative people to see that for the power elite beings, an experience is not enough. There needs to be a mental construct that puts the experience into a broader context, which ultimately is their own attempt to explain the workings of the universe so that they have never been at fault in anything.

Sanat Kumara, Ruby Fire,
you are a cosmic amplifier,
the lower forces can't withstand,
vibrations from Venusian band.

**Sanat Kumara, Ruby Ray,
bring to earth a higher way,
light this planet with your fire,
clothe her in a new attire.**

7. Gautama Buddha, awaken the most creative people to see that members of the power elite live in their own minds, which is the definition of a narcissist who cannot see beyond his own belly button.

Sanat Kumara, Ruby Fire,
I am on earth your magnifier,
the flow of love I do restore,
my chakras are your open door.

**Sanat Kumara, Ruby Ray,
bring to earth a higher way,
light this planet with your fire,
clothe her in a new attire.**

8. Gautama Buddha, awaken the most creative people to see that the power elite beings have tried to create explanations, superimposed upon the physical experience, and this can be taken into almost endless blind alleys. There is almost no end to how far we can take this creation of explanations to superimpose upon the experiences that are possible on earth.

Sanat Kumara, Ruby Fire,
Venusian song the multiplier,
as we your love reverberate,
the densest minds we penetrate.

**Sanat Kumara, Ruby Ray,
bring to earth a higher way,
light this planet with your fire,
clothe her in a new attire.**

9. Gautama Buddha, awaken the most creative people to see that the elite beings have attempted to superimpose an explanation upon any aspect of life. Such an explanation is an ideology.

Sanat Kumara, Ruby Fire,
you are for all the sanctifier,
the earth is now a holy place,
purified by cosmic grace.

**Sanat Kumara, Ruby Ray,
bring to earth a higher way,
light this planet with your fire,
clothe her in a new attire.**

Sealing

In the name of the I AM THAT I AM, I accept that Archangel Michael, Astrea and Shiva form an impenetrable shield around myself and all constructive people, sealing us from all fear-based energies in all four octaves. I accept that the Light of God is consuming and transforming all fear-based energies that make up the dark forces working against ending the era of ideology on earth!

8 INVOKING AWARENESS OF HOW SCIENCE WAS PERVERTED BY IDEOLOGY (PART 2)

In the name of the I AM THAT I AM, Jesus Christ, I use the authority that I have as a being in embodiment on earth to call upon Gautama Buddha to reinforce my calls and use my chakras to project the statements in this invocation into the collective consciousness and awaken people to the need to free ourselves from the ideological mindset. Awaken people to the reality that we are spiritual beings and that we can co-create a new future by working with the ascended masters. I especially call for …

[Make your own calls here.]

Part 1

1. Gautama Buddha, awaken the most creative people to see that an ideology projects that people cannot have the experience of enjoying physical

life. We always have to have some mental construct that we have to apply to whatever situation we encounter.

> Archangel Michael, light so blue,
> my heart has room for only you.
> My mind is one, no longer two,
> your love for me is ever true.

> **Archangel Michael, you are here,**
> **consuming now all doubt and fear.**
> **Your Presence is forever near,**
> **you are to me so very dear.**

2. Gautama Buddha, awaken the most creative people to see that instead of being immersed in the experience, we have to be a little bit separated from the experience. We have to be evaluating and analyzing it with the rational, analytical mind, otherwise, we are not sophisticated people, we are not the way people should be—according to the ideology.

> Archangel Michael, I will be,
> all one with your reality.
> No fear can hold me as I see,
> this world no power has o'er me.

> **Archangel Michael, you are here,**
> **consuming now all doubt and fear.**
> **Your Presence is forever near,**
> **you are to me so very dear.**

3. Gautama Buddha, awaken the most creative people to see that the people who are focused on the mental realm are the ones who in most cases are pulled right into the fallen beings' deception, thinking that they have to always apply some mental evaluation upon every experience they are having.

> Archangel Michael, hold me tight,
> shatter now the darkest night.
> Clear my chakras with your light,
> restore to me my inner sight.

**Archangel Michael, you are here,
consuming now all doubt and fear.
Your Presence is forever near,
you are to me so very dear.**

4. Gautama Buddha, awaken the most creative people to see that an ideology seeks to come up with an explanation, but in doing so, it distances itself from the experience. It is precisely this distancing from the experience that sets the stage for conflict between different groups of people.

Archangel Michael, now I stand,
with you the light I do command.
My heart I ever will expand,
till highest truth I understand.

**Archangel Michael, you are here,
consuming now all doubt and fear.
Your Presence is forever near,
you are to me so very dear.**

5. Gautama Buddha, awaken the most creative people to see that if everybody on earth was having their own experience and being fully immersed in it, without being concerned about other people having a different experience, what would be the basis of conflict?

Archangel Michael, in my heart,
from me you never will depart.
Of hierarchy I am a part,
I now accept a fresh new start.

**Archangel Michael, you are here,
consuming now all doubt and fear.
Your Presence is forever near,
you are to me so very dear.**

6. Gautama Buddha, awaken the most creative people to see that there are many examples throughout history where one group of people did go on a crusade to either convince other people to change their lifestyle according

to these people's ideology, or to force them to do so, or even to eradicate the people who would not be forced.

> Archangel Michael, sword of blue,
> all darkness you are cutting through.
> My Christhood I do now pursue,
> discernment shows me what is true.

> **Archangel Michael, you are here,**
> **consuming now all doubt and fear.**
> **Your Presence is forever near,**
> **you are to me so very dear.**

7. Gautama Buddha, awaken the most creative people to see that the basis for this attempt to force other people has always been an ideology that defined something that *should* happen, defined it as having epic importance, defined it as requiring a struggle against those people who did not accept the ideology.

> Archangel Michael, in your wings,
> I now let go of lesser things.
> God's homing call in my heart rings,
> my heart with yours forever sings.

> **Archangel Michael, you are here,**
> **consuming now all doubt and fear.**
> **Your Presence is forever near,**
> **you are to me so very dear.**

8. Gautama Buddha, awaken the most creative people to see that the coup de gras of the power elite beings is that an ideology defines that it is justified to force other people to come into conformity with the ideology. If those people do not want to be forced, it is justified to kill them. It is justified to override our natural instinct not to kill.

> Archangel Michael, take me home,
> in higher spheres I want to roam.
> I am reborn from cosmic foam,
> my life is now a sacred poem.

Archangel Michael, you are here,
consuming now all doubt and fear.
Your Presence is forever near,
you are to me so very dear.

9. Gautama Buddha, awaken the most creative people to see that our natural instinct not to kill is based on an experience that has accumulated in the collective consciousness over a long period of time, namely the experience that killing other human beings is not constructive for ourselves.

Archangel Michael, light you are,
shining like the bluest star.
You are a cosmic avatar,
with you I will go very far.

Archangel Michael, you are here,
consuming now all doubt and fear.
Your Presence is forever near,
you are to me so very dear.

Part 2

1. Gautama Buddha, awaken the most creative people to see that it does affect ourselves when we kill other people. It may not seem so in the short run, but it will in the long run. This is an experience that has built up over a very long time in the collective consciousness.

O Jesus, blessed brother mine,
I walk the path that you outline,
a great example to us all,
I follow now your inner call.

O Jesus, let the Fire of Joy,
consume the devil's subtle ploy,
transfigured is our planet earth,
the golden age is given birth.

2. Gautama Buddha, awaken the most creative people to see that in order to override that experience-based knowledge, we have to create a mental construct that replaces it, that makes people doubt it, that makes people feel that under certain circumstances, of epic importance, it is not only necessary but justifiable, perhaps even desirable, to kill other human beings.

> O Jesus, open inner sight,
> the ego wants to prove it's right,
> but this I will no longer do,
> I want to be all one with you.

> **O Jesus, let the Fire of Joy,**
> **consume the devil's subtle ploy,**
> **transfigured is our planet earth,**
> **the golden age is given birth.**

3. Gautama Buddha, awaken the most creative people to see that on earth free will reigns supreme. The earth is a reality simulator, an experience-machine designed to give people the experiences they want for as long as they want. Some people want to have the experience of what it is like to kill other human beings.

> O Jesus, I now clearly see,
> the Key of Knowledge given me,
> my Christ self I hereby embrace,
> as you fill up my inner space.

> **O Jesus, let the Fire of Joy,**
> **consume the devil's subtle ploy,**
> **transfigured is our planet earth,**
> **the golden age is given birth.**

4. Gautama Buddha, awaken the most creative people to see that because we have this long, instinctual experience that killing affects ourselves, people always need an ideology in order to justify their killing.

> O Jesus, show me serpent's lie,
> expose the beam in my own eye,

as Christ discernment you me give,
in oneness I forever live.

O Jesus, let the Fire of Joy,
consume the devil's subtle ploy,
transfigured is our planet earth,
the golden age is given birth.

5. Gautama Buddha, awaken the most creative people to see that one purpose of ideology is to give people the temporary feeling that they can do whatever they want, including killing other people, and they can feel at peace about it, they can set aside the instinctual knowledge that it actually hurts themselves.

O Jesus, I am truly meek,
and thus I turn the other cheek,
when the accuser attacks me,
I go within and merge with thee.

O Jesus, let the Fire of Joy,
consume the devil's subtle ploy,
transfigured is our planet earth,
the golden age is given birth.

6. Gautama Buddha, awaken the most creative people to see that through an ideology, people can believe that killing does not hurt themselves, that they can get away with it. In order to have that experience, people need to have an ideology that explains why killing is justified or necessary.

O Jesus, ego I let die,
surrender ev'ry earthly tie,
the dead can bury what is dead,
I choose to walk with you instead.

O Jesus, let the Fire of Joy,
consume the devil's subtle ploy,
transfigured is our planet earth,
the golden age is given birth.

7. Gautama Buddha, awaken the most creative people to see that it is possible to set aside for a time our instinctual knowing, when we have the sense of distance between the direct experience and some mental construct. We are superimposing that mental construct on the mind, we are using the ideology to explain why it is necessary to kill.

O Jesus, help me rise above,
the devil's test through higher love,
show me separate self unreal,
my formless self you do reveal.

O Jesus, let the Fire of Joy,
consume the devil's subtle ploy,
transfigured is our planet earth,
the golden age is given birth.

8. Gautama Buddha, awaken the most creative people to see that in an instinctual experience, or experience-based knowledge, there is no evaluation of right and wrong. The instinctual experience that killing other people affects ourselves negatively is also beyond right and wrong.

O Jesus, what is that to me,
I just let go and follow thee,
with this I do pass ev'ry test,
to find with you eternal rest.

O Jesus, let the Fire of Joy,
consume the devil's subtle ploy,
transfigured is our planet earth,
the golden age is given birth.

9. Gautama Buddha, awaken the most creative people to see that an ideology not only defines a mental construct of what should or should not happen, but it also introduces the value judgment between right and wrong, good and evil.

O Jesus, fiery master mine,
my heart now melting into thine,

I love with heart and mind and soul,
the God who is my highest goal.

**O Jesus, let the Fire of Joy,
consume the devil's subtle ploy,
transfigured is our planet earth,
the golden age is given birth.**

Part 3

1. Gautama Buddha, awaken the most creative people to see that the power elite beings are causing tremendous harm to the people on earth. They are causing tremendous harm to themselves and they have done so for a very long time. It is not a matter of saying an ideology is wrong, it is a matter of saying: What are the consequences of the ideology?

Maitreya, I am truly meek,
your counsel wise I humbly seek,
your vision I so want to see,
with you in Eden I will be.

**Maitreya, kindness is the cure,
in fires of kindness I am pure.
Maitreya, now release the fire,
that raises me forever higher.**

2. Gautama Buddha, awaken the most creative people to see that when we transcend the dualistic mindset, we transcend this value judgment between right and wrong. This is what was introduced into modern civilization by science.

Maitreya, help me to return,
to learn from you, I truly yearn,
as oneness is all I desire
I feel initiation's fire.

Maitreya, kindness is the cure,
in fires of kindness I am pure.
Maitreya, now release the fire,
that raises me forever higher.

3. Gautama Buddha, awaken the most creative people to see that science was meant as a tool for helping people get beyond ideology. Society could not progress beyond a certain point before people got beyond this attempt to define how the world *should* work.

Maitreya, I hereby decide,
from you I will no longer hide,
expose to me the very lie
that caused edenic self to die.

Maitreya, kindness is the cure,
in fires of kindness I am pure.
Maitreya, now release the fire,
that raises me forever higher.

4. Gautama Buddha, awaken the most creative people to see that science is meant to be a processes that can evaluate: How does the world actually work. What can be observed based on experiment, how does the world work, not how somebody thinks it *should* work, according to a theory, a mental construct.

Maitreya, blessed Guru mine,
my heart of hearts forever thine,
I vow that I will listen well,
so we can break the serpent's spell.

Maitreya, kindness is the cure,
in fires of kindness I am pure.
Maitreya, now release the fire,
that raises me forever higher.

5. Gautama Buddha, awaken the most creative people to see that scientific experimentation is an attempt to go beyond theory, beyond mental construct, and have a direct experience of how the universe works.

Maitreya, help me see the lie
whereby the serpent broke the tie,
the serpent now has naught in me,
in oneness I am truly free.

**Maitreya, kindness is the cure,
in fires of kindness I am pure.
Maitreya, now release the fire,
that raises me forever higher.**

6. Gautama Buddha, awaken the most creative people to see that the struggle on earth is born when we are distancing ourselves from the experience. We are creating a mental construct and by the very fact that the planet is trapped in duality, we can never create an ultimate theory, there will always be an opposing viewpoint.

Maitreya, truth does set me free
from falsehoods of duality,
the fruit of knowledge I let go,
so your true spirit I do know.

**Maitreya, kindness is the cure,
in fires of kindness I am pure.
Maitreya, now release the fire,
that raises me forever higher.**

7. Gautama Buddha, awaken the most creative people to see that when we create a theory, we must take certain things for granted. Here is a foundation that we build our theory upon, these are self-evident, absolute truths that we do not need to question. They are so valid, so absolute, that we can build an entire worldview upon these basic truths.

Maitreya, I submit to you,
intentions pure, my heart is true,
from ego I am truly free,
as I am now all one with thee.

**Maitreya, kindness is the cure,
in fires of kindness I am pure.**

Maitreya, now release the fire,
that raises me forever higher.

8. Gautama Buddha, awaken the most creative people to see that this is just a choice we are making. What we choose is not some absolute truth, it is just one relative viewpoint. It is inevitable that in duality, there will always be pairs, there will always be opposing polarities. Someone else is bound to take the opposite viewpoint and call this the self-evident truth.

Maitreya, kindness is the key,
all shades of kindness teach to me,
for I am now the open door,
the Art of Kindness to restore.

Maitreya, kindness is the cure,
in fires of kindness I am pure.
Maitreya, now release the fire,
that raises me forever higher.

9. Gautama Buddha, awaken the most creative people to see that if we build two philosophies on different foundations, they will reach different forms, different conclusions, different ultimate truths. When we add the value judgment, one philosophy will say: "I am right, so the other is wrong." And the other will say: "Well, I am right, so the other is wrong."

Maitreya, oh sweet mystery,
immersed in your reality,
the myst'ry school will now return,
for this, my heart does truly burn.

Maitreya, kindness is the cure,
in fires of kindness I am pure.
Maitreya, now release the fire,
that raises me forever higher.

Part 4

1. Gautama Buddha, awaken the most creative people to see that we now have two groups of people who are pulled into this approach, each of them are trying to convince the other group that they are right. How can this not end in a struggle?

Gautama, show my mental state
that does give rise to love and hate,
your exposé I do endure,
so my perception will be pure.

**Gautama, Flame of Cosmic Peace,
unruly thoughts do hereby cease,
we radiate from you and me
the peace to still Samsara's Sea.**

2. Gautama Buddha, awaken the most creative people to see that we can transcend the struggle by transcending both of the previous viewpoints, realizing there is more to understand than what they had defined.

Gautama, in your Flame of Peace,
the struggling self I now release,
the Buddha Nature I now see,
it is the core of you and me.

**Gautama, Flame of Cosmic Peace,
unruly thoughts do hereby cease,
we radiate from you and me
the peace to still Samsara's Sea.**

3. Gautama Buddha, awaken the most creative people to see that throughout the Middle Ages, there were two opposing ideologies, Christianity and Islam, and they had created much conflict between them.

Gautama, I am one with thee,
Mara's demons do now flee,

your Presence like a soothing balm,
my mind and senses ever calm.

**Gautama, Flame of Cosmic Peace,
unruly thoughts do hereby cease,
we radiate from you and me
the peace to still Samsara's Sea.**

4. Gautama Buddha, awaken the most creative people to see that science was meant to be a way to make observations and draw conclusions that was neutral, that was not polarized towards either of the known ideologies.

Gautama, I now take the vow,
to live in the eternal now,
with you I do transcend all time,
to live in present so sublime.

**Gautama, Flame of Cosmic Peace,
unruly thoughts do hereby cease,
we radiate from you and me
the peace to still Samsara's Sea.**

5. Gautama Buddha, awaken the most creative people to see that the scientific method in its pure form cannot be pulled into the field of ideology because it is strictly focused on observation, and making conclusions only based on the observations.

Gautama, I have no desire,
to nothing earthly I aspire,
in non-attachment I now rest,
passing Mara's subtle test.

**Gautama, Flame of Cosmic Peace,
unruly thoughts do hereby cease,
we radiate from you and me
the peace to still Samsara's Sea.**

6. Gautama Buddha, awaken the most creative people to see that the power elite beings will use any new development to try and pervert it, to prevent it from setting people free, or try to use it for controlling people even more.

Gautama, I melt into you,
my mind is one, no longer two,
immersed in your resplendent glow,
Nirvana is all that I know.

Gautama, Flame of Cosmic Peace,
unruly thoughts do hereby cease,
we radiate from you and me
the peace to still Samsara's Sea.

7. Gautama Buddha, awaken the most creative people to see that the power elite beings took the scientific method and said: "We do not need to experiment with everything because there are some things that cannot be demonstrated through experience or experiment. And therefore there must be some theory that we take for granted as a truth that does not need to be questioned."

Gautama, in your timeless space,
I am immersed in Cosmic Grace,
I know the God beyond all form,
to world I will no more conform.

Gautama, Flame of Cosmic Peace,
unruly thoughts do hereby cease,
we radiate from you and me
the peace to still Samsara's Sea.

8. Gautama Buddha, awaken the most creative people to see that the power elite then elevated the materialistic viewpoint that there is nothing beyond the material universe and that we can explain the workings of the world by only looking at the material universe.

Gautama, I am now awake,
I clearly see what is at stake,

and thus I claim my sacred right
to be on earth the Buddhic Light.

**Gautama, Flame of Cosmic Peace,
unruly thoughts do hereby cease,
we radiate from you and me
the peace to still Samsara's Sea.**

9. Gautama Buddha, awaken the most creative people to see that in taking these simple viewpoints that started with Aristotle, and reintroducing them in the modern world, they created a new ideology. They pulled the scientific method into the realm of ideology and superimposed an ideology on what was meant to be purely an investigative tool that was not dependent on ideology. It was aimed at setting people free from mental constructs, but it was pulled into the world of mental constructs.

Gautama, with your thunderbolt,
we give the earth a mighty jolt,
I know that some will understand,
and join the Buddha's timeless band.

**Gautama, Flame of Cosmic Peace,
unruly thoughts do hereby cease,
we radiate from you and me
the peace to still Samsara's Sea.**

Part 5

1. Gautama Buddha, awaken the most creative people to see that mental constructs were superimposed upon the scientific method to the point where today, scientists do not feel free to investigate anything they want. If they investigate something that points beyond the materialist ideology, they will be opposed by the scientific establishment, the ideological establishment, the thought police.

Sanat Kumara, Ruby Fire,
I seek my place in love's own choir,
with open hearts we sing your praise,
together we the earth do raise.

Sanat Kumara, Ruby Ray,
bring to earth a higher way,
light this planet with your fire,
clothe her in a new attire.

2. Gautama Buddha, awaken the most creative people to see that even science has been pulled into the realm of ideology. One result is that there is an endless conflict between science and religion.

Sanat Kumara, Ruby Fire,
initiations I desire,
I am for you an electrode,
Shamballa is my true abode.

Sanat Kumara, Ruby Ray,
bring to earth a higher way,
light this planet with your fire,
clothe her in a new attire.

3. Gautama Buddha, awaken the most creative people to see that science was meant to be beyond religion, so that it could be embraced by all religions. How could we object to making an observation of how the world works? How could this be a religious matter? How could it be a political matter?

Sanat Kumara, Ruby Fire,
I follow path that you require,
initiate me with your love,
the open door for Holy Dove.

Sanat Kumara, Ruby Ray,
bring to earth a higher way,
light this planet with your fire,
clothe her in a new attire.

4. Gautama Buddha, awaken the most creative people to see that when we are making something an ideological issue, it is because we have separated ourselves from a neutral observation of how the world actually works. We think that the world works or *should* work according to our mental construct, our ideology.

Sanat Kumara, Ruby Fire,
your great example all inspire,
with non-attachment and great mirth,
we give the earth a true rebirth.

Sanat Kumara, Ruby Ray,
bring to earth a higher way,
light this planet with your fire,
clothe her in a new attire.

5. Gautama Buddha, awaken the most creative people to see that even in a democratic nation, people can be pulled into an ideological approach to everything, to where they cannot cooperate on anything. Ideology creates conflict after conflict after conflict.

Sanat Kumara, Ruby Fire,
you are this planet's purifier,
consume on earth all spirits dark,
reveal the inner Spirit Spark.

Sanat Kumara, Ruby Ray,
bring to earth a higher way,
light this planet with your fire,
clothe her in a new attire.

6. Gautama Buddha, awaken the most creative people to understand this mechanism, free themselves from it, and say: "Let's observe how the world works. Let's not superimpose some ideological belief about how it *should* work. And let us do what is practically necessary in every facet of life, whether it be a disease, whether it be the economy, whether it be any other aspect of life."

Sanat Kumara, Ruby Fire,
you are a cosmic amplifier,
the lower forces can't withstand,
vibrations from Venusian band.

**Sanat Kumara, Ruby Ray,
bring to earth a higher way,
light this planet with your fire,
clothe her in a new attire.**

7. Gautama Buddha, awaken the most creative people to see whether we have taken a spiritual teaching and effectively turned it into an ideology. Help us consider that it is not a matter of right and wrong, it is a matter of saying: What are the consequences for us? Does it slow down or speed up our spiritual growth?

Sanat Kumara, Ruby Fire,
I am on earth your magnifier,
the flow of love I do restore,
my chakras are your open door.

**Sanat Kumara, Ruby Ray,
bring to earth a higher way,
light this planet with your fire,
clothe her in a new attire.**

8. Gautama Buddha, I call to you, based on the growth in the collective consciousness, to decide that you will no longer allow space for ideology on earth. I will do my part to shift the collective consciousness above that critical limit where it becomes possible for you to say: "No more will there be space for the mindset behind ideology."

Sanat Kumara, Ruby Fire,
Venusian song the multiplier,
as we your love reverberate,
the densest minds we penetrate.

**Sanat Kumara, Ruby Ray,
bring to earth a higher way,**

**light this planet with your fire,
clothe her in a new attire.**

9. Gautama Buddha, awaken the most creative people from the mindset that sucks people into the collective beast behind a particular ideology, or even the collective beast behind all ideologies. I call for ideology to no longer be allowed space on earth so people can be free from the ideological baggage that is obstructing the manifestation of Saint Germain's Golden Age.

Sanat Kumara, Ruby Fire,
you are for all the sanctifier,
the earth is now a holy place,
purified by cosmic grace.

**Sanat Kumara, Ruby Ray,
bring to earth a higher way,
light this planet with your fire,
clothe her in a new attire.**

Sealing

In the name of the I AM THAT I AM, I accept that Archangel Michael, Astrea and Shiva form an impenetrable shield around myself and all constructive people, sealing us from all fear-based energies in all four octaves. I accept that the Light of God is consuming and transforming all fear-based energies that make up the dark forces working against ending the era of ideology on earth!

9 HOW IDEOLOGIES BECOME CLOSED SYSTEMS

I AM the Ascended Master Gautama Buddha. I have told you about the five elements that are traditionally seen as being part of ideologies. The first one is that there is an explanation put forth of how life works. Then there is a program for social/political change, change in society and then, as we have talked about, there is … (long silence). What you see here is an example of what I talked about in my last discourse, of going beyond thinking, going beyond the thinking of the linear mind where I caused the messenger's mind to go blank where there was no thought, just the experience. This is what you all need to be open to in order to escape duality: an experience of the linear mind coming to an impasse, to a point of stillness where the mind cannot continue, the mind cannot continue being linear, step by step by step. You will not escape duality through the linear mind because you used the linear mind to go into duality.

You understand – perhaps – you glimpse perhaps, that in order to truly grasp the message that I am seeking to give here, you need to be aware that whenever a message is given in words, you tend to interpret it through the linear mind. If you *only* interpret the message through the linear mind, you will not grasp the message. There is an old anecdote that was told in the Summit Lighthouse about the difference between various masters and their approach. The story was that El Morya, as he was called at the time, and Kuthumi were both charged with ascending a mountain to meet a master there, get a message and then bring the message back down. El

Morya who was the master of the blue ray of power charged ahead, went straight up the mountain got the message, went straight down. But when he came down, he found that he had not retained the message. Kuthumi took longer to get up the mountain and on the way down he stopped to smell the flowers, to listen to the birds. But when he came back down, he had retained the message. This is an example, an illustration, of the linear mind versus the intuitive, spherical mind.

I know very well that I have started giving these discourses in a somewhat linear way. There are steps, there are elements and if you look at this, this is what the world always does. It wants to give a linear explanation for everything. It seeks to analyze, it seeks to come up with some cause-effect sequence. In doing so, you are tying people's minds into this linear, rational, analytical approach. This is the approach behind most ideologies, they take you step by step.

Why an ideology cannot explain everything

The first element described was to attempt to explain what people cannot explain themselves or what the old ideology, the dominant ideology, cannot explain. You do grasp – I assume – that when you go into duality, you cannot explain everything because in duality you are taking a particular viewpoint, a particular foundation that you take for granted and say: "This cannot be questioned and on this foundation we build our ideology." Because you are taking one aspect and not questioning it, it is a guarantee that you cannot explain everything. No ideology has ever been able to explain everything. Now, for that matter no teaching given in words can ever explain everything because you must also *experience*. That is why we have consistently in this dispensation talked about the need to go beyond understanding and seek a direct, intuitive experience.

The first element is the explanation, then there is the program for change or what must happen—not necessarily only in society, it can even be on a cosmic level as this epic fight between good and evil, God and the devil and the fight for the souls of humanity. The third element is that the implementation of this program is explained as a struggle because some people object to it, some people resist. You have now gradually taken people in a linear way from seeking to explain, setting up this carrot dangling in front of their nose of the wonderful changes that will come about as a result of implementing this ideology. Then, you also have divided those people who accept your ideology into seeing themselves as being in a separate category from those people who resist the ideology.

Ideologies encourage fanaticism

As the next step, the fourth step or element in an ideology there is this: The ideology is not merely seeking to persuade people into believing something; it is seeking to attract some people who are willing to make a greater commitment, a commitment that goes beyond intellectual understanding and mere belief. It is a commitment to a cause, to the cause of implementing the ideology by doing whatever is necessary to overcome the resistance to the ideology. You see that gradually people are being taken by an ideology towards the point where they go through a change, not just in their minds but in their four lower bodies. They literally come to see themselves as having a different form of identity, an identity that is defined by their ideology. You are a Christian. You are a Muslim. You are a revolutionary. You are one of the true faithful communists, the party elite. Then, you have the intellectual level where you have now used the intellect's ability to filter out information that *does not* validate your ideology and to focus on information that *does* validate your ideology. Then, you have people decide that from this point on they do not need to question the ideology because: "It is true, it must be true, it can only be true, so there is no need to question it."

Then, you have the emotional component where people begin to feel very strongly that they are the right kind of people, they belong to the elite, to the select few that are part of implementing this great program of change that will have some epic importance on earth. Of course, then comes the fact that when you have shifted their identity, their mental mind and their emotions, you will also have shifted their actions. In many cases these people who have made the commitment are willing to do anything they are told, as long as they believe it furthers the cause and that it is necessary in order to further the cause. This of course first of all means that now they are willing to force others, they are willing to even kill others if that is necessary.

This is as far as the world goes. It talks about an ideology seeking to attract those who are willing to make that commitment. What is really going on in this process is that an ideology seeks to attract a group of committed people who have been turned into fanatics. You take some of our teachings on fanaticism and you will see that the true followers of any ideology, be it a religion or political ideology or even scientific Materialism, have become fanatics. Not all of them are willing to kill others in order to further their cause, but they have still gone into this fanatical mindset where they are not willing to question the ideology, they do not think it needs to be questioned. It is, as Mother Mary said about fanaticism: "You have an idea that you do not think can ever be expanded upon—it is absolute, it is the final truth, you do not need to question it, you do not need to look beyond it." This is the broadest definition of fanaticism. A more narrow definition is that you are willing to kill in order to further your cause, but even those who are not willing to kill can still be in the fanatical mindset. This is of course the ultimate outcome of an ideology: to create this group of fanatics that are willing to do anything in order to force the ideology upon a society or upon the entire planet. You can see for example, when you look at Nazism, how they attracted these groups of very devoted fanatical people who became part of the SS, the Gestapo, the Nazi apparatus and they were absolutely fanatical about forcing Nazism upon not only German society but other societies.

The architects behind an ideology

There were other groups of people who were not quite as fanatical but who were still pulled into this vortex of energy that was created by the Nazi ideology. You saw in the Soviet Union how there was a group of people that were willing to do anything to force communism upon not only Russia but other nations. Their ultimate goal was to force it upon the world. What you often see in these fanatical people is that you have two groupings. You have the architects, the ones that are in the leadership, they are often very intellectual and they are the ones who are defining not only what the ideology is but also how it needs to be implemented. Many of these are, as I talked about, the intellectuals who are looking at everything from a distance. They are sitting in their ivory tower, whether it is the Kremlin or the Nazi high command, and they are looking at society or they are looking at a battlefield and they are making decisions.

Now, in a sense they know that this decision might lead to war. This particular battle might cause thousands of their own soldiers to be killed, thousands of the enemy to be killed. Or this particular program of implementing or creating these camps will cause millions of people to die. They know this, they understand this but because they are intellectuals, they are centered in the mental mind, they see it all at a distance. They are not really thinking they are killing flesh-and-blood human beings because they have convinced themselves that the Jews, or those who oppose communism, are not really human beings like themselves. Therefore, they do not deserve the same consideration, they do not even have the same rights. They can set aside what we have called the basic humanity and implement these sweeping programs that they know will lead to the killing of tens of thousands, hundreds of thousands or millions of people and it does not affect them whatsoever. It is like they are moving chess pieces around on a chessboard and they have no more feelings involved (because their intellects, their mental minds, blocks their feelings) than if you move chess pieces on a chessboard.

The executioners behind an ideology

Now, of course you can clearly see throughout history that these architects of ideology, they cannot implement the ideology, they cannot go out there and do the dirty work of forcing that ideology upon others, so they need another group of people that have made this commitment, this absolute commitment to the cause, and they are the executioners, those who not only execute the ideology but also execute the people who resist the ideology. You see in the Nazi regime how you had these leaders in the party apparatus, some of them were in the military, some of them were not even military leaders. If you looked at these people individually, you would see that many of them were highly intelligent people, they were even quite aware. They were certainly very, very capable of using their intellectual faculties to see the shortcomings of Nazism, the contradictions of Nazi ideology. But they were not using their faculties to do this because they had made the decision that the Nazi ideology had to be true, that Hitler had to be right and therefore they did not need to question this.

Then, you will look at the people who were part of the SS, the Gestapo, the prison guards in the concentration camps, many of the army commanders at lower levels and they were the executioners. They did not have the intellectual capacity to see the contradictions of Nazism but they were not concerned about it. They did not really understand Nazi ideology. They did not really care about understanding it because these are people who were centered in the emotional and physical levels. They did not question the orders. They had made the commitment and for them the commitment meant: "I do whatever I am told from the leaders. I have made a commitment to obey the leaders and execute the orders that they tell me to execute, and execute the people that they tell me to execute, or whatever they tell me to do." You see here that there is a group of people who do not question the ideology, they are the leaders, then there is a group of people who do not question the leaders. They do not question the ideology either, but primarily for them it is a matter of not questioning the leaders.

We have said before that you and all people have a certain basic humanity. You have a sense that there are certain things you are not supposed to do to other people, such as killing other people. You have the instinct, the instinctual urge, not to kill other human beings. Once people make that commitment to the ideology, those instincts, that basic humanity, is set aside. Not necessarily towards all people but certainly towards the people who resist the ideology. You have here a group of leaders, the architects, who believe they do not need to question the ideology, or question the person who ultimately defined the ideology whether it is Hitler, Karl Marx, Mao or whomever. Then, you have the executioners who believe they do not have to question the architects. Normal considerations concerning what you do to other people do not come into play for either of these groups.

In most cases, certainly the architects have not lost all humanity, and you can see an example we have used before that the commander of the Auschwitz death camp could spend his day at work carrying out the execution of thousands of children. But then, when he was done with work, he would go home to his house in the camp and there he would play like a normal family father with his own children—and he saw no contradiction there. He saw no problem switching from one role to the next.

Ideologies divide people into separate categories

Why was this? Well, it was because he did not consider the Jewish children that were being executed in the gas chambers as human beings the same as his own children. This points to another element that is not normally defined in the worldly definition of ideology. You see here that there is an explanation that is part of the ideology and it attempts to explain how the world works. The explanation usually talks about how there are certain mechanisms that come into play and usually, even at this level of the explanation, there is a division of people. You see in the ideology of Marxism how there is a fundamental division of people into classes. Now you may say: "Are there actually classes of people?" As we have said, all human beings are connected, all human beings were created equal. They were created with equal rights. There are no classes that were created.

We have said before, there were no races. God did not create races. The concept of race is a man-made, artificial construct and so is the concept of class. Now, it is understandable that Karl Marx would look at society, the society of his time, and conclude that there were classes. Why is this understandable? Because during medieval times the medieval philosophy created the feudal society where there, in effect, was a fundamental difference between the kings and the noble class and the peasants. It was even considered that God had created the noble class and the Kings to rule. There was talk about the divine rights of kings. There was talk about the noble class having blue blood, being therefore created differently than ordinary people.

You see that in a sense there were, in the medieval mindset, classes of people. This of course was based on the Catholic ideology, which was based on the Roman ideology, which had at a certain point come to define that the Roman emperor was not just a human being who had been elevated to a leadership position. When the Roman emperor became emperor, he became God in embodiment. This was somewhat mitigated by the Catholic ideology that said that only Jesus was God, but Jesus needed representatives on earth and during medieval times that became expanded to the ideology of the clergy, the Pope and the Catholic priests and bishops being in a special class of people because they were talking directly to God. Of course, the kings and noblemen being in another special class of people that were meant to rule secular society, but it was all connected in this Catholic ideology that some people are special, created by God in a special class.

It is understandable that Karl Marx looked at this kind of society and then created the concept of classes. What few people were able to see, and what Karl Marx was not able to see himself, was that he thereby created a fundamental contradiction. What was the declared goal of Marxism, communism, socialism? It was to create the classless society. What was the entire ideology of Marxism based on: History is a class struggle. By its very foundation, Marxism defined "class" as the distinctive feature of human beings. Class was the very way to divide human beings into separate categories. How can an ideology that is based on the definition of classes ever produce a classless society? *It cannot be done.* I understand that most people in the world who use the linear mind cannot see this, but when you understand what we have given you about the dualistic mind, you can see that this cannot be done. An ideology that divides people based on the concept of class, cannot produce a classless society because how could the classless society be produced? Only by transcending the ideology of classes—and how can an ideology transcend itself?

An ideology cannot transcend itself

You look at history and you look at the different ideologies (religious, political, what have you). Do you see any example in known history of an ideology that came to a point where it said: "We have reached the end of the line here. We see that our ideology is based on an inherent contradiction that we can never overcome and therefore, we are just giving up. We are just laying down all our claims, abandoning all of our claims and walking away from the whole thing." It has not happened in *known* history. I can assure you, it has not happened in *unknown* history and why does it not happen? Because once an ideology has started to attain power in society, it attracts these people who make the commitment to the ideology. These people will not voluntarily give up what they have and what do they have? Well, when an ideology begins to have real power in a society, it attracts these two classes of people, as I said, the architects, the executioners. What do these people get out of making the commitment to the ideology? They get *power.* They get a *sense* of power.

The architects have what they consider a benevolent intent for wanting that power. They desire to see changes in society. They have a genuine (in many cases constructive, you might even say) desire to see change in society. Once they have convinced themselves that the only way to implement that change is through this ideology, then their minds become closed to seeing the shortcomings of the ideology. In fact, their minds become closed to evaluating: "Can we achieve the society we desire through the ideology? Can the ideology actually produce the result that it promises to produce?" As I said, go back to the Soviet Union. Look at all the Marxists (the intellectuals in the Western world that were convinced Marxists during the 1960s and 70s) and consider: Did any of them really see what I just said: Marxism can never produce the classless society? You will see that very few had even a hint of this understanding. You see that the architects become closed to considering whether the ideology can produce its results. Therefore, how could they ever come to a point where they realize that the ideology is not going to work, we are going to have to abandon it?

The other aspect is of course that if they were to question the ideology, they would feel they would lose their power, and for them power is important, not power in itself but the power to bring about change. Many of you have been programmed to look at Nazism as an entirely evil ideology, as an entirely evil event. You have been programmed to think that all of the Nazi leaders were evil people, but most of the Nazi leaders were not evil people. Some of them were avatars, as we have said before. They were pulled in by their desire to see positive change on earth, they were not driven by this quest to have unlimited power. Hitler himself was to a large degree driven by this, but even Hitler had some desire to see change at least in his outer mind. Many of the architects of Nazism had a desire to see positive change and they were driven by this. They did not want power just to execute power. They wanted power in order to bring about the positive change that they thought they could bring about. The same goes for many of the leaders of Marxism, at least in the early years where it was still a revolutionary movement.

After Stalin came to power, there was a change in the Soviet Union where the architects, the thinking people, the intellectuals, were systematically rooted out of communist leadership. Stalin was not an intellectual, he was not an architect, actually he was not a thinker and therefore those who could think were a threat to him. Stalin was an example where a person who really is an executioner comes to power. He is not the only example. You see many other dictators throughout history who have been executioners who came to power out of their willingness to kill anyone who opposed them. After Stalin came to power, there were no longer any architects in the leadership of the Soviet Union, which is why it became more focused on power, on the Red Terror, of not necessarily killing everybody but the *willingness* to kill everybody if necessary. That is why you saw in the Soviet Union how it became more brutal, how it attracted a larger group of what we call the executioners who were willing to kill anybody that they were told to kill.

Those who want power for its own sake

You see Beria, who was another example of an executioner who simply enjoyed having power for its own sake. You see that the architects desire power because they think they can then implement positive change as they see it. Then, an ideology, in order to gain power in society, it attracts the kind of people who want power for its own sake. They enjoy having power over other people. They enjoy being like gods on earth who can decide who lives and who dies. This is Stalin, this is Beria. This is some of the Nazi leaders and it is many of the people who were attracted to Mao and were doing the bidding of Mao who was, in a sense, a mixture of an architect and an executioner.

You see that there is a clear grouping of architects who want power to implement change. There is a clear grouping of executioners who want power for the sake of having power. Then, there are a few people who are a mixture of the two, somewhere in between, where they are not really great thinkers but they are willing to be brutal and they are not satisfied with having a lower position as an executioner, they want the highest position they could possibly get in that society.

Of course, all of this, once people have made this commitment and become fanatical adherents, fanatical followers of the ideology, is based on the division of humankind into different groups. This is the concept that is known, even in worldly psychology, of scapegoating. However, worldly psychology often considers it more at the individual level where there are certain people who are always blaming other people for their situation and their misfortune, always projecting out that the problem is outside themselves. These people are very difficult to help from a traditional psychological perspective. They are also very difficult to help with an ascended master teaching because how can we help people if they are always projecting out that the problem is outside their self? We can only help people who are willing to look at themselves.

Ideologies must have a scapegoat

Nevertheless, the point is that if you take this concept of scapegoating to the higher level, to the level of ideology, you see that most ideologies, sometimes even from the very beginning, define this division between those who are *for* the ideology and those who are *opposing* the ideology and therefore become the scapegoats. You often have an ideology that by the very explanation it gives of how life works, it divides people into separate categories. Marxism divides them into classes. Christianity divides them into Christians and non-Christians, Islam divides them into Muslims and non-Muslims, the Jews divided them into Jews and Gentiles and so on. From the very theory that is put forth, there is a division of people and there is a scapegoat defined.

Then, you also see that when an ideology defines the program of change that needs to happen, it is also defined that there is a certain group of people who can be the driving force of implementing these changes and there is a certain group of people who will oppose it. This of course leads to the concept of the struggle where those who are the people who are implementing the ideology (whose task it is, whose destiny it is to implement the ideology), they must be in a struggle against those who oppose the ideology, the scapegoat. This then leads to the point where those who feel they are destined to implement the ideology, they make the commitment that now makes them willing to execute the scapegoats who are opposing the ideology.

When you look at history, when you look at various nations, you can see what is the deciding factor of whether a nation becomes trapped in this vortex of a particular ideology. Why did the Roman empire become trapped in this ideology where the emperor was seen as God? There was a very centralized form of government with absolute power at the top that was filtered down, even to the willingness to kill anyone who opposed the decrees of the emperor. How could such a society exist? How could you have this centralized power structure? Well, you could have it because at the top you had a group of people who were the architects who were willing to implement the system. Now, in the Roman society you can say: Was there really a clearly defined ideology or was it mainly self-interest? In other words, there were a group of people around the emperor who saw it in their own self-interest to support the emperor because it gave them a position, it gave them power, it gave them riches, it gave them a privileged lifestyle.

Opportunists who use an ideology for themselves

You can look at history and see that I have talked about architects and executioners but we might need to add a third group of people who are the opportunists. They are not really intellectuals. They are not really into defining a certain ideology. They are not thinkers but they want privilege. They do not necessarily so much want power as they want a privileged lifestyle. This can involve having a position, having money so that they can have an affluent, lavish lifestyle, living in great palaces, having enough money to spend, having servants who can do whatever they want. What you see in Roman society was that there was a group of people around the emperor who were not really ideologists in the sense that they were thinking or were in the mental level. They were simply opportunists, they wanted a privileged lifestyle and they could get this by supporting the emperor. You also saw that at lower levels, first of all in the armed forces and the police of Roman society, we had the executioners who were willing to kill anyone who did not obey the decree of the emperor.

In any society with a centralized power structure you have these four groupings. I am deliberately not saying classes even though you could apply that terminology, but you have these four groupings. You have the ultimate leader, often just one person who wants to have ultimate power. Then you have the architects who are convinced by some ideology of that society. Then you have the opportunists who want a privileged position and then you have the executioners who enjoy having the power, the low-level power to arrest people, to kill people, to torture people, whatever you have. Based on this division of these groupings, you can look at the societies that have had a centralized power structure, and you can see that how these societies were actually formed, depended on the balance between these four groupings. You saw that in most such societies there was just one person who was the ultimate leader. It could be Hitler, it could be Lenin, it could be Stalin, it could be Mao, it could be any dictator seen throughout history. He wanted the absolute power. Nobody could question him and his judgments.

You see some dictatorships that were dominated by this person, and the person who had ultimate power was not really a thinker, he was a power person. They were always fallen beings at that level and he was simply brutal in exercising that power, eradicating anyone who opposed it. You see this in many dictators, and in many of these dictatorships you did not see a very prominent group of architects. They almost did not have any presence there because there was not much of an ideology. There was not much need to think, it was just a matter of killing anyone who opposed the dictator. You still saw a group of opportunists around the dictator who were the ones who were willing to take his commands and carry them out, spread them down to lower levels of society. In other words, they were the ones who were supporting the dictator and some of them were in the command structure so they were passing his dictates on to the executioners who were, then, carrying them out.

There was also part of the opportunists who were simply in it for the privilege they could get. What did they give to the dictator? Well, they were the ones who participated in social events and gave him the impression that he was special. Some dictators needed this more than others. Some of the kings of medieval Europe, you see how they had gathered around themselves this group of noble class people who were simply there to make the king feel special by creating these social events, elaborate parties, lavish parties. You saw that in the Roman civilization where parties became more and more extreme, more and more extravagant, in order to make the emperor and the people around him feel special. You can look at some of these centralized societies, and you can see how the interaction of these groups determined the society.

How the Soviet Union became more extreme

You saw for example in the Soviet Union how in the beginning the architects played a prominent role. You also had the opportunists, not in terms of the lavish lifestyle, but more those who were willing to bring on the command to the executioners who could then carry it out. Still, under Lenin the architects had a much greater influence. There was a certain amount of opportunists but they were mainly those who would carry out the orders. Then, there was a certain group of executioners but the executioners did not really have so much of an influence. Then, with the shift to Stalin, you see that now you have this ultimate dictator who wants ultimate power. You did have a certain group of people around him who were willing to carry out that power and you even had some people around Stalin who were there for his social events to make him feel special. But with Stalin, you saw that he became so paranoid that none of them could feel really secure. This is something that the opportunists desired. They desired to feel secure in their positions.

What Stalin actually did was he pushed out the architects, pushed out many of the opportunists and therefore ended up having to take some of the executioners and elevate them to higher positions because they were willing to do his bidding and they were not really capable of thinking:

"What is going to happen to me in six months when I fall out of favor with Stalin?" You saw that under Stalin the executioners attained a much more prominent position and influence in Soviet society and you can look at this and you can say: "Well, how could the leadership under Stalin find so many people in Russia who were willing to arrest, torture and execute their own citizens, their own fellow citizens?" This shows you that at the time of Stalin there was a large group of people in Russia who were at such a low level of consciousness that they did not have the basic humanity. They were so focused on themselves that killing another human being was not a problem for them. It was not something they had to think about. If they felt they were ordered to do so, they would do so without reflecting on it. Some of them would even enjoy the power they had, many of them would enjoy the power they had. You can go to Nazism and you can see that certainly there was a group of executioners who enjoyed having their power, as you saw some of the sadistic guards in the concentration camps, and there was a certain amount of opportunists that were willing to execute the orders. But the architects had a much more prominent position in Nazi society because they were still driven by this desire to create the ideal society.

Ideologies create self-reinforcing spirals

These are just some thoughts that I wanted to put out there that help you evaluate societies that have come under the influence of an ideology. It helps you understand what happens when people are pulled into making this shift in the mind where now they make the commitment to the ideology. You might say that at the moment an ideology gains this influence in society, where people can see that they can gain a personal advantage out of making the commitment, at that moment the ideology creates a self-reinforcing downward spiral.

There is no longer any chance that the ideology could transcend itself or could even fall apart from within. The people who have made the commitment are not willing to question the ideology because doing so would mean they would lose the position they have attained. Once these people have attained that position, it is so important to them (it even becomes part of their identity) that they will do anything to avoid losing it. There is always a certain possibility that some among the architects could decide to reactivate their critical thinking and see some of the shortcomings, either in the ideology itself or at least in how it is being implemented. When that happens, they would either be executed, frozen out, or they would leave voluntarily because there is no chance that they can persuade the ultimate leader, the opportunists or the executioners to abandon the ideology.

You can look at any society, for example you can take Germany during the 1930s, and you can see that there came a certain point that was the tipping point. I do not want to put a deliberate date on it but certainly we could say that when Hitler was elected Chancellor was one of these tipping points. There are different ways to look at it because there was actually a tipping point in the physical, there was one in the emotional, one in the mental and one in the identity level. The identity level of course came first and then the mental, then the emotional and then the physical. There were tipping points where you can see that from this point on, Nazi ideology had created a self-reinforcing spiral that could not be stopped or reformed from within because all of the people who had made that absolute commitment, that firm commitment, they were unable to stop the spiral.

That is why the only thing that could stop the spiral was a collapse, was the defeat of the Nazi Empire. Nazism made a certain mistake, you could say. They started engaging in this military campaign to take over the entire world and because of Hitler's delusions of grandeur he took on the entire world at the same time. He started the war on two fronts and once you engage in an all-out war like this, a war must have a winner and a loser so it is only a question of who becomes the winner, who becomes the loser. In this case Nazism lost. You can see that for centuries the Roman society won the military confrontation but even they were eventually defeated.

What you see here is a mechanism where once you have a society that is based on an ideology, and once that society engages in violent military actions to spread the ideology, then it is only a matter of time before that society will be defeated. It will collapse either through an outer defeat or sometimes from within. You can see that the Soviet Union, despite all of the military buildup during the cold war, they avoided a war with the West. That is why they survived as long as they did until they eventually collapsed from within because the economy that was defined by Marxist ideology was not sustainable. You can see in China how Mao, once he took power in China, consolidated his power and did not engage in a military campaign to spread ideology to other nations. This is why his society could survive as long as it did. Now you may say: "Why then, has not the Chinese economy collapsed from within?" Because the Chinese economy is no longer a Marxist ideological economy but China has opened up to an influx of capital from outside the country. That is why it can survive economically although you can debate whether China has survived ideologically as a truly Marxist-communist society. It is by name, but not really in reality, a Marxist society.

After Mao died there was an emergence of a group of people who saw the need to transform society in a certain direction, and that is why China has so far survived. Based on this you could debate whether China is an example of a nation where the ideology has been transformed from within and this is an open question because it is a very complex equation that simply depends on what you focus on to be the decisive factors in what has happened in China. We see here again, that there is always the possibility that the architects might gain a greater influence on society but it will not happen as long as you have that one dictator who wants absolute power.

Ideologies give a simplistic explanation of the world

With this I have given you what I wanted to give you in this installment. I trust you will grasp that what I am seeking to do here is to give you a somewhat simplified and therefore, somewhat simplistic understanding. I am seeking to help you understand ideology without creating a new ideology. While I am seeking to point out certain tendencies in ideology, I am not telling you that what I am giving you is the ultimate, complete and final understanding.

What is it that ideology does if you step back from ideology? It seeks to explain the world, but how does it do so? It seeks to explain the world in very simple terms. Any ideology seeks to explain the world in a way that is simple and easy to grasp for people. Now, what have we said before many times? The world is very complex. We have in Buddhism the concept of the interdependent originations where everything is connected. Everything is part of this enormously complex tapestry of life and you cannot single out a particular event, a particular cause, and say: "Here is the real cause of our problems." There is always many, many complex facets of any situation. What does an ideology do? It does single out one or a few aspects of life and it then simplifies the explanations to say: "This is the real cause of humanity's problems and if we remove that cause, we will have utopia on earth."

The real feature of ideology is this simplification of the complexity of life. I trust you will realize that understanding how ideology influences people is also a very complex topic that does not have just a simple explanation. I am attempting to give you a simplified understanding of it so that you can at least have a foundation for freeing yourself from the ideological mindset. If you are willing to look at yourselves as spiritual people, and if you could look at your past embodiments, you would see that especially those of you who are avatars (but even those of you who are the original inhabitants of the earth who have reached a higher level of consciousness), you all have a desire to see improvement on earth. At some point in your lives you have been pulled into the vortex or what I call the ideological mindset. You have been convinced of a certain ideology, whether it be Christianity, Islam, Marxism, or whatever you have. You came to that point where you made that commitment to the cause, to the ideology.

Now, there may have been a particular outer situation, a particular ideology, that caused you to make that commitment. Once you have made that commitment, you have stepped into a particular state of mind and you may go out of embodiment still being in that particular state of mind, as for example a committed Christian or committed Marxist. When you come back into your next embodiment after that, you are most likely not going to come back as a committed Christian or committed Marxist, but you are going to come back with the ideological mindset and that means you are looking for another cause, for another ideology. This means that when you find a spiritual teaching, even an ascended master teaching, you are going to approach that teaching with the ideological mindset. This is what we have seen in previous ascended master dispensations where a large group of the students clearly made that ideological commitment to the teachings, to the organization, to the movement, to saving the world for Saint Germain, bringing the Golden Age, however they saw it.

It is perfectly understandable that you did this, but the question I want to pose at the end of this discourse is: "Does it enhance your spiritual growth or does it slow down your spiritual growth? Furthermore, can the ideological approach to the spiritual path, to ascended master teachings qualify you for the ascension?"

I will of course talk more about this as we move on. For now, I thank you for your attention, for your willingness to be the open doors for letting these teachings go far and wide into the collective consciousness of this planet, where they are having a dramatic, distinctive effect in awakening some of the people who are close to being awakened to seeing the shortcomings of the ideological approach, the ideological state of mind.

With this, I seal you in the joy of the Buddha, the joy of being able to teach on earth. My greatest joy in my last embodiment on earth was to teach and here I am, able to teach again.

10 INVOKING AWARENESS OF IDEOLOGIES AS CLOSED SYSTEMS (PART 1)

In the name of the I AM THAT I AM, Jesus Christ, I use the authority that I have as a being in embodiment on earth to call upon Gautama Buddha to reinforce my calls and use my chakras to project the statements in this invocation into the collective consciousness and awaken people to the need to free ourselves from the ideological mindset. Awaken people to the reality that we are spiritual beings and that we can co-create a new future by working with the ascended masters. I especially call for ...

[Make your own calls here.]

Part 1

1. Gautama Buddha, awaken the most creative people to see that in order to escape duality, we need to experience that the linear mind is coming to an impasse where the mind cannot continue being linear, going step by step by step.

O Jesus, blessed brother mine,
I walk the path that you outline,
a great example to us all,
I follow now your inner call.

**O Jesus, let the Fire of Joy,
consume the devil's subtle ploy,
transfigured is our planet earth,
the golden age is given birth.**

2. Gautama Buddha, awaken the most creative people to see that we will not escape duality through the linear mind because we used the linear mind to go into duality.

O Jesus, open inner sight,
the ego wants to prove it's right,
but this I will no longer do,
I want to be all one with you.

**O Jesus, let the Fire of Joy,
consume the devil's subtle ploy,
transfigured is our planet earth,
the golden age is given birth.**

3. Gautama Buddha, awaken the most creative people to see that whenever a message is given in words, we tend to interpret it through the linear mind. If we *only* interpret the message through the linear mind, we will not grasp the message.

O Jesus, I now clearly see,
the Key of Knowledge given me,
my Christ self I hereby embrace,
as you fill up my inner space.

**O Jesus, let the Fire of Joy,
consume the devil's subtle ploy,
transfigured is our planet earth,
the golden age is given birth.**

4. Gautama Buddha, awaken the most creative people to see that the world wants to give a linear explanation for everything. It seeks to analyze and come up with some cause-effect sequence. In doing so, we are tying our minds into this linear, rational, analytical approach. This is the approach behind most ideologies, they take us step by step.

> O Jesus, show me serpent's lie,
> expose the beam in my own eye,
> as Christ discernment you me give,
> in oneness I forever live.

> **O Jesus, let the Fire of Joy,**
> **consume the devil's subtle ploy,**
> **transfigured is our planet earth,**
> **the golden age is given birth.**

5. Gautama Buddha, awaken the most creative people to see that when we go into duality, we cannot explain everything because in duality we are taking a particular viewpoint that we take for granted and say: "This cannot be questioned and on this foundation we build our ideology."

> O Jesus, I am truly meek,
> and thus I turn the other cheek,
> when the accuser attacks me,
> I go within and merge with thee.

> **O Jesus, let the Fire of Joy,**
> **consume the devil's subtle ploy,**
> **transfigured is our planet earth,**
> **the golden age is given birth.**

6. Gautama Buddha, awaken the most creative people to see that because we are taking one aspect and not questioning it, it is a guarantee that we cannot explain everything. No ideology has ever been able to explain everything.

> O Jesus, ego I let die,
> surrender ev'ry earthly tie,

the dead can bury what is dead,
I choose to walk with you instead.

**O Jesus, let the Fire of Joy,
consume the devil's subtle ploy,
transfigured is our planet earth,
the golden age is given birth.**

7. Gautama Buddha, awaken the most creative people to see that no teaching given in words can ever explain everything because we must also experience. We need to go beyond understanding and seek a direct, intuitive experience.

O Jesus, help me rise above,
the devil's test through higher love,
show me separate self unreal,
my formless self you do reveal.

**O Jesus, let the Fire of Joy,
consume the devil's subtle ploy,
transfigured is our planet earth,
the golden age is given birth.**

8. Gautama Buddha, awaken the most creative people to see that an ideology defines a program of change that is a struggle, and then it sets up this carrot dangling in front of us of the wonderful changes that will come about as a result of implementing the ideology.

O Jesus, what is that to me,
I just let go and follow thee,
with this I do pass ev'ry test,
to find with you eternal rest.

**O Jesus, let the Fire of Joy,
consume the devil's subtle ploy,
transfigured is our planet earth,
the golden age is given birth.**

9. Gautama Buddha, awaken the most creative people to see that an ideology guides those people who accept the ideology into seeing themselves as being in a separate category from those people who resist the ideology.

> O Jesus, fiery master mine,
> my heart now melting into thine,
> I love with heart and mind and soul,
> the God who is my highest goal.
>
> **O Jesus, let the Fire of Joy,**
> **consume the devil's subtle ploy,**
> **transfigured is our planet earth,**
> **the golden age is given birth.**

Part 2

1. Gautama Buddha, awaken the most creative people to see that an ideology is not merely seeking to persuade people into believing something. It is seeking to attract some people who are willing to make a greater commitment, a commitment that goes beyond intellectual understanding and mere belief.

> Maitreya, I am truly meek,
> your counsel wise I humbly seek,
> your vision I so want to see,
> with you in Eden I will be.
>
> **Maitreya, kindness is the cure,**
> **in fires of kindness I am pure.**
> **Maitreya, now release the fire,**
> **that raises me forever higher.**

2. Gautama Buddha, awaken the most creative people to see that an ideology encourages commitment to a cause, to the cause of implementing the ideology by doing whatever is necessary to overcome the resistance to the ideology.

Maitreya, help me to return,
to learn from you, I truly yearn,
as oneness is all I desire
I feel initiation's fire.

Maitreya, kindness is the cure,
in fires of kindness I am pure.
Maitreya, now release the fire,
that raises me forever higher.

3. Gautama Buddha, awaken the most creative people to see that gradually people are being taken by an ideology towards the point where they go through a change, not just in their minds but in their four lower bodies. They literally come to see themselves as having a different form of identity, an identity that is defined by their ideology.

Maitreya, I hereby decide,
from you I will no longer hide,
expose to me the very lie
that caused edenic self to die.

Maitreya, kindness is the cure,
in fires of kindness I am pure.
Maitreya, now release the fire,
that raises me forever higher.

4. Gautama Buddha, awaken the most creative people to see that this causes people to use the intellect's ability to filter out information that *does not* validate their ideology and to focus on information that *does* validate the ideology.

Maitreya, blessed Guru mine,
my heart of hearts forever thine,
I vow that I will listen well,
so we can break the serpent's spell.

Maitreya, kindness is the cure,
in fires of kindness I am pure.

**Maitreya, now release the fire,
that raises me forever higher.**

5. Gautama Buddha, awaken the most creative people to see that people decide that from this point on, they do not need to question the ideology because: "It is true, it must be true, it can only be true, so there is no need to question it."

Maitreya, help me see the lie
whereby the serpent broke the tie,
the serpent now has naught in me,
in oneness I am truly free.

**Maitreya, kindness is the cure,
in fires of kindness I am pure.
Maitreya, now release the fire,
that raises me forever higher.**

6. Gautama Buddha, awaken the most creative people to see that there is also an emotional component so that people begin to feel that they are the right kind of people, they belong to the elite, to the select few that are part of implementing this great program of change that will have some epic importance on earth.

Maitreya, truth does set me free
from falsehoods of duality,
the fruit of knowledge I let go,
so your true spirit I do know.

**Maitreya, kindness is the cure,
in fires of kindness I am pure.
Maitreya, now release the fire,
that raises me forever higher.**

7. Gautama Buddha, awaken the most creative people to see that when they have shifted their identity, their mental mind and their emotions, they will also have shifted their actions.

Maitreya, I submit to you,
intentions pure, my heart is true,
from ego I am truly free,
as I am now all one with thee.

Maitreya, kindness is the cure,
in fires of kindness I am pure.
Maitreya, now release the fire,
that raises me forever higher.

8. Gautama Buddha, awaken the most creative people to see that in many cases people who have made the commitment are willing to do anything they are told, as long as they believe it furthers the cause defined by the ideology. This means that now they are willing to force others, they are willing to even kill others if that is necessary.

Maitreya, kindness is the key,
all shades of kindness teach to me,
for I am now the open door,
the Art of Kindness to restore.

Maitreya, kindness is the cure,
in fires of kindness I am pure.
Maitreya, now release the fire,
that raises me forever higher.

9. Gautama Buddha, awaken the most creative people to see that an ideology seeks to attract those who are willing to make that commitment, but what is really going on is that an ideology seeks to attract a group of committed people who have been turned into fanatics.

Maitreya, oh sweet mystery,
immersed in your reality,
the myst'ry school will now return,
for this, my heart does truly burn.

Maitreya, kindness is the cure,
in fires of kindness I am pure.

**Maitreya, now release the fire,
that raises me forever higher.**

Part 3

1. Gautama Buddha, awaken the most creative people to see that the true followers of any ideology, be it a religion or political ideology or even scientific Materialism, have become fanatics. Not all of them are willing to kill, but they have still gone into the fanatical mindset.

Gautama, show my mental state
that does give rise to love and hate,
your exposé I do endure,
so my perception will be pure.

**Gautama, Flame of Cosmic Peace,
unruly thoughts do hereby cease,
we radiate from you and me
the peace to still Samsara's Sea.**

2. Gautama Buddha, awaken the most creative people to see that such people are not willing to question the ideology, they do not think it needs to be questioned. Fanaticism is when we have an idea that we do not think can ever be expanded upon—it is absolute, it is the final truth, we do not need to question it, we do not need to look beyond it.

Gautama, in your Flame of Peace,
the struggling self I now release,
the Buddha Nature I now see,
it is the core of you and me.

**Gautama, Flame of Cosmic Peace,
unruly thoughts do hereby cease,
we radiate from you and me
the peace to still Samsara's Sea.**

3. Gautama Buddha, awaken the most creative people to see that this is the broadest definition of fanaticism. A more narrow definition is that we are willing to kill in order to further our cause but even those who are not willing to kill can still be in the fanatical mindset.

> Gautama, I am one with thee,
> Mara's demons do now flee,
> your Presence like a soothing balm,
> my mind and senses ever calm.

> **Gautama, Flame of Cosmic Peace,**
> **unruly thoughts do hereby cease,**
> **we radiate from you and me**
> **the peace to still Samsara's Sea.**

4. Gautama Buddha, awaken the most creative people to see that the ultimate outcome of an ideology is to create this group of fanatics that are willing to do anything in order to force the ideology upon a society or upon the entire planet.

> Gautama, I now take the vow,
> to live in the eternal now,
> with you I do transcend all time,
> to live in present so sublime.

> **Gautama, Flame of Cosmic Peace,**
> **unruly thoughts do hereby cease,**
> **we radiate from you and me**
> **the peace to still Samsara's Sea.**

5. Gautama Buddha, awaken the most creative people to see that there are often two groupings among such fanatical people. There are the architects, the ones that are in the leadership, and they are often very intellectual. They are the ones defining not only what the ideology is but also how it needs to be implemented.

> Gautama, I have no desire,
> to nothing earthly I aspire,

in non-attachment I now rest,
passing Mara's subtle test.

**Gautama, Flame of Cosmic Peace,
unruly thoughts do hereby cease,
we radiate from you and me
the peace to still Samsara's Sea.**

6. Gautama Buddha, awaken the most creative people to see that the architects are looking at everything from a distance. They know that a decision might lead to war, but they are centered in the mental mind, they see it all from a distance.

Gautama, I melt into you,
my mind is one, no longer two,
immersed in your resplendent glow,
Nirvana is all that I know.

**Gautama, Flame of Cosmic Peace,
unruly thoughts do hereby cease,
we radiate from you and me
the peace to still Samsara's Sea.**

7. Gautama Buddha, awaken the most creative people to see that ideological leaders are not really thinking they are killing flesh-and-blood human beings, because they have convinced themselves that those who oppose their ideology are not human beings like themselves. Therefore, they do not deserve the same consideration, they do not even have the same rights.

Gautama, in your timeless space,
I am immersed in Cosmic Grace,
I know the God beyond all form,
to world I will no more conform.

**Gautama, Flame of Cosmic Peace,
unruly thoughts do hereby cease,
we radiate from you and me
the peace to still Samsara's Sea.**

8. Gautama Buddha, awaken the most creative people to see that ideological leaders can set aside basic humanity and implement sweeping programs that they know will lead to the killing of thousands or millions of people and it does not affect them whatsoever.

Gautama, I am now awake,
I clearly see what is at stake,
and thus I claim my sacred right
to be on earth the Buddhic Light.

Gautama, Flame of Cosmic Peace,
unruly thoughts do hereby cease,
we radiate from you and me
the peace to still Samsara's Sea.

9. Gautama Buddha, awaken the most creative people to see that such leaders are moving chess pieces around on a chessboard and they have no more feelings involved, because their intellects, their mental minds, block their feelings.

Gautama, with your thunderbolt,
we give the earth a mighty jolt,
I know that some will understand,
and join the Buddha's timeless band.

Gautama, Flame of Cosmic Peace,
unruly thoughts do hereby cease,
we radiate from you and me
the peace to still Samsara's Sea.

Part 4

1. Gautama Buddha, awaken the most creative people to see that the architects of ideology cannot implement the ideology, they cannot go out there and do the dirty work of forcing that ideology upon others, so they need

another group of people that have made this commitment, and they are the executioners.

Sanat Kumara, Ruby Fire,
I seek my place in love's own choir,
with open hearts we sing your praise,
together we the earth do raise.

**Sanat Kumara, Ruby Ray,
bring to earth a higher way,
light this planet with your fire,
clothe her in a new attire.**

2. Gautama Buddha, awaken the most creative people to see that the executioners not only execute the ideology but also execute the people who resist the ideology. They do not understand the ideology and they do not care about understanding it because they are centered in the emotional and physical levels.

Sanat Kumara, Ruby Fire,
initiations I desire,
I am for you an electrode,
Shamballa is my true abode.

**Sanat Kumara, Ruby Ray,
bring to earth a higher way,
light this planet with your fire,
clothe her in a new attire.**

3. Gautama Buddha, awaken the most creative people to see that the executioners do not question the orders from the architects. They have made the commitment and for them the commitment means: "I do whatever I am told from the leaders. I have made a commitment to obey the leaders and execute the orders that they tell me to execute, and execute the people they tell me to execute."

Sanat Kumara, Ruby Fire,
I follow path that you require,

initiate me with your love,
the open door for Holy Dove.

**Sanat Kumara, Ruby Ray,
bring to earth a higher way,
light this planet with your fire,
clothe her in a new attire.**

4. Gautama Buddha, awaken the most creative people to see that there is a group of people who do not question the ideology, they are the leaders, then there is a group of people who do not question the leaders. They do not question the ideology either, but primarily it is a matter of not questioning the leaders.

Sanat Kumara, Ruby Fire,
your great example all inspire,
with non-attachment and great mirth,
we give the earth a true rebirth.

**Sanat Kumara, Ruby Ray,
bring to earth a higher way,
light this planet with your fire,
clothe her in a new attire.**

5. Gautama Buddha, awaken the most creative people to see that once people make a commitment to an ideology, the basic humanity is set aside, not necessarily towards all people but certainly towards the people who resist the ideology.

Sanat Kumara, Ruby Fire,
you are this planet's purifier,
consume on earth all spirits dark,
reveal the inner Spirit Spark.

**Sanat Kumara, Ruby Ray,
bring to earth a higher way,
light this planet with your fire,
clothe her in a new attire.**

6. Gautama Buddha, awaken the most creative people to see that there is a group of leaders, the architects, who believe they do not need to question the ideology, or question the person who ultimately defined the ideology. Then, there are the executioners who believe they do not have to question the architects. Normal considerations concerning what to do to other people do not come into play for either of these groups.

> Sanat Kumara, Ruby Fire,
> you are a cosmic amplifier,
> the lower forces can't withstand,
> vibrations from Venusian band.

> **Sanat Kumara, Ruby Ray,**
> **bring to earth a higher way,**
> **light this planet with your fire,**
> **clothe her in a new attire.**

7. Gautama Buddha, awaken the most creative people to see that there is always an inherent contradiction because an ideology ignores the basic fact that all people were created of equal value. Instead, the ideology divides people into separate groupings.

> Sanat Kumara, Ruby Fire,
> I am on earth your magnifier,
> the flow of love I do restore,
> my chakras are your open door.

> **Sanat Kumara, Ruby Ray,**
> **bring to earth a higher way,**
> **light this planet with your fire,**
> **clothe her in a new attire.**

8. Gautama Buddha, awaken the most creative people to see that one example is Marxism that defined "class" as the distinctive feature of human beings. Class was the way to divide human beings into separate categories.

> Sanat Kumara, Ruby Fire,
> Venusian song the multiplier,

as we your love reverberate,
the densest minds we penetrate.

**Sanat Kumara, Ruby Ray,
bring to earth a higher way,
light this planet with your fire,
clothe her in a new attire.**

9. Gautama Buddha, awaken the most creative people to see that an ideology that is based on the definition of classes can never produce a classless society? *It cannot be done.* An ideology that divides people based on the concept of class, cannot produce a classless society because how could the classless society be produced? Only by transcending the ideology of classes—and how can an ideology transcend itself?

Sanat Kumara, Ruby Fire,
you are for all the sanctifier,
the earth is now a holy place,
purified by cosmic grace.

**Sanat Kumara, Ruby Ray,
bring to earth a higher way,
light this planet with your fire,
clothe her in a new attire.**

Sealing

In the name of the I AM THAT I AM, I accept that Archangel Michael, Astrea and Shiva form an impenetrable shield around myself and all constructive people, sealing us from all fear-based energies in all four octaves. I accept that the Light of God is consuming and transforming all fear-based energies that make up the dark forces working against ending the era of ideology on earth!

11 INVOKING AWARENESS OF IDEOLOGIES AS CLOSED SYSTEMS (PART 2)

In the name of the I AM THAT I AM, Jesus Christ, I use the authority that I have as a being in embodiment on earth to call upon Gautama Buddha to reinforce my calls and use my chakras to project the statements in this invocation into the collective consciousness and awaken people to the need to free ourselves from the ideological mindset. Awaken people to the reality that we are spiritual beings and that we can co-create a new future by working with the ascended masters. I especially call for ...

[Make your own calls here.]

Part 1

1. Gautama Buddha, awaken the most creative people to see that there is no example in known history of an ideology that came to a point where it said: "We have reached the end of the line. We see that our ideology is based on an inherent contradiction that we can never overcome and therefore, we are just giving up. We are abandoning all of our claims and walking away from the whole thing."

Gautama, show my mental state
that does give rise to love and hate,
your exposé I do endure,
so my perception will be pure.

**Gautama, Flame of Cosmic Peace,
unruly thoughts do hereby cease,
we radiate from you and me
the peace to still Samsara's Sea.**

2. Gautama Buddha, awaken the most creative people to see that this cannot happen because once an ideology has started to attain power in society, it attracts people who make the commitment to the ideology. These people will not voluntarily give up the power they have.

Gautama, in your Flame of Peace,
the struggling self I now release,
the Buddha Nature I now see,
it is the core of you and me.

**Gautama, Flame of Cosmic Peace,
unruly thoughts do hereby cease,
we radiate from you and me
the peace to still Samsara's Sea.**

3. Gautama Buddha, awaken the most creative people to see that once an ideology begins to have real power in a society, it attracts these two classes of people, the architects and the executioners. By making the commitment to the ideology, these people get *power.* They get a *sense* of power.

Gautama, I am one with thee,
Mara's demons do now flee,
your Presence like a soothing balm,
my mind and senses ever calm.

**Gautama, Flame of Cosmic Peace,
unruly thoughts do hereby cease,
we radiate from you and me
the peace to still Samsara's Sea.**

4. Gautama Buddha, awaken the most creative people to see that the architects have what they consider a benevolent intent for wanting power. They desire to see changes in society. They have a genuine desire to see change in society. Once they have convinced themselves that the only way to implement that change is through this ideology, then their minds become closed to seeing the shortcomings of the ideology.

Gautama, I now take the vow,
to live in the eternal now,
with you I do transcend all time,
to live in present so sublime.

**Gautama, Flame of Cosmic Peace,
unruly thoughts do hereby cease,
we radiate from you and me
the peace to still Samsara's Sea.**

5. Gautama Buddha, awaken the most creative people to see that their minds become closed to evaluating: "Can we achieve the society we desire through the ideology? Can the ideology actually produce the result that it promises to produce?"

Gautama, I have no desire,
to nothing earthly I aspire,
in non-attachment I now rest,
passing Mara's subtle test.

**Gautama, Flame of Cosmic Peace,
unruly thoughts do hereby cease,
we radiate from you and me
the peace to still Samsara's Sea.**

6. Gautama Buddha, awaken the most creative people to see that none of the Marxists in the Soviet Union or the intellectuals in the Western world could see that Marxism could never produce the classless society.

Gautama, I melt into you,
my mind is one, no longer two,

immersed in your resplendent glow,
Nirvana is all that I know.

**Gautama, Flame of Cosmic Peace,
unruly thoughts do hereby cease,
we radiate from you and me
the peace to still Samsara's Sea.**

7. Gautama Buddha, awaken the most creative people to see that the architects become closed to considering whether the ideology can produce its results. Therefore, how could they ever come to a point where they realize that the ideology is not going to work?

Gautama, in your timeless space,
I am immersed in Cosmic Grace,
I know the God beyond all form,
to world I will no more conform.

**Gautama, Flame of Cosmic Peace,
unruly thoughts do hereby cease,
we radiate from you and me
the peace to still Samsara's Sea.**

8. Gautama Buddha, awaken the most creative people to see that if people were to question the ideology, they would feel they would lose their power, and for them power is important, not power in itself but the power to bring about change.

Gautama, I am now awake,
I clearly see what is at stake,
and thus I claim my sacred right
to be on earth the Buddhic Light.

**Gautama, Flame of Cosmic Peace,
unruly thoughts do hereby cease,
we radiate from you and me
the peace to still Samsara's Sea.**

9. Gautama Buddha, awaken the most creative people to see that there is a clear grouping of architects who want power to implement change. There is a clear grouping of executioners who want power for the sake of having power.

> Gautama, with your thunderbolt,
> we give the earth a mighty jolt,
> I know that some will understand,
> and join the Buddha's timeless band.

> **Gautama, Flame of Cosmic Peace,**
> **unruly thoughts do hereby cease,**
> **we radiate from you and me**
> **the peace to still Samsara's Sea.**

Part 2

1. Gautama Buddha, awaken the most creative people to see that when people make the commitment to become fanatical followers of the ideology, this is based on the division of humankind into different groups. This is the concept of scapegoating.

> O Shiva, God of Sacred Fire,
> It's time to let the past expire,
> I want to rise above the old,
> a golden future to unfold.

> **O Shiva, clear the energy,**
> **O Shiva, bring the synergy,**
> **O Shiva, make all demons flee,**
> **O Shiva, bring back peace to me.**

2. Gautama Buddha, awaken the most creative people to see that most ideologies, even from the very beginning, define this division between those who are *for* the ideology and those who are *opposing* the ideology and therefore become the scapegoats.

O Shiva, come and set me free,
from forces that do limit me,
with fire consume all that is less,
paving way for my success.

O Shiva, clear the energy,
O Shiva, bring the synergy,
O Shiva, make all demons flee,
O Shiva, bring back peace to me.

3. Gautama Buddha, awaken the most creative people to see that an ideology, by the very explanation it gives of how life works, divides people into separate categories. From the very theory that is put forth, there is a division of people and there is a scapegoat defined.

O Shiva, Maya's veil disperse,
clear my private universe,
dispel the consciousness of death,
consume it with your Sacred Breath.

O Shiva, clear the energy,
O Shiva, bring the synergy,
O Shiva, make all demons flee,
O Shiva, bring back peace to me.

4. Gautama Buddha, awaken the most creative people to see that when an ideology defines the program of change that needs to happen, it is also defined that there is a certain group of people who can be the driving force of implementing these changes and there is a certain group of people who will oppose it.

O Shiva, I hereby let go,
of all attachments here below,
addictive entities consume,
the upward path I do resume.

O Shiva, clear the energy,
O Shiva, bring the synergy,

O Shiva, make all demons flee,
O Shiva, bring back peace to me.

5. Gautama Buddha, awaken the most creative people to see that this leads to the concept of the struggle where those who are implementing the ideology must be in a struggle against those who oppose the ideology, the scapegoat.

O Shiva, I recite your name,
come banish fear and doubt and shame,
with fire expose within my mind,
what ego seeks to hide behind.

O Shiva, clear the energy,
O Shiva, bring the synergy,
O Shiva, make all demons flee,
O Shiva, bring back peace to me.

6. Gautama Buddha, awaken the most creative people to see that this leads to the point where those who feel they are destined to implement the ideology make the commitment that now makes them willing to execute the scapegoats who are opposing the ideology.

O Shiva, I am not afraid,
my karmic debt hereby is paid,
the past no longer owns my choice,
in breath of Shiva I rejoice.

O Shiva, clear the energy,
O Shiva, bring the synergy,
O Shiva, make all demons flee,
O Shiva, bring back peace to me.

7. Gautama Buddha, awaken the most creative people to see that an ideology often leads to a centralized form of government with absolute power vested in one leader. Yet there is always a group of people around the leader who see it as their own self-interest to support the leader because it gives them a position, power, riches or a privileged lifestyle.

O Shiva, show me spirit pairs,
that keep me trapped in their affairs,
I choose to see within my mind,
the spirits that you surely bind.

O Shiva, clear the energy,
O Shiva, bring the synergy,
O Shiva, make all demons flee,
O Shiva, bring back peace to me.

8. Gautama Buddha, awaken the most creative people to see that beyond the architects and executioners, an ideology attracts a third group of people who are the opportunists.

O Shiva, naked I now stand,
my mind in freedom does expand,
as all my ghosts I do release,
surrender is the key to peace.

O Shiva, clear the energy,
O Shiva, bring the synergy,
O Shiva, make all demons flee,
O Shiva, bring back peace to me.

9. Gautama Buddha, awaken the most creative people to see that the opportunists are not intellectuals. They are not into defining a certain ideology. They are not thinkers but they want privilege. They do not so much want power as they want a privileged lifestyle.

O Shiva, all-consuming fire,
with Parvati raise me higher,
when I am raised your light to see,
all men I will draw onto me.

O Shiva, clear the energy,
O Shiva, bring the synergy,
O Shiva, make all demons flee,
O Shiva, bring back peace to me.

Part 3

1. Gautama Buddha, awaken the most creative people to see that this can involve having a position, having money so that they can have an affluent, lavish lifestyle, living in great palaces, having enough money to spend, having servants who can do whatever they want.

Surya, cosmic being bright,
your balance is my pure delight,
I am in orbit round God Star,
in perfect unity we are.

Surya, banish all extremes,
Surya, shatter Serpent's schemes,
Surya, balance to me bring,
Surya, making my heart sing.

2. Gautama Buddha, awaken the most creative people to see that in Roman society there was a group of people around the emperor who were not ideologists. They were simply opportunists who wanted a privileged lifestyle and they could get this by supporting the emperor.

Surya, there is more to life,
than human conflict, war and strife,
your balance gives me inner peace,
all outer conflicts do now cease.

Surya, banish all extremes,
Surya, shatter Serpent's schemes,
Surya, balance to me bring,
Surya, making my heart sing.

3. Gautama Buddha, awaken the most creative people to see that in any society with a centralized power structure, we have these groupings. There is the ultimate leader, the architects who are convinced by some ideology, the opportunists who want a privileged position and the executioners who enjoy having the low-level power to arrest, kill or torture people.

Surya, what a wondrous sight,
from Sirius you send the light,
of one mind, I now call to thee,
for your apprentice I would be.

Surya, banish all extremes,
Surya, shatter Serpent's schemes,
Surya, balance to me bring,
Surya, making my heart sing.

4. Gautama Buddha, awaken the most creative people to see that the particular form of a society with a centralized power structure depends on the balance between these four groupings. For example, in the beginning days of the Soviet Union the architects played a prominent role.

Surya, radiate your light,
with balance you set all things right,
consuming energetic dross,
my letting go is not a loss.

Surya, banish all extremes,
Surya, shatter Serpent's schemes,
Surya, balance to me bring,
Surya, making my heart sing.

5. Gautama Buddha, awaken the most creative people to see that Stalin pushed out the architects, pushed out many of the opportunists and therefore ended up having to take some of the executioners and elevate them to higher positions because they were willing to do his bidding.

Surya, your light is alive,
for inner balance I do strive,
the alchemy is now begun,
my heart transformed into a sun.

Surya, banish all extremes,
Surya, shatter Serpent's schemes,
Surya, balance to me bring,
Surya, making my heart sing.

6. Gautama Buddha, awaken the most creative people to see that the most brutal regimes can only happen in nations where a large group of people are at such a low level of consciousness that they do not have the basic humanity. They are so focused on themselves that killing another human being is not a problem for them.

Surya, come enlighten me,
duality you help me see,
extremes they cannot pull me in,
on Middle Way I always win.

Surya, banish all extremes,
Surya, shatter Serpent's schemes,
Surya, balance to me bring,
Surya, making my heart sing.

7. Gautama Buddha, awaken the most creative people to see that when an ideology gains such influence in society that people can gain a personal advantage out of making the commitment, the ideology creates a self-reinforcing downward spiral.

Surya, in your cosmic sphere,
with Cuzco I your light revere,
from your perspective o so grand,
life finally I understand.

Surya, banish all extremes,
Surya, shatter Serpent's schemes,
Surya, balance to me bring,
Surya, making my heart sing.

8. Gautama Buddha, awaken the most creative people to see that there is no longer any chance that the ideology could transcend itself or could fall apart from within. The people who have made the commitment are not willing to question the ideology because doing so would mean they would lose the position they have attained.

Surya, show me God's design,
I see that God is all benign,

you calm my feeling body's storm,
I know the God beyond all form.

Surya, banish all extremes,
Surya, shatter Serpent's schemes,
Surya, balance to me bring,
Surya, making my heart sing.

9. Gautama Buddha, awaken the most creative people to see that once these people have attained a position, it is so important to them that they will do anything to avoid losing it.

Surya, I come from afar,
and as you show me my home star,
I see now my internal light,
a star I am in my own right.

Surya, banish all extremes,
Surya, shatter Serpent's schemes,
Surya, balance to me bring,
Surya, making my heart sing.

Part 4

1. Gautama Buddha, awaken the most creative people to see that Nazi ideology had created a self-reinforcing spiral that could not be stopped or reformed from within, because all of the people who had made that absolute commitment were unable to stop the spiral. The only thing that could stop the spiral was the total defeat of the Nazi Empire.

I see how my senses can only deceive,
for nothing they tell me, I fully believe.
Behind all appearances is only light,
they only seem real to our limited sight.

O Padmasambhava, in your Flame of Peace,
all human opinions I hereby release.

**I see now the ultimate truth you reveal,
earth is an appearance, where nothing is real.**

2. Gautama Buddha, awaken the most creative people to see that there is a mechanism where once we have a society that is based on an ideology, and once that society engages in violent military actions to spread the ideology, then it is only a matter of time before that society will be defeated. It will collapse either through an outer defeat or sometimes from within.

My mind and my senses are only a tool,
and I am determined to not be a fool.
My personal self, is no more who I am,
the earthly identity is but a scam.

**O Padmasambhava, in your Flame of Peace,
all human opinions I hereby release.
I see now the ultimate truth you reveal,
earth is an appearance, where nothing is real.**

3. Gautama Buddha, awaken the most creative people to see that the Soviet Union avoided a war with the West and that is why they survived so long. They eventually collapsed from within because the economy that was defined by Marxist ideology was not sustainable.

From sense-based perception I want to be free,
clear my inner sight, so I truly can see.
My human opinions, they do make me blind,
with neutral awareness, new visions I find.

**O Padmasambhava, in your Flame of Peace,
all human opinions I hereby release.
I see now the ultimate truth you reveal,
earth is an appearance, where nothing is real.**

4. Gautama Buddha, awaken the most creative people to see that our challenge is to understand ideology without creating a new ideology. An ideology seeks to explain the world in very simple terms. Any ideology seeks to explain the world in a way that is simple and easy to grasp.

A self is what makes an opinion seem real,
it projects there's a problem, with which I must deal.
I will not be free, till I see through this lie,
and say to the self: I am letting you die.

O Padmasambhava, in your Flame of Peace,
all human opinions I hereby release.
I see now the ultimate truth you reveal,
earth is an appearance, where nothing is real.

5. Gautama Buddha, awaken the most creative people to see that the world is very complex. Because of interdependent originations, everything is connected. Everything is part of this enormously complex tapestry of life.

Through human opinions, I simply can't see,
the higher perspective—Christ reality,
When the self dualistic, I truly let die,
the Christ mind does open, up my inner eye.

O Padmasambhava, in your Flame of Peace,
all human opinions I hereby release.
I see now the ultimate truth you reveal,
earth is an appearance, where nothing is real.

6. Gautama Buddha, awaken the most creative people to see that we cannot single out a particular event, a particular cause, and say: "Here is the real cause of our problems." There will always be many complex facets of any situation. An ideology does single out one or a few aspects of life and it then simplifies the explanation to say: "This is the real cause of humanity's problems and if we remove that cause, we will have utopia on earth." The real feature of ideology is this simplification of the complexity of life.

O Padmasambhava, the world has gone mad,
as dualistic thinking, defines good and bad.
The judgment of Christ, upon forces so dark,
rekindle in people, our spiritual spark.

O Padmasambhava, in your Flame of Peace,
all human opinions I hereby release.

I see now the ultimate truth you reveal,
earth is an appearance, where nothing is real.

7. Gautama Buddha, awaken the most creative people to free ourselves from the ideological mindset. Help us see how our desire to see improvement on earth has caused us to be pulled into the vortex of the ideological mindset, often in past lifetimes.

O Padmasambhava, set all people free,
from mindset so epic, from duality.
Cut all people free from the serpentine lie,
so that to Christ Jesus, we all can draw nigh.

O Padmasambhava, in your Flame of Peace,
all human opinions I hereby release.
I see now the ultimate truth you reveal,
earth is an appearance, where nothing is real.

8. Gautama Buddha, awaken the most creative people to see that we may overcome the fixation on a particular ideology, but when we come back into embodiment, we can come back with the ideological mindset and that means we are looking for another cause. When we find a spiritual teaching, we are going to approach that teaching with the ideological mindset.

The serpentine lie, says that what we now see,
is all that our lives, on this planet can be.
Yet with the Christ mind, we can see there is more,
the earth will be brighter than ever before.

O Padmasambhava, in your Flame of Peace,
all human opinions I hereby release.
I see now the ultimate truth you reveal,
earth is an appearance, where nothing is real.

9. Gautama Buddha, awaken the most creative people to free ourselves from the ideological mindset so we can be the open doors for letting these teachings go into the collective consciousness and awakening the people who are close to being awakened to seeing the shortcomings of the ideological approach, the ideological state of mind.

Saint Germain has the plans, for a bright Golden Age,
to receive them, our minds must be free from the cage,
O Padmasambhava, with your Flame of Peace,
the vision of Oneness, to all you release.

**O Padmasambhava, in your Flame of Peace,
all human opinions I hereby release.
I see now the ultimate truth you reveal,
earth is an appearance, where nothing is real.**

Sealing

In the name of the I AM THAT I AM, I accept that Archangel Michael, Astrea and Shiva form an impenetrable shield around myself and all constructive people, sealing us from all fear-based energies in all four octaves. I accept that the Light of God is consuming and transforming all fear-based energies that make up the dark forces working against ending the era of ideology on earth!

12 IDEOLOGIES AS A MEANS OF CONTROL

I AM the Ascended Master Gautama Buddha. In this next installment in the discourses I have planned for this conference, we are going to look at the last of the five elements that traditional sources define as part of ideology. We have talked about the explanation of how the world works, the program for change, the portrayal of a struggle and the quest or the demand for commitment. The fifth element defined is that, although an ideology seeks to appeal to a broad range of people, the broad population, it always defines that there is a particular group that are more suited to grasping, interpreting and implementing the ideology.

These are often portrayed as intellectuals. As you very clearly saw how in many Western nations during the 60s and 70s, it was the intellectuals who were enamored by the ideology of Marxism. They were clearly enamored with it from a distance because they had not experienced how it actually was to live in a Marxist society, such as the Soviet Union. Had they experienced this, most of them would have been disillusioned and very disappointed and would have had to question their ideology. When you only see it from a distance, how do you question the ideology? What frame of reference do you have once you have entered the ideological mindset that I talked about in my last discourse?

Now, it is of course correct that many ideologies first of all are appealing to intellectuals. Ideologies are based on ideas. Ideas are dealt with by the mental mind. Therefore, of course people who are focused in the mental mind are more likely to be enamored by the ideas and to feel that they are the only ones who can really understand and interpret the ideas. As I have said, an ideology must appeal to various groups of people so when you go beyond the worldly interpretation, what is really going on here? What is it that an ideology really seeks to do?

Well, an ideology of course seeks to control people, and it wants to control their actions. It is not so easy to directly control people's actions. You can just see how you yourself can be walking through a store and suddenly you feel an impulse to buy a certain type of food that you do not normally buy. So on a whim, your behavior can change. With "you" of course I mean people in general. It is not that easy to control people at the level of actions.

How ideologies are used to control people

The fallen beings know that in order to really control people, you also have to work with the three higher bodies. You have to attempt to control their emotions. Again, controlling the emotions at the level of emotions is not so easy either. Emotions can also change on a whim. For seemingly no obvious reason, you can suddenly feel an emotion that you have not felt for some time.

You also need to control people's thoughts. Controlling people's thoughts at the level of the mental mind is actually easier than controlling the emotions and the actions. But it is still not completely easy because the intellectual mind can, as we have said, argue for or against any point. At the mental level, a person who has convinced himself or herself that a certain ideology is true, could at any moment suddenly consider the opposite argument that questions the ideology. In order to really control people, you actually have to go to the highest level, the level of identity.

What an ideology seeks to do is to control people's sense of identity, how they see themselves, how they see themselves in relation to the world. What ideologies generally do is that they tend to create three groupings of people. First of all, we have the people who are convinced, are converted, by the ideology. They enter the ideological mindset. They are the ones who are actively promoting and implementing the ideology. This is one group and they identify themselves in that way. They identify themselves as belonging to the elite who can grasp, interpret and implement this ideology and thereby be the driving force in bringing the defined changes.

Then, the next group you have, which is usually the largest part of the population, are the people who do not particularly grasp or understand the ideology. They have at least some sense or some hope that the ideology can fulfill its promises, can deliver the kind of society and give them the benefits that have been outlined in the ideology. They have so to speak submitted themselves to the ideology. They may have submitted because they believe it can work and they believe that the ruling class, the architects, will be able to make it work. They have in a sense voluntarily submitted themselves, thinking that the changes will come at some point.

There is also another gradation of this submission where people felt/feel that there was/is no point in resisting the ideology, or they cannot resist the ideology. You saw in the Soviet Union for example how in the beginning, there was a larger group of people that had the hope that communism could deliver. After the ascent of Stalin and the brutality that he implemented, the vast majority of people simply submitted themselves because they felt they could not resist. There was no point in resisting and it was better to be alive than to be dead. You see that what actually happens to this second group of people is that they become pacified. They go into a pacified state of mind, a passive state of mind. They submit to what we might call the ruling elite of society.

Then, of course you have the third group of people, those who are resisting the ideology. They become the scapegoat, they become the enemy. You will see that for all three groups, their sense of identity can be affected. During communism, you saw that there was a certain group of people who identified themselves as the ruling class of the classless society. They were the party elite, they were those who implemented the will of the party by doing whatever was necessary to force the people to conform. They identified themselves as the most advanced people, the most powerful people, the ones who were right and the ones who were the guardians of the ideology. Then, you had the large group of people who simply submitted to conditions as they were, and they accepted that they were basically powerless. They were powerless to change the system, to change the fundamentals. They had to just make the best of whatever situation was perpetrated upon them from above.

Then, of course you saw during communist times there was a group of people who came to identify themselves as anti-communists, those who were fighting against communism. There were not so many of them in the Soviet Union because of the brutality of Stalin. There were many of them outside the Soviet Union, primarily in the United States. You can see that there were people in the United States during the height of the Cold War, who identified themselves as those whose destiny it was to prevent or stop the spread of communism. Even though they rejected communist ideology, they were still identifying themselves in relation to the communist ideology. You had those who accepted the ideology, and who identified themselves based on the ideology. You had those who rejected the ideology, but still identified themselves as being in opposition to the ideology, as the anti-communists. Then, you had the large group of people in between who just identified themselves as normal human beings trying to get by and make the best of whatever situation there was, but they still identified themselves as passive.

Locking people in a struggle against each other

You see the groupings of people, those who are *for,* those who are *against.* Both groups are active, feel empowered. Then, you see the large group of people who are passive. You may think, if you look at the communist ideology, that it was aimed primarily at those who identified themselves as communists, but it was not. It was aimed equally at those who resisted communism because communism also forced these people to enter a certain sense of identity that was unbalanced. It was very much in relation to communism and therefore, they were simply dualistic polarities. The communists, the anti-communists, both had their sense of identity profoundly affected by it. Then, there was the large group of people who identified themselves as passive, and this is exactly what the fallen beings want.

The fallen beings want the majority of the people to be passive because that makes them easy to control. The fallen beings know (at least the ones in the lower identity realm) that you cannot pacify all people. There is a certain group of people in embodiment at any time that you cannot pacify because they are more active people. They have some kind of ambition, some kind of desire, some kind of vision—and you cannot pacify them. What do you do? Well, you cause them to polarize into those who are actively working *for* a particular ideology, and those who are actively working *against* it.

Now, you have managed to take the most active people and lock them into a struggle against each other, a struggle that ultimately is inconsequential. We have said before that whether communism or capitalism had come to dominate the world, it would still in either way have been a system controlled by a small power elite of fallen beings. It was simply a matter of how you achieve this ultimate control. Do we achieve it by the state taking over all means of production, or by one corporation gradually becoming so powerful that it could destroy all the other competing corporations, and therefore it owned the means of production? That is essentially the idea, the ideology of Marxism and the ideology of capitalism.

Beyond that, you also have another consideration. The fallen beings know that among the active people on earth, there are two groupings. One group of people are the fallen beings in embodiment. They cannot be pacified, and of course the fallen beings in the higher realms do not want to pacify them. They want the fallen beings in embodiment to work for their agenda, and their agenda is *not* to spread a certain ideology. It was ultimately the fallen beings in the lower identity realm who inspired both capitalism and communism. There were of course fallen beings in the mental realm that were also involved and even some in the emotional realm, but they inspired both ideologies.

Both capitalism and communism undermine democracy

They knew that whenever you create one ideology, you also create an opposite dualistic polarity so they were quite content with creating these two opposing ideologies. Their purpose was not really to make one dominant. At a certain level, yes, this was the goal of both ideologies. But for the fallen beings who started this entire confrontation, they did not care whether it was communism or capitalism that ultimately won because either way, they would get the kind of society that they could control. Both of these ideologies were actually an attempt to undermine democracy because they saw that democracy was on its way, that they could not hold it back. They attempted to create these two ideologies where communism claimed to be some form of democracy where people could vote, even though there was only one party to vote for. Of course, capitalism was meant to undermine the democratic nations from an economic angle, taking over through money what they could not take through direct power in a democratic nation where each person has one vote.

Really, the declared goal of these ideologies was not a major concern to the fallen beings who started the whole spiral. It was a goal to some fallen beings in the mental realm. There were fallen beings in the mental realm who were convinced that communism was the only true ideology, there were those who were convinced that capitalism was the only true ideology. They were working to make their ideology win. They were competing with the other fallen beings to see who could win. This is one reason the fallen beings cannot completely take over a planet because, as we have said, they are always divided, they are always competing against each other about who has ultimate power. In this competition for ultimate power, they lose ultimate power.

Now, there is a group among the active people who are fallen beings in embodiment, and the fallen beings in the higher realms are seeking to activate these people and draw them into working for them. There were falling beings in the mental realm who were trying to recruit some fallen beings in embodiment to fight for communism, and other fallen beings who were trying to recruit fallen beings to fight for capitalism—many among the huge capitalists and basically the monopoly capitalists of the 1800s. Even later, business leaders have been fallen beings and are fallen beings today.

Fooling avatars into fighting for or against an ideology

There is another group among the active people, and those are the avatars and the most advanced of the original inhabitants of the earth. With avatars I use this term broadly, for people who have come to earth from other planets. Not all of them have necessarily been natural planets, but most of them have been more advanced than earth.

You have this group of people who are on earth, and they have (whether it is avatars or the original inhabitants) a higher state of consciousness than the average person. That is why they cannot be pacified. They know they are here to do something positive, to make a difference. They need a sense of purpose, they need a sense that they are useful, that they are doing something good, that they are making a difference and all of these feelings.

These people are of course the major threat to the fallen beings, and they know this very, very well. They know that especially the avatars, but also the more mature original inhabitants, are a threat to their control of the earth. What do they do? Well, they attempt to do many different schemes, but in terms of our current topic of ideology, they seek to draw the avatars into supporting an ideology, or fighting against that same ideology. They do this primarily to prevent them from doing what is their highest potential, which is of course to raise their consciousness to the level of the Christ consciousness and begin to express their Christhood. This is what they want to prevent. They, with all might, want to prevent another Jesus from walking the earth in a physical body, another person with that level of Christhood from walking the earth—or even lower levels of Christhood.

One of their main diversionary tactics has always been to get these avatars to fight for a cause that they think is a just cause, a beneficial cause, a constructive cause, but it is just another dualistic game. It is just another dualistic struggle that in the long run will be inconsequential. This ties up people's attention, their energy, their resources, their thoughts, feelings, actions, and it ties up their sense of identity so they do not identify themselves as spiritual beings. They identify themselves as either communists or anti-communists, or Nazis, or materialists, or whatever you have.

What is it then that happens when people allow their identity to be affected by an ideology? Well, as I said, they go into the ideological mindset. The big group of people that are pacified do not, but the active people, whether they are *for* or *against* the ideology, they go into the ideological mindset. They are very, very focused on the ideology. They believe that the ideology gives either a completely *accurate* portrayal of how life works, or a completely *inaccurate* portrayal of how life works. They are either *for* or *against*. They are polarized. Their minds are focused on the ideology and they are evaluating everything based on the ideology. It is easy enough to see that people who are *for* communism will evaluate everything based on a communist ideology. Those who are against it are also evaluating everything based on a communist ideology because they see it of course as wrong. Anything that opposes communism, they tend to see as right, and this can lead you to go into many blind alleys. You clearly saw many people for example in the United States, in the CIA, in the military, in the government, who were so consumed by this anti-communist mindset that they were open to all kinds of anti-democratic ideas, anti-christ ideas.

Naturally, for the fallen beings in embodiment, it is not a problem that they go into the ideological mindset. They are already in this mindset and they have been in it since they fell because they have been in this mindset of trying to prove an idea, and trying to prove that the idea is superior to direct experience. They are denying the experience they had of encountering the ascended masters, realizing that they could change. They are denying this experience by creating some ideology in their minds that is a denial of experience. This is the state of mind that the fallen beings have been in since they fell whether it was in the fourth, fifth or sixth sphere. It is not a problem that these people go into the ideological mindset. They actually do not go into it when they become pulled in by an ideology, they are already in it, and that is why they choose that ideology.

Creating false polarities

Now, what happens when you have an avatar who goes into the ideological mindset? Well, we have said that in duality there are always two polarities that oppose each other. The tricky part of duality is to realize that this can be taken too far by the linear mind, this idea that there are always two polarities. The linear mind, the serpentine mind, the fallen mind, will take any idea and will always seek to use it against those who are threatening them. For example, we expose duality with the ascended master teachings, but the fallen beings will come up and say: "Well, you are saying that duality is anti-christ, but that means that the mind of Christ is the opposite polarity of anti-christ." In other words, there is a polarity between the mind of Christ and the mind of anti-christ.

The reason they want to do this is of course that this is what they have been trying to do since they fell. When they fell, they may have seen that they became an opposition to God, but they did not become an opposition to the real Creator, as we have said before, but only to their self-made image of God. What they really did was to separate themselves from and put themselves in opposition to the ascended masters. In the fallen mind there is a polarity between the fallen beings and the ascended masters, and they see themselves as being in one polarity and that the ascended masters are in the opposite polarity. For the fallen beings, it is a matter of which polarity is going to win, which polarity is going to prove its superiority over the other. This is how the fallen beings see it. This is the only way the fallen beings *can* see it while they are trapped in a mind of anti-christ.

They are trying to pull the ascended masters into a dualistic polarity with themselves. They are trying to pull the mind of Christ into a dualistic polarity with themselves, which is what you saw the scribes and the Pharisees tried to do with Jesus, the Hindu Brahmins tried to do with me and many other examples of this. This of course is how the fallen beings see it. How do the ascended masters see it? Well, we never saw that the fallen beings, by falling, created a dualistic polarity with ourselves. We never saw them creating an opposition. We never saw them drawing us, pulling us, into a dualistic reaction to them, or forming a dualistic polarity with them. We never saw it that way because we are in the mind of Christ, and therefore we see no opposition to the mind of Christ. In a sense, you could say that one simple way to explain the mind of Christ is to say that it is the mind that is created by God in order to maintain oneness. Oneness between an individual lifestream and its source, the I AM Presence and ultimately the Creator, and oneness horizontally between all people. The Christ mind is the mind of oneness, which means it cannot be divided. The Christ mind cannot be divided within itself. This is a statement that requires some explanation, which I will give, but in its higher aspect, the Christ mind cannot be divided within itself. It always stays in oneness.

How the masters seek to help us escape duality

You now come to earth, you have a planet where virtually all people are in the duality consciousness. Therefore, they look at everything through the filter of the duality consciousness. The duality consciousness can only see two polarities, there must always be two polarities. For any statement you can formulate with words on earth, you can formulate an opposite state-ment. If I say *yes,* you can say *no.* If I say *white,* you can say *black,* there is always an opposite with words.

Here we come, we are now the ascended masters, we are in the mind of Christ. Our task is to help people who are trapped in duality escape duality. What can we do? Well, ultimately, we seek to give them an experi-ence of the mind of Christ. That is what Jesus ultimately tried to do. That is what I ultimately tried to do when I was embodied as the Buddha. I did not call it the Christ mind, but there is a higher mind, there was a mind of oneness, and I attempted to give my students that experience.

What we are attempting to do as ascended masters speaking through an embodied messenger is to give those who listen to us an experience of that mind of oneness. If you achieve that, you have attained the highest potential of what we can give you in a dictation. If you are focused at the level of words, you have not reached that highest potential. If you are try-ing to interpret, understand, evaluate, analyze and intellectualize our dicta-tions, you have not reached the highest potential.

Anyway, here we are, we are in the mind of oneness, we come to a planet like earth. Although we want to give people an experience, we have to start by appealing to them in a way they can grasp and understand, given the state of consciousness they are in. That means we must give a teach-ing in words, we must express certain ideas in words that can get people started on the process of raising their consciousness until they can have those direct experiences of the one mind, the mind of oneness.

We gave a teaching in words. Naturally, this is not something that can be easily done on a planet like earth. You see that ever since the fallen beings came to earth, one of their primary goals has been to shut out the ascended masters from earth.

Shutting the ascended masters out from earth

When the fallen beings fell, they knew very, very well that they fell not because of the ascended masters, even though they may conceive it that way because it was us who opposed them, who drew a boundary and said thus far and no farther. If you do not change your mind, you cannot ascend with the rest of your sphere, and therefore you must fall into the next sphere that is created. That was us.

Their main goal is to shut out the ascended masters from whatever sphere they feel they have some control over. So here come some fallen beings in the identity, mental, emotional and physical realms who now become attached to earth. Their first and foremost goal is to eradicate all knowledge of ascended masters so that we cannot influence people. You may say, as some people have said: "Well, why have we never heard about the concept of ascended masters until the late 1800s?" Well, it was because the fallen beings were very successful, at least in recorded history, to shut out, to destroy, to eliminate, the concept of ascended masters. There has always been the concept of spiritual beings (known or unknown) by other names, and it is not really so much the name that is important as our existence. Nevertheless, their main goal is to shut us out so we cannot influence people.

They have of course managed to densify the collective consciousness, which means that according to the Law of Free Will, we cannot manifest ourselves in some undeniable manifestation that gives people a direct sensory experience of our existence. Therefore, we must, according to the law, fulfill the principle of plausible deniability. We can only give teachings that people can deny, and this means that at the present level we are giving teachings in words. Of course, on a dualistic planet, as I said, any statement in words has an opposite. This is what the fallen beings will always do. They will first try to shut us out from giving teachings. When we then (on rare occasions if you look at it historically) manage to give a teaching by some person in embodiment raising his or her consciousness to being able to tune in to us, then they will do everything they can to first destroy that person, like they killed Jesus. If that does not work, they will destroy or distort the teaching.

This is why you have seen that the non-dualistic teachings of Jesus were turned into the clearly dualistic religion called Roman Catholicism. You can see again that Catholicism from its inception was what we have described as an ideology. It had all of the goals of an ideology: explain, set forth a program of change, present a struggle, seek a commitment and establish classes, those who could implement the religion, the priest class, and those who were the passive recipients, and those who were the enemies who needed to be destroyed. All of the elements are there in the Catholic religion. This shows you that by the time of 325, or 381, the teachings of Jesus had been virtually destroyed and turned into a tool for the fallen beings to exercise power and control over the population.

Turning a concept on its head

What will the fallen beings then do? Well, they will take any concept we give you and try to turn it on its head, or use it against itself. We have given you the concept that there is the mind of Christ, or the mind of oneness. What will they then say? Well, they will say that the mind of Christ is the opposite of the mind of anti-christ, because anti means the opposite. This means that the mind of Christ is also an anti-mind, they will say. It is "anti" our state of mind. It is anti the dualistic mind. Of course, in reality, the mind of Christ is not anti anything. *It is not anti anything.*

It is not against anything. Now, I realize that some of you are scratching your heads. "What do you mean when you say it is not against anything?" Clearly, we have given the concept that there are ascended masters who are working to liberate people and there are fallen beings who are seeking to entrap people. Does that not mean that the ascended masters are against the fallen beings? Well, many ascended master students have thought this. Many people throughout the ages have thought that there are forces in heaven fighting against the forces of darkness.

You see in the *Book of Revelation* where even though this was supposedly given as some higher revelation, there is this concept that there was a war in heaven. Lucifer, the dragon, fought and Archangel Michael fought against him and cast the devil out of heaven. There is a portrayal that supposedly there are forces in heaven who are fighting against the forces of darkness, defeating them and casting them out. As we have said before, it is not a direct and accurate interpretation because, as Archangel Michael himself has said on several occasions, he is not against the fallen beings. He is simply immovable towards them, he is not fighting them aggressively, actively, violently. He is simply immovable to their energy. Archangel Michael did not cast Lucifer out of heaven, Lucifer cast himself out of heaven. Of course, it was not out of "heaven," it was an unascended sphere, a previous sphere.

The reality here is that we of the ascended masters are not against the fallen beings, we are not fighting against the fallen beings. We are not seeing ourselves as being the enemies of the fallen beings, we are not seeing the fallen beings as being our enemies. The concept of enemies exists only in the dualistic mind because that is the only mind that can conceive of divisions into opposite polarities that must eradicate each other in some epic struggle. We do not have the epic mindset.

How ascended masters see the world

You may say: "But aren't there some of your teachings that could be interpreted as having an epic battle between the ascended masters and the fallen beings?" Yes, they can be *interpreted* that way through the epic mindset, but not through the mind of Christ because through the mind of Christ, you do not see it in terms of dualistic polarities and an epic struggle between them. We simply see that the underlying dynamic of the entire world of form is this upward movement towards wider and wider states of consciousness, higher and higher states of consciousness, a broader and broader sense of identity. This is the upward movement of the entire sphere.

The only question is: What kind of circuitous route do individual beings have to follow before they raise their consciousness and ascend? How long does it take for a sphere to ascend? How many of the inhabitants of that sphere have to go into duality, and how long do they have to stay in duality before they have had enough of it that a critical mass of lifestreams in a sphere are ready to ascend, and therefore the entire sphere is ready to ascend? That is how we look at it.

We do not look at it as a battle. For us, there is no question of whether a sphere will ascend or not. I know that you can say that when the spheres become denser and denser and denser, could there not come a point where a sphere would not ascend? It is not the mind of Christ that asks that question. We know that every sphere will ultimately ascend. It is just a matter of what the inhabitants of that sphere have to go through in order to come to that point. We know that there may be a few who do not ascend. They go through what we have called the second death. Nevertheless, even this contributes to the upward movement of the sphere because even those who have gone through the second death, they have had some experiences that have been stored in their causal bodies, and this is part of the growth of the sphere.

We do not have this dualistic mindset, win or lose, that the fallen beings could potentially win over the ascended masters, they could capture an entire sphere and they could cause that sphere to self-destruct and not ascend. The fallen beings dream of this. This is their ultimate dream: That they could prove God wrong by causing a sphere to fail to ascend. We of the ascended masters know that this cannot happen. *It cannot happen.* We are not seeing ourselves in an epic struggle, battle, with the fallen beings. We are working within the confines of free will. We are giving teachings seeking to help those who can raise their consciousness and therefore escape the downward pull of the fallen beings.

Any statement in words can be interpreted

Back to the original idea that I started out with a long time ago: the mind of Christ versus the mind of anti-christ. Whenever we make a statement in words, we are making it from the mind of Christ but as that energetic impulse that we send is translated into words, naturally words can be interpreted in different ways. That is the way it is on a planet that is unnatural and as dense as earth. We cannot give a statement in words that will cause all people to understand what we meant. There is always the plausible deniability that different people will interpret the statement we give through their state of consciousness, through their perception filter. Therefore, the same words can have vastly different interpretations in the minds of different people. The same words can lead to vastly different experiences in the minds of different people.

What the fallen beings will attempt to do is they will attempt to say that the mind of Christ is just another mind. It is not inherently superior to the mind of anti-christ. It is just one viewpoint. They will say the mind of Christ is just a viewpoint like any other viewpoint, and it is not better than any other viewpoints in duality. You see, the mind of Christ is *not* a viewpoint, it is not a perspective that can be influenced by duality. What does this mean? What did I just say? I said, when we give a statement that originates in the mind of Christ, as it is translated into words, it enters the realm of interpretation because words can always be interpreted. Even if you are not in duality, words can be interpreted. Why is that?

What did I say in my previous discourses? Why do you need an ideology? Why do you need an idea? Why do you need an explanation, an understanding? Because there is a distance between your mind and the direct experience. Your mind is not fulfilled in having the direct experience. It is not absorbed in the experience, it is looking at life from a distance and wanting to explain it from a distance. That is what happens with words. I may say the word "apple," but that does not mean that you instantly have an apple in your hand, does it? There is a difference between the word and the thing. The word refers to the thing, it points to the thing, but it is not the thing, "the thing in itself," as the philosopher Kant expressed it.

Keeping our minds trapped in words

Kant gave the idea that there is a real world but human beings can never experience that world directly. They can never experience "the thing in itself" because they always experience it though their minds, their perception. That is why people need words to describe what they cannot experience. That is why you will see that when you talk about the fallen beings and the many ideologies, the many false teachings, that they have given, they all are given in words. Now, some of them are very, very advanced, very, very sophisticated, very, very intricate, very elaborate. What is the real underlying purpose of all of the false teachings on earth? All of them, what is the underlying purpose of them? It is to keep your mind trapped in the realm of words. Your mind is focused on words instead of seeking the direct experience.

Now, some fallen teachings do not mind that you have the direct experience of something in the physical realm, or even in the emotional, mental or lower identity realm. What they really do not want you to have is an experience of the Christ mind, the Christ oneness from the ascended realm. That is the one thing that they do not want you to have, and the purpose of all these false teachings is to pull your mind into the realm of words so you do not seek the experience of the Christ mind. That is the purpose of ideology. For that matter, any teaching whatsoever on earth is meant to keep you trapped in words, arguing about words, thinking *this* word is the more accurate description of the world than *that* word.

You see that many, many people are trapped in this, but especially the intellectuals. You see, if you go back and look at philosophers who have debated between themselves, theologians who have debated, you will see how many times the interpretation of one or two words led to a conflict or division. You see that in the early years of the Catholic church there was a division between the western church, centered in Rome, and the eastern church, centered in Alexandria. It all boiled down to the interpretation of one Greek word. Was Jesus of the same substance of the father or was he not? One word led to a schism that eventually led to a split between the Catholic and the Eastern Orthodox church. The interpretation of one word. Neither side was in the mind of Christ, neither side was open to an experience of the mind of Christ, which could have settled the issue. You see how they were trapped by words, and the Catholic church and the Eastern Orthodox churches have been trapped in this level of words ever since.

Many fundamentalist Christian churches are today trapped in words. If you will go to Buddhism, you will see many different sects in Buddhism who are trapped at this level of words. What exactly did the Buddha mean when he said *that* word, or *that* next word, or the third word? The Hindu brahmins, at the time that I was in embodiment, were trapped in words. Look at the Jews, the Old Testament prophets. Look at the scribes and Pharisees who challenged Jesus. Look at the intellectuals today, the scientists, the materialists, who are endlessly debating words. The entire purpose of this is to keep your mind trapped at the level of words where everything can be interpreted.

Why can it be interpreted? Because it is not the thing in itself. It only points to the thing. You may say: "Well, the word apple cannot be interpreted." Yes, but apple is an English word. They have different words for apple in other languages. So you could still argue, no, the French word for apple is better than the English word for apple. It is a more accurate portrayal of the real thing. Of course, once you go away from physical things to ideas, the potential for an interpretation of words is endless, literally *endless*. There is no limit to how far you can go into this blind alley. The only limit is: When do you get tired of it? When have you had enough of that experience and you want something more, which is what: the Christ mind.

The ideological mindset endlessly interprets words

What is the ideological mindset? In its essence, the ideological mindset is based on the interpretation of words, ideas described in words, and this endless evaluation of whether *this* wording, *that* description, is better than the other. They are all words. They are not the real thing. That is why the fallen beings will say, when the ascended masters give a teaching about the Christ mind: "But that teaching is just words, it needs to be interpreted, it needs to be understood in a certain way." *That,* my beloved, is the essence of the ideological mindset. You take a teaching given in words and you focus your mind on the words and the interpretation of words instead of using the teaching as a stepping stone for the direct experience of the Christ mind. This is the ideological mindset. The ideological mindset does everything it can to shut out the direct experience of oneness, the direct experience of anything beyond the words and the mind that can interpret words endlessly.

My beloved, this points directly to you. I have given a discourse called *The Finger-Pointing Discourse* (In the book *Ending the Era of Dictatorships*) of how people always point the fingers at others. *Now,* I as the Buddha, because I am not in the dualistic mind, I am pointing my finger at *you.* You, each one of you individually, even the messenger, you need to consider – if you want to rise higher on the spiritual path – whether you are still affected by or even trapped in the ideological mindset. What do you do when you hear or read a dictation given by the ascended masters?

The entire idea here is that we are not in embodiment, we are not in duality. We are in a higher state of consciousness, a distinctly higher state of consciousness than you are. That is why we can be helpful to you. How do you see this? How do you relate to this? What do you do with this in your mind? Do you realize that the real value of the ascended masters is that they are in a higher state of consciousness that is not affected by human opinions, idiosyncrasies and interpretations. They are beyond words. They give a teaching in words but they are beyond words. The only way to really make use of that teaching is that I seek to experience the mind that the ascended masters are in. I seek to experience the ascended masters.

Do you grasp this? Or are you still affected by this tendency to look at the words we are giving, to seek to understand them through the linear analytical mind, to seek to fit them into your worldview and to seek to interpret them based on what you already believe when you encounter the teaching? None of you found the teachings in a vacuum—none of you.

You did not find the teaching with an open, neutral mind. Why do you think the Zen Buddhists are so often talking about the beginner's mind? Because they know that when people come to the teachings of Zen, they come with all kinds of content in their minds. You, look at yourself, how did you come into embodiment in this lifetime? It was not a matter of the outer situation, whether your parents were in this religion or that religion or no religion. What was your mindset? What did you already believe and think you knew about life?

Questioning our inherent mindset

Many of you have in past lives been associated with various thought systems, various ideologies, various spiritual teachings. You have in your mind these beliefs that are always turned into selves and these selves are guarding the belief. The self is defined based on the belief, and the self thinks it has to guard the belief so you do not really look at it, see it as incomplete or inconsistent and let it go. There is a self that actively fights your seeing beyond a certain belief that you hold and you being free of the limitations of that belief.

You come in, you have a certain worldview, you have over many lifetimes built an understanding of how you think life works. Go back to what we have said. You came here as an avatar, you were exposed to the fallen beings who questioned your reasons for coming to earth, your right to be here. This was a painful shock for you. How did you deal with it? By creating selves that could explain this situation in such a way that it did not seem like you were wrong for coming here.

You have, ever since that birth trauma, created this conglomerate of selves that think they can explain the world and how the world works. You have these selves that are absolutely unable to question a certain belief. It is not really that the self is convinced that the belief is true, the self is created based on the belief and therefore the self cannot question it. It will however resist that you question it with the conscious mind.

Here you are, maybe you have studied various spiritual teachings before you find an ascended master teaching. One day, you now find an ascended master teaching and it resonates with something in you because you know there is some reality here, there is something useful, there is something that you need in order to grow. The question is: How free are you to actually listen to the teaching with a neutral state of mind? How free are you to go beyond the words of the teaching to the direct experience? Well, that depends on how much baggage you have from past lifetimes of these beliefs that you have come to think explain the world and therefore do not need to be questioned. This is the determining factor of how you will approach the teaching. How willing are you to look at your past beliefs to have them challenged?

Many of you will, if you are willing to be honest, see that even in this lifetime, you came across a certain spiritual teaching that made some kind of claim to be superior in some way. You accepted this claim and therefore, really, what you hoped to get out of the ascended master teaching is that the ascended masters will validate that previous teaching. We will validate that this really is a superior teaching. What does this show? This shows you are focused at the level of words. You think that the words given by the previous teaching was the ultimate description of how life works. It has some superior authority. You do not need to question it. My beloved, if you are to grow towards the Christ mind, you *must* question it.

You must question all of the beliefs you have in your mind that are based on your reaction to earth. You came here as an avatar. I am not saying you came in a completely neutral state of mind because, as we have said, there were even some selves or some intentions you had for coming to earth. Nevertheless, you came as an avatar, you are exposed to the cosmic birth trauma, you start a process of creating selves in reaction to the experience you have had here on earth. What is the effect of creating all these selves? It is to tie you to earth. How are you going to get out of earth? How are you going to be free of earth? How are you going to ascend from earth? Only by freeing yourself from all of these selves and all of the beliefs behind them. Therefore, you must be willing to question any and all beliefs you have picked up here on earth. You must, beyond that, be willing to question any and all beliefs that you had that brought you to earth, that made you decide to come to earth. You must question *everything*. Every belief that can be expressed in words, you must question.

Are there any beliefs that are accurate?

You are going to say: "But aren't there at least some beliefs that are accurate?" Well, my beloved, that is an entirely different topic. What have I just said about words? They are a description of the thing, not the thing in itself. How can any belief expressed in words be *completely* accurate? You may say: "But in previous dispensations of the ascended masters, it was said that we had given you the highest spiritual teaching on the planet and does not that mean that this teaching was completely accurate, and the ultimate truth about how the world works, therefore the ultimate ideology?" Well, what is the word "highest?" Is it not a *comparative* word, a *relative* word? There is *highest* and there is *lowest,* there is *high* and *low.* Is it not relative and therefore could very easily be interpreted through the dualistic mind? Is there a highest teaching on the planet? Can there ever be a highest teaching on the planet? No, there cannot, not expressed in words.

The highest spiritual experience you can have is to go beyond duality and experience oneness, but that experience cannot be described by words. The Christ mind can be named by words. It can be said to have certain characteristics in relation to the mind of anti-christ. The mind of anti-christ is *divided,* the Christ mind is *undivided.* This is not an accurate and completely complete description of the mind of Christ. You can only know the mind of Christ by experiencing it directly, not through a description.

What is the purpose of the ascended masters giving you a teaching? It is to give you the motivation and the understanding and the tools that you need in order to seek the direct experience of the Christ mind. *That* is the only purpose of a teaching. Sure, you can say it is not a teaching that is given directly to deceive you as is the teachings of the fallen beings. We are not deceiving you by giving you the teachings we are giving you. It is not that it is incorrect but it is not the full understanding either, because you will never have the full understanding until you have completely transcended duality and you are now completely in the Christ mind. Then, you have a completely different perspective, a much broader perspective, a perspective you cannot even begin to imagine while you are in embodiment on a dense planet like earth.

You see, many of you have come to the ascended master teachings. You have certain spiritual holy cows, as we have called it. You believe: "This I know, and this is definitely accurate. This is the way it is." You may base this on a certain teaching or it comes from past lives and you do not even know where it originated. Then, you come to the ascended master teachings. Many people come to the teachings of the ascended masters only to validate, to have the validation for those spiritual holy cows. They want us to validate their holy cows and when we do not do so, people will often reject the teaching. Many people have found an ascended master teaching, then come to one particular teaching we gave that challenged one of their spiritual holy cows and they have rejected the teaching. Others have rejected the messenger. If we now say something through the messenger that challenges one of their holy cows, they say: "Well, the messenger was an accurate messenger before but now he is not anymore." There are all of these kinds of games that people can play where you again are projecting out that the problem is out there. The problem is with somebody else, the problem is with the teaching, with the messenger or with these other people. It is projecting out and that is part of the ideological mindset. You are focused at the level of words. You have a desire to be right, to be one of the superior class of people, the advanced people, however you define it. You can always make it seem like you are, by projecting that the problem, the fault, is out there. Because you have your holy cow that is untouchable and you are determined that nothing on earth is going to touch that.

Questioning our spiritual holy cows

Well, my beloved, you can have your holy cow for as long as you want until time runs out and it is time for the second death. If you want to follow the teachings of the ascended masters, you need to be willing to question those holy cows, or you are not going to get anywhere. We have said that this messenger started out with a certain potential to bring forth a certain teaching to a certain level, based on the collective consciousness and his individual consciousness. He then came to a point where he was willing to question his own spiritual holy cows, which caused him to free his mind from those particular beliefs. This opened him up to bringing forth a higher teaching that we could not bring forth through him while he had those holy cows. You need to be willing to do the same if you are to ascend after this lifetime, or for that matter, at any time in the future. In order to ascend, you must question those spiritual holy cows. The ideological mindset has not only *defined* the holy cows, it will also *defend* the holy cows to the death—that either the enemies die or the self dies, because you finally have had enough of this endless battle based on words.

We see students who come and find the teachings and engage in these discussions with other people. Endless discussions. Or they ask questions of the messenger, but they are not even listening for the answers because they have in their minds an idea of how the answer should be before it is given, or at least how it should be interpreted. These students are unreachable to us. They may follow an outer teaching, they may study it, they may even come to conferences, they may even give decrees for a long time.

They are still trapped at the level of words and in the interpretation of words, and they have not gone beyond to experience the teaching.

Is an ideology always bad?

Now you may say: "You're making it sound, Gautama, as if an ideology is always bad." Well, it *is* if it keeps people trapped in the mind of anti-christ, is it not? An ideology does not have to be that way. It does not have to trap people. An ideology could actually give people a useful foundation for expanding their consciousness. For that to happen, not only would the ideology have to meet certain criteria, but also the people who are following that ideology would have to be willing to go beyond the words and seek the direct experience. That is why you generally see, in the spiritual field, that the so-called mystical teachings have been more successful than the mainstream religions. Many mystical teachings are focused on giving people an experience of something beyond what can be expressed in words. The teaching is meant to point to an experience. This is opposite of words, as they are normally used on earth. This is something you need to consider as well. It is one of the limitations of words when it comes to a spiritual teaching.

Really, what is the practical purpose of words? Well, it is that it allows people to communicate, it allows people to communicate about practical things in the physical realm that are not there right now. For example, you can meet a friend, you are walking through the hills, and you tell him,: "There is an apple tree on the other side of that hill, and the apples are ripe." None of you are seeing the apple tree, you are not experiencing it directly, you cannot give him that experience. You can use words to point him in a direction where he can have the experience of eating the apple.

Normally, words point to something physical, they are practical means of communication. Now, when we start talking about ideas, we are not talking about something that has a direct physical parallel. You cannot necessarily go and experience it through the physical senses. This means that you can only experience it through intuition, through the intuitive faculties. It is a matter of whether people are open to using those, whether they are *willing* to use them.

Of course, for a spiritual teaching, we are not pointing to anything on earth. We are pointing to something beyond the physical realm, beyond the emotional realm, beyond the mental realm, beyond the lower identity realm, to the higher identity realm or the spiritual realm. That is what a spiritual teaching is pointing to, a direct experience of that. Some people are not able to have that experience yet because their consciousness is too low. Some people are not willing to stretch their consciousness in order to have the experience even though they *could* have it. They get trapped in taking the spiritual teaching, pulling it into the realm of words, and then interpreting it to make themselves seem superior to those who do not have that same sophisticated interpretation. It is a game that people are playing, it is an *ego* game. They are using a spiritual teaching as a tool for playing an ego game. *That,* of course is not what a spiritual teaching is meant to do.

No ideology will bring Saint Germain's Golden Age

Why am I telling you all of this? Well, partly because I want to set you free, also because I want to see you fulfill your Divine plans. Many of you have as part of your Divine plans to be in embodiment at this time to help bring Saint Germain's Golden Age, and how are we going to bring Saint Germain's Golden Age? Well, not through any ideology, I hope that much has become clear.

The golden age will not be brought by a particular ideology. What we need to do is to help humankind transcend the era of ideology, transcend the era where people thought they could define a thought system and then the universe would work according to the thought system.

In other words, an ideology is formulated with words. The words just point to the real thing, but what many people have done, based on the fallen mindset, is that they have reversed that. They think that certain words have a magical power to create the thing, or to at least change the thing, affect the thing. This is a mindset that is in complete opposition to the manifestation of the golden age, so we need to pull the collective consciousness above this ideological mindset.

Who can do this, my beloved? Certainly not those who are absolutely convinced that the way to bring the golden age is through their particular ideology. The only people who have a realistic potential for doing this are those of you who are open to either the ascended master teachings we are giving in this dispensation, or through another mystical teaching that focuses on direct experience beyond words. These are the only people who can pull the planet up. We of course hope that you who are direct students, who are listening to and reading these teachings, that you will be among the people who are pulling the planet up into the golden age mindset, instead of the ideological mindset.

How are you going to pull the planet up if you have not pulled yourself up? *It cannot be done.* You need to start with yourself, you need to pull yourself above this. This is of course one of the main reasons for giving this teaching. Another reason is of course to project it into the collective consciousness so that all people out there who may not know about ascended masters, who are not open to this teaching, they still can receive these ideas and use them to raise themselves above that mindset.

Many, many people in embodiment have been trapped in an ideological mindset for many lifetimes. They have seen over and over again how people who became fanatical and extremists in this ideological mindset have created disaster after disaster, have created suffering upon suffering, have created misery upon misery, and they have had enough of it. They are open to a different approach but they are not to the point where they can do this themselves. They need something to pull them up over that hump, as they say. You can be that impetus, but only if you start by pulling yourself up.

We have given you now tools and teachings that can help you do this, and it is of course the point. We are not pointing, *I* am not pointing the finger at you in order to make you feel bad or feel ashamed. I am simply pointing out: It is time for you, at least some of you, to look at this ideological mindset and to say: "Oh well, it's just another conglomeration of separate selves that I have to let go of. And how free I will feel when I let go of those also, as I have let go of others already." You *will* feel free, you will feel like the weight of the world has been lifted from your shoulders when you finally escape that ideological mindset. Because suddenly you do not have this responsibility of changing the world according to an idea in your mind, an idea that could never actually produce the result of changing the world.

We have all gone through it before we ascended. We all had an ideology, a set of ideas, a certain mindset that we could change the world. It was a huge relief for all of us to let go of it, and to realize that I can, and I *will* ascend even though the world has not changed, as I once thought it *had* to change. Regardless of the fact that the world is in the state it is in, I can look at earth and say: "There's nothing here for me anymore." If you are in the ideological mindset, you cannot say this because there is some change that *must* happen. Even if you have the concept of the ascension, you will think: "I can't ascend until this change has happened." *Then,* you can ascend. If you are waiting for some change to happen on earth before you ascend, your ascension could be delayed indefinitely.

Some of you are at this point where the next logical step on your path is to consider this. Many are not at the point yet, but they may be so in a year, in five years, in 10 years, in 20 years, so the teaching will be valid, as new rungs of people reach that level where this is the next hindrance they need to dissolve in order to rise to a new level of spiritual freedom.

You can have spiritual holy cows or spiritual freedom, but you cannot have both. How do you overcome the holy cows? By shifting your mind and deciding: "That cow is no longer untouchable. I am going to touch it, I am going to pull it out into the open, I am going to pick it apart, I am going to look at that belief behind it and dismiss it with an experience and a realization from the Christ mind."

My beloved, I have said what I want to say for now. Again, my gratitude for you being willing to be the broadcast stations for this, to consider it in your own minds. I know that there is a certain group of people who are following these teachings who are always open to the next level of teaching we give, and who are always willing to consider it. I also know there is a certain group of people who are not open to considering the teaching, but will always interpret it through words. This is the way it must be. How else can it be, given the Law of Free Will? You must be allowed to come to an ascended master teaching and do with it whatever you want, according to your individual decision. I am at peace with this, and therefore I seal you in that peace of the Buddha, which I hope that you can one day experience directly.

13 EXPOSING IDEOLOGY AS A MEANS OF CONTROL (PART 1)

In the name of the I AM THAT I AM, Jesus Christ, I use the authority that I have as a being in embodiment on earth to call upon Gautama Buddha to reinforce my calls and use my chakras to project the statements in this invocation into the collective consciousness and awaken people to the need to free ourselves from the ideological mindset. Awaken people to the reality that we are spiritual beings and that we can co-create a new future by working with the ascended masters. I especially call for …

[Make your own calls here.]

Part 1

1. Gautama Buddha, awaken the most creative people to see that although an ideology seeks to appeal to a broad range of people, it always defines that there is a particular group of people who are more suited to implementing the ideology.

Archangel Michael, light so blue,
my heart has room for only you.
My mind is one, no longer two,
your love for me is ever true.

**Archangel Michael, you are here,
consuming now all doubt and fear.
Your Presence is forever near,
you are to me so very dear.**

2. Gautama Buddha, awaken the most creative people to see that these are often portrayed as intellectuals, as the intellectuals in the West who were enamored by the ideology of Marxism from a distance because they had not experienced how it was to live in a Marxist society.

Archangel Michael, I will be,
all one with your reality.
No fear can hold me as I see,
this world no power has o'er me.

**Archangel Michael, you are here,
consuming now all doubt and fear.
Your Presence is forever near,
you are to me so very dear.**

3. Gautama Buddha, awaken the most creative people to see that when we only see it from a distance, how do we question the ideology? What frame of reference do we have once we have entered the ideological mindset?

Archangel Michael, hold me tight,
shatter now the darkest night.
Clear my chakras with your light,
restore to me my inner sight.

**Archangel Michael, you are here,
consuming now all doubt and fear.
Your Presence is forever near,
you are to me so very dear.**

4. Gautama Buddha, awaken the most creative people to see that ideologies are based on ideas and ideas are dealt with by the mental mind. People who are focused in the mental mind are more likely to be enamored by ideas and feel that they are the only ones who can understand and interpret the ideas.

Archangel Michael, now I stand,
with you the light I do command.
My heart I ever will expand,
till highest truth I understand.

Archangel Michael, you are here,
consuming now all doubt and fear.
Your Presence is forever near,
you are to me so very dear.

5. Gautama Buddha, awaken the most creative people to see that what an ideology really seeks to do is to control people, and it wants to control their actions.

Archangel Michael, in my heart,
from me you never will depart.
Of hierarchy I am a part,
I now accept a fresh new start.

Archangel Michael, you are here,
consuming now all doubt and fear.
Your Presence is forever near,
you are to me so very dear.

6. Gautama Buddha, awaken the most creative people to see that it is not easy to directly control people's actions. In order to control people, one also has to work with the emotional, mental and identity bodies.

Archangel Michael, sword of blue,
all darkness you are cutting through.
My Christhood I do now pursue,
discernment shows me what is true.

**Archangel Michael, you are here,
consuming now all doubt and fear.
Your Presence is forever near,
you are to me so very dear.**

7. Gautama Buddha, awaken the most creative people to see that controlling the emotions at the level of emotions is not easy because emotions can change so easily. It is easier to control people's thoughts at the level of the mental mind than controlling the emotions and the actions.

Archangel Michael, in your wings,
I now let go of lesser things.
God's homing call in my heart rings,
my heart with yours forever sings.

**Archangel Michael, you are here,
consuming now all doubt and fear.
Your Presence is forever near,
you are to me so very dear.**

8. Gautama Buddha, awaken the most creative people to see that the intellectual mind can argue for or against any point. At the mental level, people who are convinced by an ideology could at any moment consider the opposite argument that questions the ideology.

Archangel Michael, take me home,
in higher spheres I want to roam.
I am reborn from cosmic foam,
my life is now a sacred poem.

**Archangel Michael, you are here,
consuming now all doubt and fear.
Your Presence is forever near,
you are to me so very dear.**

9. Gautama Buddha, awaken the most creative people to see that in order to control people, one has to go to the highest level, the level of identity. An ideology seeks to control people's sense of identity, how they see themselves in relation to the world.

Archangel Michael, light you are,
shining like the bluest star.
You are a cosmic avatar,
with you I will go very far.

Archangel Michael, you are here,
consuming now all doubt and fear.
Your Presence is forever near,
you are to me so very dear.

Part 2

1. Gautama Buddha, awaken the most creative people to see that ideologies generally create three groupings of people. There are people who are convinced by the ideology. They enter the ideological mindset and are actively promoting and implementing the ideology.

O Saint Germain, you do inspire,
my vision raised forever higher,
with you I form a figure-eight,
your Golden Age I co-create.

O Saint Germain, what love you bring,
it truly makes all matter sing,
your violet flame does all restore,
with you we are becoming more.

2. Gautama Buddha, awaken the most creative people to see that the next group is usually the largest part of the population, namely the people who do not particularly understand the ideology. They have some hope that the ideology can bring the kind of society outlined in the ideology.

O Saint Germain, what Freedom Flame,
released when we recite your name,
acceleration is your gift,
our planet it will surely lift.

O Saint Germain, what love you bring,
it truly makes all matter sing,
your violet flame does all restore,
with you we are becoming more.

3. Gautama Buddha, awaken the most creative people to see that such people have submitted themselves to the ideology, either because they believe it can work, or they feel there is no point in resisting the ideology. These people have become pacified by the ideology or the ruling elite of society.

O Saint Germain, in love we claim,
our right to bring your violet flame,
from you Above, to us below,
it is an all-transforming flow.

O Saint Germain, what love you bring,
it truly makes all matter sing,
your violet flame does all restore,
with you we are becoming more.

4. Gautama Buddha, awaken the most creative people to see that the third group of people are resisting the ideology. They become the scapegoat, they become the enemy. For all three groups, their sense of identity can be affected.

O Saint Germain, I love you so,
my aura filled with violet glow,
my chakras filled with violet fire,
I am your cosmic amplifier.

O Saint Germain, what love you bring,
it truly makes all matter sing,
your violet flame does all restore,
with you we are becoming more.

5. Gautama Buddha, awaken the most creative people to see that those who identify themselves as working against the ideology are identifying

themselves in opposition to the ideology. Both those who accept the ideology and those who reject it still identify themselves based on the ideology.

> O Saint Germain, I am now free,
> your violet flame is therapy,
> transform all hang-ups in my mind,
> as inner peace I surely find.

> **O Saint Germain, what love you bring,**
> **it truly makes all matter sing,**
> **your violet flame does all restore,**
> **with you we are becoming more.**

6. Gautama Buddha, awaken the most creative people to see that a large group of people identify themselves as normal human beings trying to get by and make the best of whatever situation there is, but they identify themselves as passive or powerless.

> O Saint Germain, my body pure,
> your violet flame for all is cure,
> consume the cause of all disease,
> and therefore I am all at ease.

> **O Saint Germain, what love you bring,**
> **it truly makes all matter sing,**
> **your violet flame does all restore,**
> **with you we are becoming more.**

7. Gautama Buddha, awaken the most creative people to see that the groupings of people who are *for* or *against* are active and feel empowered. The general population are passive.

> O Saint Germain, I'm karma-free,
> the past no longer burdens me,
> a brand new opportunity,
> I am in Christic unity.

> **O Saint Germain, what love you bring,**
> **it truly makes all matter sing,**

your violet flame does all restore,
with you we are becoming more.

8. Gautama Buddha, awaken the most creative people to see that an ideology is partly aimed at those who accept it, but it is equally aimed at those who resist it.

O Saint Germain, we are now one,
I am for you a violet sun,
as we transform this planet earth,
your Golden Age is given birth.

O Saint Germain, what love you bring,
it truly makes all matter sing,
your violet flame does all restore,
with you we are becoming more.

9. Gautama Buddha, awaken the most creative people to see that an ideology forces people to enter a sense of identity that is either for or against, and thus divides people based on dualistic polarities. The communists and the anti-communists both had their sense of identity affected by communism.

O Saint Germain, the earth is free,
from burden of duality,
in oneness we bring what is best,
your Golden Age is manifest.

O Saint Germain, what love you bring,
it truly makes all matter sing,
your violet flame does all restore,
with you we are becoming more.

Part 3

1. Gautama Buddha, awaken the most creative people to see that there is a large group of people who identify themselves as passive, and this

is exactly what the power elite wants. The elite wants the majority of the people to be passive, because that makes them easy to control.

> O Godfre, your ascension light,
> leads us through the darkest night,
> it is a trail that you have carved,
> for all who are for freedom starved.

> **O Godfre, I am free to be,**
> **one with God and one with thee,**
> **there is no greater love I see,**
> **than what I feel for God in me.**

2. Gautama Buddha, awaken the most creative people to see that power elite beings know that they cannot pacify all people. There is a certain group of people in embodiment at any time that they cannot pacify because they are active people. They have ambition, desire and vision.

> O Godfre, I surrender all,
> as I now follow inner call.
> The providence that is Divine,
> will show me plan uniquely mine.

> **O Godfre, I am free to be,**
> **one with God and one with thee,**
> **there is no greater love I see,**
> **than what I feel for God in me.**

3. Gautama Buddha, awaken the most creative people to see that the power elite can cause them to polarize into those who are actively working *for* a particular ideology, and those who are actively working *against* it. The elite has now managed to lock the most active people into a struggle against each other, a struggle that is ultimately inconsequential.

> O Godfre, show me how to be,
> from man's ambitions clearly free.
> I can of my self nothing do,
> and this I want to learn from you.

**O Godfre, I am free to be,
one with God and one with thee,
there is no greater love I see,
than what I feel for God in me.**

4. Gautama Buddha, awaken the most creative people to see that whether communism or capitalism had come to dominate the world, it would in either way have been a system controlled by a small power elite.

O Godfre, I would know your flame,
so I will never be the same.
I want to grow forever more,
and help God's kingdom to restore.

**O Godfre, I am free to be,
one with God and one with thee,
there is no greater love I see,
than what I feel for God in me.**

5. Gautama Buddha, awaken the most creative people to see that for the elite, it was a matter of how to achieve ultimate control. Do they achieve it by the state taking over all means of production, or by one corporation gradually becoming so powerful that it could destroy all competing corporations, and therefore it owned the means of production.

O Godfre, help me now to see,
complete surrender is the key.
All problems can be solved by me,
when I surrender all to thee.

**O Godfre, I am free to be,
one with God and one with thee,
there is no greater love I see,
than what I feel for God in me.**

6. Gautama Buddha, awaken the most creative people to see that the elite knows that whenever they create one ideology, they also create an opposite dualistic polarity. They were content with creating these two opposing ideologies.

O Godfre, for your flame I call,
a great example to us all.
You stand so firm in time of need,
so we can move with true God-speed.

O Godfre, I am free to be,
one with God and one with thee,
there is no greater love I see,
than what I feel for God in me.

7. Gautama Buddha, awaken the most creative people to see that for the power elite, the purpose is not to make one ideology dominant. The power elite beings who started the confrontation did not care whether it was communism or capitalism that ultimately won because either way, they would get the kind of society that they could control.

O Godfre, I would know your mind,
to see the secret you did find.
of when to do and when to stop,
so I am always going up.

O Godfre, I am free to be,
one with God and one with thee,
there is no greater love I see,
than what I feel for God in me.

8. Gautama Buddha, awaken the most creative people to see that both of these ideologies were an attempt to undermine democracy, because the power elite saw that democracy was on its way and they could not hold it back.

O Godfre, you are always free,
for you obedience is the key,
we go beyond all human flaw,
by following the greater law.

O Godfre, I am free to be,
one with God and one with thee,

there is no greater love I see,
than what I feel for God in me.

9. Gautama Buddha, awaken the most creative people to see that the power elite attempted to create these two ideologies, where communism claimed to be some form of democracy even though there was only one party to vote for. Capitalism was meant to undermine the democratic nations from an economic angle, taking over through money what they could not take through direct power in a democratic nation.

O Godfre, light is shining clear,
the mighty I AM Presence near,
I go with you beyond the fray,
to set example in my day.

O Godfre, I am free to be,
one with God and one with thee,
there is no greater love I see,
than what I feel for God in me.

Part 4

1. Gautama Buddha, awaken the most creative people to see that the declared goal of these ideologies was not a major concern to the power elite beings at the highest level.

Divine Director, I now see,
the world is unreality,
in my heart I now truly feel,
the Spirit is all that is real.

Divine Director, send the light,
from blindness clear my inner sight,
my vision free, my vision clear,
your guidance is forever here.

2. Gautama Buddha, awaken the most creative people to see that some power elite beings were convinced that communism was the only true ideology, and some were convinced that capitalism was the only true ideology. They were competing with each other to see who would win.

Divine Director, vision give,
in clarity I want to live,
I now behold my plan Divine,
the plan that is uniquely mine.

Divine Director, send the light,
from blindness clear my inner sight,
my vision free, my vision clear,
your guidance is forever here.

3. Gautama Buddha, awaken the most creative people to see that this is why the power elite beings cannot completely take over a planet. They are always divided, they are competing against each other about who has ultimate power. In this competition for ultimate power, they lose ultimate power.

Divine Director, show in me,
the ego games, and set me free,
help me escape the ego's cage,
to help bring in the golden age.

Divine Director, send the light,
from blindness clear my inner sight,
my vision free, my vision clear,
your guidance is forever here.

4. Gautama Buddha, awaken the most creative people to see that the most spiritually aware people are the major threat to the power elite beings. That is why they seek to draw spiritual people into supporting an ideology, or fighting against that same ideology.

Divine Director, I'm with you,
my vision one, no longer two,

as karma's veil you do disperse,
I see a whole new universe.

Divine Director, send the light,
from blindness clear my inner sight,
my vision free, my vision clear,
your guidance is forever here.

5. Gautama Buddha, awaken the most creative people to see that the power elite beings do this primarily to prevent us from doing what is our highest potential, which is to raise our consciousness to the level of the Christ consciousness and begin to express our Christhood.

Divine Director, I go up,
electric light now fills my cup,
consume in me all shadows old,
bestow on me a vision bold.

Divine Director, send the light,
from blindness clear my inner sight,
my vision free, my vision clear,
your guidance is forever here.

6. Gautama Buddha, awaken the most creative people to see that one of their main diversionary tactics has always been to get spiritual people to fight for a cause that they think is a just cause, but it is just another dualistic game. It is just another dualistic struggle that in the long run will be inconsequential.

Divine Director, heart of gold,
my sacred labor I unfold,
o blessed Guru, I now see,
where my own plan is taking me.

Divine Director, send the light,
from blindness clear my inner sight,
my vision free, my vision clear,
your guidance is forever here.

7. Gautama Buddha, awaken the most creative people to see that this ties up our resources, and it ties up our sense of identity so we do not identify ourselves as spiritual beings. We identify ourselves as communists, anti-communists, Nazis, materialists or something else.

Divine Director, by your grace,
in grander scheme I find my place,
my individual flame I see,
uniqueness God has given me.

Divine Director, send the light,
from blindness clear my inner sight,
my vision free, my vision clear,
your guidance is forever here.

8. Gautama Buddha, awaken the most creative people to see that when we allow our identity to be affected by an ideology, we go into the ideological mindset. Whether we are *for* or *against* the ideology, we go into the ideological mindset and are focused on the ideology.

Divine Director, vision one,
I see that I AM God's own Sun,
with your direction so Divine,
I am now letting my light shine.

Divine Director, send the light,
from blindness clear my inner sight,
my vision free, my vision clear,
your guidance is forever here.

9. Gautama Buddha, awaken the most creative people to see that we then believe that the ideology gives either a completely *accurate* portrayal of how life works, or a completely *inaccurate* portrayal of how life works. We are either *for* or *against*. We are polarized. Our minds are focused on the ideology and we are evaluating everything based on the ideology.

Divine Director, what a gift,
to be a part of Spirit's lift,

to raise mankind out of the night,
to bask in Spirit's loving sight.

**Divine Director, send the light,
from blindness clear my inner sight,
my vision free, my vision clear,
your guidance is forever here.**

Sealing

In the name of the I AM THAT I AM, I accept that Archangel Michael, Astrea and Shiva form an impenetrable shield around myself and all constructive people, sealing us from all fear-based energies in all four octaves. I accept that the Light of God is consuming and transforming all fear-based energies that make up the dark forces working against ending the era of ideology on earth!

14 EXPOSING IDEOLOGY AS A MEANS OF CONTROL (PART 2)

In the name of the I AM THAT I AM, Jesus Christ, I use the authority that I have as a being in embodiment on earth to call upon Gautama Buddha to reinforce my calls and use my chakras to project the statements in this invocation into the collective consciousness and awaken people to the need to free ourselves from the ideological mindset. Awaken people to the reality that we are spiritual beings and that we can co-create a new future by working with the ascended masters. I especially call for …

[Make your own calls here.]

Part 1

1. Gautama Buddha, awaken the most creative people to see that those who are *for* communism will evaluate everything based on a communist ideology. Those who are against it are also evaluating everything based on a communist ideology because they see it as wrong. Anything that opposes communism, they tend to see as right.

O Jesus, blessed brother mine,
I walk the path that you outline,
a great example to us all,
I follow now your inner call.

**O Jesus, let the Fire of Joy,
consume the devil's subtle ploy,
transfigured is our planet earth,
the golden age is given birth.**

2. Gautama Buddha, awaken the most creative people to see that the idea that there are always two polarities in duality can be taken too far by the linear mind. The linear mind, the serpentine mind, will take any idea and seek to use it against those who are threatening the ideology.

O Jesus, open inner sight,
the ego wants to prove it's right,
but this I will no longer do,
I want to be all one with you.

**O Jesus, let the Fire of Joy,
consume the devil's subtle ploy,
transfigured is our planet earth,
the golden age is given birth.**

3. Gautama Buddha, awaken the most creative people to see that the power elite beings will say that if duality is anti-christ, that means the mind of Christ is the opposite polarity of anti-christ. There is a polarity between the mind of Christ and the mind of anti-christ.

O Jesus, I now clearly see,
the Key of Knowledge given me,
my Christ self I hereby embrace,
as you fill up my inner space.

**O Jesus, let the Fire of Joy,
consume the devil's subtle ploy,
transfigured is our planet earth,
the golden age is given birth.**

4. Gautama Buddha, awaken the most creative people to see that the power elite beings are trying to pull the mind of Christ into a dualistic polarity with themselves. In reality, it is their own minds that create the duality. The mind of Christ sees only oneness and that which is separated from oneness.

O Jesus, show me serpent's lie,
expose the beam in my own eye,
as Christ discernment you me give,
in oneness I forever live.

**O Jesus, let the Fire of Joy,
consume the devil's subtle ploy,
transfigured is our planet earth,
the golden age is given birth.**

5. Gautama Buddha, awaken the most creative people to see that the mind of Christ is created in order to maintain oneness between an individual lifestream and its source, the I AM Presence and ultimately the Creator, and oneness horizontally between all people.

O Jesus, I am truly meek,
and thus I turn the other cheek,
when the accuser attacks me,
I go within and merge with thee.

**O Jesus, let the Fire of Joy,
consume the devil's subtle ploy,
transfigured is our planet earth,
the golden age is given birth.**

6. Gautama Buddha, awaken the most creative people to see that the Christ mind is the mind of oneness, which means it cannot be divided. The Christ mind cannot be divided within itself.

O Jesus, ego I let die,
surrender ev'ry earthly tie,
the dead can bury what is dead,
I choose to walk with you instead.

**O Jesus, let the Fire of Joy,
consume the devil's subtle ploy,
transfigured is our planet earth,
the golden age is given birth.**

7. Gautama Buddha, awaken the most creative people to see that on earth, virtually all people are in the duality consciousness. They look at everything through the filter of the duality consciousness. The duality consciousness can only see two polarities, there must always be two polarities.

O Jesus, help me rise above,
the devil's test through higher love,
show me separate self unreal,
my formless self you do reveal.

**O Jesus, let the Fire of Joy,
consume the devil's subtle ploy,
transfigured is our planet earth,
the golden age is given birth.**

8. Gautama Buddha, awaken the most creative people to see that for any statement we can formulate with words, we can formulate an opposite statement. There is always an opposite with words.

O Jesus, what is that to me,
I just let go and follow thee,
with this I do pass ev'ry test,
to find with you eternal rest.

**O Jesus, let the Fire of Joy,
consume the devil's subtle ploy,
transfigured is our planet earth,
the golden age is given birth.**

9. Gautama Buddha, awaken the most creative people to see that the ascended masters are in the mind of Christ and your task is to help people who are trapped in duality escape duality. Ultimately, the masters seek to give us an experience of the mind of Christ, which is what Jesus and the Buddha tried to do.

O Jesus, fiery master mine,
my heart now melting into thine,
I love with heart and mind and soul,
the God who is my highest goal.

**O Jesus, let the Fire of Joy,
consume the devil's subtle ploy,
transfigured is our planet earth,
the golden age is given birth.**

Part 2

1. Gautama Buddha, awaken the most creative people to see that although the ascended masters want to give us an experience, they have to start by appealing to us in a way we can grasp, given the state of consciousness we are in.

Maitreya, I am truly meek,
your counsel wise I humbly seek,
your vision I so want to see,
with you in Eden I will be.

**Maitreya, kindness is the cure,
in fires of kindness I am pure.
Maitreya, now release the fire,
that raises me forever higher.**

2. Gautama Buddha, awaken the most creative people to see that the masters must give a teaching in words that can get us started on the process of raising our consciousness until we can have those direct experiences of the one mind that are beyond words.

Maitreya, help me to return,
to learn from you, I truly yearn,
as oneness is all I desire
I feel initiation's fire.

Maitreya, kindness is the cure,
in fires of kindness I am pure.
Maitreya, now release the fire,
that raises me forever higher.

3. Gautama Buddha, awaken the most creative people to see that the main goal of the power elite beings is to shut out the ascended masters from earth so they themselves can have control over the planet. Their foremost goal is to eradicate all knowledge of ascended masters so that the masters cannot set us free.

Maitreya, I hereby decide,
from you I will no longer hide,
expose to me the very lie
that caused edenic self to die.

Maitreya, kindness is the cure,
in fires of kindness I am pure.
Maitreya, now release the fire,
that raises me forever higher.

4. Gautama Buddha, awaken the most creative people to see that the power elite beings have managed to densify the collective consciousness, which means that according to the Law of Free Will, the ascended masters cannot manifest themselves in an undeniable manifestation. The masters must fulfill the principle of plausible deniability.

Maitreya, blessed Guru mine,
my heart of hearts forever thine,
I vow that I will listen well,
so we can break the serpent's spell.

Maitreya, kindness is the cure,
in fires of kindness I am pure.
Maitreya, now release the fire,
that raises me forever higher.

5. Gautama Buddha, awaken the most creative people to see that the ascended masters can only give teachings that people can deny, meaning

you are giving teachings in words. On a dualistic planet, any statement in words has an opposite. The power elite beings will use this to destroy or distort the teaching.

Maitreya, help me see the lie
whereby the serpent broke the tie,
the serpent now has naught in me,
in oneness I am truly free.

Maitreya, kindness is the cure,
in fires of kindness I am pure.
Maitreya, now release the fire,
that raises me forever higher.

6. Gautama Buddha, awaken the most creative people to see that the non-dualistic teachings of Jesus were turned into the clearly dualistic religion called Roman Catholicism. Catholicism was from its inception an ideology that attempted to explain, set forth a program of change, present a struggle, seek a commitment and establish classes of people.

Maitreya, truth does set me free
from falsehoods of duality,
the fruit of knowledge I let go,
so your true spirit I do know.

Maitreya, kindness is the cure,
in fires of kindness I am pure.
Maitreya, now release the fire,
that raises me forever higher.

7. Gautama Buddha, awaken the most creative people to see that by the time of 381, the teachings of Jesus had been virtually destroyed and turned into a tool for the power elite beings to exercise control over the population.

Maitreya, I submit to you,
intentions pure, my heart is true,
from ego I am truly free,
as I am now all one with thee.

**Maitreya, kindness is the cure,
in fires of kindness I am pure.
Maitreya, now release the fire,
that raises me forever higher.**

8. Gautama Buddha, awaken the most creative people to see that the power elite beings will take any concept and try to turn it on its head, or use it against itself. They will say that the mind of Christ is the opposite of the mind of anti-christ, meaning it is also an anti-mind. In reality, the mind of Christ is not anti anything.

Maitreya, kindness is the key,
all shades of kindness teach to me,
for I am now the open door,
the Art of Kindness to restore.

**Maitreya, kindness is the cure,
in fires of kindness I am pure.
Maitreya, now release the fire,
that raises me forever higher.**

9. Gautama Buddha, awaken the most creative people to see that the ascended masters are not against the power elite beings. The concept of enemies exists only in the dualistic mind because that is the only mind that can conceive of divisions into opposite polarities that must eradicate each other in some epic struggle.

Maitreya, oh sweet mystery,
immersed in your reality,
the myst'ry school will now return,
for this, my heart does truly burn.

**Maitreya, kindness is the cure,
in fires of kindness I am pure.
Maitreya, now release the fire,
that raises me forever higher.**

Part 3

1. Gautama Buddha, awaken the most creative people to see that when the ascended masters make a statement in words, they are making it from the mind of Christ but as that energetic impulse is translated into words, they can be interpreted in different ways.

> Gautama, show my mental state
> that does give rise to love and hate,
> your exposé I do endure,
> so my perception will be pure.
>
> **Gautama, Flame of Cosmic Peace,**
> **unruly thoughts do hereby cease,**
> **we radiate from you and me**
> **the peace to still Samsara's Sea.**

2. Gautama Buddha, awaken the most creative people to see that the ascended masters cannot give a statement in words that will cause all people to understand what is meant. There is always the plausible deniability that different people will interpret the statement through their state of consciousness or perception filter.

> Gautama, in your Flame of Peace,
> the struggling self I now release,
> the Buddha Nature I now see,
> it is the core of you and me.
>
> **Gautama, Flame of Cosmic Peace,**
> **unruly thoughts do hereby cease,**
> **we radiate from you and me**
> **the peace to still Samsara's Sea.**

3. Gautama Buddha, awaken the most creative people to see that the power elite beings will attempt to say that the mind of Christ is just another mind. It is not inherently superior to the mind of anti-christ. It is just one

viewpoint. They will say the mind of Christ is just a viewpoint like any other viewpoint, and it is not better than any other viewpoints in duality.

> Gautama, I am one with thee,
> Mara's demons do now flee,
> your Presence like a soothing balm,
> my mind and senses ever calm.

> **Gautama, Flame of Cosmic Peace,**
> **unruly thoughts do hereby cease,**
> **we radiate from you and me**
> **the peace to still Samsara's Sea.**

4. Gautama Buddha, awaken the most creative people to see that the mind of Christ is *not* a viewpoint, it is not a perspective that can be influenced by duality. Even if we are not in duality, words can be interpreted.

> Gautama, I now take the vow,
> to live in the eternal now,
> with you I do transcend all time,
> to live in present so sublime.

> **Gautama, Flame of Cosmic Peace,**
> **unruly thoughts do hereby cease,**
> **we radiate from you and me**
> **the peace to still Samsara's Sea.**

5. Gautama Buddha, awaken the most creative people to see that we need an ideology only because there is a distance between our minds and the direct experience. Our minds are not fulfilled in having the direct experience, are not absorbed in the experience. We are looking at life from a distance and wanting to explain it from a distance.

> Gautama, I have no desire,
> to nothing earthly I aspire,
> in non-attachment I now rest,
> passing Mara's subtle test.

Gautama, Flame of Cosmic Peace,
unruly thoughts do hereby cease,
we radiate from you and me
the peace to still Samsara's Sea.

6. Gautama Buddha, awaken the most creative people to see that this is what happens with words. There is a difference between the word and the thing. The word refers to the thing, it points to the thing, but it is not the "thing in itself," as the philosopher Kant expressed it.

Gautama, I melt into you,
my mind is one, no longer two,
immersed in your resplendent glow,
Nirvana is all that I know.

Gautama, Flame of Cosmic Peace,
unruly thoughts do hereby cease,
we radiate from you and me
the peace to still Samsara's Sea.

7. Gautama Buddha, awaken the most creative people to see that Kant gave the idea that there is a real world but human beings can never experience that world directly. We can never experience "the thing in itself" because we always experience it though our perception. That is why we need words to describe what we cannot experience.

Gautama, in your timeless space,
I am immersed in Cosmic Grace,
I know the God beyond all form,
to world I will no more conform.

Gautama, Flame of Cosmic Peace,
unruly thoughts do hereby cease,
we radiate from you and me
the peace to still Samsara's Sea.

8. Gautama Buddha, awaken the most creative people to see that the many ideologies given by the power elite beings are given in words. The real underlying purpose of all of the teachings on earth is to keep our minds

trapped in the realm of words. Our minds are focused on words instead of seeking the direct experience.

> Gautama, I am now awake,
> I clearly see what is at stake,
> and thus I claim my sacred right
> to be on earth the Buddhic Light.

> **Gautama, Flame of Cosmic Peace,**
> **unruly thoughts do hereby cease,**
> **we radiate from you and me**
> **the peace to still Samsara's Sea.**

9. Gautama Buddha, awaken the most creative people to see that what the power elite beings do not want is for us to have an experience of the Christ mind. The purpose of all false teachings is to pull our minds into the realm of words so we do not seek the experience of the Christ mind. That is the purpose of ideology.

> Gautama, with your thunderbolt,
> we give the earth a mighty jolt,
> I know that some will understand,
> and join the Buddha's timeless band.

> **Gautama, Flame of Cosmic Peace,**
> **unruly thoughts do hereby cease,**
> **we radiate from you and me**
> **the peace to still Samsara's Sea.**

Part 4

1. Gautama Buddha, awaken the most creative people to see that any teaching is meant to keep us trapped in words, arguing about words, thinking *this* word is the more accurate description of the world than *that* word.

Sanat Kumara, Ruby Fire,
I seek my place in love's own choir,
with open hearts we sing your praise,
together we the earth do raise.

**Sanat Kumara, Ruby Ray,
bring to earth a higher way,
light this planet with your fire,
clothe her in a new attire.**

2. Gautama Buddha, awaken the most creative people to see that many people are trapped in this, especially intellectuals. For philosophers and theologians, the interpretation of one or two words can lead to a conflict or division.

Sanat Kumara, Ruby Fire,
initiations I desire,
I am for you an electrode,
Shamballa is my true abode.

**Sanat Kumara, Ruby Ray,
bring to earth a higher way,
light this planet with your fire,
clothe her in a new attire.**

3. Gautama Buddha, awaken the most creative people to see that the entire purpose of this is to keep our minds trapped at the level of words where everything can be interpreted. It can be interpreted because it is not the thing in itself. It only points to the thing.

Sanat Kumara, Ruby Fire,
I follow path that you require,
initiate me with your love,
the open door for Holy Dove.

**Sanat Kumara, Ruby Ray,
bring to earth a higher way,
light this planet with your fire,
clothe her in a new attire.**

4. Gautama Buddha, awaken the most creative people to see that in the realm of ideas, the potential for an interpretation of words is endless. There is no limit to how far we can go into this blind alley. The only limit is: When do we get tired of it? When have we had enough of that experience and want something more, which is the Christ mind.

Sanat Kumara, Ruby Fire,
your great example all inspire,
with non-attachment and great mirth,
we give the earth a true rebirth.

**Sanat Kumara, Ruby Ray,
bring to earth a higher way,
light this planet with your fire,
clothe her in a new attire.**

5. Gautama Buddha, awaken the most creative people to see that the ideological mindset is based on the interpretation of words, and an endless evaluation of whether *this* wording is better than *that* description. Yet they are all words.

Sanat Kumara, Ruby Fire,
you are this planet's purifier,
consume on earth all spirits dark,
reveal the inner Spirit Spark.

**Sanat Kumara, Ruby Ray,
bring to earth a higher way,
light this planet with your fire,
clothe her in a new attire.**

6. Gautama Buddha, awaken the most creative people to see that words are not the real thing. When the ascended masters give a teaching about the Christ mind, the power elite beings will say that the teaching is just words, it needs to be interpreted, it needs to be understood in a certain way.

Sanat Kumara, Ruby Fire,
you are a cosmic amplifier,

the lower forces can't withstand,
vibrations from Venusian band.

**Sanat Kumara, Ruby Ray,
bring to earth a higher way,
light this planet with your fire,
clothe her in a new attire.**

7. Gautama Buddha, awaken the most creative people to see that the essence of the ideological mindset is that we take a teaching given in words and we focus our minds on the words and the interpretation of words, instead of using the teaching as a stepping stone for the direct experience of the Christ mind.

Sanat Kumara, Ruby Fire,
I am on earth your magnifier,
the flow of love I do restore,
my chakras are your open door.

**Sanat Kumara, Ruby Ray,
bring to earth a higher way,
light this planet with your fire,
clothe her in a new attire.**

8. Gautama Buddha, awaken the most creative people to see that the ideological mindset does everything it can to shut out the direct experience of oneness, the direct experience of anything beyond the words and the mind that can interpret words endlessly.

Sanat Kumara, Ruby Fire,
Venusian song the multiplier,
as we your love reverberate,
the densest minds we penetrate.

**Sanat Kumara, Ruby Ray,
bring to earth a higher way,
light this planet with your fire,
clothe her in a new attire.**

9. Gautama Buddha, awaken the most creative people to see that if we want to rise higher on the spiritual path, we need to openly consider whether we are still affected by or even trapped in the ideological mindset.

Sanat Kumara, Ruby Fire,
you are for all the sanctifier,
the earth is now a holy place,
purified by cosmic grace.

Sanat Kumara, Ruby Ray,
bring to earth a higher way,
light this planet with your fire,
clothe her in a new attire.

Sealing

In the name of the I AM THAT I AM, I accept that Archangel Michael, Astrea and Shiva form an impenetrable shield around myself and all constructive people, sealing us from all fear-based energies in all four octaves. I accept that the Light of God is consuming and transforming all fear-based energies that make up the dark forces working against ending the era of ideology on earth!

15 EXPOSING IDEOLOGY AS A MEANS OF CONTROL (PART 3)

In the name of the I AM THAT I AM, Jesus Christ, I use the authority that I have as a being in embodiment on earth to call upon Gautama Buddha to reinforce my calls and use my chakras to project the statements in this invocation into the collective consciousness and awaken people to the need to free ourselves from the ideological mindset. Awaken people to the reality that we are spiritual beings and that we can co-create a new future by working with the ascended masters. I especially call for …

[Make your own calls here.]

Part 1

1. Gautama Buddha, awaken the most creative people to see that we need to transcend the tendency to look at words and seek to understand them through the linear analytical mind, where we seek to fit them into our worldview and interpret them based on what we already believe.

Gautama, show my mental state
that does give rise to love and hate,
your exposé I do endure,
so my perception will be pure.

**Gautama, Flame of Cosmic Peace,
unruly thoughts do hereby cease,
we radiate from you and me
the peace to still Samsara's Sea.**

2. Gautama Buddha, awaken the most creative people to see that we need
to strive for what Zen Buddhists call beginner's mind. We need to question our mindset, what we already believe and think we know about life.

Gautama, in your Flame of Peace,
the struggling self I now release,
the Buddha Nature I now see,
it is the core of you and me.

**Gautama, Flame of Cosmic Peace,
unruly thoughts do hereby cease,
we radiate from you and me
the peace to still Samsara's Sea.**

3. Gautama Buddha, awaken the most creative people to see that we have
in past lives been associated with various thought systems and ideologies,
and we have in our minds these beliefs that we don't think we need to
question.

Gautama, I am one with thee,
Mara's demons do now flee,
your Presence like a soothing balm,
my mind and senses ever calm.

**Gautama, Flame of Cosmic Peace,
unruly thoughts do hereby cease,
we radiate from you and me
the peace to still Samsara's Sea.**

4. Gautama Buddha, awaken the most creative people to see that we need to question how free we are to listen to a spiritual teaching with a neutral state of mind. How free are we to go beyond the words of the teaching to the direct experience?

Gautama, I now take the vow,
to live in the eternal now,
with you I do transcend all time,
to live in present so sublime.

Gautama, Flame of Cosmic Peace,
unruly thoughts do hereby cease,
we radiate from you and me
the peace to still Samsara's Sea.

5. Gautama Buddha, awaken the most creative people to see that we may have come across a spiritual teaching that made the claim to be superior in some way. We accepted this claim and we hope the ascended masters will validate that previous belief. If we are to grow towards the Christ mind, we *must* question this mindset.

Gautama, I have no desire,
to nothing earthly I aspire,
in non-attachment I now rest,
passing Mara's subtle test.

Gautama, Flame of Cosmic Peace,
unruly thoughts do hereby cease,
we radiate from you and me
the peace to still Samsara's Sea.

6. Gautama Buddha, awaken the most creative people to see that we must question all beliefs that are based on our reaction to earth. We have been exposed to trauma, and we create selves in reaction to the experience we have had on earth.

Gautama, I melt into you,
my mind is one, no longer two,

immersed in your resplendent glow,
Nirvana is all that I know.

**Gautama, Flame of Cosmic Peace,
unruly thoughts do hereby cease,
we radiate from you and me
the peace to still Samsara's Sea.**

7. Gautama Buddha, awaken the most creative people to see that this ties us to earth. We are going to be free of earth only by freeing ourselves from all of these selves and all of the beliefs behind them. Therefore, we must be willing to question any and all beliefs we have picked up here on earth.

Gautama, in your timeless space,
I am immersed in Cosmic Grace,
I know the God beyond all form,
to world I will no more conform.

**Gautama, Flame of Cosmic Peace,
unruly thoughts do hereby cease,
we radiate from you and me
the peace to still Samsara's Sea.**

8. Gautama Buddha, awaken the most creative people to see that words are a description of the thing, not the thing in itself. How can any belief expressed in words be completely accurate? There can never be a highest teaching on the planet, not expressed in words.

Gautama, I am now awake,
I clearly see what is at stake,
and thus I claim my sacred right
to be on earth the Buddhic Light.

**Gautama, Flame of Cosmic Peace,
unruly thoughts do hereby cease,
we radiate from you and me
the peace to still Samsara's Sea.**

9. Gautama Buddha, awaken the most creative people to see that the highest spiritual experience we can have is to go beyond duality and experience oneness, but that experience cannot be described by words. The Christ mind can be named by words, but we can only know the mind of Christ by experiencing it directly.

> Gautama, with your thunderbolt,
> we give the earth a mighty jolt,
> I know that some will understand,
> and join the Buddha's timeless band.

> **Gautama, Flame of Cosmic Peace,**
> **unruly thoughts do hereby cease,**
> **we radiate from you and me**
> **the peace to still Samsara's Sea.**

Part 2

1. Gautama Buddha, awaken the most creative people to see that many of us have certain spiritual holy cows and believe: "This I know, and this is definitely accurate. This is the way it is." We may base this on a certain teaching or it comes from past lives and we don't even know where it originated.

> I see how my senses can only deceive,
> for nothing they tell me, I fully believe.
> Behind all appearances is only light,
> they only seem real to our limited sight.

> **O Padmasambhava, in your Flame of Peace,**
> **all human opinions I hereby release.**
> **I see now the ultimate truth you reveal,**
> **earth is an appearance, where nothing is real.**

2. Gautama Buddha, awaken the most creative people to see that if we come to ascended master teachings only to have the validation for those spiritual holy cows, we cannot make use of the teaching.

My mind and my senses are only a tool,
and I am determined to not be a fool.
My personal self, is no more who I am,
the earthly identity is but a scam.

**O Padmasambhava, in your Flame of Peace,
all human opinions I hereby release.
I see now the ultimate truth you reveal,
earth is an appearance, where nothing is real.**

3. Gautama Buddha, awaken the most creative people to see that there are all kinds of games that people can play where they are projecting that the problem is out there. The problem is with somebody else, the problem is with the teaching, with the messenger or with other people.

From sense-based perception I want to be free,
clear my inner sight, so I truly can see.
My human opinions, they do make me blind,
with neutral awareness, new visions I find.

**O Padmasambhava, in your Flame of Peace,
all human opinions I hereby release.
I see now the ultimate truth you reveal,
earth is an appearance, where nothing is real.**

4. Gautama Buddha, awaken the most creative people to see that projecting out is part of the ideological mindset. We are focused at the level of words, we have a desire to be right, and we can always make it seem like we are right by projecting that the problem is out there.

A self is what makes an opinion seem real,
it projects there's a problem, with which I must deal.
I will not be free, till I see through this lie,
and say to the self: I am letting you die.

**O Padmasambhava, in your Flame of Peace,
all human opinions I hereby release.
I see now the ultimate truth you reveal,
earth is an appearance, where nothing is real.**

5. Gautama Buddha, awaken the most creative people to see that in order to ascend and be free of earth, we must question our spiritual holy cows. The ideological mindset has not only *defined* the holy cows, it will also *defend* the holy cows to the death, where either the enemies die or the self dies, because we finally have had enough of this endless battle based on words.

Through human opinions, I simply can't see,
the higher perspective—Christ reality,
When the self dualistic, I truly let die,
the Christ mind does open, up my inner eye.

**O Padmasambhava, in your Flame of Peace,
all human opinions I hereby release.
I see now the ultimate truth you reveal,
earth is an appearance, where nothing is real.**

6. Gautama Buddha, awaken the most creative people to see that an ideology is always bad if it keeps people trapped in the mind of anti-christ. Yet an ideology does not have to trap people. An ideology could give people a useful foundation for expanding their consciousness.

O Padmasambhava, the world has gone mad,
as dualistic thinking, defines good and bad.
The judgment of Christ, upon forces so dark,
rekindle in people, our spiritual spark.

**O Padmasambhava, in your Flame of Peace,
all human opinions I hereby release.
I see now the ultimate truth you reveal,
earth is an appearance, where nothing is real.**

7. Gautama Buddha, awaken the most creative people to see that for this to happen, the ideology has to meet certain criteria, but also the people who are following that ideology must be willing to go beyond the words and seek the direct experience.

O Padmasambhava, set all people free,
from mindset so epic, from duality.

Cut all people free from the serpentine lie,
so that to Christ Jesus, we all can draw nigh.

**O Padmasambhava, in your Flame of Peace,
all human opinions I hereby release.
I see now the ultimate truth you reveal,
earth is an appearance, where nothing is real.**

8. Gautama Buddha, awaken the most creative people to see that so-called mystical teachings have been more successful than mainstream religions. Many mystical teachings are focused on giving people an experience of something beyond what can be expressed in words. The teaching is meant to point to an experience.

The serpentine lie, says that what we now see,
is all that our lives, on this planet can be.
Yet with the Christ mind, we can see there is more,
the earth will be brighter than ever before.

**O Padmasambhava, in your Flame of Peace,
all human opinions I hereby release.
I see now the ultimate truth you reveal,
earth is an appearance, where nothing is real.**

9. Gautama Buddha, awaken the most creative people to see that the purpose of words is that it allows people to communicate about practical things in the physical realm that are not there right now.

Saint Germain has the plans, for a bright Golden Age,
to receive them, our minds must be free from the cage,
O Padmasambhava, with your Flame of Peace,
the vision of Oneness, to all you release.

**O Padmasambhava, in your Flame of Peace,
all human opinions I hereby release.
I see now the ultimate truth you reveal,
earth is an appearance, where nothing is real.**

Part 3

1. Gautama Buddha, awaken the most creative people to see that normally words point to something physical. When we start talking about ideas, we are not talking about something that has a physical parallel we can experience through the senses. This means that we can only experience it through intuition. It is a matter of whether people are open to using intuition, whether they are willing to use it.

> Gautama, show my mental state
> that does give rise to love and hate,
> your exposé I do endure,
> so my perception will be pure.

> **Gautama, Flame of Cosmic Peace,**
> **unruly thoughts do hereby cease,**
> **we radiate from you and me**
> **the peace to still Samsara's Sea.**

2. Gautama Buddha, awaken the most creative people to see that a spiritual teaching is pointing to something beyond the physical realm, beyond the emotional realm, beyond the mental realm, beyond the lower identity realm, to the higher identity realm or the spiritual realm.

> Gautama, in your Flame of Peace,
> the struggling self I now release,
> the Buddha Nature I now see,
> it is the core of you and me.

> **Gautama, Flame of Cosmic Peace,**
> **unruly thoughts do hereby cease,**
> **we radiate from you and me**
> **the peace to still Samsara's Sea.**

3. Gautama Buddha, awaken the most creative people to see that some people are not able to have that experience yet, others are not willing to stretch their consciousness in order to have the experience. They get

trapped in pulling the teaching into the realm of words and then interpreting it to make themselves seem superior.

> Gautama, I am one with thee,
> Mara's demons do now flee,
> your Presence like a soothing balm,
> my mind and senses ever calm.

> **Gautama, Flame of Cosmic Peace,**
> **unruly thoughts do hereby cease,**
> **we radiate from you and me**
> **the peace to still Samsara's Sea.**

4. Gautama Buddha, awaken the most creative people to see that it is a game that people are playing, it is an *ego* game. They are using a spiritual teaching as a tool for playing an ego game, and that is not what a spiritual teaching is meant to do.

> Gautama, I now take the vow,
> to live in the eternal now,
> with you I do transcend all time,
> to live in present so sublime.

> **Gautama, Flame of Cosmic Peace,**
> **unruly thoughts do hereby cease,**
> **we radiate from you and me**
> **the peace to still Samsara's Sea.**

5. Gautama Buddha, awaken the most creative people to see that many of us have as part of our Divine plans to be in embodiment at this time to help bring Saint Germain's Golden Age. Yet we are not going to bring Saint Germain's Golden Age through any ideology.

> Gautama, I have no desire,
> to nothing earthly I aspire,
> in non-attachment I now rest,
> passing Mara's subtle test.

**Gautama, Flame of Cosmic Peace,
unruly thoughts do hereby cease,
we radiate from you and me
the peace to still Samsara's Sea.**

6. Gautama Buddha, awaken the most creative people to see that the golden age will not be brought by a particular ideology. We need to help humankind transcend the era of ideology, transcend the era where people thought they could define a thought system and then the universe would work according to the thought system.

Gautama, I melt into you,
my mind is one, no longer two,
immersed in your resplendent glow,
Nirvana is all that I know.

**Gautama, Flame of Cosmic Peace,
unruly thoughts do hereby cease,
we radiate from you and me
the peace to still Samsara's Sea.**

7. Gautama Buddha, awaken the most creative people to see that an ideology is formulated with words. The words point to the real thing, but many people have reversed that. They think that certain words have a magical power to create the thing, or to at least change the thing.

Gautama, in your timeless space,
I am immersed in Cosmic Grace,
I know the God beyond all form,
to world I will no more conform.

**Gautama, Flame of Cosmic Peace,
unruly thoughts do hereby cease,
we radiate from you and me
the peace to still Samsara's Sea.**

8. Gautama Buddha, awaken the most creative people to see that this is a mindset that is in complete opposition to the manifestation of the golden

age, so we need to pull the collective consciousness above this ideological mindset.

> Gautama, I am now awake,
> I clearly see what is at stake,
> and thus I claim my sacred right
> to be on earth the Buddhic Light.

> **Gautama, Flame of Cosmic Peace,**
> **unruly thoughts do hereby cease,**
> **we radiate from you and me**
> **the peace to still Samsara's Sea.**

9. Gautama Buddha, awaken the most creative people to see that this cannot be done by those who are convinced that the way to bring the golden age is through their particular ideology.

> Gautama, with your thunderbolt,
> we give the earth a mighty jolt,
> I know that some will understand,
> and join the Buddha's timeless band.

> **Gautama, Flame of Cosmic Peace,**
> **unruly thoughts do hereby cease,**
> **we radiate from you and me**
> **the peace to still Samsara's Sea.**

Part 4

1. Gautama Buddha, awaken the most creative people to see that the only people who have a realistic potential for shifting the collective consciousness are those of who are open to a mystical teaching that focuses on direct experience beyond words. These are the only people who can pull the planet up.

> I see how my senses can only deceive,
> for nothing they tell me, I fully believe.

Behind all appearances is only light,
they only seem real to our limited sight.

**O Padmasambhava, in your Flame of Peace,
all human opinions I hereby release.
I see now the ultimate truth you reveal,
earth is an appearance, where nothing is real.**

2. Gautama Buddha, awaken the most creative people to see that we are not going to pull the planet up if we have not pulled ourselves up. It cannot be done. We need to start with ourselves, we need to pull ourselves above the ideological mindset.

My mind and my senses are only a tool,
and I am determined to not be a fool.
My personal self, is no more who I am,
the earthly identity is but a scam.

**O Padmasambhava, in your Flame of Peace,
all human opinions I hereby release.
I see now the ultimate truth you reveal,
earth is an appearance, where nothing is real.**

3. Gautama Buddha, use my mind and chakras to project this teaching into the collective consciousness so that people, who may not know about ascended masters, still can receive these ideas and use them to raise themselves above the ideological mindset.

From sense-based perception I want to be free,
clear my inner sight, so I truly can see.
My human opinions, they do make me blind,
with neutral awareness, new visions I find.

**O Padmasambhava, in your Flame of Peace,
all human opinions I hereby release.
I see now the ultimate truth you reveal,
earth is an appearance, where nothing is real.**

4. Gautama Buddha, awaken the most creative people to see that many people have been trapped in the ideological mindset for lifetimes. They have seen how people who became fanatical and extremists in this ideological mindset have created disaster after disaster, have created suffering upon suffering, have created misery upon misery, and they have had enough of it.

> A self is what makes an opinion seem real,
> it projects there's a problem, with which I must deal.
> I will not be free, till I see through this lie,
> and say to the self: I am letting you die.

> **O Padmasambhava, in your Flame of Peace,**
> **all human opinions I hereby release.**
> **I see now the ultimate truth you reveal,**
> **earth is an appearance, where nothing is real.**

5. Gautama Buddha, awaken those who are open to a different approach. Use my aura and chakras to pull them up over that hump, as I start pulling myself up.

> Through human opinions, I simply can't see,
> the higher perspective—Christ reality,
> When the self dualistic, I truly let die,
> the Christ mind does open, up my inner eye.

> **O Padmasambhava, in your Flame of Peace,**
> **all human opinions I hereby release.**
> **I see now the ultimate truth you reveal,**
> **earth is an appearance, where nothing is real.**

6. Gautama Buddha, awaken the most creative people to see that it is time for us to look at this ideological mindset and say: "Oh well, it's just another conglomeration of separate selves that I have to let go of. And how free I will feel when I let go of those also, as I have let go of others already."

> O Padmasambhava, the world has gone mad,
> as dualistic thinking, defines good and bad.

The judgment of Christ, upon forces so dark,
rekindle in people, our spiritual spark.

O Padmasambhava, in your Flame of Peace,
all human opinions I hereby release.
I see now the ultimate truth you reveal,
earth is an appearance, where nothing is real.

7. Gautama Buddha, awaken the most creative people to see that we *will* feel free, we will feel like the weight of the world has been lifted from our shoulders when we finally escape that ideological mindset. Suddenly, we do not have the responsibility of changing the world according to an idea in our minds, an idea that could never produce the result of changing the world.

O Padmasambhava, set all people free,
from mindset so epic, from duality.
Cut all people free from the serpentine lie,
so that to Christ Jesus, we all can draw nigh.

O Padmasambhava, in your Flame of Peace,
all human opinions I hereby release.
I see now the ultimate truth you reveal,
earth is an appearance, where nothing is real.

8. Gautama Buddha, awaken the most creative people to see that it is a huge relief to let go of an ideology, a set of ideas, a certain mindset that we could change the world. It is a huge relief to let go of it, and to realize that we can ascend even though the world has not changed.

The serpentine lie, says that what we now see,
is all that our lives, on this planet can be.
Yet with the Christ mind, we can see there is more,
the earth will be brighter than ever before.

O Padmasambhava, in your Flame of Peace,
all human opinions I hereby release.
I see now the ultimate truth you reveal,
earth is an appearance, where nothing is real.

9. Gautama Buddha, awaken the most creative people to see that we can have spiritual holy cows or spiritual freedom, but we cannot have both. I am willing to shift my mind and I hereby decide: "That cow is no longer untouchable. I am going to touch it, I am going to pull it out into the open, I am going to pick it apart, I am going to look at that belief behind it and dismiss it with an experience and a realization from the Christ mind."

> Saint Germain has the plans, for a bright Golden Age,
> to receive them, our minds must be free from the cage,
> O Padmasambhava, with your Flame of Peace,
> the vision of Oneness, to all you release.

> **O Padmasambhava, in your Flame of Peace,**
> **all human opinions I hereby release.**
> **I see now the ultimate truth you reveal,**
> **earth is an appearance, where nothing is real.**

Sealing

In the name of the I AM THAT I AM, I accept that Archangel Michael, Astrea and Shiva form an impenetrable shield around myself and all constructive people, sealing us from all fear-based energies in all four octaves. I accept that the Light of God is consuming and transforming all fear-based energies that make up the dark forces working against ending the era of ideology on earth!

16 HOW IDEOLOGY LED TO THE FALL

I AM the Ascended Master Gautama Buddha. I have now taken you through the worldly definition of ideology and I have given you the ascended master perspective on this definition. We will now go beyond the worldly definition and consider ideology from a broader perspective, an ascended master perspective.

One of the things we have given you is that the basic law of an unascended sphere is free will. We have explained this several times from various perspectives, but I want to give it again here even though it may overlap what we have said previously. What does free will mean? Well, it means essentially that all individual beings have been given *unrestricted* free will. This does not mean that they can choose anything, because they can only choose among the options they can see. In other words, the options they can see in their minds based on their level of understanding, their level of consciousness, the current worldview that they have—among these options, they are free to choose.

Exercising free will on a natural planet

Now, when you consider a natural planet, how do beings on a natural planet exercise their free will? Well, on a natural planet, you have an awareness that even though you are an individual being, you are part of a whole, you are connected to something greater than yourself. You have a sense of connection to your I AM Presence, whether you call it that or not, and you have a sense of connection to the other beings on your planet. Therefore, you know that you are living in a world that you did not personally create. You know that someone else has defined or created this world, and you are starting out as a new being and you have a limited sense of self, a limited sense of awareness. You are seeking to expand it, but you know you do not have the awareness to have created the world in which you live. You know that some being with a greater awareness than you created this world and you also have at least some understanding that this being designed the world based on certain principles. Part of the purpose was to create a world that was sustainable, that would not self-destruct, that would not cause suffering for the inhabitants. In other words, there is a benevolent intent behind the definition of the basic principles that created your world, and it is to give people a positive, uplifting experience where they do not suffer.

Based on this, on a natural planet, how are you seeking to expand your awareness? Well, you are doing so by experimenting with your co-creative abilities, your *co*-creative abilities. You are experimenting, you are formulating an image in your mind, you are superimposing it upon the Mat-er Light. When you see the result out-pictured by the Mat-er Light, you use this to evaluate your own state of consciousness, your own vision, and therefore, to expand your own vision.

What is it that enables you to look at what you have manifested and learn from it? Well, it is that you know there are certain principles, and you understand (and certainly you are told by the teachers you have) that the way to maximize your creative potential is to come to understand the design principles upon which your world is based. Now, you could say: "Well, but if you have spiritual teachers on a natural planet, why don't they just explain these creative principles to all the other people on the planet?" What would be the purpose of that? How would that help you grow?

You are put in an environment where you cannot easily hurt yourself and other people. You are given guidance as to how to interpret the results that you manifest, but there is a lot of room for you to make your own discovery, to have your own insights coming to you from within. As a co-creator, you are not meant to be told from without. You are meant to discover from within so that you *internalize* what you discover, instead of just learning it as some intellectual understanding. Again, I have talked about the difference between the thing and the understanding of it. On a natural planet, you are seeking to get the experience so that you internalize what you learn, instead of just understanding it at a distance. It becomes part of your being and therefore, you truly have internalized the lesson. As you grow on a natural planet, you gradually discover the design principles upon which the world works. You learn how to co-create in a way that not only does not harm yourself and others, but actually benefits others, benefits the whole to the maximum degree. This is how free will is exercised on a natural planet.

How the first beings fell

Now, we have said that after the first beings fell in the fourth sphere, the fifth sphere was created with two levels so that there was a level where the fallen beings could exist and where the new beings in that sphere could exist. What you see is that the fallen beings of course were not experimenting this way, so we now go to the fourth sphere, and we say: "Well, if the fourth sphere was created with just one level, would it not stand to reason that all planets were created as what we call natural planets?" The question is: How could beings who have evolved on a natural planet, how could they come to the point where they could fall? What created the situation in the fourth sphere where the first beings could get themselves in a state of consciousness that they were not willing to give up, causing them to fall instead of ascending with their sphere?

In order to understand this, you need to look at the full range of free will. You can, for a very long time, experiment with your free will within the framework, the design principles, that determined the design of your particular planet. You can learn how these design principles work. You can even learn how the general design principles for the entire universe work. Therefore, you can come to a greater understanding of the consequences of your choices. You understand that if you follow the design principles that guide your particular planet, you will not harm yourself, you will not harm other beings, you will not harm the planet—you will create in a positive spiral.

One of the logical consequences of giving beings free will is that there is a possibility that some beings can come to the point where they have a certain understanding of the design principles that were defined by those who had created their planet. They may see them as ascended masters, they may see them as God, however they conceive of it. They are saying: "I have now lived on this planet for a long time. I have learned how the planet works, but I have learned this within the context of principles designed by other beings. Now, why should I always be confined to exercising my free will within those restraints created by other beings? Why couldn't I define my own environment in which to exercise my free will?"

Now, you will see that already in thinking this way, something has happened to these beings that does not happen to *all* beings. The vast majority of co-creators do not feel that the design principles for their particular planet, or for the universe, are a *limitation* for them. In fact, they are a *liberation* for them because it allows them to create something that is sustainable. In the fourth sphere, there were a few beings who came to the point where they started thinking: "If I really have free will, I should be allowed to create my own environment, to define my own principles for how life works on my planet." Of course, this is within the principle of free will.

When a co-creator comes to this particular mindset (and again, not everybody has to come to that), but when a particular co-creator comes to this mindset, adopts this mindset, then the co-creator must be allowed to act out that mindset in order to experience the consequences of it. This is why you had these few planets where a certain being had set itself up as the ultimate authority on that planet. This being was the one who now defined the principles for how life should work on that planet. Now, does this mean that this being could define these principles any way it wanted, any way it could conceive off? Yes, it does. There were a few beings who came to this point where they desired to define their own world, and the Mater Light, the reality simulator on that particular planet, then conformed to this vision, especially as that being began to convince others that these principles were the real principles so that a greater number of people began to accept this vision.

Now, what did I just say? The vast majority of co-creators are using the real world as a frame of reference for their co-creative activities. They are seeking to discover more and more of the design principles for how the world works. They are not seeking to define these principles, they are seeking to discover how the ascended masters who created their planet, or the Elohim, defined those principles. This is a process of *discovery,* not a process of *definition.*

There is a constant interaction here where these beings are not having a fixed image in their minds. They will have a certain image in their minds. As you grow up, as you evolve even on a natural planet, you need to have some kind of image of how you think the world works because otherwise you cannot even start co-creating. You are given a certain image as a foundation and then you gradually expand upon it, but you are constantly seeking to compare your image to the results you get back from the material universe. In other words, does the universe actually work the way I think it works? Then, of course you have the other option on a natural planet, which is that you do have spiritual teachers and as you expand your consciousness, you can ask for their help and their direction.

Basically, you could say that there are two ways that a co-creator can discover the design principles. One is through asking for help, asking for direction from those who know more and the other is by experimenting and comparing the results that are produced to your understanding. Do the results match your understanding, and if they do not, then you realize you need to raise your understanding. How else could it be, because you know that if you had the full understanding, you would be able to co-create anything you wanted. These are the two ways: There is a frame of reference you have from outside yourself, you know there are spiritual teachers who have a higher level of consciousness than you have. Then, there is the constant comparing of your mental image to the results you produce.

Now, as a result of free will outplaying itself, there were a few people in the fourth sphere, a few beings, who came to this point where they decided that this was a restriction for them. Why should they have to listen to spiritual teachers? Why should they have to compare their vision to the results being produced? Why should they not be able to define their own environment, their own principles, where there were no advanced teachers who could tell them what to do, and where matter would simply conform to their vision—not that they would have to refine their vision and conform to matter. Again, this was allowed as an outplaying of free will,.

You now have a being on a planet who gets itself into this state of mind where it decides that it wants to define its own environment. It does not want anyone to interfere—these were not really necessarily ascended masters on all natural planets, there were beings embodied on the natural planets who had a higher level of awareness so that they could interact directly with the beings on the planet. In other words, you did not need revelation from the ascended realm because you had teachers right there in physical embodiment, we might say, on a natural planet. On these specific planets, there was a being who decided: "I do not want these teachers on the planet." By the law of free will, then, these teachers withdrew out of physical embodiment so that there was no teacher that could serve as a frame of reference.

Co-creating without a frame of reference

Then, the being who had set itself up as the leader on this planet, decided that it did not want to compare its results to its frame of mind, to its mental image, because it wanted the experience that its mental image would be out-pictured by matter in its exact form. In other words, its mental image did not need to be refined, did not need to be expanded upon. It was complete, it was the way it should be and matter just had to conform to that image.

Now, what happened in this process? Well, this being created a mental image of how the universe was supposed to work and that mental image became what we have called an ideology. It was a set of ideas of how the universe is supposed to work and now this being not only attempted to use its co-creative abilities to project that image on the Ma-ter Light, but it also attempted to convince other people that this vision was true so that they would use their co-creative abilities to project the image upon the Ma-ter Light.

In other words, this being now said: "Away with the authority of the spiritual teachers. Away with the authority of comparing our mental images to observations. I am the ultimate authority on this planet." If the being could convince a critical mass of people on the planet to accept this mental image and to start projecting according to that image, then the Law of Free Will mandated that the reality simulator would reflect back physical conditions that corresponded to the image. Now, this led to a situation where, for a very, very long period of time, the inhabitants of one of these planets could make quite dramatic changes to what you would call, in your sphere, physical matter. They could create a change to how the planet looked. They could even change a lot of things according to their vision of how they could manifest whatever they desired.

You look at this situation and you realize that the being who was the leader on such a planet had of course gone into a state of separation. It had separated itself from its spiritual teachers, it had separated itself from observation so it had no frame of reference from outside itself. This being had become a law unto itself, a self-referential system, the ultimate authority. It had even begun to believe that it had a certain godlike status because it could define how the universe is supposed to work.

The question now is: You have a world of form that is created by your Creator, who has defined certain principles. Now, your Creator was not created as a creator with the creator consciousness. It went through a long process of attaining the creator consciousness, and during this process, your Creator learned what can create a sustainable creation, a sustainable world of form, a world a form that will not self-destruct, that will not cause the inhabitants of that world to suffer. This is what you learn in order to become a creator: How to create something sustainable, that does not cause suffering. The basic, we might say, design principle for any world of form is sustainability and that it does not create suffering. Because of free will, the inhabitants of a world of form can create their own suffering, but the Creator of the world of form does not define the world in such a way that it inevitably creates suffering. In other words, suffering is never forced upon anyone; it can only be the result of choices. We now see that the Creator of your world of form has this creator level consciousness, has this understanding of how to create a world that is sustainable, that does not force suffering upon the inhabitants. Of course, those beings in the fourth sphere who had set themselves up as god-like creatures on their particular planet, they had not gone through this process. They were created as new co-creators in the fourth sphere. They did not have the experience. Therefore, they were not able to function as creators, they were not able to define a world that was sustainable and that would not force suffering upon its inhabitants.

The experience of being like a god

Why would they then be allowed to go into this state of mind? Because of free will. In other words, free will does not mandate that a being in an unascended sphere is allowed to set itself up as a god in its sphere on a particular planet. What free will mandates is that a being in an unascended sphere must be allowed to have the *experience* of being like a god who is defining the principles on its planet and imposing those principles upon others. You see, it is not that an unascended being can become a god who can define its own principles, but it is allowed to have the *experience*.

What is the purpose of allowing a being to have this experience? Well, once the being has had the experience and has realized the limitations of this approach, then the being has learned an important lesson that can bring it closer to the creator consciousness. Not that it will be close, but it will be closer. In other words, the experience of thinking you can define your own world and your own principles can be part of the growth process. That is why the being is not allowed to become a god, but it is being allowed to have the *experience* of being as a god who is defining how matter works on this particular planet. Of course, the basic principle behind your creation is sustainability and that suffering is not forced upon anyone.

What is sustainability? Sustainability means self-transcendence. In other words, it is impossible in any world of form to create something that never changes. It is simply one of the design principles behind any world of form. You have innumerable worlds of forms created by innumerable creators. They are very, very different in the actual form they take. They are all based on this principle of sustainability, which means self-transcendence. A world of form can only sustain itself in the long run by constantly transcending itself. This is a universal principle that was not even designed by your Creator. This means that when a being on one of these planets sets itself up as defining the principles, sets itself up as a god we might say, then it is allowed to have the experience, *but only for a time*. If it could have that experience *forever*, it would go against the principle of sustainability through transcendence.

What inevitably will happen is that this being can set itself up as having the experience that it is the god who can define how the world works and it can have that experience for a time. After some time, there are certain things that will begin to happen. First of all, even though this leader and all of those who follow the leader on the planet, have a certain freedom to manifest whatever they want on their planet, there will come a point where what they manifest begins to have certain limitations. There is a certain break-down process that begins to happen. This causes a certain tension, and this causes suffering. It can cause physical suffering, but it also causes a certain mental suffering because suddenly, the beings on the planet and the leader begin to doubt that the principles they have created or defined, work the way they are supposed to work. Can they really give them the results they want?

This is simply the safety mechanism that is applied when people use their free will to go into this state of mind. For a time, you can have the experience: "Yes, I am a god, I can do anything I want. I can manifest anything I want. I can define how this planet should be." Then, after a time that sense begins to break down. The purpose is of course, the highest potential is, that this leader will come to the point where he realizes: "I have had this experience of being like a god long enough, I have had enough of this experience, I am tired of it, I want something more." Then, it can again join the upward path of the rest of its sphere. There are examples, both from the fourth sphere and from later spheres, where a planet has gone into this kind of a spiral. After a time, the leader and a critical mass of the followers have come to this realization: We have had enough of this experience. The planet has been turned back into an upward spiral and become a natural planet again and it has ascended with the rest of the universe, with the rest of the sphere.

When beings go into total denial

In the fourth sphere, there were a few planets where the leaders had not been willing to make this switch. They had not been willing to admit that they actually were not capable of defining principles that would not cause suffering. What these leaders did was they reinforced their ideology, their mental image of how the world *should* work. They fixated their minds on it to the point where they had convinced themselves that this image was actually right. It was absolutely right, regardless of the evidence to the contrary, regardless of the fact that things were breaking down on the planet, that people were suffering, that there were all kinds of phenomena. They convinced themselves and they stayed convinced that their definition, their ideology, was still correct. They managed to have a certain number of beings on the planet who believed in this vision and therefore uncritically followed the leader.

The Law of Free Will then mandates that such beings have to be confronted by the ascended masters, because they have to be given a frame of reference to see that there is an alternative to their ideology. This happens as the sphere has begun to enter the ascension spiral because the vast majority of planets have ascended or are ready to ascend. They have to be given the opportunity, a final opportunity, to choose to abandon their ideology. Some did and then received help to ascend with their sphere, but a few were not willing to do so. Then again, free will mandates (once you have been given that opportunity by the ascended masters), you must then be allowed to exercise your free will by denying this opportunity. That means you cannot remain in the sphere that ascends so you must of necessity fall into the next sphere that is created.

In this fifth sphere, there were two levels. For a long time, the new co-creators created in the fifth sphere evolved in a level where there were no fallen beings. The fallen beings were given certain planets where they could continue to experiment with this ideology, forcing their ideology upon the Ma-ter Light. They would again experience that there was suffering.

Then, what happened in the fifth sphere was that after a long period of time, there were a few planets that had gone into that same pattern where a leader had set itself up as being the ultimate authority wanting to define how the world *should* work. A critical mass of beings on the planet followed them so the planet was for a time allowed to out-picture the ideology created by the leader and give these people an experience that they could define their own world.

There came a time where the sphere was again nearing the ascension point. What did we do with one of these planets where they have not realized the shortcomings of their ideology? Well, the solution in the fifth sphere was that you first allowed the fallen beings in the other realm to embody on these planets. These fallen beings not only had experience, but they also had their own ideology that would naturally clash with the ideology of those who were already on the planet.

This gave the beings on this planet an opportunity to see the shortcomings of their approach. It gave the fallen beings an opportunity to see how they affected other people. There was the potential for growth. Some of the leaders on these planets (that were suddenly confronted with fallen beings) did awaken because they saw that the fallen beings had taken their own approach to an even greater extreme than they had done. They saw the consequences of it and realized it did not work—but some did not. Some either decided to fight the fallen beings (they were not successful because the fallen beings had more momentum, having fallen from another sphere) or they decided to submit to the fallen beings and follow them. Again, you had the situation where, on a few planets, these beings were confronted by the ascended masters, given that ultimate choice and again, a few of them chose to reject it and therefore fell into the next sphere. This was then repeated until you have your sphere where the same pattern has repeated itself.

How ideology created a downward spiral on earth

On planet earth there was a point (after a very, very long time of this planet existing, and the first waves of lifestreams ascending because they aligned themselves with the design principles, aligned with Elohim) where in the fourth wave of beings, there were many beings that again went into this wanting to define their own environment, their own principles, and they developed an ideology. The ideology was that it was essentially important, epically important, to have uniformity in society by eradicating differences and so on. This then created this downward spiral where suffering started to manifest, things started to break down, even though these leaders were convinced that they had the right ideology and that therefore, they were creating a sustainable society. Nevertheless, society started to break down, but the leaders were not willing to abandon their ideology.

Then, as an interim step, fallen beings were allowed to embody on earth so that they would give another opportunity to the inhabitants of the earth and they would themselves receive another opportunity. Then, you also had a situation where certain avatars on natural planets were looking at the earth and desiring to help the inhabitants of the earth change (for whatever reasons that motivated the avatars, which I will not go into here). The avatars were allowed to embody here as a counterbalance to the fallen beings. You had the fallen beings with an intent to control the population of earth, and you had the avatars with an intent to liberate, as they could see it, the inhabitants of the earth. This gave a certain balance between the two, which meant that the fallen beings did not have unrestricted reign to take over and control the inhabitants of the earth. There was at least an alternative that there were beings with a different state of consciousness.

What do you now see in relation to ideology? In a sense you could say that all co-creators start out having a certain ideology, they have a certain mental image of how they think their world works. Now (as I said), on a natural planet, they are given this by their spiritual teacher. They start out with a correct foundation. They can then build upon this and come to a point where now they have attained what we here on earth call the Christ consciousness. This means that they have now abandoned any ideology, any mental image. They do not need a mental image anymore because now they have come into alignment, into oneness, with the design principles so that they do not need to have a mental image of what they want to create (and how to create it) and superimpose that. They have a direct experience of the design principles and based on that experience, instead of a mental image, they are co-creating. This is how you co-create through the Christ consciousness, but that requires a certain level of maturity.

Levels of the mind of anti-christ

When you go into this state of wanting to create your own ideology, then of course this is not through the Christ mind. This is through what we might call the anti-christ mind, but this is a concept that needs to be explained further. There are levels of the mind of anti-christ. There is a level that is what Maitreya in the Christ discernment seminar (see *www.ascendedmaster-light.com*) talked about as *innocent ignorance* of going into duality, just without having an aggressive intent. You are just experimenting with duality. Then, you have the level of the aggressive intent of the fallen beings. This is the deeper level of the mind of anti-christ. We might say that there is a mind that is non-christ because it is simply ignorant of how the Christ mind is and how the design principles work, but it is an innocent ignorance of people that are willing to learn. Then, there is the real mind of anti-christ, which is based on a denial of the guidance coming from spiritual teachers or the ascended masters and the guidance coming from simply observing the difference between your mental image and what is manifest.

You can then say that, as a co-creator grows towards the Christ mind, it transcends the need to have an ideology and a mental image. In the Christ mind there is no ideology. If a co-creator grows in awareness but grows away from oneness, grows away from the Christ mind, then it reinforces the ideology. It takes the ideology to another level. As I said, when a new co-creator is experimenting, it sees this ideology as just a working hypothesis: "I have a certain understanding of how the world works, I know it is not the full understanding, so I am just experimenting and based on the outcome of my experiments, I am going to look at my understanding and see how I can refine it." When you go into creating this ideology based on the denial of the mind of anti-christ, then you are no longer experimenting. You are no longer comparing: "Does my ideology actually give me the results I want?" Now you have decided your ideology is absolute, it is infallible, and this *is* the way the world works.

Now, this is all very complex. It is of course, not something that we expect that the general population will come to understand and accept anytime soon. It is given for you who are our direct students so that you can gain a deeper understanding of this. Those of you who are avatars, and even those who are the more advanced members of the original inhabitants, in order to fulfill your highest potential on earth and raise the collective consciousness, you need to understand the dynamic of the fallen beings so that you can first of all avoid going into this reaction of fighting them. Also, so that you can raise yourself above their state of consciousness and thereby pull up the collective. Some of you might even at some point fill the role of being teachers that can help others.

Innocent ideology versus ideology based on denial

When you now take this to another level, you can say there is what we might call an *innocent ideology*. In other words, you have these first planets in the fourth sphere where a being decided it wanted to define its own environment, its own design principles. It did this by creating an ideology. This was allowed by the Law of Free Will, it was sort of an innocent ideology. They are being innocently flawed in thinking that they could define their own principles and create a sustainable environment.

Then comes the process whereby a being falls and this takes away the innocence because now the being denies the ascended masters, their frame of reference, it denies that there are shortcomings to its ideology. This means that when a being falls, it now goes into a different dynamic where its entire approach to existence is based on denial. You could say that in the fourth sphere, these beings defined an ideology. Even though they saw it as being valid, they did not think it was necessarily absolute and it was not based on denial. It was based on whatever vision they had when they defined the ideology.

When the being falls, it goes into this state of denial and now, in order to justify and uphold the denial, it defines an ideology, which has the only purpose to uphold this denial. Nothing must challenge the denial. This is what the fallen beings are trapped in. Now, you may say, well what hope is there that fallen beings can ever escape this? There is always a possibility that they *can*. They can come to the point where the strain of upholding this denial simply becomes too much. There are fallen beings who (for a very, very long time, even through several spheres) have been in this state of denial, have been in a state of constant tension and suddenly, for seemingly no obvious rational reason, they had a moment where they saw the tension and they asked themselves: "Why am I doing this?" In asking that question, they suddenly had the vision of what they were doing, and how utterly pointless it was, how *utterly* pointless it was.

A fallen being can have this experience at any point. It is a little bit similar to the road to Damascus experience of Paul where he saw the futility of persecuting the Christians and seeking to suppress the Christian religion. Why then, you could say, are the fallen beings allowed to influence others? Well, it is simply because by seeing how the fallen beings act, other beings on a certain planet that have not fallen can also have that experience of seeing the utter futility, the utter madness of what the fallen beings are doing.

As we have said, there were avatars that were pulled in by the ideology of Nazism, by the hypnotic field created by Hitler. When they came closer to Hitler and saw how he acted, or in some cases when they saw the consequences of how the war was lost and even the Holocaust was exposed (which they had not known about before), they had that moment of realization, of suddenly seeing that Hitler was a complete madman. What he did was utter madness and this then awakened them from this hypnotic state, which really is what we have called the ideological state of mind.

The ideological state of mind is hypnotic

It *is* hypnotic. Once you have entered into it, you are hypnotized, you are *literally* hypnotized but you can be awakened from it. In many cases, it takes these dramatic physical circumstances but in other cases it takes just observing how the fallen beings act, observing the mindset of the fallen beings, observing the utter pointlessness of it. This is what is portrayed in some of the Shakespearean plays, and in many other works of fiction throughout the ages, this utter madness that causes some people here and there to see it, and to see that there is a mindset that leads to this madness and I do not want to be in it, nor do I want to be a follower of leaders who are in this state of madness.

The fallen beings then serve, as we have said, as the substitute teachers because they are willing to do what the ascended masters cannot do because we ascended. They are willing to act out the duality consciousness to a greater extreme than the original inhabitants of the earth could conceive of acting it out. When the original inhabitants see the fallen beings act it out to that extreme, they have that moment of realization: "This is just too much. I do not want to go there." This has had the effect of awakening many people on earth, which is essentially why you see the emergence of democracies. The mad kings and emperors of the Middle Ages acted out to such an extreme that many people saw this, saw the madness of having a dictatorial form of government where one person had all power and could wage war on a whim or could cause the execution of thousands of people. They saw that there is a need to find a different form of government where one person's madness cannot be carried out into physical events. You might say, if you look at democracy, one way to define democracy is to create a form of government where one person's madness cannot determine the course of a nation.

Transcending the ideological mindset

These are some thoughts that I wanted to give you as ascended master students, for your own benefit, especially for those of you who are avatars, where you can begin to see that if you are to fulfill your highest potential here on earth, you cannot do so by entering into this ideological mindset that originates with the fallen beings. You need to step up to the Christ mind and we have given you many, many teachings on the Christ mind, on the path to Christhood, on how to attain that state of consciousness. Therefore, I must, because it is a requirement by the Law of Free Will, tell you: "You have the teachings, you have the tools, the only question is, do you have the will to apply them by looking at yourself and seeing if you are still affected by that ideological mindset?"

This messenger transcended the ideological mindset quite some time ago, even though he had it as a young man and he also had it during his time at the Summit Lighthouse, which was very much affected by the ideological mindset, but he transcended it. He saw how we systematically gave teachings to help people transcend this mindset. He kind of got himself into a state of mind where he thought that anyone who is sincere about this particular dispensation, who is studying our teachings and practicing some of the decrees and invocations, they must be in the process of transcending this mindset. They cannot be completely hypnotized by it. He was awakened by the situation after the United States' election, when he realized that some people who had been ascended master students for decades, were in fact in the ideological mindset and had been hypnotized by Donald Trump and his claims of a stolen election and his claim to be the only president that could save America from whatever he defined it as.

He realized that it is actually possible to seemingly be an ascended master student, to study the teachings, read the dictations, practice the decrees and invocations, but you have not really started seeing the limitations of the ideological mindset and you have not sincerely started looking at yourself and freeing yourself from this mindset. This is just a reinforcement of the fact that on a planet with free will, on a planet as dense as earth, there is no guarantee. We can give a teaching but there is no guarantee that everyone who studies the teaching will be able to grasp it, will be willing to apply it to themselves, instead of projecting it upon others. This is simply one of these realizations that all of you who are avatars have to come to.

You have to come to this realization that on a planet like earth, as dense as it is, as dense as the collective consciousness is, with free will reigning supreme, there is no guarantee that you can fulfill the mission that you defined for yourself before you came. There is no guarantee that you can have the result that you desire to have. You need to come to a point where you accept fully that the vision you had before you came, there is no guarantee that it can be fulfilled. You may have been a mature co-creator on a natural planet, you may have been able to manifest anything you desired on the natural planet. Therefore, you may have thought that you could come to an unnatural planet and still manifest what you desired to manifest, namely freeing the people of earth.

On an unnatural planet there is no guarantee that you can manifest it. You need to accept this, and then you need to also work on realizing, fully realizing and accepting, that the fact that you cannot manifest your vision is not a fault of yours. It is not because *you* are deficient, but it is because your *vision* was not realistic on an unnatural plant. You do not need to go into this state of mind—you need to be careful, *very* careful, not to go into this state of mind of blaming yourself or feeling like you are a failure (which is what the fallen beings want you to feel) because you could not do what you came to earth to do. You need to realize that one of your purposes for coming to earth was precisely to free yourself from this vision that you had, from this ideology that you had, that you could do something on an unnatural plant and that you could do what perhaps no one else could do. You could be the savior, the one who came and saved the day, the prince on the white horse.

Many of the avatars who came to earth had that kind of attitude: We can free the people from the fallen beings. Therefore, you have in your mind this evaluation that if you cannot do what you came here to do, you have failed, and there must be something wrong with you. That is of course what happens when you receive that cosmic birth trauma. You come with the best of intentions. You are not intending to force anybody. Then, you experience that the fallen beings are forcing *you* and that the people are rejecting you, perhaps even aggressively wanting to silence or kill you. All of a sudden, you have this moment of realization, this shock: "What if I cannot fulfill what I came here to do? I must be a failure then." The fallen beings will mercilessly exploit this, make you feel this way, and this can cause you to go into this state of denial where you create this primal self that is meant to make sure that you can never again have that experience of feeling like you have failed and there is something wrong with you and that you made a mistake for coming to earth and all of these things. You need to realize that you came here with an unrealistic vision, we might say an *unrealistic ideology,* of what you could accomplish on earth. It does not mean there is something wrong with *you.* You did the best you could based on the level of consciousness you had reached on a natural planet. It could have been a high level of consciousness but it was not the full Christ consciousness. There is no guarantee that beings evolving on a natural planet will necessarily attain Christ Consciousness on that planet. You made the choice you needed to make in order to grow further and that was to come to an unnatural planet, experience what it was like and therefore, you now have the opportunity to evaluate the vision that brought you to earth versus what you can see manifest on earth and what you have been able to accomplish on earth. Then, you can do what you did on a natural planet: evaluate whether your vision was the highest possible. *Then,* you just refine it.

It is not a matter of saying it was wrong in some epic way, and you were wrong and you are a failure and all of this. It is a matter of saying: "But I had the best of intentions for coming to earth. I wanted to free the people on earth from suffering so that they could have the kind of life that I had seen on a natural planet. I formulated the vision based on my good intentions and my level of consciousness and now I have the opportunity to realize that my vision was not realistic, given how earth works, given how the fallen beings are here and how the fallen beings, their state of consciousness, works, given how duality works." You can use this sojourn on planet earth as a tremendous stepping-stone, *many* stepping-stones for your further growth. You have an opportunity to grow because you have come to earth that you could never have gotten on a natural planet.

This can be a tremendous boost for your growth, once you overcome those separate selves and the primal self that caused you to go into that state of denial, that state of wanting to defend the ideology that brought you here, rather than transcending it. You do not grow by *defending,* only by *transcending.*

Seeing earth as a tremendous learning opportunity

You need to come to the point as an avatar where you can step back, you can look at your interaction with this earth and you can see it as a stepping-stone for your growth, as a tremendous learning opportunity. How can you come to that? Well, only by resolving the primal self and the other selves that you have created in reaction to the conditions on earth because it is in these selves that the pain is centered. It is these selves that have the pain, that feel the pain. *You* experience the pain when you identify with the selves, but when you let those selves die, *you* are free of the pain and that is when you can look at your interaction with earth as a tremendous learning opportunity.

Pain comes from the self. The self is based on a certain belief and what the self believes is that there is a specific outer condition, a specific problem, here on earth that caused your pain. Therefore, there is another self that says: "The only way to overcome the pain is to change that condition." What have we said from the moment we started giving these teachings on the primal self and the separate selves? You do not become free of a self by solving the problem that the self projects you have to solve. You become free of the self only by seeing that *there is no problem to solve. You just need to let the self die.*

You will not escape the pain you have experienced on earth by solving the problems, by removing the conditions, that the self thinks caused your pain. It was not the outer conditions that caused the pain. It was the selves you created that caused the pain. Even sometimes the selves you brought with you, thinking you always had to be successful in achieving whatever you set as your goal. It is these selves that are causing the pain, and the only way to escape the pain is to let the selves die by accepting that you will never solve the problem and you *do not need* to solve the problem. You are not on earth to solve problems and to do anything, as this messenger realized. As he has talked about several times, he came to this complete realization: "There is nothing I *have* to do on earth."

Before you came here, you thought: "There is something I *have* to do on earth. There is something I *have* to achieve on earth." The greatest outcome of your sojourn to earth is that you free yourself from the self that has this belief, and where you could just *be* on earth. That is how you pull up the collective consciousness, that is how you free yourself from any selves on earth, any reaction to earth, even the selves that brought you here, and that is how you qualify for your ascension.

With this, I have given you what I wanted you to give you in this installment, and again my gratitude for being willing to be those in embodiment who are holding the spiritual balance that made it possible for me to release this teaching. For if there are not enough people in embodiment who are willing to receive the teaching and send it on into the collective consciousness, then a teaching cannot be given.

Again, I seal you in the peace of the Buddha, the joyful peace of the Buddha, which is why the Buddha is often depicted as having this mysterious smile. He is not ecstatic in smiling, he is smiling in complete peace. When you go through the process I have described here, you will be able to be here on earth and encounter whatever you encounter, and you will be able to sit there, as I sat under the Bo tree being confronted with the demons of Mara, and give that mysterious Buddhic smile. When *that* is your ultimate reaction to anything on earth, you are free to move on—if you desire.

17 INVOKING THE JUDGMENT OF THE FALLEN BEINGS BEHIND IDEOLOGY

In the name of the I AM THAT I AM, Jesus Christ, I use the authority that I have as a being in embodiment on earth to call upon Gautama Buddha to reinforce my calls and use my chakras to project the statements in this invocation into the collective consciousness and awaken people to the need to free ourselves from the ideological mindset. Awaken people to the reality that we are spiritual beings and that we can co-create a new future by working with the ascended masters. I especially call for …

[Make your own calls here.]

Part 1

1. Gautama Buddha, I call forth the judgment of Christ upon those beings in the fourth sphere who said: "I have now lived on this planet for a long time. I have learned how the planet works, but I have learned this within the context of principles designed by other beings. Now, why should I always be confined to exercising my free will within those restraints created

by other beings? Why couldn't I define my own environment in which to exercise my free will?"

O Jesus, blessed brother mine,
I walk the path that you outline,
a great example to us all,
I follow now your inner call.

**O Jesus, let the Fire of Joy,
consume the devil's subtle ploy,
transfigured is our planet earth,
the golden age is given birth.**

2. Gautama Buddha, I call forth the judgment of Christ upon those beings in the fourth sphere who said: "If I really have free will, I should be allowed to create my own environment, to define my own principles for how life works on my planet."

O Jesus, open inner sight,
the ego wants to prove it's right,
but this I will no longer do,
I want to be all one with you.

**O Jesus, let the Fire of Joy,
consume the devil's subtle ploy,
transfigured is our planet earth,
the golden age is given birth.**

3. Gautama Buddha, I call forth the judgment of Christ upon those beings in the fourth sphere who set themselves up as the ultimate authority on various planets. They defined the principles for how life should work on "their" planet.

O Jesus, I now clearly see,
the Key of Knowledge given me,
my Christ self I hereby embrace,
as you fill up my inner space.

**O Jesus, let the Fire of Joy,
consume the devil's subtle ploy,
transfigured is our planet earth,
the golden age is given birth.**

4. Gautama Buddha, I call forth the judgment of Christ upon those beings in the fourth sphere who desired to define their own world and convinced others that its self-defined principles were the real principles, so that a greater number of people began to accept this vision.

O Jesus, show me serpent's lie,
expose the beam in my own eye,
as Christ discernment you me give,
in oneness I forever live.

**O Jesus, let the Fire of Joy,
consume the devil's subtle ploy,
transfigured is our planet earth,
the golden age is given birth.**

5. Gautama Buddha, I call forth the judgment of Christ upon those beings in the fourth sphere who decided that learning from the ascended masters and comparing their theories to actual results was a restriction for them.

O Jesus, I am truly meek,
and thus I turn the other cheek,
when the accuser attacks me,
I go within and merge with thee.

**O Jesus, let the Fire of Joy,
consume the devil's subtle ploy,
transfigured is our planet earth,
the golden age is given birth.**

6. Gautama Buddha, I call forth the judgment of Christ upon those beings in the fourth sphere who refused to listen to spiritual teachers or compare their vision to the results being produced.

O Jesus, ego I let die,
surrender ev'ry earthly tie,
the dead can bury what is dead,
I choose to walk with you instead.

**O Jesus, let the Fire of Joy,
consume the devil's subtle ploy,
transfigured is our planet earth,
the golden age is given birth.**

7. Gautama Buddha, I call forth the judgment of Christ upon those beings in the fourth sphere who wanted to define their own environment, their own principles, where there were no advanced teachers who could tell them what to do, and where matter would conform to their vision—not that they would have to refine their vision and conform to matter.

O Jesus, help me rise above,
the devil's test through higher love,
show me separate self unreal,
my formless self you do reveal.

**O Jesus, let the Fire of Joy,
consume the devil's subtle ploy,
transfigured is our planet earth,
the golden age is given birth.**

8. Gautama Buddha, I call forth the judgment of Christ upon those beings in the fourth sphere who got themselves into this state of mind where they decided that they wanted to define their own environment, and they did not want anyone to interfere. They said: "I do not want any teachers on 'my' planet."

O Jesus, what is that to me,
I just let go and follow thee,
with this I do pass ev'ry test,
to find with you eternal rest.

**O Jesus, let the Fire of Joy,
consume the devil's subtle ploy,**

**transfigured is our planet earth,
the golden age is given birth.**

9. Gautama Buddha, I call forth the judgment of Christ upon those beings in the fourth sphere who had set themselves up as leaders on a planet and who decided that they did not want to compare their results to their frame of mind, to their mental image, because they wanted the experience that their mental image would be out-pictured by matter in its exact form.

O Jesus, fiery master mine,
my heart now melting into thine,
I love with heart and mind and soul,
the God who is my highest goal.

**O Jesus, let the Fire of Joy,
consume the devil's subtle ploy,
transfigured is our planet earth,
the golden age is given birth.**

Part 2

1. Gautama Buddha, I call forth the judgment of Christ upon those beings in the fourth sphere who refused to refine their mental image or expand upon it. They decided it was complete, it was the way it should be and matter just had to conform to that image.

Maitreya, I am truly meek,
your counsel wise I humbly seek,
your vision I so want to see,
with you in Eden I will be.

**Maitreya, kindness is the cure,
in fires of kindness I am pure.
Maitreya, now release the fire,
that raises me forever higher.**

  Ending the Era of Ideology

2. Gautama Buddha, I call forth the judgment of Christ upon those beings in the fourth sphere who created a mental image of how the universe was supposed to work, and the mental image became an ideology.

> Maitreya, help me to return,
> to learn from you, I truly yearn,
> as oneness is all I desire
> I feel initiation's fire.

> **Maitreya, kindness is the cure,**
> **in fires of kindness I am pure.**
> **Maitreya, now release the fire,**
> **that raises me forever higher.**

3. Gautama Buddha, I call forth the judgment of Christ upon those beings in the fourth sphere who created a set of ideas of how the universe is supposed to work and then they attempted to use their co-creative abilities to project that image on the Ma-ter Light.

> Maitreya, I hereby decide,
> from you I will no longer hide,
> expose to me the very lie
> that caused edenic self to die.

> **Maitreya, kindness is the cure,**
> **in fires of kindness I am pure.**
> **Maitreya, now release the fire,**
> **that raises me forever higher.**

4. Gautama Buddha, I call forth the judgment of Christ upon those beings in the fourth sphere who attempted to convince other people that this vision was true, so that they would use their co-creative abilities to project the image upon the Ma-ter Light.

> Maitreya, blessed Guru mine,
> my heart of hearts forever thine,
> I vow that I will listen well,
> so we can break the serpent's spell.

**Maitreya, kindness is the cure,
in fires of kindness I am pure.
Maitreya, now release the fire,
that raises me forever higher.**

5. Gautama Buddha, I call forth the judgment of Christ upon those beings in the fourth sphere who said: "Away with the authority of the spiritual teachers. Away with the authority of comparing our mental images to observations. I am the ultimate authority on this planet."

Maitreya, help me see the lie
whereby the serpent broke the tie,
the serpent now has naught in me,
in oneness I am truly free.

**Maitreya, kindness is the cure,
in fires of kindness I am pure.
Maitreya, now release the fire,
that raises me forever higher.**

6. Gautama Buddha, I call forth the judgment of Christ upon those beings in the fourth sphere who accepted a mental image created by their leader, and who then projected according to that image, making changes to physical matter.

Maitreya, truth does set me free
from falsehoods of duality,
the fruit of knowledge I let go,
so your true spirit I do know.

**Maitreya, kindness is the cure,
in fires of kindness I am pure.
Maitreya, now release the fire,
that raises me forever higher.**

7. Gautama Buddha, I call forth the judgment of Christ upon those beings in the fourth sphere who had gone into a state of separation, had separated themselves from their spiritual teachers, had separated themselves from observation so they had no frame of reference from outside themselves.

Maitreya, I submit to you,
intentions pure, my heart is true,
from ego I am truly free,
as I am now all one with thee.

**Maitreya, kindness is the cure,
in fires of kindness I am pure.
Maitreya, now release the fire,
that raises me forever higher.**

8. Gautama Buddha, I call forth the judgment of Christ upon those beings in the fourth sphere who had become a law unto themselves, self-referential systems, the ultimate authority. They had even begun to believe that they had a certain godlike status because they could define how the universe is supposed to work.

Maitreya, kindness is the key,
all shades of kindness teach to me,
for I am now the open door,
the Art of Kindness to restore.

**Maitreya, kindness is the cure,
in fires of kindness I am pure.
Maitreya, now release the fire,
that raises me forever higher.**

9. Gautama Buddha, I call forth the judgment of Christ upon those beings in the fourth sphere who had set themselves up as god-like creatures on their particular planet, without having the experience of how to define a world that was sustainable and that would not force suffering upon its inhabitants.

Maitreya, oh sweet mystery,
immersed in your reality,
the myst'ry school will now return,
for this, my heart does truly burn.

**Maitreya, kindness is the cure,
in fires of kindness I am pure.**

**Maitreya, now release the fire,
that raises me forever higher.**

Part 3

1. Gautama Buddha, I call forth the judgment of Christ upon those beings in the fourth sphere who used their free will to go into a state of mind of wanting the experience: "Yes, I am a god, I can do anything I want. I can manifest anything I want. I can define how this planet should be."

Gautama, show my mental state
that does give rise to love and hate,
your exposé I do endure,
so my perception will be pure.

**Gautama, Flame of Cosmic Peace,
unruly thoughts do hereby cease,
we radiate from you and me
the peace to still Samsara's Sea.**

2. Gautama Buddha, I call forth the judgment of Christ upon those beings in the fourth sphere who refused to acknowledge that they had not become gods, and that their creative efforts had produced a planet that was not sustainable and that did produce suffering.

Gautama, in your Flame of Peace,
the struggling self I now release,
the Buddha Nature I now see,
it is the core of you and me.

**Gautama, Flame of Cosmic Peace,
unruly thoughts do hereby cease,
we radiate from you and me
the peace to still Samsara's Sea.**

3. Gautama Buddha, I call forth the judgment of Christ upon those beings in the fourth sphere who were not willing to admit that they were not capable of defining principles that would not cause suffering.

Gautama, I am one with thee,
Mara's demons do now flee,
your Presence like a soothing balm,
my mind and senses ever calm.

**Gautama, Flame of Cosmic Peace,
unruly thoughts do hereby cease,
we radiate from you and me
the peace to still Samsara's Sea.**

4. Gautama Buddha, I call forth the judgment of Christ upon those beings in the fourth sphere who reinforced their ideology, their mental image of how the world *should* work. They fixated their minds on it to the point where they had convinced themselves that this image was actually right.

Gautama, I now take the vow,
to live in the eternal now,
with you I do transcend all time,
to live in present so sublime.

**Gautama, Flame of Cosmic Peace,
unruly thoughts do hereby cease,
we radiate from you and me
the peace to still Samsara's Sea.**

5. Gautama Buddha, I call forth the judgment of Christ upon those beings in the fourth sphere who decided that their ideology was absolutely right, regardless of the evidence to the contrary, regardless of the fact that things were breaking down on the planet and that people were suffering.

Gautama, I have no desire,
to nothing earthly I aspire,
in non-attachment I now rest,
passing Mara's subtle test.

Gautama, Flame of Cosmic Peace,
unruly thoughts do hereby cease,
we radiate from you and me
the peace to still Samsara's Sea.

6. Gautama Buddha, I call forth the judgment of Christ upon those beings in the fourth sphere who convinced themselves and stayed convinced that their definition, their ideology, was still correct. They managed to have a certain number of beings on the planet who believed in this vision and therefore uncritically followed the leader.

Gautama, I melt into you,
my mind is one, no longer two,
immersed in your resplendent glow,
Nirvana is all that I know.

Gautama, Flame of Cosmic Peace,
unruly thoughts do hereby cease,
we radiate from you and me
the peace to still Samsara's Sea.

7. Gautama Buddha, I call forth the judgment of Christ upon those beings in the fourth sphere who were confronted by the ascended masters and given a frame of reference to see that there is an alternative to their ideology. They were given, a final opportunity to choose to abandon their ideology.

Gautama, in your timeless space,
I am immersed in Cosmic Grace,
I know the God beyond all form,
to world I will no more conform.

Gautama, Flame of Cosmic Peace,
unruly thoughts do hereby cease,
we radiate from you and me
the peace to still Samsara's Sea.

8. Gautama Buddha, I call forth the judgment of Christ upon those beings in the fourth sphere who were not willing to abandon their ideology, and

therefore could not remain in the sphere that ascended so they fell into the next sphere that was created.

> Gautama, I am now awake,
> I clearly see what is at stake,
> and thus I claim my sacred right
> to be on earth the Buddhic Light.

> **Gautama, Flame of Cosmic Peace,**
> **unruly thoughts do hereby cease,**
> **we radiate from you and me**
> **the peace to still Samsara's Sea.**

9. Gautama Buddha, I call forth the judgment of Christ upon the fallen beings in the fifth sphere who were given certain planets where they could continue to experiment with their ideology, forcing it upon the Ma-ter Light.

> Gautama, with your thunderbolt,
> we give the earth a mighty jolt,
> I know that some will understand,
> and join the Buddha's timeless band.

> **Gautama, Flame of Cosmic Peace,**
> **unruly thoughts do hereby cease,**
> **we radiate from you and me**
> **the peace to still Samsara's Sea.**

Part 4

1. Gautama Buddha, I call forth the judgment of Christ upon the beings in the fifth sphere who took some planets into the same pattern where a leader had set itself up as being the ultimate authority, wanting to define how the world *should* work.

Sanat Kumara, Ruby Fire,
I seek my place in love's own choir,
with open hearts we sing your praise,
together we the earth do raise.

Sanat Kumara, Ruby Ray,
bring to earth a higher way,
light this planet with your fire,
clothe her in a new attire.

2. Gautama Buddha, I call forth the judgment of Christ upon the beings who followed such leaders, so the planet was allowed to out-picture the ideology created by the leader and give these people an experience that they could define their own world.

Sanat Kumara, Ruby Fire,
initiations I desire,
I am for you an electrode,
Shamballa is my true abode.

Sanat Kumara, Ruby Ray,
bring to earth a higher way,
light this planet with your fire,
clothe her in a new attire.

3. Gautama Buddha, I call forth the judgment of Christ upon the fallen beings from the fourth sphere who were allowed to embody on the new planets where they had not realized the shortcomings of their ideology.

Sanat Kumara, Ruby Fire,
I follow path that you require,
initiate me with your love,
the open door for Holy Dove.

Sanat Kumara, Ruby Ray,
bring to earth a higher way,
light this planet with your fire,
clothe her in a new attire.

4. Gautama Buddha, I call forth the judgment of Christ upon the beings who received an opportunity to see the shortcomings of their approach, and the fallen beings who had an opportunity to see how they affected other people.

Sanat Kumara, Ruby Fire,
your great example all inspire,
with non-attachment and great mirth,
we give the earth a true rebirth.

**Sanat Kumara, Ruby Ray,
bring to earth a higher way,
light this planet with your fire,
clothe her in a new attire.**

5. Gautama Buddha, I call forth the judgment of Christ upon the leaders in the fifth sphere who refused to learn from the fallen beings who had taken their own approach to an even greater extreme than they had done.

Sanat Kumara, Ruby Fire,
you are this planet's purifier,
consume on earth all spirits dark,
reveal the inner Spirit Spark.

**Sanat Kumara, Ruby Ray,
bring to earth a higher way,
light this planet with your fire,
clothe her in a new attire.**

6. Gautama Buddha, I call forth the judgment of Christ upon the leaders in the fifth sphere who decided to fight the fallen beings or they decided to submit to the fallen beings and follow them.

Sanat Kumara, Ruby Fire,
you are a cosmic amplifier,
the lower forces can't withstand,
vibrations from Venusian band.

Sanat Kumara, Ruby Ray,
bring to earth a higher way,
light this planet with your fire,
clothe her in a new attire.

7. Gautama Buddha, I call forth the judgment of Christ upon the beings in the fifth sphere who were confronted by the ascended masters, given the ultimate choice and who chose to reject it and therefore fell into the next sphere.

Sanat Kumara, Ruby Fire,
I am on earth your magnifier,
the flow of love I do restore,
my chakras are your open door.

Sanat Kumara, Ruby Ray,
bring to earth a higher way,
light this planet with your fire,
clothe her in a new attire.

8. Gautama Buddha, I call forth the judgment of Christ upon the beings in the fourth wave of beings on earth, who went into wanting to define their own environment, their own principles, and who developed an ideology.

Sanat Kumara, Ruby Fire,
Venusian song the multiplier,
as we your love reverberate,
the densest minds we penetrate.

Sanat Kumara, Ruby Ray,
bring to earth a higher way,
light this planet with your fire,
clothe her in a new attire.

9. Gautama Buddha, I call forth the judgment of Christ upon the leaders on earth who developed an ideology that it was essentially important, epically important, to have uniformity in society by eradicating differences.

Sanat Kumara, Ruby Fire,
you are for all the sanctifier,
the earth is now a holy place,
purified by cosmic grace.

**Sanat Kumara, Ruby Ray,
bring to earth a higher way,
light this planet with your fire,
clothe her in a new attire.**

Part 5

1. Gautama Buddha, I call forth the judgment of Christ upon the people who created a downward spiral where suffering started to manifest, things started to break down, even though the leaders were convinced that they had the right ideology and that therefore, they were creating a sustainable society.

Astrea, loving Being white,
your Presence is my pure delight,
your sword and circle white and blue,
the astral plane is cutting through.

**Astrea, come accelerate,
with purity I do vibrate,
release the fire so blue and white,
my aura filled with vibrant light.**

2. Gautama Buddha, I call forth the judgment of Christ upon the leaders who, even though society started to break down, were not willing to abandon their ideology.

Astrea, calm the raging storm,
so purity will be the norm,
my aura filled with blue and white,
with shining armor, like a knight.

**Astrea, come accelerate,
with purity I do vibrate,
release the fire so blue and white,
my aura filled with vibrant light.**

3. Gautama Buddha, I call forth the judgment of Christ upon the fallen beings who were allowed to embody on earth, so that they would give another opportunity to the inhabitants of the earth and they would themselves receive another opportunity.

Astrea, come and cut me free,
from every binding entity,
let astral forces all be bound,
true freedom I have surely found.

**Astrea, come accelerate,
with purity I do vibrate,
release the fire so blue and white,
my aura filled with vibrant light.**

4. Gautama Buddha, I call forth the judgment of Christ upon the avatars from natural planets who were desiring to help the inhabitants of the earth change, and who were allowed to embody here as a counterbalance to the fallen beings.

Astrea, I sincerely urge,
from demons all, do me purge,
consume them all and take me higher,
I will endure your cleansing fire.

**Astrea, come accelerate,
with purity I do vibrate,
release the fire so blue and white,
my aura filled with vibrant light.**

5. Gautama Buddha, I call forth the judgment of Christ upon the beings on earth who went into a state of wanting to create their own ideology through the anti-christ mind.

Astrea, do all spirits bind,
so that I am no longer blind,
I see the spirit and its twin,
the victory of Christ I win.

Astrea, come accelerate,
with purity I do vibrate,
release the fire so blue and white,
my aura filled with vibrant light.

6. Gautama Buddha, I call forth the judgment of Christ upon the aggressive intent of the fallen beings from the deeper level of the mind of anti-christ.

Astrea, clear my every cell,
from energies of death and hell,
my body is now free to grow,
each cell emits an inner glow.

Astrea, come accelerate,
with purity I do vibrate,
release the fire so blue and white,
my aura filled with vibrant light.

7. Gautama Buddha, I call forth the judgment of Christ upon the mind of anti-christ, which is based on a denial of the guidance coming from spiritual teachers or the ascended masters and the guidance coming from simply observing the difference between our mental image and what is manifest.

Astrea, clear my feeling mind,
in purity my peace I find,
with higher feeling you release,
I co-create in perfect peace.

Astrea, come accelerate,
with purity I do vibrate,
release the fire so blue and white,
my aura filled with vibrant light.

8. Gautama Buddha, I call forth the judgment of Christ upon all beings on earth who went into creating an ideology based on the denial from the mind of anti-christ, thinking they had an ideology that is infallible, and this *is* the way the world works.

Astrea, clear my mental realm,
my Christ self always at the helm,
I see now how to manifest,
the matrix that for all is best.

**Astrea, come accelerate,
with purity I do vibrate,
release the fire so blue and white,
my aura filled with vibrant light.**

9. Gautama Buddha, I call forth the judgment of Christ upon all beings who have fallen and who have lost their innocence because they deny the ascended masters, they deny that there are shortcomings to their ideology.

Astrea, with great clarity,
I claim a new identity,
etheric blueprint I now see,
I co-create more consciously.

**Astrea, come accelerate,
with purity I do vibrate,
release the fire so blue and white,
my aura filled with vibrant light.**

Part 6

1. Gautama Buddha, I call forth the judgment of Christ upon the fallen beings whose entire approach to existence is based on denial.

O Shiva, God of Sacred Fire,
It's time to let the past expire,

I want to rise above the old,
a golden future to unfold.

O Shiva, clear the energy,
O Shiva, bring the synergy,
O Shiva, make all demons flee,
O Shiva, bring back peace to me.

2. Gautama Buddha, I call forth the judgment of Christ upon the fallen beings who have gone into this state of denial and who, in order to justify and uphold the denial, have defined an ideology, which has the only purpose to uphold this denial—nothing must challenge the denial.

O Shiva, come and set me free,
from forces that do limit me,
with fire consume all that is less,
paving way for my success.

O Shiva, clear the energy,
O Shiva, bring the synergy,
O Shiva, make all demons flee,
O Shiva, bring back peace to me.

3. Gautama Buddha, I call forth the judgment of Christ upon the fallen beings who are trapped in this state of denial.

O Shiva, Maya's veil disperse,
clear my private universe,
dispel the consciousness of death,
consume it with your Sacred Breath.

O Shiva, clear the energy,
O Shiva, bring the synergy,
O Shiva, make all demons flee,
O Shiva, bring back peace to me.

4. Gautama Buddha, I call forth the judgment of Christ upon these fallen beings so they might come to the point where the strain of upholding this denial becomes too much.

O Shiva, I hereby let go,
of all attachments here below,
addictive entities consume,
the upward path I do resume.

O Shiva, clear the energy,
O Shiva, bring the synergy,
O Shiva, make all demons flee,
O Shiva, bring back peace to me.

5. Gautama Buddha, I call forth the judgment of Christ upon the fallen beings who for a very long time, even through several spheres, have been in this state of denial, have been in a state of constant tension, so they might have a moment where they see the tension and ask themselves: "Why am I doing this?"

O Shiva, I recite your name,
come banish fear and doubt and shame,
with fire expose within my mind,
what ego seeks to hide behind.

O Shiva, clear the energy,
O Shiva, bring the synergy,
O Shiva, make all demons flee,
O Shiva, bring back peace to me.

6. Gautama Buddha, I call forth the judgment of Christ upon all beings who have encountered fallen beings, so they might have the experience of seeing the utter futility, the utter madness of what the fallen beings are doing.

O Shiva, I am not afraid,
my karmic debt hereby is paid,
the past no longer owns my choice,
in breath of Shiva I rejoice.

O Shiva, clear the energy,
O Shiva, bring the synergy,

O Shiva, make all demons flee,
O Shiva, bring back peace to me.

7. Gautama Buddha, I call forth the judgment of Christ upon the avatars who were pulled in by the ideology of Nazism, by the hypnotic field created by Hitler, so they might be awakened from this hypnotic state, the ideological state of mind.

O Shiva, show me spirit pairs,
that keep me trapped in their affairs,
I choose to see within my mind,
the spirits that you surely bind.

O Shiva, clear the energy,
O Shiva, bring the synergy,
O Shiva, make all demons flee,
O Shiva, bring back peace to me.

8. Gautama Buddha, I call forth the judgment of Christ upon all people who are hypnotized by the ideological state of mind, so they might be awakened without having to experience dramatic physical circumstances.

O Shiva, naked I now stand,
my mind in freedom does expand,
as all my ghosts I do release,
surrender is the key to peace.

O Shiva, clear the energy,
O Shiva, bring the synergy,
O Shiva, make all demons flee,
O Shiva, bring back peace to me.

9. Gautama Buddha, I call forth the judgment of Christ upon all people in the ideological state of mind, so they might acknowledge how the fallen beings act, observe the mindset of the fallen beings, observe the utter pointlessness of it.

O Shiva, all-consuming fire,
with Parvati raise me higher,

when I am raised your light to see,
all men I will draw onto me.

O Shiva, clear the energy,
O Shiva, bring the synergy,
O Shiva, make all demons flee,
O Shiva, bring back peace to me.

Part 7

1. Gautama Buddha, I call forth the judgment of Christ upon the fallen beings who serve as the substitute teachers because they are willing to do what the ascended masters cannot do.

Surya, cosmic being bright,
your balance is my pure delight,
I am in orbit round God Star,
in perfect unity we are.

Surya, banish all extremes,
Surya, shatter Serpent's schemes,
Surya, balance to me bring,
Surya, making my heart sing.

2. Gautama Buddha, I call forth the judgment of Christ upon the fallen beings who are willing to act out the duality consciousness to a greater extreme than the original inhabitants of the earth could conceive of acting it out.

Surya, there is more to life,
than human conflict, war and strife,
your balance gives me inner peace,
all outer conflicts do now cease.

Surya, banish all extremes,
Surya, shatter Serpent's schemes,

Surya, balance to me bring,
Surya, making my heart sing.

3. Gautama Buddha, I call forth the judgment of Christ upon the original inhabitants, so they might see the fallen beings and have a moment of realization: "This is just too much. I do not want to go there."

Surya, what a wondrous sight,
from Sirius you send the light,
of one mind, I now call to thee,
for your apprentice I would be.

Surya, banish all extremes,
Surya, shatter Serpent's schemes,
Surya, balance to me bring,
Surya, making my heart sing.

4. Gautama Buddha, I call forth the judgment of Christ upon the fallen beings who were the mad kings and emperors of the Middle Ages, acting out the madness of a dictatorial form of government where one person had all power and could wage war on a whim or could cause the execution of thousands of people.

Surya, radiate your light,
with balance you set all things right,
consuming energetic dross,
my letting go is not a loss.

Surya, banish all extremes,
Surya, shatter Serpent's schemes,
Surya, balance to me bring,
Surya, making my heart sing.

5. Gautama Buddha, I call forth the judgment of Christ upon all people, so they might see that democracy is a form of government where one person's madness cannot determine the course of a nation.

Surya, your light is alive,
for inner balance I do strive,

the alchemy is now begun,
my heart transformed into a sun.

**Surya, banish all extremes,
Surya, shatter Serpent's schemes,
Surya, balance to me bring,
Surya, making my heart sing.**

6. Gautama Buddha, I call forth the judgment of Christ upon all avatars, so they might see that if they are to fulfill their highest potential on earth, they cannot do so by entering into the ideological mindset that originates with the fallen beings.

Surya, come enlighten me,
duality you help me see,
extremes they cannot pull me in,
on Middle Way I always win.

**Surya, banish all extremes,
Surya, shatter Serpent's schemes,
Surya, balance to me bring,
Surya, making my heart sing.**

7. Gautama Buddha, I call forth the judgment of Christ upon all avatars, so they might see the need and develop the willingness to step up to the Christ mind.

Surya, in your cosmic sphere,
with Cuzco I your light revere,
from your perspective o so grand,
life finally I understand.

**Surya, banish all extremes,
Surya, shatter Serpent's schemes,
Surya, balance to me bring,
Surya, making my heart sing.**

8. Gautama Buddha, I call forth the judgment of Christ upon all ascended master students, who study the teachings but who have not started seeing

the limitations of the ideological mindset, so they might free themselves from this mindset.

> Surya, show me God's design,
> I see that God is all benign,
> you calm my feeling body's storm,
> I know the God beyond all form.

> **Surya, banish all extremes,**
> **Surya, shatter Serpent's schemes,**
> **Surya, balance to me bring,**
> **Surya, making my heart sing.**

9. Gautama Buddha, I call forth the judgment of Christ upon all avatars who came to earth with the vision that we could do what perhaps no one else could do, that we could be the saviors, the ones who came and saved the day, the prince on the white horse.

> Surya, I come from afar,
> and as you show me my home star,
> I see now my internal light,
> a star I am in my own right.

> **Surya, banish all extremes,**
> **Surya, shatter Serpent's schemes,**
> **Surya, balance to me bring,**
> **Surya, making my heart sing.**

Part 8

1. Gautama Buddha, awaken all avatars to see that because of the density of the collective consciousness and free will, we cannot accomplish the vision we had before we came here, yet this does not mean that we have failed.

> Beloved Alpha, God's great plan,
> in Central Sun it all began,

what wondrous vision of a world,
the cosmic spheres were then unfurled.

Beloved Alpha, in your light,
I now see God with inner sight,
as man I will no longer live,
my life to God I fully give.

2. Gautama Buddha, I call forth the judgment of Christ upon the fallen beings who targeted all incoming avatars and exposed us to the cosmic birth trauma.

Beloved Alpha, serve the All,
this is Creator's timeless call,
from out Creator's perfect whole,
sprang lifestreams with a sacred goal.

Beloved Alpha, in your light,
I now see God with inner sight,
as man I will no longer live,
my life to God I fully give.

3. Gautama Buddha, I call forth the judgment of Christ upon the fallen beings who were forcing avatars, and the people who were rejecting us, even aggressively wanting to silence or kill us.

Beloved Alpha, all was one,
as we were sent from Central Sun,
to you we shall in time return,
for cosmic union we do yearn.

Beloved Alpha, in your light,
I now see God with inner sight,
as man I will no longer live,
my life to God I fully give.

4. Gautama Buddha, I call forth the judgment of Christ upon the fallen beings who mercilessly exploit our sense of having failed, perhaps causing us to go into a state of denial where we create the primal self to make sure

that we can never again have that experience of feeling like we have failed and there is something wrong with us.

Beloved Alpha, I now see,
you with Omega form the key,
it was from your polarity,
that I received identity.

Beloved Alpha, in your light,
I now see God with inner sight,
as man I will no longer live,
my life to God I fully give.

5. Gautama Buddha, awaken all avatars to realize that we came here with an unrealistic vision, an *unrealistic ideology,* of what we could accomplish on earth. It does not mean there is something wrong with *us.* We did the best we could based on the level of consciousness we had reached on a natural planet.

Beloved Alpha, cosmic gate,
the nexus of your figure-eight,
I sprang from Cosmic Cube so bright,
I am at heart a spark of light.

Beloved Alpha, in your light,
I now see God with inner sight,
as man I will no longer live,
my life to God I fully give.

6. Gautama Buddha, awaken all avatars to see that it is not a matter of saying we were wrong in some epic way. It is a matter of saying: "But I had the best of intentions for coming to earth. I wanted to free the people on earth from suffering so that they could have the kind of life that I had seen on a natural planet. I formulated the vision based on my good intentions and my level of consciousness and now I have the opportunity to realize that my vision was not realistic, given how earth works, given that the fallen beings are here and how the fallen beings, their state of consciousness, works, given how duality works."

Beloved Alpha, from your womb,
I did descend to matter's tomb,
but buried I will be no more,
my inner vision you restore.

Beloved Alpha, in your light,
I now see God with inner sight,
as man I will no longer live,
my life to God I fully give.

7. Gautama Buddha, awaken all avatars to see our sojourn on planet earth as a tremendous stepping-stone, *many* stepping-stones for our further growth. We have an opportunity to grow because we have come to earth that we would not have had otherwise.

Beloved Alpha, I now know,
the love you did on me bestow,
a co-creator, I will bring,
the light to make all matter sing.

Beloved Alpha, in your light,
I now see God with inner sight,
as man I will no longer live,
my life to God I fully give.

8. Gautama Buddha, awaken all avatars to see that the pain we feel is coming from separate selves that are not who we are. We can transcend the pain by resolving those selves, so we can be free of the pain and look at our interaction with earth as a tremendous learning opportunity. We become free of a self only by seeing that *there is no problem to solve. We just need to let the self die.*

Beloved Alpha, on this earth,
a new age we are giving birth,
for we are here to bring the love,
that you are sending from Above.

Beloved Alpha, in your light,
I now see God with inner sight,

**as man I will no longer live,
my life to God I fully give.**

9. Gautama Buddha, help all avatars see that before we came here, we thought: "There is something I have to do on earth. There is something I have to achieve on earth." The greatest outcome of our sojourn to earth is that we free ourselves from the self that has this belief, so we can just *be* on earth. That is how we pull up the collective consciousness and qualify for our ascension.

Beloved Alpha, you and me,
we form a true polarity,
as up Above, so here below,
with life's own river I do flow.

**Beloved Alpha, in your light,
I now see God with inner sight,
as man I will no longer live,
my life to God I fully give.**

Sealing

In the name of the I AM THAT I AM, I accept that Archangel Michael, Astrea and Shiva form an impenetrable shield around myself and all constructive people, sealing us from all fear-based energies in all four octaves. I accept that the Light of God is consuming and transforming all fear-based energies that make up the dark forces working against ending the era of ideology on earth!

18 THE INESCAPABLE TENSION OF THE IDEOLOGICAL MINDSET

I AM the Ascended Master Gautama Buddha. I trust that those of you who have heard and are willing to study and read the dictation I gave as my last discourse, will realize that free will gives you the right to go into the mindset where you think that you are capable of defining your own environment, the principles that should guide the unfoldment of your world, at least on a planetary level. I trust you recognize that this is an experience that is allowed. It is an *experience* that is allowed. You are allowed to change your *experience*, but you are of course not allowed or capable of changing the way the entire creation works, the way your world of form works, or even the design principles that the Elohim defined when they created your particular planet.

You are allowed to *think* you have changed reality but you are not allowed to change reality—and why is this? Partly because you have a lower state of consciousness, you are still focused on yourself instead of one with the whole. Partly because there are many other beings in your unascended sphere and *your* free will cannot override *their* free will. The purpose of allowing this outplaying of free will in this way, is to give you an experience until you have had enough of the experience and therefore, you are willing to transcend that state of consciousness. What I have called the ideological state of consciousness where you are creating an image in your mind that is out of touch with the reality of how your world of form works. You are allowed to do this to get the experience, but you do not have the power to actually change reality. What does this mean? Well, it means that when you are in the ideological state of mind, you are out of touch with reality, with the reality of how life actually works.

Now, as I said, you are allowed to have the experience that you are creating your own world and you are defining how it should work, but you are not allowed to have that experience forever because that is not what you actually want as the highest self that created the extension of itself that is in embodiment. There has to be a mechanism that can bring you back to an upward path. You are allowed to go into a blind alley but there has to be, no matter how far you go into that blind alley, some mechanism that can pull you back. What is that mechanism? Well, it is the fact that you can create the experience that you are in command, that you are in control of your planet, but the experience exists only in your mind. It does not exist in reality. There is always a tension between reality and the image you have created in your mind. The tension exists only in your mind, but the mechanism works this way that the more you go into seeking to reinforce your image, the more tension you create in your mind. Therefore, there will come a point where your mind breaks, your mind can no longer handle the strain, it can no longer uphold the effort that it takes to reinforce the image. Now, this is something that you can benefit from considering.

The ideological mindset has an element of force

We have talked about natural planets. Those of you who are avatars will be able to lock in to the reality of what we are saying because deep in your memory, you have the experience of being on a natural planet. For the inhabitants of the earth, it can be somewhat more difficult, but some of you will at least remember that there was a state before the planet went into duality. Not necessarily consciously, but you can tune in to it so that you can intuitively sense the reality of what we are saying. What is it that happens on a natural planet? How do you create on a natural planet? We have said that you create essentially the same way you do on an unnatural planet. You formulate a mental image, you project it upon the Ma-ter Light, and the Ma-ter Light takes on the form of the image.

The difference between a natural and an unnatural planet is that on a natural planet, you are formulating the image, first of all, based on a sense that you are connected to your higher self, you are connected to other people, you are part of a whole. You are also formulating it with a fluid mind, an open mind, a liquid mind, a flexible mind. You are doing it for the purpose of learning something. You formulate the image, you project it, you look at the result. Then, you evaluate: "Do I want to refine my mental image based on the results I see?" What does this mean? This means that for you, when you are on a natural planet, you are experiencing that co-creation is an *effortless* process. It does not take effort to co-create on a natural planet, the way it does on an unnatural planet. The reason for this is that the vision you formulate may not be the highest vision, but it is not in opposition to the basic design principles of how your planet operates. It is not seeking to force other people. There is no element of force in your mind. You do not have the attitude that you live in a hostile universe where you need to force your will upon the universe or upon other people. You do not see a need to force anything. You are just projecting the image, you are seeing the result, you are adjusting the image in your mind. Your mind is constantly flexible. You are not fixated on a particular point. You are constantly learning, constantly transcending yourself, constantly growing. For you, co-creation is a process of self-transcendence. It is not a matter of achieving specific outer results. The purpose is not to produce results, but to transcend your level of consciousness.

Now, when you make the switch that we have talked about: We have said you can go into duality, you can become self-centered, you can (as we now say in this teaching) go into the "ideological mindset," there is a switch that happens. You are now no longer in touch with the basic design principles because your whole idea is that you can design your own principles and you can do it better than the beings who designed your world, whether you see it as Elohim, or you see it as God in some ultimate sense. You think, or at least the fallen beings who fell in the fourth sphere, think that they can do better than God, they can design a world in a better way than God can. Now, as I said, the Creator has spent a long time attaining the creator consciousness and therefore has experiences of what works and what does not work.

Even those beings who have set themselves up on these planets in the fourth sphere, they had only had the span of that one sphere and it was an unascended sphere. They had never even experienced an ascended sphere. Naturally, they did not have the awareness of the Creator, but they thought that they were still capable of defining how a world *should* work and they could do it better than God. When you go into this state of mind, you are not seeking to learn, you are formulating a mental image, but it is not as an experiment. Your mental image is a final, absolute image. You believe in your mind: "This is the truth. This is how the world *should* work." Therefore, you are projecting it upon the Ma-ter Light. You are not doing this in order to get feedback that can help you refine your image or your state of consciousness. You want the Ma-ter Light to conform to your mental image and validate your mental image and never challenge your mental image. In this very process, there is an element of force in your mind. There is a tension that has happened because you feel that your image must be out-pictured in exact detail by the Ma-ter Light. If it is not, *you* have failed, you have made a mistake, you are wrong. This is the mindset you go into. Naturally, there is that element of force where you want the Ma-ter Light to conform to your mental image.

The inescapable strain of seeking to force matter

We now have a subtle distinction to make here. We have said that free will reigns supreme and that the inhabitants of a planet have a right to change a lot of things on their planet, including the basic thing of densifying matter, making matter more dense. It is clear that not necessarily one unascended being, but certainly a critical mass of inhabitants of a planet, can change the planet in certain ways, they can change matter on their planet in certain ways. However, they cannot uphold this indefinitely. In order to change matter or to densify matter, force is needed. There needs to be a constant force applied through the minds of people and this means that there is that strain. Individuals feel it. Collectively, humanity on earth feels that strain. This is part of what creates the Sea of Samsara, part of what creates suffering, the constant strain of forcing a mental image upon matter because naturally matter can be changed but only temporarily.

As we have said, the earth is a reality simulator. Matter really is not matter. It is an image that is projected, but there is always a "force" that seeks to return matter to its natural state. There is a possibility that the inhabitants of the planet can take the planet to a lower level, and thereby make the planet an unnatural planet. There is always a "force" that seeks to return matter or return the planet to a natural planet. In other words, de-densifying matter. We have called this "force" the second law of thermo-dynamics to refer to modern science. In Hinduism, it could be called the wrath of Shiva that breaks down all structures. Whatever you call it, there is this "force" and this means that in order to keep matter in a certain state, constant force needs to be applied. This is of course the mechanism that makes it possible for people to get out of duality because they can come to that point where they have just had enough of the strain. They do not want to go into this struggle, this suffering, anymore, they want a way out of it.

What can be changed and what cannot be changed

On the one hand, there is a certain change that can happen on a planet. The inhabitants of a planet can create actual changes in matter, which they then experience through their physical senses. We can say, as just one effect, that human beings on earth are, through your physical senses and your minds, only perceiving the material realm, the physical octave. You are not perceiving the emotional, mental or identity realms or the spiritual realm. A few people, maybe they have clairvoyance, they have second sight whatever you call it, they have intuitive experiences. In general, people are perceiving through their minds only what comes through the physical senses. This is one effect of the densification of matter. There are many others, but as an example. However, has this changed the fact that the world of form, the unascended sphere, earth, has four octaves? Of course not. There are still four octaves. It is just that people cannot see them.

This points to the second aspect of what makes it possible for people to experience that they are in control of their world and they have changed their world. It is that the real change that happens is of course in people's minds. People cannot perceive the three higher octaves, but it does not mean those octaves are not there. It is just that there has been a change in people's minds instead of being a change in how the world actually works.

There are some changes that *can* happen, that the people *can* manifest. You can densify the physical octave and matter in the physical octave, you can also densify the emotional realm and create these energetic vortexes in the mass consciousness, create these beasts, create even demons. You can densify the mental realm so it becomes much more difficult for people to think clearly. You can densify the identity realm that limits how people see what they *can* and *cannot* do as human beings. It does not change reality as such. It changes what the reality simulator is projecting as a temporary image, but the moment your projection upon the Ma-ter Light stops, the Ma-ter Light will start going back to a natural state. In order to uphold it, you need this constant tension.

Now, as I said, people are not actually seeing that there is anything beyond the material world. This is because matter has been densified. There is an energy veil that blocks them, most people, from seeing this. Beyond this, when it comes to the ideology, the mental image that beings are projecting, there is a process that takes place in their own minds. It is the process we have talked about many times where your basic view of life, your worldview, your *ideology* (as we now say) forms a perception filter. The fallen beings are completely obsessive-compulsive, completely frantic, completely fanatic, about maintaining their mental image. They are in as absolute of a state of denial as you can go into. Nothing is absolute in an unascended sphere, nevertheless, they are in a very, very deep state of denial. They absolutely *must* uphold the illusion that they are right, that they cannot be wrong. In order to uphold that illusion, they go into this state of denial, they use a perception filter to filter out anything that contradicts the illusion.

The difference between projection and reality

What you see is that people go into this state of denying certain things that contradicts their ideology, the mental image that they are projecting and that they believe is the reality of how the world actually works. Just to give an example, Marxism defines a certain ideology (whether Karl Marx called it an ideology or not) of how the economy *should* work. In other words, it is stated in Marxism that in a capitalist society, you have an elite, the bourgeoisie, who are exploiting the workers. The only way to avoid having a society where an elite is exploiting the broad population is to have a Marxist economy where everyone consumes according to their need and produces according to their ability. This is the basic principle behind a Marxist economy. The ideology of Marxism, as it was applied in the Soviet Union, projected the mental image that the economy can work this way. People produce according to their ability, but they will still produce enough that everybody can consume according to their need.

In the Soviet Union, there was created this perception filter, which was based on a complete denial of the possibility that the Marxist economy might not work, that the economy might not actually work this way, that it would not be possible to create an economy where everybody produces according to their ability and consumes according to their need. What if the collective need of the entire population was bigger than the collective ability of the population to produce? In other words, what if there were some people that simply did not want to make an effort to produce, they were just focused on consuming everything they could get. You got to a point where the collective level of production was lower than the collective need. Therefore, it limited the economy at a certain level. There was a complete denial of the possibility that this could be a fact, this could be the reality. There was a very, very strong perception filter that was created, that a Marxist economy *must* work. It was also created in China under Mao. What you see is that first of all, from the very beginning, it would have been possible to see that this principle simply does not work. From the very beginning, the Soviet economy was not able to produce enough that everybody could consume according to their need. What did the architects, the ideologists of Marxism have to do? They had to redefine what people were supposed to need. They had to redefine what it meant to be a human being in the Soviet-Marxist state.

They even defined that communism would bring forth a new type of human being. Homo Sovieticus they sometimes called it, and it was defined here that essentially the Homo Sovieticus, would only consume what the economy Sovieticus could produce. This was not what Marxism originally promised. This was an adaptation in order to avoid the realization that a Marxist economy cannot work. You see here that this denial was kept up for decades. You also see the fact that people in the Soviet Union lived at a much lower material standard of living than people in the West did, or in other parts of the world, for that matter.

You see here that the reality is that the mental image created through the Marxist ideology was out of touch with certain economic principles. You do see that, for some time, the Marxist economy could work in the sense that there was not mass starvation and people did have enough to get by. They could live in these very simple apartments, they could go to work, they could buy just enough furniture, just enough food, and so forth. But it was a much lower material standard of living than what you see in nations who are not under the Marxist ideology. Then, gradually, over the decades, there were people in the Soviet Union who started realizing, or at least questioning, whether a Marxist economy could actually work.

There were some people that interacted with the West for example and had a vision, a direct experience, of how people live in the West. They realized there was a huge difference between the standard of living of the average person in the West and the average person in the Soviet Union. It gradually led to where more and more people started overcoming this denial, being able to see beyond the perception filter and ask the question: "Can a Marxist economy actually work?" You also saw, as I said yesterday about China, that after Mao, the ideological approach started fading and there were people in China who questioned whether a Marxist economy could work, which is why they were open to starting more interaction with the West, more economic interaction so that there was an infusion of capital from outside the Marxist economy into China.

Now, there are of course some of you who will know that even during Soviet times, there was an infusion of capital from the West into the Soviet Union because there were certain forces in the western world who wanted to maintain the Soviet Union for a variety of reasons, including of course maintaining the arms race that they were profiting by. Also, simply fallen beings who wanted to maintain that conflict. They did not want the Soviet Union to fall apart. They tried to extend the lifespan of the Soviet Union as far as they could, by this injection of capital from the outside. We can debate whether the Marxist economy actually did work, even to maintain the meager standard of living they had, and could have worked if there was not that influx of capital. But that is beside the point here.

The point is that, if you look at the reality of how the economy works, then from its inception, the Marxist economy was out of touch with reality. You cannot create a society where everybody consumes according to their need and produces according to their ability. You cannot do this on an unnatural planet. You can create it on a natural planet because there is not the resistance. The moment you have the resistance that you have on an unnatural planet, then it cannot work because the basic principle of the economy is what Jesus described in his parable about the talents. When everybody is multiplying their talents, then more will be added from the spiritual realm, which is what happens constantly on a natural planet and that is how an economy on a planet can continue to grow and therefore, the standard of living can continue to be raised.

The only real way to make an economy work is to have the figure-eight flow between the unascended realm and the ascended realm, whereby when people do make an effort to multiply and transcend, then we can multiply their efforts and people receive more in return. That is the only way an economy can function. This is of course not how the ideology of Marxism conceives it, nor the ideology of capitalism, nor the ideology of Neoliberalism, or any other economic philosophy currently there on earth.

Any ideology has an element of denial

What I am pointing out here is this. What beings are having on an unnatural planet is an *experience*. An experience, which is based on this thinking that they can define the principles for how life should work and then the matter world is going to conform to their vision. It is an attempt to create a mental image and force the universe to conform to the image. You can have the experience that you are doing this, but only by going into a state of denial, denying anything that challenges your ideology.

You see that in any ideology, there is that element of denial. I know very well that the teachings that I gave yesterday about avatars and fallen beings, this is beyond what the general public is ready to understand. What I am pointing out here is not beyond what many among the more creative people in the top 10% are ready to grasp. Not in a context that it comes from an ascended being, but I am projecting these ideas into the collective consciousness, using your chakras to magnify this projection. Many people are ready to pick up on the ideas and they are ready to realize that in any ideology, there is an element of denial.

People are refusing to look at: "Does the world actually work as our ideology says it should work?" Whenever there is some indication, some evidence, that the world does not work that way, people go into denial about it. Many people will be able to look back at history and see that there was a certain point where the Catholic church had projected the image that Catholic doctrine was infallible. They had also projected the image that Catholic doctrine about the movements of the stars in the sky was infallible, and they had projected the image that the earth was the center of the universe and all of the heavenly bodies were moving around the earth.

Now, as observations started becoming more accurate, especially after the invention of telescopes, then observations were clearly not in alignment with Catholic doctrine about the earth being the center of the universe. Catholic doctrine attempted to adapt by creating this theory of epicycles, which basically said that whenever there is an anomaly in the movement of the heavenly bodies, this can be explained by some kind of epicycle, meaning we can still maintain the mental image, the ideology, that the earth is the center of the universe. If the earth was proven not to be the center of the universe, then it would be proven that Catholic doctrine was not infallible on this point. If it was not infallible on *this* point, perhaps it was not infallible on *other* points.

The ideological claim of infallibility

You see here, there is another feature of ideologies. Most ideologies have this built-in claim that the mental image that they project, of how the universe works, is infallible in its totality. This means that you now go into a state of mind, which is what I call the denial, where you must deny any evidence to the contrary because if your ideology is proven wrong in one little detail, it questions the claim to infallibility of the entire ideology. When people are in the ideological state of mind, they believe that it is all or nothing. If one little aspect of the ideology is disproved, the entire ideology falls apart. This is of course not necessarily the case. As we have even said before, there are some aspects of Marxist theory, Marxist ideology, that are valid observations. It does not mean that if one aspect of Marxist ideology is disproved, then the entire thing is disproved. It does not mean for example that if the doctrine of the earth being the center of the universe was disproved, necessarily all Catholic doctrine was disproved. But what would be disproved would be the claim to infallibility.

Now, as I have explained, the claim to infallibility comes ultimately from the fallen beings. Nevertheless, many, many people out there are able to see that when you look at history, you see that some of the worst disasters created in history, some of the worst conflicts, have sprung from this desire of one group to uphold the infallibility of the ideology, be it a religion or any other kind of ideology. People will be able to see that the claim of infallibility simply is not constructive, it is not useful. It becomes a straitjacket for human thought because suddenly, you have to think within the boundaries defined by your ideology. If you question the ideology, if you go beyond the ideology, it is a threat to this claim of infallibility and the claim of infallibility overrides everything else and therefore, it becomes a straitjacket. Not just for human thought, but even for human society and behavior.

The feudal societies of the Middle Ages were very tied in to this claim of infallibility of the Catholic doctrine because they were based on, supported by, Catholic doctrine. The entire order of society was threatened if Catholic doctrine was proven not to be infallible. At least that was how it was perceived by the leaders of society. That is why they resisted it. Many, many people today are able to see that this claim of infallibility has created some of the worst disasters and it is time to go beyond it. Many people will be able to see that the claim to infallibility is actually out of touch with the essential process of science.

Ideologies are out of touch with pure science

When you look at science today, you will say that science has been perverted, as I have said before, from its original open process of experimentation or observation, to being restrained by the ideology of Materialism. This is actually out of touch with the basic principles of science, which were expounded upon by a philosopher called Karl Popper, who came up with the observation that a scientific theory is just a working hypothesis. It is not infallible, it is not the final theory, it is not an absolute theory. It is simply a foundation for conducting scientific experiments. Then, when we see the outcome of these scientific experiments, we adjust our theory accordingly.

Now, if you look at what Karl Popper explained, quite a long time ago, you will see it is exactly what I have described here as the very process for co-creation. You have a mental image that is your starting point, you project it onto the Ma-ter Light, but then you evaluate the results and you refine your image. That is what science is meant to do because that is exactly how Saint Germain, in his previous embodiment, set up the scientific method. The scientific method is an attempt to turn planet earth back towards the essential process of co-creation: experimentation, observation, adjustment. *Experimentation, observation, adjustment.* Many people today are able to grasp this, are able to see that the claim to infallibility is out of touch with the reality of how science is supposed to work. Therefore, they can also come to see that Materialism, as an ideology, is out of touch with the basic scientific process, because Materialism is also based on this claim to infallibility.

You look at some of the most ardent materialists, sometimes called the militant atheists, and how they attempt to use science to disprove religion. In the process of doing so, they are making the claim that the absolute reality in the universe is that there is nothing beyond the material world. They also make the implicit claim that this is an infallible ideology. They do not call it an ideology, but it *is* an ideology according to what I have given you here. Many people could come to see that this is simply another ideology. This is simply another attempt to formulate a man-made mental image and project that this image is infallible, and then the state of denial of refusing to see any evidence that challenges the claim to infallibility, challenges the ideology.

We have two aspects of an ideology, there is a mental image and then there is the claim to infallibility. Then, of course you have the denial of anything that challenges the mental image because then the illusion of infallibility would be lost. Who is it that cannot stand losing the illusion of infallibility? Ultimately, the fallen beings, but many, many people can come to see (without knowing about fallen beings) that there is a certain type of people who are attached to, who are obsessive-compulsive about this claim to infallibility.

Infallibility leads to disaster

There is a growing awareness of the psychological phenomenon of narcissists. It is just a matter of time before people start applying this to world leaders known through history and even today, realizing that this person has the narcissistic tendencies and has this obsessive need for infallibility. You see so many of these leaders in the past, you see some of the leaders today that cannot admit they were wrong. It is like the overarching modus operandi for their entire position of power that they can never be wrong.

You see that many of these leaders have attempted to set themselves up in a position where, not only can they not be challenged in their lifetime, but they even want to create a legacy that will endure past their physical lifetime and still maintain this aura of infallibility. You can see in China today, how there is an enormous cult of idolatry around Chairman Mao, the *great* Chairman Mao. It is focused in this physical mausoleum where his mummified body is on display every day, being lowered into a vault and refrozen every night. Or rather, not really his body because most of it is wax, but they still are maintaining the illusion that Mao's body is there, as they are maintaining the illusion that Mao's legacy has never been challenged and that his vision for the communist society of China is still infallible, even though the reality of course is very, very different. You see that many other leaders have attempted to do the same; create this kind of legacy. Many people are able to see this. Many people are able, especially when you make the calls for this, to make that switch and suddenly realize: "When we make this claim to have an infallible ideology, disaster follows." It could be construed as a natural law: *Infallibility leads to disaster.*

Why is this so? Because the claim to infallibility keeps people stuck in a certain framework defined by the ideology. You have an ideology that defines a framework for what human beings can be or not be, do or not do, how a society can function or should function. You have this claim of how society should be and for a time, society might actually function somewhat according to that mental image. You saw that the medieval society, for almost a thousand years, functioned according to the mental image projected by the Catholic church. Society is very much affected by the image, but it is also limited by the image. What really limits society is the claim to infallibility because if there is a claim to infallibility, how can you adjust the ideology? If you cannot adjust the ideology, there will be certain problems in society that you cannot solve. When you look at the feudal societies in the Middle Ages, you could say that there were certain problems that could not be solved. One of those problems was that you could not give the general population a better standard of living than what they had. They lived a very poor material existence, barely surviving, barely having a place to live, barely having enough food to eat, having to work very, very hard without getting any personal benefit from it other than mere survival.

Of course, the general population has a desire to have a certain material standard of living. This is simply something you can observe in human history. There has always been a drive to have better living conditions. Now, we have said that there is a built-in desire for self-transcendence, for experiencing what is more. This ultimately means there is a desire to transcend your level of consciousness and walk the spiritual path. This is the underlying desire that drives this. But because planet earth has sunk to such a low level, matter has been densified, the collective consciousness has been densified, the majority of people are not attuned to this need for self-transcendence, for raising consciousness. There is still the drive that you even see in nature (which is actually the drive behind what Darwin observed as the evolutionary process) and that is the drive for self-transcendence, for growth, for evolution towards a higher state. You see it built into nature and it is also built into human psychology. There has always been a drive for improvement. For the majority of the people on a dense planet like earth, it has been this focus on improving their material lifestyle.

You can go and you can see that in medieval society, there was an artificial economy where the noble class siphoned off the fruits of the people's labor. This caused the people, the general population, to live in an artificial state of poverty, and the people knew this, they knew this was not the way it was supposed to be. Some were not able to formulate it clearly, but there was a general dissatisfaction with the living conditions. There was a general desire for better living conditions and this problem could not be solved in medieval society, partly because there was an ideology that defined a clearly elitist society. A small elite had a privileged position and they could only maintain that position by siphoning off the fruits of the people's labor, which condemned the population to living in a state of poverty.

Then, there was the claim that this society, the structure of society, was tied to the ideology of the Catholic church and that this ideology was infallible. The only way to really have changed the living conditions of the common people was to overthrow the feudal system and the feudal lords. Since this was supported by the Catholic doctrine, which was infallible, this would then mean overthrowing the power that the Catholic Church had over society. You saw that it was not really until the Protestant Reformation that some of the countries in northern Europe overthrew the claim that the Catholic church was infallible and therefore were able to suddenly experience an improvement, at least over time, of the living conditions of the general population. They started a process that caused the feudal system to fall apart, eventually leading to modern democracies, a more liberal economy that then created more affluence for the population.

No ideology could ever be infallible

Many, many people in today's world are ready to make that switch and therefore realize that the first thing that needs to be done away with is the claim to infallibility. There never has been in known history any ideology, any thought and belief system that has been infallible. Some have endured for a time, but they have all eventually been overthrown, or replaced, or refined and changed.

Of course, if something is infallible, it cannot be changed, can it? Because infallibility means it must be perfect and in perfection, there can be no change, at least that is the way it is seen from a state of duality. What many people can come to realize here is that we must do away with this concept that any ideology could be infallible. We must get back to the founding principles of the scientific method where we see our current understanding of the world, our current worldview, our current *ideology*, only as a stepping stone to further progress. Therefore, it is not fixed, it is liquid. Our minds are not fixed on a particular worldview, our minds are liquid. We are willing to search for a higher understanding and we do this by experimenting and then making observations of the results of our experiments. Does it actually work? You observe a Marxist economy. Did it work? Was it possible to raise the standard of living of the general population in an economy where everybody consumed according to their desire and produced according to their ability? Well, clearly it was not. Then, you look at a capitalist economy, does it actually work in terms of increasing the material standard of living of the general population? Well, of course it did not.

You see that back in the 1900s, with the early industrialists who created factories that might have improved the standard of living compared to people living in an agricultural society, but they were still stuck at a certain level of poverty that everybody knew was not enough. There was a need to go away from this strictly capitalist economy (that allowed the capitalist to exploit the workers) and create a more compassionate economy, which is what you see in the modern democracies. The government stepped in and, so to speak, spread the wealth, prevented that the wealth was concentrated in the hands of the elite, but instead spread out in the general population. This is what created an economy that, up until the 1960s, increased the standard of living of the general population.

Then, there was a change in the 1960s and beyond, where many modern democracies shifted into the Neoliberal ideology, which said that there was nothing wrong with concentrating wealth in the hands of an elite because it would increase the amount of wealth. The rising tide would lift all boats, meaning that even though the rich got richer, the general population would also improve its standard of living. As has been proven by the study by the RAND Corporation that we have referred to in several dictations, this is not the case. Since the 1960s, in the United States, the average citizen has experienced a dramatic decrease in their affluence. Money has been pulled away from the general population and concentrated in the hands of a small elite, a *smaller and smaller* elite who have *more and more* money. This is the outcome of a Neoliberal ideology. By looking at this neutrally, we can draw the conclusion: "The Neoliberal ideology does not work in terms of improving the living conditions of the general population."

Since we claim to be a democracy, how can we actually have an economic ideology that concentrates wealth in the hands of a small elite by taking it away from the general population? In other words, as we have said before, Neoliberalism is completely out of touch with basic democratic principles. Once there is a wider recognition of that, people will be able, societies will be able, to say: "It is time to do away with Neoliberalism," as some in the United States have already started saying and acting upon.

How ideologies hold back progress

When you make the switch in your own minds, when you make the calls based on our invocations, you will see that this realization will spread like rings in the water in the collective consciousness. People will be able to recognize that infallibility is a claim that must be given up. It is time to give it up. By doing this one thing, realizing that no ideology is infallible, it is only a stepping stone to progress, this can make a fundamental shift in how societies approach life. It can have many widespread consequences that will improve how societies deal with problems. Instead of formulating an ideology of how the world is *supposed* to work, they can begin to look at: How does the world *actually* work. How does society work? How does the economy work? How does human psychology work? This of course is another topic that I will not go into here because I have given you what I wanted to give you in this installment.

An ideological mindset leads to the formulation of a mental image, the projecting of this mental image upon society and a claim that the ideology is infallible. Therefore, there is no need to even look at how the world actually works. There is no need to look at the actual consequences of implementing this ideology because we need to uphold the infallibility of the ideology, regardless of what the consequences are for people. It is this refusal, this denial, of the need to look at the consequences that an ideology has for the people, that blocks human progress more than any other single factor. When people start realizing this, then all of a sudden, so much progress can be attained that you can barely even conceive of it, that most people will not be able to accept that this would even be possible. As Saint Germain has said several times, he has such wide-ranging plans for the golden age that most people today would not be able to even conceive it, let alone accept it, but it is amazing how much progress can happen.

When you look back at the Western world, you may say: A few hundred years ago, you still had feudal societies and look how limited they were. Look how much growth has happened in those few centuries and look how much the general population's standard of living has improved. I can assure you that when this switch happens (that people give up the infallibility of the ideological approach and go back to an experimental approach) even more progress will happen. Much more progress can happen in the next two or three centuries than has happened in the last two or three centuries. The world can change, society can change, so dramatically that you can really talk about future shock. Of course, when people give up the claim that the ideology is infallible, they will not experience future shock because they will not experience improvement as a threat. Do you see, my beloved, the basic psychology here? To those who were in the ideological mindset and had fixated their minds on the need to uphold the feudal society and the infallibility of Catholic doctrine, the progress that you are now seeing was a threat. It was a direct threat to them. Most people today will say: "Well, clearly, we are better off. Clearly the world is better off today than it was during your feudal societies." For those who were the architects and the leaders of the feudal societies, this improvement was a threat because it was a threat to their privileged position and their sense that they had an infallible worldview.

You can see how, when you give up this claim to infallibility, your minds are no longer fixated, they become liquid. This means that instead of resisting change, resisting improvement, you are flowing with it so there is no future shock. There is just this sense of wonder: "How incredible that life could change so fast, change so much so quickly. How wondrous it is that we have such a better life today than what our parents and grandparents had." This is of course what Saint Germain wants to see. This is of course what all members of the Ascended Host, all ascended masters, want to see.

It is, quite frankly, what a substantial portion of the people on earth want to see. Many, many people, who are what we often call the creative people, the top 10%, they have that genuine desire to see improvement. When they make that switch in the mind of realizing that ideology and the claim of infallibility and the denial that is the inevitable consequence, is really the main hindrance to progress, then they will be willing to give up the ideology—instead of seeking to come up with the ultimate ideology. For that of course is another mechanism that many people are trapped in, the belief that there must be an ultimate theory, a theory of everything, but that is another topic for another discourse.

With this, I seal you in the joyful peace of the Buddha. Gautama Buddha, I AM.

19 INVOKING AWARENESS OF THE INESCAPABLE TENSION (PART 1)

In the name of the I AM THAT I AM, Jesus Christ, I use the authority that I have as a being in embodiment on earth to call upon Gautama Buddha to reinforce my calls and use my chakras to project the statements in this invocation into the collective consciousness and awaken people to the need to free ourselves from the ideological mindset. Awaken people to the reality that we are spiritual beings and that we can co-create a new future by working with the ascended masters. I especially call for …

[Make your own calls here.]

Part 1

1. Gautama Buddha, awaken the most creative people to see that the purpose of allowing the outplaying of free will is to give us an experience, until we have had enough of the experience and therefore, we are willing to transcend that state of consciousness.

Archangel Michael, light so blue,
my heart has room for only you.
My mind is one, no longer two,
your love for me is ever true.

**Archangel Michael, you are here,
consuming now all doubt and fear.
Your Presence is forever near,
you are to me so very dear.**

2. Gautama Buddha, awaken the most creative people to see that we need to transcend the ideological state of consciousness where we are creating an image in our minds that is out of touch with the reality of how our world of form works.

Archangel Michael, I will be,
all one with your reality.
No fear can hold me as I see,
this world no power has o'er me.

**Archangel Michael, you are here,
consuming now all doubt and fear.
Your Presence is forever near,
you are to me so very dear.**

3. Gautama Buddha, awaken the most creative people to see that we are allowed to do this to get the experience, but we do not have the power to actually change reality. When we are in the ideological state of mind, we are out of touch with the reality of how life works.

Archangel Michael, hold me tight,
shatter now the darkest night.
Clear my chakras with your light,
restore to me my inner sight.

**Archangel Michael, you are here,
consuming now all doubt and fear.
Your Presence is forever near,
you are to me so very dear.**

4. Gautama Buddha, awaken the most creative people to see that we are allowed to have the experience that we are creating our own world and we are defining how it should work, but we are not allowed to have that experience forever because that is not what we actually want as the highest self that sent us into embodiment.

Archangel Michael, now I stand,
with you the light I do command.
My heart I ever will expand,
till highest truth I understand.

**Archangel Michael, you are here,
consuming now all doubt and fear.
Your Presence is forever near,
you are to me so very dear.**

5. Gautama Buddha, awaken the most creative people to see that there has to be a mechanism that can bring us back to an upward path. This mechanism is the fact that we can create the experience that we are in command of our planet, but the experience exists only in our minds. It does not exist in reality.

Archangel Michael, in my heart,
from me you never will depart.
Of hierarchy I am a part,
I now accept a fresh new start.

**Archangel Michael, you are here,
consuming now all doubt and fear.
Your Presence is forever near,
you are to me so very dear.**

6. Gautama Buddha, awaken the most creative people to see that there is always a tension between reality and the image we have created in our minds. The tension exists only in our minds, but the mechanism works so that the more we go into seeking to reinforce our image, the more tension we create in our minds.

Archangel Michael, sword of blue,
all darkness you are cutting through.
My Christhood I do now pursue,
discernment shows me what is true.

**Archangel Michael, you are here,
consuming now all doubt and fear.
Your Presence is forever near,
you are to me so very dear.**

7. Gautama Buddha, awaken the most creative people to see that there will come a point where the mind breaks, the mind can no longer handle the strain, it can no longer uphold the effort that it takes to reinforce the image.

Archangel Michael, in your wings,
I now let go of lesser things.
God's homing call in my heart rings,
my heart with yours forever sings.

**Archangel Michael, you are here,
consuming now all doubt and fear.
Your Presence is forever near,
you are to me so very dear.**

8. Gautama Buddha, awaken the most creative people to use their intuition to lock in to the memory of how it was to live on a planet before it went into duality.

Archangel Michael, take me home,
in higher spheres I want to roam.
I am reborn from cosmic foam,
my life is now a sacred poem.

**Archangel Michael, you are here,
consuming now all doubt and fear.
Your Presence is forever near,
you are to me so very dear.**

9. Gautama Buddha, awaken the most creative people to see that ideally, we are formulating our mental image based on a sense that we are connected to our higher selves, we are connected to other people, we are part of a whole.

> Archangel Michael, light you are,
> shining like the bluest star.
> You are a cosmic avatar,
> with you I will go very far.

> **Archangel Michael, you are here,**
> **consuming now all doubt and fear.**
> **Your Presence is forever near,**
> **you are to me so very dear.**

Part 2

1. Gautama Buddha, awaken the most creative people to see that ideally, we are formulating our mental image with a fluid mind, an open mind. We are doing it for the purpose of learning something. We formulate the image, we project it, we look at the result. Then, we evaluate: "Do I want to refine my mental image based on the results I see?"

> O Jesus, blessed brother mine,
> I walk the path that you outline,
> a great example to us all,
> I follow now your inner call.

> **O Jesus, let the Fire of Joy,**
> **consume the devil's subtle ploy,**
> **transfigured is our planet earth,**
> **the golden age is given birth.**

2. Gautama Buddha, awaken the most creative people to see that ideally, co-creation is an effortless process. It does not take effort to co-create on

a natural planet, because our vision is not in opposition to the basic design principles and it is not seeking to force other people.

> O Jesus, open inner sight,
> the ego wants to prove it's right,
> but this I will no longer do,
> I want to be all one with you.

> **O Jesus, let the Fire of Joy,**
> **consume the devil's subtle ploy,**
> **transfigured is our planet earth,**
> **the golden age is given birth.**

3. Gautama Buddha, awaken the most creative people to see that before we go into duality, there is no element of force in our minds. We do not have the attitude that we live in a hostile universe where we need to force our will upon the universe or upon other people.

> O Jesus, I now clearly see,
> the Key of Knowledge given me,
> my Christ self I hereby embrace,
> as you fill up my inner space.

> **O Jesus, let the Fire of Joy,**
> **consume the devil's subtle ploy,**
> **transfigured is our planet earth,**
> **the golden age is given birth.**

4. Gautama Buddha, awaken the most creative people to see that before duality, we do not see a need to force anything. We are just projecting the image, we are seeing the result, we are adjusting the image in our minds. Our minds are constantly flexible, not fixated on a particular point.

> O Jesus, show me serpent's lie,
> expose the beam in my own eye,
> as Christ discernment you me give,
> in oneness I forever live.

**O Jesus, let the Fire of Joy,
consume the devil's subtle ploy,
transfigured is our planet earth,
the golden age is given birth.**

5. Gautama Buddha, awaken the most creative people to see that before duality, we are constantly learning, constantly transcending ourselves, constantly growing. Co-creation is a process of self-transcendence. It is not a matter of achieving specific outer results. The purpose is not to produce results, but to transcend our level of consciousness.

O Jesus, I am truly meek,
and thus I turn the other cheek,
when the accuser attacks me,
I go within and merge with thee.

**O Jesus, let the Fire of Joy,
consume the devil's subtle ploy,
transfigured is our planet earth,
the golden age is given birth.**

6. Gautama Buddha, awaken the most creative people to see that when we make the switch and become self-centered, we go into the "ideological mindset." We are now no longer in touch with the basic design principles because our whole idea is that we can design our own principles and we can do it better than the beings who designed our world.

O Jesus, ego I let die,
surrender ev'ry earthly tie,
the dead can bury what is dead,
I choose to walk with you instead.

**O Jesus, let the Fire of Joy,
consume the devil's subtle ploy,
transfigured is our planet earth,
the golden age is given birth.**

7. Gautama Buddha, awaken the most creative people to see that when we go into this state of mind, we are not seeking to learn. We are formulating

a mental image, but it is not as an experiment. Our mental image is a final, absolute image. We believe in our minds: "This is the truth. This is how the world should work."

O Jesus, help me rise above,
the devil's test through higher love,
show me separate self unreal,
my formless self you do reveal.

**O Jesus, let the Fire of Joy,
consume the devil's subtle ploy,
transfigured is our planet earth,
the golden age is given birth.**

8. Gautama Buddha, awaken the most creative people to see that we are projecting the image upon the Ma-ter Light, but not in order to get feedback that can help us refine our state of consciousness. We want the Ma-ter Light to conform to our mental image and validate the image.

O Jesus, what is that to me,
I just let go and follow thee,
with this I do pass ev'ry test,
to find with you eternal rest.

**O Jesus, let the Fire of Joy,
consume the devil's subtle ploy,
transfigured is our planet earth,
the golden age is given birth.**

9. Gautama Buddha, awaken the most creative people to see that in this process, there is an element of force in our minds. There is a tension that has happened because we feel that our image *must* be out-pictured in exact detail by the Ma-ter Light. If it is not, we have failed, we have made a mistake, we are wrong.

O Jesus, fiery master mine,
my heart now melting into thine,
I love with heart and mind and soul,
the God who is my highest goal.

**O Jesus, let the Fire of Joy,
consume the devil's subtle ploy,
transfigured is our planet earth,
the golden age is given birth.**

Part 3

1. Gautama Buddha, awaken the most creative people to see that because free will reigns supreme, the inhabitants of a planet have a right to change their planet, including densifying matter. They cannot uphold this indefinitely because in order to change or densify matter, force is needed.

Maitreya, I am truly meek,
your counsel wise I humbly seek,
your vision I so want to see,
with you in Eden I will be.

**Maitreya, kindness is the cure,
in fires of kindness I am pure.
Maitreya, now release the fire,
that raises me forever higher.**

2. Gautama Buddha, awaken the most creative people to see that there needs to be a constant force applied through the minds of people and this means that there is a strain. Individuals feel it. Collectively, humanity on earth feels that strain. This is part of what creates the Sea of Samsara, part of what creates suffering, the constant strain of forcing a mental image upon matter because matter can be changed only temporarily.

Maitreya, help me to return,
to learn from you, I truly yearn,
as oneness is all I desire
I feel initiation's fire.

**Maitreya, kindness is the cure,
in fires of kindness I am pure.**

**Maitreya, now release the fire,
that raises me forever higher.**

3. Gautama Buddha, awaken the most creative people to see that the earth is a reality simulator. Matter really is not matter. It is an image that is projected, but there is always a "force" that seeks to return matter to its natural state.

Maitreya, I hereby decide,
from you I will no longer hide,
expose to me the very lie
that caused edenic self to die.

**Maitreya, kindness is the cure,
in fires of kindness I am pure.
Maitreya, now release the fire,
that raises me forever higher.**

4. Gautama Buddha, awaken the most creative people to see that there is a possibility that the inhabitants can take a planet to a lower level, and thereby make the planet an unnatural planet. There is always a "force" that seeks to return matter or return the planet to a natural state.

Maitreya, blessed Guru mine,
my heart of hearts forever thine,
I vow that I will listen well,
so we can break the serpent's spell.

**Maitreya, kindness is the cure,
in fires of kindness I am pure.
Maitreya, now release the fire,
that raises me forever higher.**

5. Gautama Buddha, awaken the most creative people to see that in order to keep matter in a certain state, constant force needs to be applied. This is the mechanism that makes it possible for people to get out of duality, because they can come to a point where they have had enough of that strain. They do not want to go into this struggle, this suffering, anymore, they want a way out of it.

Maitreya, help me see the lie
whereby the serpent broke the tie,
the serpent now has naught in me,
in oneness I am truly free.

**Maitreya, kindness is the cure,
in fires of kindness I am pure.
Maitreya, now release the fire,
that raises me forever higher.**

6. Gautama Buddha, awaken the most creative people to see that the inhabitants of a planet can create actual changes in matter, which they then experience through their physical senses. On earth, people are, through our physical senses and minds, only perceiving the material realm, the physical octave. We are not perceiving the emotional, mental or identity realms or the spiritual realm.

Maitreya, truth does set me free
from falsehoods of duality,
the fruit of knowledge I let go,
so your true spirit I do know.

**Maitreya, kindness is the cure,
in fires of kindness I am pure.
Maitreya, now release the fire,
that raises me forever higher.**

7. Gautama Buddha, awaken the most creative people to see that in general, people are perceiving through their minds only what comes through the physical senses. This is one effect of the densification of matter.

Maitreya, I submit to you,
intentions pure, my heart is true,
from ego I am truly free,
as I am now all one with thee.

**Maitreya, kindness is the cure,
in fires of kindness I am pure.**

**Maitreya, now release the fire,
that raises me forever higher.**

8. Gautama Buddha, awaken the most creative people to see that this
has not changed the fact that earth has four octaves. There are still four
octaves, it is just that people cannot see them.

Maitreya, kindness is the key,
all shades of kindness teach to me,
for I am now the open door,
the Art of Kindness to restore.

**Maitreya, kindness is the cure,
in fires of kindness I am pure.
Maitreya, now release the fire,
that raises me forever higher.**

9. Gautama Buddha, awaken the most creative people to see that what
makes it possible for people to experience that they are in control of their
world and that they have changed their world, is that the real change that
happens is in people's minds. People cannot perceive the three higher
octaves, but it does not mean those octaves are not there. There has been
a change in people's minds instead of a change in how the world works.

Maitreya, oh sweet mystery,
immersed in your reality,
the myst'ry school will now return,
for this, my heart does truly burn.

**Maitreya, kindness is the cure,
in fires of kindness I am pure.
Maitreya, now release the fire,
that raises me forever higher.**

Part 4

1. Gautama Buddha, awaken the most creative people to see that there are some changes that people can manifest. We can densify the physical octave, the emotional realm, the mental realm and the identity realm so we limit how we see ourselves and the world.

> Gautama, show my mental state
> that does give rise to love and hate,
> your exposé I do endure,
> so my perception will be pure.
>
> **Gautama, Flame of Cosmic Peace,**
> **unruly thoughts do hereby cease,**
> **we radiate from you and me**
> **the peace to still Samsara's Sea.**

2. Gautama Buddha, awaken the most creative people to see that this changes what the reality simulator is projecting as a temporary image, but the moment our projection upon the Ma-ter Light stops, the Ma-ter Light will start going back to a natural state. In order to uphold a limited state, we need constant tension.

> Gautama, in your Flame of Peace,
> the struggling self I now release,
> the Buddha Nature I now see,
> it is the core of you and me.
>
> **Gautama, Flame of Cosmic Peace,**
> **unruly thoughts do hereby cease,**
> **we radiate from you and me**
> **the peace to still Samsara's Sea.**

3. Gautama Buddha, awaken the most creative people to see that because matter has been densified, there is an energy veil that blocks our vision of anything beyond the physical realm. Yet there is also a process that takes

place in our own minds. Our worldview, our ideology, forms a perception filter.

Gautama, I am one with thee,
Mara's demons do now flee,
your Presence like a soothing balm,
my mind and senses ever calm.

Gautama, Flame of Cosmic Peace,
unruly thoughts do hereby cease,
we radiate from you and me
the peace to still Samsara's Sea.

4. Gautama Buddha, awaken the most creative people to see that the power elite beings are completely obsessive-compulsive, completely frantic, completely fanatical, about maintaining their mental image. They are in as absolute of a state of denial as one can go into.

Gautama, I now take the vow,
to live in the eternal now,
with you I do transcend all time,
to live in present so sublime.

Gautama, Flame of Cosmic Peace,
unruly thoughts do hereby cease,
we radiate from you and me
the peace to still Samsara's Sea.

5. Gautama Buddha, awaken the most creative people to see that the power elite beings are in a very deep state of denial. They absolutely must uphold the illusion that they are right, that they cannot be wrong. In order to uphold that illusion, they use a perception filter to filter out anything that contradicts the illusion.

Gautama, I have no desire,
to nothing earthly I aspire,
in non-attachment I now rest,
passing Mara's subtle test.

Gautama, Flame of Cosmic Peace,
unruly thoughts do hereby cease,
we radiate from you and me
the peace to still Samsara's Sea.

6. Gautama Buddha, awaken the most creative people to see that many people go into a state of denying certain things that contradict their ideology, the mental image that they are projecting and that they believe is a reality of how the world works.

Gautama, I melt into you,
my mind is one, no longer two,
immersed in your resplendent glow,
Nirvana is all that I know.

Gautama, Flame of Cosmic Peace,
unruly thoughts do hereby cease,
we radiate from you and me
the peace to still Samsara's Sea.

7. Gautama Buddha, awaken the most creative people to see that in the Soviet Union, there was created this perception filter, which was based on a complete denial of the possibility that the Marxist economy might not work, that it would not be possible to create an economy where everybody produces according to their ability and consumes according to their need.

Gautama, in your timeless space,
I am immersed in Cosmic Grace,
I know the God beyond all form,
to world I will no more conform.

Gautama, Flame of Cosmic Peace,
unruly thoughts do hereby cease,
we radiate from you and me
the peace to still Samsara's Sea.

8. Gautama Buddha, awaken the most creative people to see that there was a very strong perception filter that was created, saying that a Marxist

economy *must* work. From the very beginning, the Soviet economy was not able to produce enough that everybody could consume according to their need.

> Gautama, I am now awake,
> I clearly see what is at stake,
> and thus I claim my sacred right
> to be on earth the Buddhic Light.

> **Gautama, Flame of Cosmic Peace,**
> **unruly thoughts do hereby cease,**
> **we radiate from you and me**
> **the peace to still Samsara's Sea.**

9. Gautama Buddha, awaken the most creative people to see that the architects of Marxism had to redefine what people were supposed to need, they even defined that communism would bring forth a new type of human being, Homo Sovieticus, that would only consume what the economy Sovieticus could produce.

> Gautama, with your thunderbolt,
> we give the earth a mighty jolt,
> I know that some will understand,
> and join the Buddha's timeless band.

> **Gautama, Flame of Cosmic Peace,**
> **unruly thoughts do hereby cease,**
> **we radiate from you and me**
> **the peace to still Samsara's Sea.**

Part 5

1. Gautama Buddha, awaken the most creative people to see that this was not what Marxism originally promised. This was an adaptation in order to avoid the realization that a Marxist economy cannot work. This denial was

kept up for decades and people in the Soviet Union lived at a much lower material standard of living than people in the West.

> Sanat Kumara, Ruby Fire,
> I seek my place in love's own choir,
> with open hearts we sing your praise,
> together we the earth do raise.

> **Sanat Kumara, Ruby Ray,**
> **bring to earth a higher way,**
> **light this planet with your fire,**
> **clothe her in a new attire.**

2. Gautama Buddha, awaken the most creative people to see that the mental image created through Marxist ideology was out of touch with certain economic principles. For some time, the Marxist economy could work in the sense that there was not mass starvation and people did have enough to get by.

> Sanat Kumara, Ruby Fire,
> initiations I desire,
> I am for you an electrode,
> Shamballa is my true abode.

> **Sanat Kumara, Ruby Ray,**
> **bring to earth a higher way,**
> **light this planet with your fire,**
> **clothe her in a new attire.**

3. Gautama Buddha, awaken the most creative people to see that if we look at the reality of how the economy works, then from its inception, the Marxist economy was out of touch with reality.

> Sanat Kumara, Ruby Fire,
> I follow path that you require,
> initiate me with your love,
> the open door for Holy Dove.

Sanat Kumara, Ruby Ray,
bring to earth a higher way,
light this planet with your fire,
clothe her in a new attire.

4. Gautama Buddha, awaken the most creative people to see that on an unnatural planet, we cannot create a society where everybody consumes according to their need and produces according to their ability. Because of the resistance on an unnatural planet, it cannot work.

Sanat Kumara, Ruby Fire,
your great example all inspire,
with non-attachment and great mirth,
we give the earth a true rebirth.

Sanat Kumara, Ruby Ray,
bring to earth a higher way,
light this planet with your fire,
clothe her in a new attire.

5. Gautama Buddha, awaken the most creative people to see that the basic principle of the real economy is that when everybody is multiplying their talents, then more will be added from the spiritual realm, and that is how an economy on a planet can continue to grow and the standard of living can continue to be raised.

Sanat Kumara, Ruby Fire,
you are this planet's purifier,
consume on earth all spirits dark,
reveal the inner Spirit Spark.

Sanat Kumara, Ruby Ray,
bring to earth a higher way,
light this planet with your fire,
clothe her in a new attire.

6. Gautama Buddha, awaken the most creative people to see that the only real way to make an economy work is to have the figure-eight flow between the unascended realm and the ascended realm, whereby when people do

make an effort to multiply and transcend, then the ascended masters can multiply our efforts and we receive more in return.

> Sanat Kumara, Ruby Fire,
> you are a cosmic amplifier,
> the lower forces can't withstand,
> vibrations from Venusian band.

> **Sanat Kumara, Ruby Ray,**
> **bring to earth a higher way,**
> **light this planet with your fire,**
> **clothe her in a new attire.**

7. Gautama Buddha, awaken the most creative people to see that on an unnatural planet people are having an *experience*, based on thinking that they can define the principles for how life *should* work and then the matter world is going to conform to their vision.

> Sanat Kumara, Ruby Fire,
> I am on earth your magnifier,
> the flow of love I do restore,
> my chakras are your open door.

> **Sanat Kumara, Ruby Ray,**
> **bring to earth a higher way,**
> **light this planet with your fire,**
> **clothe her in a new attire.**

8. Gautama Buddha, awaken the most creative people to see that this is an attempt to create a mental image and force the universe to conform to the image. We can have the experience that we are doing this, but only by going into a state of denial, denying anything that challenges our ideology.

> Sanat Kumara, Ruby Fire,
> Venusian song the multiplier,
> as we your love reverberate,
> the densest minds we penetrate.

**Sanat Kumara, Ruby Ray,
bring to earth a higher way,
light this planet with your fire,
clothe her in a new attire.**

9. Gautama Buddha, awaken the most creative people to see that in any ideology, there is that element of denial. People are refusing to look at: "Does the world actually work as our ideology says it *should* work?" Whenever there is some indication that the world does not work that way, people go into denial about it.

Sanat Kumara, Ruby Fire,
you are for all the sanctifier,
the earth is now a holy place,
purified by cosmic grace.

**Sanat Kumara, Ruby Ray,
bring to earth a higher way,
light this planet with your fire,
clothe her in a new attire.**

Sealing

In the name of the I AM THAT I AM, I accept that Archangel Michael, Astrea and Shiva form an impenetrable shield around myself and all constructive people, sealing us from all fear-based energies in all four octaves. I accept that the Light of God is consuming and transforming all fear-based energies that make up the dark forces working against ending the era of ideology on earth!

20 INVOKING AWARENESS OF THE INESCAPABLE TENSION (PART 2)

In the name of the I AM THAT I AM, Jesus Christ, I use the authority that I have as a being in embodiment on earth to call upon Gautama Buddha to reinforce my calls and use my chakras to project the statements in this invocation into the collective consciousness and awaken people to the need to free ourselves from the ideological mindset. Awaken people to the reality that we are spiritual beings and that we can co-create a new future by working with the ascended masters. I especially call for …

[Make your own calls here.]

Part 1

1. Gautama Buddha, awaken the most creative people to see that there was a certain point where the Catholic church had projected the image that Catholic doctrine was infallible. They had also projected the image that the earth was the center of the universe and all of the heavenly bodies were moving around it.

Astrea, loving Being white,
your Presence is my pure delight,
your sword and circle white and blue,
the astral plane is cutting through.

Astrea, come accelerate,
with purity I do vibrate,
release the fire so blue and white,
my aura filled with vibrant light.

2. Gautama Buddha, awaken the most creative people to see that as observations became more accurate, they were clearly not in alignment with Catholic doctrine. If the earth was proven not to be the center of the universe, then it would be proven that Catholic doctrine was not infallible.

Astrea, calm the raging storm,
so purity will be the norm,
my aura filled with blue and white,
with shining armor, like a knight.

Astrea, come accelerate,
with purity I do vibrate,
release the fire so blue and white,
my aura filled with vibrant light.

3. Gautama Buddha, awaken the most creative people to see that most ideologies have this built-in claim that the mental image they project, of how the universe works, is infallible in its totality. This means that we now go into a state of mind, where we must deny any evidence to the contrary because if our ideology is proven wrong in one detail, it questions the claim to infallibility.

Astrea, come and cut me free,
from every binding entity,
let astral forces all be bound,
true freedom I have surely found.

Astrea, come accelerate,
with purity I do vibrate,

release the fire so blue and white,
my aura filled with vibrant light.

4. Gautama Buddha, awaken the most creative people to see that when people are in the ideological state of mind, they believe that it is all or nothing. If one little aspect of the ideology is disproven, the entire ideology falls apart.

Astrea, I sincerely urge,
from demons all, do me purge,
consume them all and take me higher,
I will endure your cleansing fire.

Astrea, come accelerate,
with purity I do vibrate,
release the fire so blue and white,
my aura filled with vibrant light.

5. Gautama Buddha, awaken the most creative people to see that when we look at history, we see that some of the worst disasters, some of the worst conflicts, have sprung from this desire of one group to uphold the infallibility of the ideology, be it a religion or any other kind of ideology.

Astrea, do all spirits bind,
so that I am no longer blind,
I see the spirit and its twin,
the victory of Christ I win.

Astrea, come accelerate,
with purity I do vibrate,
release the fire so blue and white,
my aura filled with vibrant light.

6. Gautama Buddha, awaken the most creative people to see that the claim of infallibility is not constructive, it is not useful. It becomes a straitjacket for human thought because suddenly, we have to think within the boundaries defined by our ideology.

Astrea, clear my every cell,
from energies of death and hell,
my body is now free to grow,
each cell emits an inner glow.

Astrea, come accelerate,
with purity I do vibrate,
release the fire so blue and white,
my aura filled with vibrant light.

7. Gautama Buddha, awaken the most creative people to see that if we question the ideology, it is a threat to the claim of infallibility. The claim of infallibility overrides everything else and therefore, it becomes a straitjacket—not just for human thought, but even for human society and behavior.

Astrea, clear my feeling mind,
in purity my peace I find,
with higher feeling you release,
I co-create in perfect peace.

Astrea, come accelerate,
with purity I do vibrate,
release the fire so blue and white,
my aura filled with vibrant light.

8. Gautama Buddha, awaken the most creative people to see that the feudal societies of the Middle Ages were tied in to the claim of infallibility of Catholic doctrine. The entire order of society was threatened if Catholic doctrine was proven not to be infallible. At least that was how it was perceived by the leaders of society.

Astrea, clear my mental realm,
my Christ self always at the helm,
I see now how to manifest,
the matrix that for all is best.

Astrea, come accelerate,
with purity I do vibrate,

**release the fire so blue and white,
my aura filled with vibrant light.**

9. Gautama Buddha, awaken the most creative people to see that this claim of infallibility has created some of the worst disasters and it is time to go beyond it. The claim to infallibility is out of touch with the essential process of science.

Astrea, with great clarity,
I claim a new identity,
etheric blueprint I now see,
I co-create more consciously.

**Astrea, come accelerate,
with purity I do vibrate,
release the fire so blue and white,
my aura filled with vibrant light.**

Part 2

1. Gautama Buddha, awaken the most creative people to see that science has been perverted from its original open process of experimentation or observation, to being restrained by the ideology of Materialism.

O Saint Germain, you do inspire,
my vision raised forever higher,
with you I form a figure-eight,
your Golden Age I co-create.

**O Saint Germain, what love you bring,
it truly makes all matter sing,
your violet flame does all restore,
with you we are becoming more.**

2. Gautama Buddha, awaken the most creative people to see that this is out of touch with the basic principles of science, namely that a scientific theory is a working hypothesis. It is not infallible, it is not the final theory, it is

not an absolute theory. It is simply a foundation for conducting scientific experiments. When we see the outcome of these scientific experiments, we adjust our theory accordingly.

> O Saint Germain, what Freedom Flame,
> released when we recite your name,
> acceleration is your gift,
> our planet it will surely lift.

> **O Saint Germain, what love you bring,**
> **it truly makes all matter sing,**
> **your violet flame does all restore,**
> **with you we are becoming more.**

3. Gautama Buddha, awaken the most creative people to see that this is the very process for co-creation. The scientific method is an attempt to turn planet earth back towards the essential process of co-creation: experimentation, observation, adjustment.

> O Saint Germain, in love we claim,
> our right to bring your violet flame,
> from you Above, to us below,
> it is an all-transforming flow.

> **O Saint Germain, what love you bring,**
> **it truly makes all matter sing,**
> **your violet flame does all restore,**
> **with you we are becoming more.**

4. Gautama Buddha, awaken the most creative people to see that the claim to infallibility is out of touch with the reality of how science is supposed to work. Materialism, as an ideology, is out of touch with the basic scientific process, because Materialism is also based on this claim to infallibility.

> O Saint Germain, I love you so,
> my aura filled with violet glow,
> my chakras filled with violet fire,
> I am your cosmic amplifier.

**O Saint Germain, what love you bring,
it truly makes all matter sing,
your violet flame does all restore,
with you we are becoming more.**

5. Gautama Buddha, awaken the most creative people to see that the most ardent materialists attempt to use science to disprove religion. In the process of doing so, they are making the claim that the absolute reality in the universe is that there is nothing beyond the material world. They also make the implicit claim that this is an infallible ideology.

O Saint Germain, I am now free,
your violet flame is therapy,
transform all hang-ups in my mind,
as inner peace I surely find.

**O Saint Germain, what love you bring,
it truly makes all matter sing,
your violet flame does all restore,
with you we are becoming more.**

6. Gautama Buddha, awaken the most creative people to see that atheists do not call it an ideology, but it *is* simply another ideology. This is another attempt to formulate a man-made mental image and project that this image is infallible, and then people go into the state of denial of refusing to see any evidence that challenges the claim to infallibility.

O Saint Germain, my body pure,
your violet flame for all is cure,
consume the cause of all disease,
and therefore I am all at ease.

**O Saint Germain, what love you bring,
it truly makes all matter sing,
your violet flame does all restore,
with you we are becoming more.**

7. Gautama Buddha, awaken the most creative people to see that there are two aspects of an ideology, a mental image and the claim to infallibility.

Then, there is the denial of anything that challenges the mental image because then the illusion of infallibility would be lost.

> O Saint Germain, I'm karma-free,
> the past no longer burdens me,
> a brand new opportunity,
> I am in Christic unity.

> **O Saint Germain, what love you bring,**
> **it truly makes all matter sing,**
> **your violet flame does all restore,**
> **with you we are becoming more.**

8. Gautama Buddha, awaken the most creative people to see that there is a certain type of people who are attached to, who are obsessive-compulsive about this claim to infallibility. They are called narcissists, and it is time to apply this to world leaders known throughout history and today.

> O Saint Germain, we are now one,
> I am for you a violet sun,
> as we transform this planet earth,
> your Golden Age is given birth.

> **O Saint Germain, what love you bring,**
> **it truly makes all matter sing,**
> **your violet flame does all restore,**
> **with you we are becoming more.**

9. Gautama Buddha, awaken the most creative people to see that members of the power elite have narcissistic tendencies and an obsessive need for infallibility. Many of the leaders in the past and some of the leaders today cannot admit they were wrong. The overarching modus operandi for their entire position of power is that they can never be wrong.

> O Saint Germain, the earth is free,
> from burden of duality,
> in oneness we bring what is best,
> your Golden Age is manifest.

O Saint Germain, what love you bring,
it truly makes all matter sing,
your violet flame does all restore,
with you we are becoming more.

Part 3

1. Gautama Buddha, awaken the most creative people to see that many leaders have attempted to set themselves up in a position where, not only can they not be challenged in their lifetime, but they even want to create a legacy that will endure past their physical lifetime and still maintain this aura of infallibility.

Divine Director, I now see,
the world is unreality,
in my heart I now truly feel,
the Spirit is all that is real.

Divine Director, send the light,
from blindness clear my inner sight,
my vision free, my vision clear,
your guidance is forever here.

2. Gautama Buddha, awaken the most creative people to see that many leaders have attempted to create a legacy of infallibility. Yet when we make this claim to have an infallible ideology, disaster follows. It is a natural law: *Infallibility leads to disaster.*

Divine Director, vision give,
in clarity I want to live,
I now behold my plan Divine,
the plan that is uniquely mine.

Divine Director, send the light,
from blindness clear my inner sight,

**my vision free, my vision clear,
your guidance is forever here.**

3. Gautama Buddha, awaken the most creative people to see that the claim to infallibility keeps people stuck in a certain framework defined by an ideology. We have an ideology that defines a framework for what human beings can be or not be, do or not do, how a society can function or should function.

Divine Director, show in me,
the ego games, and set me free,
help me escape the ego's cage,
to help bring in the golden age.

**Divine Director, send the light,
from blindness clear my inner sight,
my vision free, my vision clear,
your guidance is forever here.**

4. Gautama Buddha, awaken the most creative people to see that we have a claim of how society should be, and for a time society might actually function somewhat according to the mental image. Yet if there is a claim to infallibility, how can society adjust to changes?

Divine Director, I'm with you,
my vision one, no longer two,
as karma's veil you do disperse,
I see a whole new universe.

**Divine Director, send the light,
from blindness clear my inner sight,
my vision free, my vision clear,
your guidance is forever here.**

5. Gautama Buddha, awaken the most creative people to see that if we cannot adjust the ideology, there will be certain problems in society that we cannot solve. In the feudal societies in the Middle Ages, certain problems could not be solved.

Divine Director, I go up,
electric light now fills my cup,
consume in me all shadows old,
bestow on me a vision bold.

**Divine Director, send the light,
from blindness clear my inner sight,
my vision free, my vision clear,
your guidance is forever here.**

6. Gautama Buddha, awaken the most creative people to see that the general population has a desire to have a certain material standard of living. The drive for self-transcendence, for growth, for evolution towards a higher state is built into nature and it is also built into human psychology.

Divine Director, heart of gold,
my sacred labor I unfold,
o blessed Guru, I now see,
where my own plan is taking me.

**Divine Director, send the light,
from blindness clear my inner sight,
my vision free, my vision clear,
your guidance is forever here.**

7. Gautama Buddha, awaken the most creative people to see that in medieval society, there was an artificial economy where the noble class siphoned off the fruits of the people's labor. This caused the general population to live in an artificial state of poverty, and the people knew this was not the way it was supposed to be.

Divine Director, by your grace,
in grander scheme I find my place,
my individual flame I see,
uniqueness God has given me.

**Divine Director, send the light,
from blindness clear my inner sight,**

my vision free, my vision clear,
your guidance is forever here.

8. Gautama Buddha, awaken the most creative people to see that there was a general desire for better living conditions and this problem could not be solved in medieval society, partly because there was an ideology that defined a clearly elitist society with a small elite in a privileged position.

Divine Director, vision one,
I see that I AM God's own Sun,
with your direction so Divine,
I am now letting my light shine.

Divine Director, send the light,
from blindness clear my inner sight,
my vision free, my vision clear,
your guidance is forever here.

9. Gautama Buddha, awaken the most creative people to see that there was also the claim that this society was tied to the ideology of the Catholic church and that this ideology was infallible. The only way to have changed the living conditions of the common people was to overthrow the power that the Catholic church had over society.

Divine Director, what a gift,
to be a part of Spirit's lift,
to raise mankind out of the night,
to bask in Spirit's loving sight.

Divine Director, send the light,
from blindness clear my inner sight,
my vision free, my vision clear,
your guidance is forever here.

Part 4

1. Gautama Buddha, awaken the most creative people to see that it was only when countries in northern Europe overthrew the claim that the Catholic church was infallible that a process began that caused the feudal system to fall apart, eventually leading to modern democracies, and a more liberal economy that created more affluence for the population.

O Shiva, God of Sacred Fire,
It's time to let the past expire,
I want to rise above the old,
a golden future to unfold.

O Shiva, clear the energy,
O Shiva, bring the synergy,
O Shiva, make all demons flee,
O Shiva, bring back peace to me.

2. Gautama Buddha, awaken the most creative people to see that the first thing that needs to be done away with is the claim to infallibility. There never has been any ideology, any thought and belief system that has been infallible. Some have endured for a time, but they have all eventually been overthrown, replaced or changed.

O Shiva, come and set me free,
from forces that do limit me,
with fire consume all that is less,
paving way for my success.

O Shiva, clear the energy,
O Shiva, bring the synergy,
O Shiva, make all demons flee,
O Shiva, bring back peace to me.

3. Gautama Buddha, awaken the most creative people to see that if something is infallible, it cannot be changed. Infallibility means it must be perfect and in perfection, there can be no change, at least that is the way it is seen from a state of duality.

O Shiva, Maya's veil disperse,
clear my private universe,
dispel the consciousness of death,
consume it with your Sacred Breath.

O Shiva, clear the energy,
O Shiva, bring the synergy,
O Shiva, make all demons flee,
O Shiva, bring back peace to me.

4. Gautama Buddha, awaken the most creative people to see that we must do away with this concept that any ideology could be infallible. We must get back to the founding principles of the scientific method where we see our current understanding of the world, our current worldview, our current *ideology,* only as a stepping stone to further progress.

O Shiva, I hereby let go,
of all attachments here below,
addictive entities consume,
the upward path I do resume.

O Shiva, clear the energy,
O Shiva, bring the synergy,
O Shiva, make all demons flee,
O Shiva, bring back peace to me.

5. Gautama Buddha, awaken the most creative people to accept that our world view is not fixed; it is liquid. Our minds are not fixed on a particular worldview, our minds are liquid. We are willing to search for a higher understanding and we do this by experimenting and then making observations of the results of our experiments. Does it actually work?

O Shiva, I recite your name,
come banish fear and doubt and shame,
with fire expose within my mind,
what ego seeks to hide behind.

O Shiva, clear the energy,
O Shiva, bring the synergy,

O Shiva, make all demons flee,
O Shiva, bring back peace to me.

6. Gautama Buddha, awaken the most creative people to see that a Marxist economy did not raise the standard of living of the general population, but concentrated power in the hands of the party elite. Yet a capitalist economy also tends to concentrate wealth and power in the hands of a small elite, decreasing the material standard of living of the general population.

O Shiva, I am not afraid,
my karmic debt hereby is paid,
the past no longer owns my choice,
in breath of Shiva I rejoice.

O Shiva, clear the energy,
O Shiva, bring the synergy,
O Shiva, make all demons flee,
O Shiva, bring back peace to me.

7. Gautama Buddha, awaken the most creative people to see that there is a need to go away from a strictly capitalist economy and create a more compassionate economy, as we see in some modern democracies. The government must prevent that the wealth is concentrated in the hands of the elite, but instead spread out in the general population.

O Shiva, show me spirit pairs,
that keep me trapped in their affairs,
I choose to see within my mind,
the spirits that you surely bind.

O Shiva, clear the energy,
O Shiva, bring the synergy,
O Shiva, make all demons flee,
O Shiva, bring back peace to me.

8. Gautama Buddha, awaken the most creative people to see that in the 1960s and beyond, many modern democracies shifted into the Neoliberal ideology, which has caused the average citizen to have a dramatic decrease in their affluence.

O Shiva, naked I now stand,
my mind in freedom does expand,
as all my ghosts I do release,
surrender is the key to peace.

O Shiva, clear the energy,
O Shiva, bring the synergy,
O Shiva, make all demons flee,
O Shiva, bring back peace to me.

9. Gautama Buddha, awaken the most creative people to see that a Neo-liberal ideology does not work in terms of improving the living conditions of the general population. Neoliberalism is completely out of touch with basic democratic principles. It is time to do away with Neoliberalism.

O Shiva, all-consuming fire,
with Parvati raise me higher,
when I am raised your light to see,
all men I will draw onto me.

O Shiva, clear the energy,
O Shiva, bring the synergy,
O Shiva, make all demons flee,
O Shiva, bring back peace to me.

Part 5

1. Gautama Buddha, awaken the most creative people to see that infallibility is a claim that must be given up. By doing this one thing, realizing that no ideology is infallible, it is only a stepping stone to progress, this can make a fundamental shift in how societies approach life.

Surya, cosmic being bright,
your balance is my pure delight,
I am in orbit round God Star,
in perfect unity we are.

Surya, banish all extremes,
Surya, shatter Serpent's schemes,
Surya, balance to me bring,
Surya, making my heart sing.

2. Gautama Buddha, awaken the most creative people to see that instead of formulating an ideology of how the world is supposed to work, we can begin to look at: How does the world actually work. How does society work? How does the economy work? How does human psychology work?

Surya, there is more to life,
than human conflict, war and strife,
your balance gives me inner peace,
all outer conflicts do now cease.

Surya, banish all extremes,
Surya, shatter Serpent's schemes,
Surya, balance to me bring,
Surya, making my heart sing.

3. Gautama Buddha, awaken the most creative people to see that the ideological mindset leads to the formulation of a mental image, the projecting of this mental image upon society and a claim that the ideology is infallible. Therefore, there is no need to even look at how the world actually works.

Surya, what a wondrous sight,
from Sirius you send the light,
of one mind, I now call to thee,
for your apprentice I would be.

Surya, banish all extremes,
Surya, shatter Serpent's schemes,
Surya, balance to me bring,
Surya, making my heart sing.

4. Gautama Buddha, awaken the most creative people to see that in the ideological mindset, there is no need to look at the actual consequences of implementing this ideology, because we need to uphold the infallibility of the ideology, regardless of what the consequences are for people.

Surya, radiate your light,
with balance you set all things right,
consuming energetic dross,
my letting go is not a loss.

**Surya, banish all extremes,
Surya, shatter Serpent's schemes,
Surya, balance to me bring,
Surya, making my heart sing.**

5. Gautama Buddha, awaken the most creative people to see that this refusal, this denial, of the need to look at the consequences that an ideology has for the people, blocks human progress more than any other single factor.

Surya, your light is alive,
for inner balance I do strive,
the alchemy is now begun,
my heart transformed into a sun.

**Surya, banish all extremes,
Surya, shatter Serpent's schemes,
Surya, balance to me bring,
Surya, making my heart sing.**

6. Gautama Buddha, awaken the most creative people to see that when we realize this, so much progress can be attained that most people can barely even conceive of it.

Surya, come enlighten me,
duality you help me see,
extremes they cannot pull me in,
on Middle Way I always win.

**Surya, banish all extremes,
Surya, shatter Serpent's schemes,
Surya, balance to me bring,
Surya, making my heart sing.**

7. Gautama Buddha, awaken the most creative people to see that when we give up the infallibility of the ideological approach and go back to an experimental approach, more progress can happen in the next two or three centuries than has happened in the last two or three centuries. The world can change so dramatically that we can really talk about future shock.

Surya, in your cosmic sphere,
with Cuzco I your light revere,
from your perspective o so grand,
life finally I understand.

Surya, banish all extremes,
Surya, shatter Serpent's schemes,
Surya, balance to me bring,
Surya, making my heart sing.

8. Gautama Buddha, awaken the most creative people to see that when we give up the claim that the ideology is infallible, we will not experience future shock because we will not experience improvement as a threat. People in the ideological mindset see progress as a direct threat to them.

Surya, show me God's design,
I see that God is all benign,
you calm my feeling body's storm,
I know the God beyond all form.

Surya, banish all extremes,
Surya, shatter Serpent's schemes,
Surya, balance to me bring,
Surya, making my heart sing.

9. Gautama Buddha, awaken the most creative people to see that we have that genuine desire to see improvement. When we realize that ideology and the claim of infallibility is the main hindrance to progress, then we will be willing to give up the ideology, instead of seeking to come up with the ultimate ideology. This will bring the changes we desire to see.

Surya, I come from afar,
and as you show me my home star,

I see now my internal light,
a star I am in my own right.

Surya, banish all extremes,
Surya, shatter Serpent's schemes,
Surya, balance to me bring,
Surya, making my heart sing.

Sealing

In the name of the I AM THAT I AM, I accept that Archangel Michael, Astrea and Shiva form an impenetrable shield around myself and all constructive people, sealing us from all fear-based energies in all four octaves. I accept that the Light of God is consuming and transforming all fear-based energies that make up the dark forces working against ending the era of ideology on earth!

21 HOW IDEOLOGY LIMITS HUMAN PROGRESS

I AM the Ascended Master Gautama Buddha. What have I said about people's reaction to ideology? Let us exemplify it. In many European nations, you saw that during the 60s and 70s, there was a certain group of young people that were pulled into the ideological mindset created by Marxism, socialism, or whatever you want to call it. These people then later came to the realization that Marxism, Marxist ideology, was not what they believed it was and could not fulfill the promises it was making. Some came to this realization when the Soviet Union collapsed. Some came to it before, some after the Soviet Union collapsed. They transferred their allegiance to China, thinking that China would be the communist utopia. But most of them later had to give up on that also, when they started realizing what was actually happening in China and how there was a lack of fundamental human rights.

What was the reaction that people had to this? Some people went into the state of thinking that even though Marxism was not the ultimate ideology, there had to be an ultimate ideology. They started looking for it, and some of them are still looking for the ultimate ideology. Some have found what they think is an ultimate ideology. Some have even found a spiritual teaching that they think is the ultimate ideology. Other people have become discouraged with ideology and have, so to speak, switched into the opposite extreme of what we might call agnosticism or complete disillusionment. They think that either there is no ultimate ideology, or you can never know what the ultimate truth is, or there is no truth whatsoever, there are no higher principles, there is no way to really determine what is a higher truth because human beings are what human beings are. They are trapped in a lower state of consciousness, and they are always fighting, and we will never get beyond it. In other words, there is a certain group of people that have been very enthusiastic about the ideological approach and have become very disillusioned and disappointed with that approach, giving up on the quest to find a higher understanding.

Some of these people can by your calls be able to snap out of this mindset and realize that this is exactly what the fallen beings want to see happen. As I have said before, the fallen beings want to pull those who have the capacity to bring change into either submitting to an ideology or opposing it so that they are fighting the ideology, which means they are trapped in reacting to an ideology defined by the fallen beings. Therefore, their minds are not open to looking for a higher view. There is of course also the possibility that the fallen beings can make some of these people so disillusioned with an ideology that they give up trying to think there is any kind of higher understanding—I am deliberately not saying "higher truth." I am saying, higher understanding. This of course is a very unfortunate occurrence, and some people will be able to snap out of it and see that they cannot allow themselves to be discouraged this way. The reality of the situation is that, as I have attempted to explain in great detail, there is no ultimate ideology.

There is no ultimate truth on earth

There is in fact no ultimate truth that could ever be brought forth, but there is always the possibility of attaining a higher understanding than what you have right now. This is the basic principle behind science. As I described it, you need to have a foundation for your scientific inquiry. You need to have some foundation for understanding life on earth. You have a starting point, but when you do not see it as an ultimate ideology that has to be infallible and perfect, you see it as just a starting point for increasing your understanding. You experiment, you make observations, and then you use that to refine your understanding.

Many people are ready to see that if you look back at known history, you can say that the process that human beings have been going through is a process of raising the understanding of life. Why do you have so much more knowledge today than people had 2,000 or 5,000 years ago? Why do you have so much more technology? Why do many people (in the developed world at least) have a better standard of living than people had in past millennia and centuries? It is because you have a greater understanding of how life works.

You can see when you look at human history that there has been a certain progression in understanding. Many people will be able to see, and are able to see, that this has not been an entirely smooth process. There have been some dramatic shifts. There have been certain periods of time where the expansion of understanding almost came to a halt for a very long time. As we have said, during the so-called Dark Ages, there was still some expansion of understanding, but much slower than it has been in the last century or so. Many people are able to see this and are able to consider why this happens. Therefore, they can come to see that what actually slowed down the expansion of knowledge was that society had become trapped in a specific ideology. They thought it was infallible, and the effect was that this closed people's minds. The society was not able to think beyond the ideology; it was not able to ask questions beyond the ideology. This of course slows down the expansion of knowledge.

What is the basis for the expansion of knowledge? It is that you expand your present understanding. How do you do this? By asking questions that go *beyond* your present understanding. If you could not ask questions that are beyond a certain framework, how could you ever transcend that framework? *It cannot be done,* my beloved. This is just simple mechanics of how the expansion of knowledge works.

Some principles are independent of human beliefs

This then leads to another perspective, or another way of saying the same thing, where many people today are ready to realize that when you observe life on earth, you can see that there are certain mechanics of how the world works that are not dependent on human beliefs. They are timeless. They are universal principles. Regardless of what people have believed in certain time periods, the mechanics were not changed by that. It is very, very simple. There have been time periods where people had the belief that a particular ideology was infallible, and they should never question it or think beyond it. This always slowed down the expansion of knowledge. It can be no other way. You look at the medieval societies and the Dark

Ages and you see it so clearly. You look at the Soviet Union, and you see it so clearly.

Why did the Soviet Union collapse? For a variety of reasons. As we have talked about, one reason was that because of the belief in Marxist ideology and this ideology being infallible, there was a limit to what Soviet scientists could discover. There was a limit to how much knowledge could be expanded in the Soviet Union because of the ideological constraints. In the West, where they did not have those strict ideological constraints, science during the 60s and 70s and 80s started making progress beyond what was being made in the Soviet Union. Therefore, it was simply inevitable that there would come a time where the West would be so far ahead of the Soviet Union scientifically that the Soviet Union could not keep up in the arms race. They could not keep creating weapons that could defend themselves against what the West was creating. You see this exemplified in the entire debate created when Ronald Reagan proposed his Star Wars Defense, space-based weapons that could shoot down ICBMs with nuclear warheads. Therefore, in essence, make nuclear war obsolete or impossible. Whether this was a realistic technology at the time or not, this actually caused many people in the Soviet Union to realize that they were in the process of falling irreversibly behind the West. They simply could not keep up this sort of stalemate in technology that had kept the Cold War from becoming a hot war, that had maintained some kind of peaceful coexistence between the two systems. Therefore, they started realizing that the Soviet Union had an expiration date, and it was coming up quicker than anyone thought.

Many, many people around the world are able to see this or come to see this very quickly as you reinforce these ideas with your calls, even as they have been projected into the collective consciousness during this conference. Many people will see it. They will be able to give up this ideological approach, at least the belief that an ideology is infallible or that there must be some ultimate ideology that has not yet been discovered or developed. Therefore, they can take the more pragmatic scientific approach of saying: "Let us attempt to discover the mechanics of how life actually works. We can base our society on those mechanics instead."

A society based on observations of how life works

What will such a society based on an observation of the mechanics of the world look like? Well, first of all, it will not be a dictatorship. It will not be a society that is steeped in fanaticism. It will not be a society that is elitist. Therefore, it will be a society that has quite some resemblance with what you see in what we call the modern democracies. Democracy is a society that is based on some observation, some understanding, of the mechanics of how life works, which is that all people are connected, all people are equal. This is what you can actually see when you look at human history where you see that elitist societies, as you have seen so many times in the past, have always led to some form of conflict or disaster. There has always been an internal tension, and there has always been the suppression of the majority of the population who have been limited by the elite.

When you observe how human history has unfolded, you see that you can either have these kinds of unbalanced elitist societies, dictatorships, or you can move towards a more democratic form of government where all of the people have some influence, and where there is more of an equality between people. You can also see that the elitist societies were very deeply divided societies. There was a fundamental difference between the elite and the population, perhaps even different groups in the population, as you have seen divisions based on many different things. Many people today are able to see that in order to move into a better society that gives better living conditions to the people, greater freedom, then humankind needs to make an effort to overcome division; the entire idea that people can be divided into separate groups.

Division is inherent in ideologies

Now, what is it that divides people? When you take my explanation of the worldly definition of ideology, you will see that there is a very deep division inherent in all ideologies. They give a certain explanation of how the world works. It is claimed to be ultimate and infallible usually, which creates a greater division between those who accept this explanation and those who do not. As I have said, because of duality and the mechanics of duality, you can never get all people to accept the same idea. A democracy is actually not based on an attempt (in its purest form at least) of getting all people to accept one idea. It is based on a new form of tolerance of different ideas, different beliefs, different kinds of people, and their right to live accordingly. Instead of trying to get everybody to live the same way, according to a particular worldview, a democracy has the tolerance for different beliefs, different ideas, different ways of living, at least to some degree. The only thing that is required in a democracy is that most people have that same tolerance for those who are different. If that tolerance is not there, then a democracy has various problems, which I am not going to go into right now.

What many people can see is that democracy is really a logical step in the evolution of humankind. When you look back at history, you can see that there have been so many examples of how divisions between people have caused conflict, and conflict always causes suffering. Therefore, the only way to really overcome suffering is to overcome conflict, and the only way to overcome conflict is to overcome division. This is of course in alignment with the Christ mind, who is pulling the world up, pulling humanity up, towards the recognition that all life is one and comes from the same source, and there are no real divisions between human beings.

Even if people are not ready to grasp this, they can at least grasp that democracies prove that the world is moving towards less and less division between people. This means that many people are ready to acknowledge that the function of ideologies has really been defining and reinforcing divisions between people, and they are therefore ready to take a look at ideologies and use ideologies in the broadest possible sense as any kind of thought system that defines or reinforces fundamental, inescapable, unbreachable divisions between people. They literally define that people are fundamentally different, whether they were created that way by God or created that way by nature.

Based on this recognition that we need to overcome division, and that many ideologies reinforce or define divisions, many people will be able to take a look at the thought systems, the beliefs that they have. Of course, it is fairly easy to look at what you normally would consider an ideology and see how many ideologies have defined fundamental divisions. We have talked about the Christian religion defining a division between Christians and non-Christians. The Muslim religion is doing the same. We can see that the Hindu religion defined the concept that there are four castes of human beings that are fundamental divisions created by God, and you can never move between the castes. This is a system that society, after thousands of years, has not completely freed itself from.

Beliefs that people never question

You can also begin to see, and many people *will* begin to see, that there are many different thought systems that are not normally seen as ideologies, but they still reinforce these divisions. This can open up a new awareness where many, many people begin to question many different things. This of course leads to another realization that there is a need to broaden people's understanding of what is an ideology or at least what is a thought system that creates division. This leads to a realization that there are actually many of these thought systems that function exactly the same as an ideology, but people would never consider them to be ideologies. They do not even think that they are thought systems that have been particularly defined by anybody. They are just simply beliefs that people have been brought up with and take for granted and never question.

It is almost as if there has been this veil over humankind for a very long time. You look back at every historical period, every generation, they have had certain ideas and beliefs that they took for granted and could not question. They did not see them as ideas that had been defined by some source. They thought this is just the way life is. It is self-evident. It is obvious, and that is the way it is, and there is no reason to question it. In other words, they did not see it as an ideology that could be opposed by an opposing ideology. There was nothing in people's minds that prompted them to challenge these beliefs. Now, what you who are ascended master students can grasp is that this is not a correct view. There are no beliefs on earth that just happened to appear. They were all engineered by the fallen beings for the specific purpose of controlling people, trapping their minds in blind alleys. They are, in a sense, all ideologies because they are defined specifically to control people.

What is the most effective way to imprison people? Well, you can take a person, you can put them in chains, you can chain him inside a dark cell in a basement where the sun never shines and he is, in a very effective way, imprisoned. The only problem is, he cannot fail to realize that he is imprisoned, and therefore he has a desire to escape. The most effective way to imprison people is to do it in such a way that they do not even realize they are imprisoned. They do not realize they are limited. They do not realize how limited they are. They might even think they are free because they do not recognize that their chains are chains that limit them, that limit their movement.

During the Middle Ages, here in Europe, most people believed that the earth was flat. They believed that they lived on the one and only continent there was, which was like an island surrounded by an ocean. If you sailed out in the same direction across the ocean, you would reach the edge of this disc, this round disc of the earth, and you would fall off and there would be dragons and it would be very unpleasant for you. What was the effect of this? The effect was that nobody dared to sail out on the ocean and continue to go in the same direction. There were some discoverers that started, but they followed land. They followed the contours of the land. You see that medieval people, medieval Europeans, were imprisoned, but they did not realize they were imprisoned because they did not believe that the belief in a flat earth was a belief. They thought it was a fact. That is just the way it is. There is nothing we can do about it.

This is an example of how you can use an idea, which everybody today realizes was unrealistic, was an illusion, to imprison people without them realizing they were imprisoned. Many people are ready to grasp this, and look at history and see how many past civilizations have been imprisoned by ideas that people in today's world, at least in the modern democracies, can clearly see were illusions. They were simply wrong, they were out of touch with reality.

Ideas that limit us in ways we do not see

This means that many people are then able (not the general population, not the bottom 10%, but many among the top 10%) to stand in front of the mirror and say: "Okay, do we in our civilization have some ideas, some beliefs, that we take for granted but they are in reality illusions? Is it possible that people a century or two centuries or five centuries from now will look back at our civilization and think that some of our beliefs were just as primitive as what we think about the belief in a flat earth?" Many, many people are ready to make this shift in their awareness and then start looking at today's world and see how many of the things that are not clearly defined as ideologies, as religions, as thought systems, that are so to speak floating around in the collective consciousness. It is difficult to pin down exactly where they came from, whether anybody has defined them or not, but what can be seen is that very few people have questioned them.

There is a group of people in embodiment, many of whom never need to hear about ascended masters, but it is part of their Divine plan to start this entire movement of questioning the unquestionable, questioning what has not been questioned before. Of course, the concept of ideology as we have given it here can be helpful where people can begin to say: "Do we have ideologies? Do we have beliefs that are functioning as ideologies in terms of limiting us and creating conflict and division but we do not see it? We have not seen it as an idea that can be questioned just like any other idea. We take it for granted, we think it is a fact, something that should never be questioned."

This can of course open up for major progress in society. Let me give just a few examples here because there are so many that I could not possibly go into them. Let us take a very obvious one. We have said that democracy is a society that moves humanity beyond division. Most democracies are based on the concept that all human beings are created equally, that they have the same rights, each person has one vote, all those should be counted, all votes count the same. This is one of the founding principles of democracy. Now, this means that a democratic society, in principle, gives complete equality to all people, complete equal opportunity. Therefore, a democracy should in principle be open to looking at whether it has certain divisions between people intended to divide people and whether it has overcome this and given complete equality to different groups of people.

What is one of the fundamental divisions that you see in all democratic societies? Well, it is the division between men and women. Many democratic societies, many of the modern democracies, have made very considerable and very applaudable progress towards giving equality between men and women, but no society has fully questioned where the division between men and women comes from. Many people take it for granted. "There is a physical difference between the physical bodies, of course there is a difference between men and women." You of course who are ascended master students have our teachings that the division between men and women was inflated and was turned into an ideology by the fallen beings for specific purposes. As we have said, men are more prone to go to war than women and that is why they decided to make men the superior sex and women the inferior sex.

This of course most people are not really open to seeing, but they are open to seeing that the division between men and women needs to be questioned. The whole idea that there is some fundamental difference between men and women needs to be questioned. Yes, of course there is the differences in the physical bodies, but does a difference in the physical body mean that there is a difference in the minds of men and women in the sense that women are somehow inferior in their minds, incapable of understanding politics or understanding science or other topics? Of course many people are open to realize that there is no such difference.

This really requires people to come to understand that you are not a man or a woman. You are a spiritual being, you are a soul or a spiritual being. It really cannot be complete equality until reincarnation is recognized because then you recognize that all people have incarnated in both male and female bodies. Therefore, you as a being, as a soul, as a spiritual being, you are not male or female, you are androgynous. You can embody in both bodies and you have the same level of intelligence, the same level of understanding, whether you are in a male or female body, it makes no difference. There is no fundamental difference between the ability of men and women to grasp even the most complicated topics.

There may be a certain cultural difference that has been imposed upon men and women where some women come to accept that: "Oh, I cannot understand math" and they give up before they have even tried. There is no fundamental difference in their ability to grasp these topics and this means that there is absolutely no validity to the idea that men are more suited to doing politics than women or men are more suited to doing science than women. This is something that absolutely needs to be questioned and done away with. Many modern democracies are of course in the process, but there is still much more work to be done, especially by questioning the mentality behind it all.

Women are the forerunners for questioning ideology

Many other examples can be mentioned, but what I want to say here is that when it comes to ending the era of ideology, it is actually more likely that men will have to take a back seat and that women be the forerunners. This is again because women have been suppressed for so long that it is time for them to step forward and overcome the suppression, and demonstrate that they actually have an ability to take society in a direction that men currently cannot do because of the programming of men.

You may say that when you look realistically at many societies, there is a difference between the minds of men and women, but what I am saying is: There is no *inherent* division, they were not created with a division. There may be a *cultural* division that has been imposed upon people over many generations, but all societies have young people that have incarnated who did not come from that civilization in past lifetimes and who are therefore not programmed by these divisions. Therefore, you can find in every society men who are not trapped in the same mindset as most men in that society and you can find women who are not trapped in the mindset of most women. This means that there is a possibility in every society that there are people who can give an alternative, give a frame of reference, that there is something outside of this cultural programming. On a planetary scale it is far more likely that women can step up and challenge these subtle ideologies, beginning with the entire idea that there is a difference between men and women and their abilities and therefore they should have different positions in society.

Questioning the ideology of racism

Now, you can take this further and look at many other examples and one example I want to comment on is race, racism. Racism is normally not considered an ideology, but it *is*. It is an ideology based on defining a fundamental division in humanity depending on these artificial criteria that you call racial characteristics, whether it be skin color or the shape of your nose or whatever it may be. This is clearly an ideology that divides people, it is clearly something that needs to be questioned. Of course, most modern democracies have already started this, but there is still more that can be questioned.

Where does it actually come from? There are still many, many people in the modern democracies who are concerned about racism and who are very, very concerned about not appearing to be racist, not doing anything that be can be construed as racist, but they still, deep within their minds (often at such a deep level that they will not consciously acknowledge it) wonder: "Why do we have these differences? Why do people have different skin color? Why do they have these different characteristics? Could there be something to it? Are there some differences?" In other words, you have people in the democratic world who will be the first to say that society must not discriminate based on race, but in their minds they are still wondering where the whole concept of race came from. This needs to be questioned where they realize that when you go to the very core of something, you see that there is no reality there—there is only illusion, layers upon layers of illusion. It was a completely artificial construct and it is necessary to realize there is no biological basis for dividing human beings into different races. You have the same genes, my beloved, no matter what your skin color is. You see in the United States for example how there is, as we have talked about before, this very clear movement, especially among evangelical Christians and those who call themselves conservatives or patriots, where they think that the white people, that white men especially, should continue to rule America. This is simply a racist ideology. There is no other way to put it, but on the other side of the political spectrum you have many among what you might call progressive Democrats who are very, very concerned about not appearing to be racist, not discriminating based on racism, but they are still looking at black people and they are wondering: "Are they really different? Do they have a mindset that's different? Are there certain things they can't do? Are they more lazy? Are they not able to pull themselves up?" They wonder, they do not dare to say it or discuss it amongst themselves, but they wonder about it in their own minds. Until they overcome that doubt, that wonderment, they cannot really be the spearheads for removing racism in America. It is in fact this doubt that allows those on the opposite side to continue and to become even more bold in expressing their racism.

You see here that one of the realizations you come to, when you understand duality, is that for one dualistic polarity to exist, there must be another. You see now in America that there is a growing racism, white supremacy. They are becoming more and more bold in demonstrating and expressing themselves, using social media and so on. It can only exist because there is the opposite polarity of those who have reformed their actions, but who have not truly seen through the racist mindset and freed themselves from it. The same of course can be applied to all ideologies.

Why is it still possible for some people in China to maintain the illusion that Marxism is a valid ideology? It is because there is still a group of people in the democratic world, especially in the United States, who are believing in capitalism as a valid economic system, as an ideology. You see that there is always this pairing and the key to overcoming it is that some people in one of the polarities must begin to question the mindset behind it.

Questioning the ideology of scientific Materialism

Now, another hidden ideology, camouflaged ideology, that I want to comment on is what is sometimes called scientific Materialism, but which is basically just Materialism. You look at this ideology of Materialism and you can see all the characteristics are there. There is an attempt to give an explanation of how the world works and it is claimed that this explanation is absolute, it is infallible, at least in its basic premise that there is nothing beyond the material universe and that everything that happens on earth, in life, in society, in human beings can be explained based on a materialistic explanation. This is the basic tenet of the ideology of Materialism. So this is the first element: There is an explanation of how the world works.

The second element to find in traditional views of ideology is that there is a program for change of society, a program for social change. Well, the materialists have a very clear program for social change and it is to create a society where religion has been eradicated and where everybody is basing their worldview on science, or rather the materialist interpretation of science, the materialist ideology that has been superimposed upon science—which of course materialists will not see as an ideology. They think this is based on scientific fact, just as all of the other ideologies (including the religious people) have believed that their ideology was based on some unquestionable authority. That is why the materialists feel they are right, they have a right to force society and force other people, they have a right to go out and undermine religion. Most of them are fortunately not violent, but nevertheless they still are willing to use force to impose their program upon society.

You will also see the third element: the struggle, the concept of a struggle. The materialists are clearly portraying that implementing their program requires a struggle to overcome the resistance from religion because religious people will not voluntarily give up their religion and therefore there must be a struggle. The question is how far should this go? You can see already that a materialistic view was incorporated in Marxist ideology, it was found in the Soviet Union and there was definitely violence used to eradicate religion in many of the countries in the Soviet bloc and Warsaw Pact countries. You see the same in China. You see it even today, in the way religious minorities are dealt with. You may say that the Western materialists are not violent, but certainly there are materialists who are violent, have been violent.

Then, the fourth element is that an ideology seeks to convert the broad population, as the materialists are clearly doing, but the ideology also seeks to create an elite that has a greater commitment. You can see how, over the last couple of decades, there has been this rise in what has been called militant atheism, where certain writers have published these books that are aimed at convincing the broad public about the fallacy of religion. They have also appealed to a smaller elite that has been more committed to spreading this ideology of Materialism.

Of course, the fifth element is that even though they seek to persuade the general public, they also define that there is a certain elite that are the ones that are really able, capable, of grasping the ideology and implementing it. That is clearly also present. There are some of these militant atheists who see themselves as the elite and they appeal to others as well. There is also a clear tendency to think that it is primarily intellectuals who can drive this because it is seen that it is primarily the rational, intellectual, analytical people who can see the fallacies of religion. You clearly see here that Materialism is in all respects functioning as an ideology and therefore, it also has the same dynamic as other ideologies. One of the primary dynamics is that it limits human thought.

I have commented on it before, but I want to go into it more because what have I said about the scientific method in its essence? It is, as Karl Popper said, that our current worldview is simply a starting point for explaining and formulating experiments that can be performed. As we observe how the world works and observe the results of our experiments, we are meant to refine our worldview. Therefore, we never have a final worldview.

This means that a principle he defined is that any worldview is falsifiable, it is not complete, it is not infallible. There is always more to understand and when we understand that more, we might actually see that our current worldview is incomplete, perhaps even in some ways out of touch with reality, based on an illusion. You see that even though the materialists are constantly referring to science as the ultimate authority, or what *should be* the ultimate authority on earth and certainly what gives them the authority, they are in fact completely out of touch with this basic principle of science. They are not seeing the materialist philosophy as just a starting point for further observation and inquiry. They are seeing it as the final truth: There is nothing beyond the material universe.

Now, if you take Karl Popper's idea that a true scientific theory should be falsifiable and apply that to materialism, how exactly is materialism falsifiable? How could you demonstrate that the claim that there is nothing beyond the material universe is false? Now, of course you *can* through a spiritual, intuitive approach, but you cannot through the materialistic approach. There is no way in Materialism that you could prove the existence of something beyond the material universe. It is defined out of existence, there is no possibility of doing this. Now, you will see that there are some of these materialists who have gone to great lengths to try to spread this belief that there can be nothing beyond the material universe. One of them is called Randy who is recently deceased and now has a proof, an *experiential* proof, that there *is* something beyond the material universe and that there is more to him than his physical brain, but of course he has not communicated that to his followers. He instituted a prize of $1 million to anyone who could prove a psychic phenomenon, a supernatural phenomenon, but of course in his mindset and in how he defined this, there was no proof that could really satisfy him. What you see here is that the materialists have violated Karl Popper's principle of falsifiability by defining the materialist ideology in such a way that within the ideology itself, there is no possibility of proving that the ideology is wrong. This of course is very similar to many other ideologies, such as the Christian religion, the Muslim religion, Marxism, communism and so forth and so on.

The one factor holding back scientific progress

Many, many people in the world are ready to see this. We have before talked about the fact that there were many people in past ages who grew up in a Christian society and who came to believe in the Christian promise that if they obeyed the Christian priesthood, they would go to heaven after that lifetime. Here, they pass from the physical body and they realize they are not going to go to heaven, they are going to be sent back into embodiment. When they have done it a certain number of times, they come back into embodiment with this deep distrust of the Christian religion and its promises. There are now also people who, after giving up on the Christian religion, became pulled into the materialist ideology and they have lived several lifetimes believing in this ideology. They have believed with their outer minds that there would be nothing after they died, but then they have experienced: "Hello, my body is dead but I am still conscious, I am still experiencing, I am still alive so Materialism was wrong." After you have done this for some lifetimes, then you come back into embodiment and now you are ready to actually question the materialist claim.

Many, many people are in this state. Many of these people are not necessarily openly spiritual, they are not into any spiritual movement or philosophy, but they are open to questioning this claim, and saying: "What if there really is something beyond the material universe?" Many of them can see, as we have explained before, Einstein said: "Everything is energy." Energy is different levels of vibration, there is really nothing to prevent the existence of energetic realms, vibratory realms, beyond what you today call the physical universe. We have described how quantum physicists have pointed to the existence of such realms. Many people are open to seeing that Materialism has limited scientific inquiry and human thought, human philosophical inquiry.

One of the ways that materialism has done this is by its definition, its doctrine, that the human mind can and must be explained as a material phenomenon. In other words, everything that goes on in your mind is the result of material, physical, chemical, electromagnetic processes in your physical brain. There is nothing to you, your mind, your personality, that does not come from the brain.

This is what is currently the one factor that more than anything else is holding back scientific progress. It is also holding back the development in society because, as I have said, how can you in a democratic nation fully overcome division? Only when you begin to see a connection between different people, and this connection is clearly not physical; your bodies are separate. If you kill the body of another person, your body does not die at the same time. You cannot really create this sense of oneness, connection, equality between people through physical means. If there is a connection between people, it must be a connection at the level of the mind, which is of course why many people are open to the concept of telepathy and connections between people who are separated by physical space.

The illusion of separate entities

Now, quantum physicists have proven that elementary particles that are separated by physical space can still be connected in a way that defies traditional science, certainly the speed of light being the ultimate speed limit. Why is it not possible that human minds can be connected even though the bodies are separated by distance? Many, many people are open to this, and many people are open to coming to see that if democracy is to be taken to a higher level, if scientific inquiry is to be taken to a higher level, the one thing that needs to happen is that we must challenge the materialist ideology that says the mind is a material phenomenon, the mind is produced by the body. When we overcome this, suddenly an entirely new plethora of opportunities open up for explaining the connection between people, overcoming the divisions and conflicts between people, realizing that all life is connected, that what we do to others really does affect ourselves. This means that politically, we can take society to a higher level, we can even overcome this division between the rich and the poor world, where the rich nations, as we have talked about before, realize that it is their opportunity and their responsibility to use their affluence to help those in other nations. Beyond this, we can open up for new scientific fields of inquiry where we start using – in a systematic, unhindered, unrestricted way – scientific tools to investigate consciousness—investigate the mind. What is the human mind? How does it really function? What are the limitations of the mind? Is it really possible that the mind can have an influence on physical matter? Certainly, is it possible that the mind can have an influence on the health of our physical bodies, which has already been proven for anyone who is not trapped in the materialist ideological mindset.

All of a sudden, new inquiries for physical healing open up, but also new inquiries for psychological healing. What have we said many times is the next logical step for the modern democracies, the welfare society? It is to go beyond *material* welfare to creating *psychological* welfare. Well, how can you do this if you do not understand how the psyche works? How can you understand how the psyche works if you are not using scientific tools to investigate the mind? It is so logical that many, many people are ready to see it. The only people who cannot see it are the ones who are blocking it out because of the denial created by the materialist ideological mindset.

New avenues for philosophical inquiry

Then, of course beyond this actual research that will be conducted by traditional scientific tools, there is an entire other field of inquiry that opens up. It is what we might call philosophical inquiry. If we begin to set aside the materialist paradigm (which as we have said goes all the way back to Aristotle and has influenced many philosophers in the past), what new avenues for philosophy open up? What can we actually explain? One of the topics of philosophy has always been: What are the limits of knowledge? What can we know? What can human beings know?

If you were to study western philosophers and the evolution of western philosophy, you will see that there is one element that has been missing in western philosophy. It is that western philosophers have based their philosophy on the rational mind. They have assumed that the rational mind is the ultimate tool for philosophical inquiry, and that the rational mind only works at one particular level, the analytical, linear level, as we have called it. This means that philosophers have generally assumed that they have the state of mind, the capacity of mind, to rationally understand all that is possible to understand about the universe.

What is missing from Western philosophy is the concept that there are different states of consciousness, higher states of consciousness, and that most human beings today are at a certain level of consciousness where they can see within a certain horizon, but they cannot see beyond that horizon. It is possible for human beings to follow a systematic process, raising their consciousness, expanding their awareness, so that they can see beyond that horizon, that event horizon, that observation horizon. They can see what people cannot see today.

In fact, this is what has caused human progress. The expansion of knowledge really means an expansion of the event horizon, the observation horizon, how far people can see. In medieval times they could only see out to the edges of the flat earth. Now, people can see much further, but it does not mean that they have discovered the ultimate limits for knowledge. By raising consciousness even more, we can expand that observation horizon and come to see things that we cannot see today. Of course, the key to doing this is to understand how the mind works and apply these principles, these universal principles, for how you can expand your consciousness.

Ideology is always profoundly elitist

This then leads to another area of philosophical inquiry, which is: Do all human beings have the potential to understand how life works? Do all human beings have the capacity to raise their consciousness and fathom fundamental principles that guide life and how life works? We have talked about the mechanics—can all people understand this?

This means that when you now consider this, you can look back at ideology, and you can see that beyond the worldly definition, ideology has always been profoundly elitist. Ideology is created by, or at least brought into the physical by, one person or a few people. It attracts a few adherents that consider themselves the people who really understand the ideology, the superior elite, who can understand and implement the ideology. This elite, even though it may appeal to a broader range of intellectuals, they define in their worldview that there are some people who can grasp the ideology, but the broad population cannot. That is why the elite needs to force the ideology on society "for the greater good." In other words, the majority of the people, they do not need to be educated into grasping the ideology, they need to be forced into compliance with the ideology because they are not capable of grasping what the elite can grasp. This is clearly a division. It is also clearly an illusion, when you look at it from the ascended perspective. Many people in embodiment are ready to come to question this and see that it is an illusion, see that democracy actually proves that all people have the capacity to understand certain principles, certain mechanics of how the world works.

This means that you can look at democratic societies, and you can see that the vast majority of people in many democratic societies have risen beyond a certain level of consciousness. You will see, not all democratic societies, but certainly many democratic societies, where the vast majority of the people are not violent, they would not even dream of committing violence against another human being. They would in fact be very reluctant to use violence to defend themselves if they were attacked. There are many, many people who have overcome this old mindset that is built into most ideologies, what we have called the epic mindset, namely, that the ends can justify the means. There may be many people in democratic nations who have not consciously dismissed this idea, but they have at least reached the point where they realize that regardless of what goals you may have defined, using violence, killing and torturing other people is not justified in order to reach those goals. This again could be said to be one of the fundamental principles, one of the mechanics, of a democratic society because if a democratic society is using violence to force people to become democratic, then it is not really a democracy.

Many people are then able to make this switch of realizing that all human beings have the same potential. Now, naturally you can look at even the most modern democracies and see that there is a range of consciousness in the population. There is a range of what people understand, how aware they are. Clearly, there are some people that are more mature than others, but the basic principle of democracy is that people were not created with different capacities of the mind. All people were created with the same potential to expand their awareness and come to understand even complex topics. It is just a matter of how willing they have been to apply it, and how they have been able to apply it based on the knowledge they were given of how the mind works.

For example, as we have said, many democracies fail in educating their children about the basic mechanics of the human psyche. Nevertheless, all have the potential to do this. This means what? It means that many people in embodiment are ready to give up this hidden ideology that acquiring knowledge is reserved for an elite and not for the general population. When this is overcome, there will be such an opening of new experimentation, new speculation, new questions. People will begin to receive many more ideas from the ascended realm than what is possible today.

The horizontal and the vertical way to knowledge

This means that in the little more long term, many people will be open to realizing that there are actually two distinct ways of acquiring knowledge. One is the horizontal way where you, for example through science or through observing what you can see about life (such as observing history or observing how nature works), you can make certain observations that lead to certain conclusions. Based on these observations you can deduce certain general principles, as Saint Germain defined in the scientific method. You can make observations of specifics and expand this to certain generalities, and therefore discover these natural laws or principles, the mechanics of how the universe works.

This is the horizontal way of acquiring knowledge, but a growing number of people are coming very close to consciously being able to acknowledge that there is also a vertical way of acquiring knowledge. The vertical way in a traditional sense has been what has been called the mystical religions or the mystical path, that has been taught in many different societies. Of course, many, many people in the Western world and modern democracies have discovered some kind of spiritual teaching, some kind of spiritual movement that talks about a path, so they have started experimenting with this. Many more people are ready to grasp this idea in a more universal terminology. In other words, instead of it being a specific teaching brought forth by a particular guru, or by an ascended master organization, they can grasp in more universal terms that it is possible to expand the capacity of your mind to where you can intuitively receive certain insights, certain ideas, certain impressions, certain images, that give you a greater understanding. This is clearly the first step.

The next step up is that many more people will be willing to acknowledge that, however you see it, there is actually a realm where all knowledge that is possible about how the universe works, is found. If you want a visual image, you can consider that there is somewhere this library that contains books that describe every aspect of how the universe works, every aspect of new technology that could be brought forth, new ideas in any area of society: new philosophies, new political ideas, new economic ideas. Everything that could possibly be brought forth, in terms of knowledge for human beings, is contained in this library.

Many people will then be able to realize how human progress actually happened in history. It has always been because a new idea came forth but where did the idea come from? Was it really some human being who had this superior capacity of mind to formulate or discover this idea, all within his own mind? Or was it actually that throughout history, a few people have been able to attune their minds to this universal library of knowledge, and therefore receive a certain idea from there? When this awareness begins to spread, many, many people will then begin to say: "Well, I may be no Einstein, but what Einstein did was really just to receive an idea from the universal library. Why couldn't I do the same? I don't need to be as smart as Einstein, I just need to be open to receive an idea. And maybe I also need some practical knowledge of a particular field that is of interest to me. When I set that foundation of educating my mind, I use my intuitive faculties. I use the rational mind to educate my mind about what is already known, and based on that foundation I use my intuitive mind to reach for a new idea in this field, why shouldn't I be able to receive it?"

They do not even have to know where it comes from. You, of course, will know that it comes from the Ascended Host, you will know that Saint Germain has many, many ideas that he is willing to release and that are in fact already released from the spiritual into the identity, the mental and emotional. They just need somebody who can connect and bring it into the physical. The ideas are there. As Jesus said 2,000 years ago: "It rains upon the just and the unjust," in the sense that these ideas are raining from heaven. It is just a matter of: Is there someone who can open their minds to receive the idea, formulate it and bring it out so that it can be communicated to other people?

When you see this, you will see the complete overturning of elitism because now you cannot uphold the idea that only the elite can receive new ideas. You can already see this, if you are open to it. In history, you can go back to the early 1900s, and you can say: "Were there scientists at the time? Were there university professors? Was there an intellectual elite who believed that they had a monopoly on knowledge?" Well, certainly there was. Many of them thought that they were the only ones who could define human knowledge. They were the only ones who could take society in a new direction and bring forth new knowledge because only they had the capacity of mind.

My beloved, what is one of the major advantages of modern civilization? Is it not airplane travel? Because of airplanes, you can travel further, and "ordinary" people so to speak can afford to travel to distant destinations. Well, was it the intellectual elite of the time that invented the airplane? Nay, it was two brothers in America who had a bicycle repair shop. They had no education, and precisely because they had no education, their minds were open to making observations and receiving the ideas for how heavier than air flight was possible. The Wright brothers brought in the entire era of aviation, while the intellectuals are sitting back, not being willing to consider why they could not receive those ideas. Consider perhaps that it was their hidden ideology, their mindset, their elitist mindset of superiority, that blocked them from receiving these ideas that have had such a profound impact on civilization. When you have this democratization of knowledge, you will see an acceleration of invention and new ideas that you have not yet seen on this planet, even in the last century or the last few decades.

With this, I have given you what I wanted to give you in this installment. I still have some things I want to bring out. In a sense, there is almost no limit to what could be said based on this topic of ideology because it has had such a profound impact, not only on life on earth, but on this unascended sphere and even previous spheres since the fall of the first beings in the fourth sphere. It is truly a huge topic, but what I will do in the remainder of this conference is give you what I consider the most constructive knowledge to bring out in this particular phase, that can have the most impact on awakening those who are ready to be awakened to questioning not only ideology, not only specific ideologies, but the very mindset of ideology, the ideological mindset.

So with this, I seal you once again, in the peace, the joyful peace of the Buddha. Gautama Buddha I AM.

22 INVOKING AWARENESS OF HOW IDEOLOGY LIMITS PROGRESS (PART 1)

In the name of the I AM THAT I AM, Jesus Christ, I use the authority that I have as a being in embodiment on earth to call upon Gautama Buddha to reinforce my calls and use my chakras to project the statements in this invocation into the collective consciousness and awaken people to the need to free ourselves from the ideological mindset. Awaken people to the reality that we are spiritual beings and that we can co-create a new future by working with the ascended masters. I especially call for …

[Make your own calls here.]

Part 1

1. Gautama Buddha, awaken the most creative people to see that during the 60s and 70s, some young people were pulled into the ideological mindset created by Marxism or socialism. Some later abandoned this when the Soviet Union collapsed when they started realizing that in China there was a lack of fundamental human rights.

Archangel Michael, light so blue,
my heart has room for only you.
My mind is one, no longer two,
your love for me is ever true.

**Archangel Michael, you are here,
consuming now all doubt and fear.
Your Presence is forever near,
you are to me so very dear.**

2. Gautama Buddha, awaken the most creative people to see that some
were thinking that even though Marxism was not the ultimate ideology,
there had to be an ultimate ideology. They started looking for it, and some
of them are still looking for the ultimate ideology.

Archangel Michael, I will be,
all one with your reality.
No fear can hold me as I see,
this world no power has o'er me.

**Archangel Michael, you are here,
consuming now all doubt and fear.
Your Presence is forever near,
you are to me so very dear.**

3. Gautama Buddha, awaken the most creative people to see that some
have found what they think is an ultimate ideology. Some have even found
a spiritual teaching that they think is the ultimate ideology. Other people
have become discouraged with ideology and have switched into agnosticism or complete disillusionment.

Archangel Michael, hold me tight,
shatter now the darkest night.
Clear my chakras with your light,
restore to me my inner sight.

**Archangel Michael, you are here,
consuming now all doubt and fear.**

**Your Presence is forever near,
you are to me so very dear.**

4. Gautama Buddha, awaken the most creative people to see that some think that either there is no ultimate ideology, or we can never know what the ultimate truth is, or there is no truth, no higher principles, no way to determine what is a higher truth because of the way human beings are.

Archangel Michael, now I stand,
with you the light I do command.
My heart I ever will expand,
till highest truth I understand.

**Archangel Michael, you are here,
consuming now all doubt and fear.
Your Presence is forever near,
you are to me so very dear.**

5. Gautama Buddha, awaken the most creative people to see that a certain group of people have been very enthusiastic about the ideological approach and they have become very disillusioned and disappointed with that approach, giving up on the quest to find a higher understanding.

Archangel Michael, in my heart,
from me you never will depart.
Of hierarchy I am a part,
I now accept a fresh new start.

**Archangel Michael, you are here,
consuming now all doubt and fear.
Your Presence is forever near,
you are to me so very dear.**

6. Gautama Buddha, awaken the most creative people to snap out of this mindset and realize that this is exactly what the power elite beings want to see happen. The power elite wants to pull those who have the capacity to bring change into either submitting to an ideology or opposing it so that they are fighting the ideology, which means they are trapped in reacting to an ideology defined by the power elite beings.

Archangel Michael, sword of blue,
all darkness you are cutting through.
My Christhood I do now pursue,
discernment shows me what is true.

**Archangel Michael, you are here,
consuming now all doubt and fear.
Your Presence is forever near,
you are to me so very dear.**

7. Gautama Buddha, awaken the most creative people to see that the power elite beings also want to make some people so disillusioned with an ideology that they give up trying to think there is any kind of higher understanding.

Archangel Michael, in your wings,
I now let go of lesser things.
God's homing call in my heart rings,
my heart with yours forever sings.

**Archangel Michael, you are here,
consuming now all doubt and fear.
Your Presence is forever near,
you are to me so very dear.**

8. Gautama Buddha, awaken the most creative people to see that we cannot allow ourselves to be discouraged this way. The reality of the situation is that there is no ultimate ideology, but there is always the possibility of attaining a higher understanding than what we have right now.

Archangel Michael, take me home,
in higher spheres I want to roam.
I am reborn from cosmic foam,
my life is now a sacred poem.

**Archangel Michael, you are here,
consuming now all doubt and fear.
Your Presence is forever near,
you are to me so very dear.**

9. Gautama Buddha, awaken the most creative people to see that this is the basic principle behind science. We need to have a foundation for our scientific inquiry and for understanding life on earth. We have a starting point for increasing our understanding. We experiment, we make observations, and then we use that to refine our understanding.

Archangel Michael, light you are,
shining like the bluest star.
You are a cosmic avatar,
with you I will go very far.

Archangel Michael, you are here,
consuming now all doubt and fear.
Your Presence is forever near,
you are to me so very dear.

Part 2

1. Gautama Buddha, awaken the most creative people to see that when we look back at history, the process we have been going through is a process of raising our understanding of life.

Jophiel Archangel, in wisdom's great light,
all serpentine lies exposed to our sight.
So subtle the lies that creep through the mind,
yet you are the greatest teacher we find.

Jophiel Archangel, exposing all lies,
Jophiel Archangel, cutting all ties.
Jophiel Archangel, clearing the skies,
Jophiel Archangel, the mind truly flies.

2. Gautama Buddha, awaken the most creative people to see that we have more knowledge, more technology and a better standard of living than

people had in past centuries because we have a greater understanding of how life works.

> Jophiel Archangel, your wisdom we hail,
> your sword cutting through duality's veil.
> As you show the way, we know what is real,
> from serpentine doubt, we instantly heal.

> **Jophiel Archangel, exposing all lies,**
> **Jophiel Archangel, cutting all ties.**
> **Jophiel Archangel, clearing the skies,**
> **Jophiel Archangel, the mind truly flies.**

3. Gautama Buddha, awaken the most creative people to see that when we look at human history, there has been a progression in understanding. This has not been an entirely smooth process and there have been some dramatic shifts.

> Jophiel Archangel, your reality,
> the best antidote to duality.
> No lie can remain in your Presence so clear,
> with you on our side, no serpent we fear.

> **Jophiel Archangel, exposing all lies,**
> **Jophiel Archangel, cutting all ties.**
> **Jophiel Archangel, clearing the skies,**
> **Jophiel Archangel, the mind truly flies.**

4. Gautama Buddha, awaken the most creative people to see that there have been periods of time where the expansion of understanding almost came to a halt for a long time. For example, during the so-called Dark Ages, there was still some expansion of understanding, but much slower than it has been in the last century.

> Jophiel Archangel, God's mind is in me,
> and through your clear light, its wisdom we see.
> Divisions all vanish, as we see the One,
> and truly, the wholeness of mind we have won.

Jophiel Archangel, exposing all lies,
Jophiel Archangel, cutting all ties.
Jophiel Archangel, clearing the skies,
Jophiel Archangel, the mind truly flies.

5. Gautama Buddha, awaken the most creative people to see that what slowed down the expansion of knowledge was that society had become trapped in a specific ideology. They thought it was infallible, and this closed people's minds.

Jophiel Archangel, now show us the way,
that leads us beyond duality's fray,
we long to discern the truth and the lie,
so we the serpentine knots can untie.

Jophiel Archangel, exposing all lies,
Jophiel Archangel, cutting all ties.
Jophiel Archangel, clearing the skies,
Jophiel Archangel, the mind truly flies.

6. Gautama Buddha, awaken the most creative people to see that when society is not able to think beyond the ideology, is not able to ask questions beyond the ideology, this slows down the expansion of knowledge.

Jophiel Archangel, your Presence is here,
and therefore our minds are perfectly clear,
in wisdom's great fount we do take a bath,
and now we withstand the devil's own wrath.

Jophiel Archangel, exposing all lies,
Jophiel Archangel, cutting all ties.
Jophiel Archangel, clearing the skies,
Jophiel Archangel, the mind truly flies.

7. Gautama Buddha, awaken the most creative people to see that the basis for the expansion of knowledge is that we expand our present understanding. We do this by asking questions that go *beyond* our present understanding.

Jophiel Archangel, it is your great task,
to raise all mankind, if only we ask,
so now on behalf of those who are blind,
we ask for your help in wisdom to find.

**Jophiel Archangel, exposing all lies,
Jophiel Archangel, cutting all ties.
Jophiel Archangel, clearing the skies,
Jophiel Archangel, the mind truly flies.**

8. Gautama Buddha, awaken the most creative people to see that if we could not ask questions beyond a certain framework, how could we ever transcend that framework? *It cannot be done.* This is the simple mechanics of how the expansion of knowledge works.

Jophiel Archangel, your Presence we hail,
your Light cutting through the serpentine veil,
the serpents can no longer people deceive,
for all now your Flame of Wisdom receive.

**Jophiel Archangel, exposing all lies,
Jophiel Archangel, cutting all ties.
Jophiel Archangel, clearing the skies,
Jophiel Archangel, the mind truly flies.**

9. Gautama Buddha, awaken the most creative people to see that when we observe life on earth, we can see that there are certain mechanics of how the world works that are not dependent on human beliefs. They are time-less, they are universal principles.

Jophiel Archangel, where else can we go,
when we long the highest wisdom to know?
You share with us gladly all that you are,
and now our vision goes ever so far.

**Jophiel Archangel, exposing all lies,
Jophiel Archangel, cutting all ties.
Jophiel Archangel, clearing the skies,
Jophiel Archangel, the mind truly flies.**

Part 3

1. Gautama Buddha, awaken the most creative people to see that regardless of what people have believed in certain time periods, the mechanics were not changed by that.

> Chamuel Archangel, in ruby ray power,
> we know we are taking a life-giving shower.
> Love burning away all perversions of will,
> we suddenly feel our desires falling still.

> **Chamuel Archangel, descend from Above,**
> **Chamuel Archangel, with ruby-pink love,**
> **Chamuel Archangel, so often thought-of,**
> **Chamuel Archangel, o come Holy Dove.**

2. Gautama Buddha, awaken the most creative people to see that there have been time periods where people had the belief that a particular ideology was infallible, and they should never question it or think beyond it. This always slowed down the expansion of knowledge.

> Chamuel Archangel, a spiral of light,
> as ruby ray fire now pierces the night.
> All forces of darkness consumed by your fire,
> consuming all those who will not rise higher.

> **Chamuel Archangel, descend from Above,**
> **Chamuel Archangel, with ruby-pink love,**
> **Chamuel Archangel, so often thought-of,**
> **Chamuel Archangel, o come Holy Dove.**

3. Gautama Buddha, awaken the most creative people to give up the ideological approach, the belief that an ideology is infallible or that there must be some ultimate ideology that has not yet been discovered or developed. Help people take the more pragmatic scientific approach of saying: "Let us attempt to discover the mechanics of how life actually works. We can base our society on those mechanics instead."

Chamuel Archangel, your love so immense,
with clarified vision, our lives now make sense.
The purpose of life you so clearly reveal,
immersed in your love, God's oneness we feel.

Chamuel Archangel, descend from Above,
Chamuel Archangel, with ruby-pink love,
Chamuel Archangel, so often thought-of,
Chamuel Archangel, o come Holy Dove.

4. Gautama Buddha, awaken the most creative people to see that a society based on an observation of the mechanics of the world, will not be a dictatorship. It will not be a society that is steeped in fanaticism. It will not be a society that is elitist.

Chamuel Archangel, what calmness you bring,
we see now that even death has no sting.
For truly, in love there can be no decay,
as love is transcendence into a new day.

Chamuel Archangel, descend from Above,
Chamuel Archangel, with ruby-pink love,
Chamuel Archangel, so often thought-of,
Chamuel Archangel, o come Holy Dove.

5. Gautama Buddha, awaken the most creative people to see that it will be a society that resembles the modern democracies. Democracy is a society that is based on some observation, some understanding, of the mechanics of how life works, which is that all people are connected, all people are equal.

Chamuel Archangel, God's Love Flame bestow,
on all those longing God's true love to know,
conditions we know can never be real,
and this is the love you always reveal.

Chamuel Archangel, descend from Above,
Chamuel Archangel, with ruby-pink love,

Chamuel Archangel, so often thought-of,
Chamuel Archangel, o come Holy Dove.

6. Gautama Buddha, awaken the most creative people to see that elitist societies have always led to some form of conflict or disaster. There has always been an internal tension, and there has always been the suppression of the majority of the population who have been limited by the elite.

Chamuel Archangel, love's seed you have sown,
in hearts of all those who don't seek to own,
for love that possesses is nothing but fear,
that pierces the heart with duality's spear.

Chamuel Archangel, descend from Above,
Chamuel Archangel, with ruby-pink love,
Chamuel Archangel, so often thought-of,
Chamuel Archangel, o come Holy Dove.

7. Gautama Buddha, awaken the most creative people to see that we can either have these kinds of unbalanced elitist societies, dictatorships, or we can move towards a more democratic form of government where all of the people have some influence, and where there is more equality between people.

Chamuel Archangel, we don't want control,
for this is the devil's hold on the soul,
your love will now break the serpentine chain,
so we are set free God's love to reclaim.

Chamuel Archangel, descend from Above,
Chamuel Archangel, with ruby-pink love,
Chamuel Archangel, so often thought-of,
Chamuel Archangel, o come Holy Dove.

8. Gautama Buddha, awaken the most creative people to see that elitist societies were deeply divided societies. There was a fundamental difference between the elite and the population, perhaps even different groups in the population, as we have seen divisions based on many different things.

Chamuel Archangel, you are so adept,
at helping us God's true love to accept,
we know that the love for which we so yearn,
is not something we on earth have to earn.

Chamuel Archangel, descend from Above,
Chamuel Archangel, with ruby-pink love,
Chamuel Archangel, so often thought-of,
Chamuel Archangel, o come Holy Dove.

9. Gautama Buddha, awaken the most creative people to see that in order to move into a better society that gives better living conditions to the people, humankind needs to make an effort to overcome division, the entire idea that people can be divided into separate groups.

Chamuel Archangel, for love to accept,
we do not need to be so perfect,
for love is not static but always a flow,
demanding only we're willing to grow.

Chamuel Archangel, descend from Above,
Chamuel Archangel, with ruby-pink love,
Chamuel Archangel, so often thought-of,
Chamuel Archangel, o come Holy Dove.

Part 4

1. Gautama Buddha, awaken the most creative people to see that there is a deep division inherent in all ideologies. They give a certain explanation of how the world works. It is claimed to be ultimate and infallible, which creates a division between those who accept this explanation and those who do not.

Gabriel Archangel, your light we revere,
immersed in your Presence, nothing we fear.
Disciples of Christ, we do leave behind,
the ego's desire for responding in kind.

Gabriel Archangel, of this we are sure,
Gabriel Archangel, Christ light is the cure.
Gabriel Archangel, intentions so pure,
Gabriel Archangel, in you we're secure.

2. Gautama Buddha, awaken the most creative people to see that because of duality and the mechanics of duality, we can never get all people to accept the same idea. A democracy is not based on an attempt of getting all people to accept one idea. It is based on a new form of tolerance of different ideas, different beliefs, different kinds of people, and their right to live accordingly.

Gabriel Archangel, we fear not the light,
in purifications' fire, we delight.
With your hand in ours, each challenge we face,
we follow the spiral to infinite grace.

Gabriel Archangel, of this we are sure,
Gabriel Archangel, Christ light is the cure.
Gabriel Archangel, intentions so pure,
Gabriel Archangel, in you we're secure.

3. Gautama Buddha, awaken the most creative people to see that instead of trying to get everybody to live the same way, according to a particular worldview, a democracy has the tolerance for different beliefs, different ideas, different ways of living.

Gabriel Archangel, your fire burning white,
ascending with you, out of the night.
The ego has nowhere to run and to hide,
in ascension's bright spiral, with you we abide.

Gabriel Archangel, of this we are sure,
Gabriel Archangel, Christ light is the cure.
Gabriel Archangel, intentions so pure,
Gabriel Archangel, in you we're secure.

4. Gautama Buddha, awaken the most creative people to see that the only thing that is required in a democracy is that most people have that same

tolerance for those who are different. If that tolerance is not there, then a democracy has various problems.

> Gabriel Archangel, your trumpet we hear,
> announcing the birth of Christ drawing near.
> In lightness of being, we now are reborn,
> rising with Christ on bright Easter morn.

> **Gabriel Archangel, of this we are sure,**
> **Gabriel Archangel, Christ light is the cure.**
> **Gabriel Archangel, intentions so pure,**
> **Gabriel Archangel, in you we're secure.**

5. Gautama Buddha, awaken the most creative people to see that democracy is a logical step in the evolution of humankind. There have been many examples of how divisions between people have caused conflict, and conflict always causes suffering.

> Gabriel Archangel, the earth is now free,
> embracing a nondual reality,
> the judgment of Christ upon forces so dark,
> who deny that all have a spiritual spark.

> **Gabriel Archangel, of this we are sure,**
> **Gabriel Archangel, Christ light is the cure.**
> **Gabriel Archangel, intentions so pure,**
> **Gabriel Archangel, in you we're secure.**

6. Gautama Buddha, awaken the most creative people to see that the only way to overcome suffering is to overcome conflict, and the only way to overcome conflict is to overcome division. This is in alignment with the Christ mind, who is pulling the world up, pulling humanity up, towards the recognition that all life is one and comes from the same source.

> Gabriel Archangel, with angels so white,
> raising our planet out of the dark night,
> as we now intone the Word of the Lord,
> the beings who fell are bound by your sword.

Gabriel Archangel, of this we are sure,
Gabriel Archangel, Christ light is the cure.
Gabriel Archangel, intentions so pure,
Gabriel Archangel, in you we're secure.

7. Gautama Buddha, awaken the most creative people to see that democracies prove that the world is moving towards less and less division between people. The function of ideologies has been defining and reinforcing divisions between people.

Gabriel Archangel, we call now to you,
the astral plane your light burning through,
entities, demons, discarnates are bound,
as you and we intone Sacred Sound.

Gabriel Archangel, of this we are sure,
Gabriel Archangel, Christ light is the cure.
Gabriel Archangel, intentions so pure,
Gabriel Archangel, in you we're secure.

8. Gautama Buddha, awaken the most creative people to see that ideologies in the broadest sense means any kind of thought system that defines or reinforces fundamental, inescapable, unbreachable divisions between people. They define that people are fundamentally different, whether they were created that way by God or created that way by nature.

Gabriel Archangel, what glorious day,
your radiant angels have come here to stay,
your purifications fire burning white,
intentions so pure, our hearts taking flight.

Gabriel Archangel, of this we are sure,
Gabriel Archangel, Christ light is the cure.
Gabriel Archangel, intentions so pure,
Gabriel Archangel, in you we're secure.

9. Gautama Buddha, awaken the most creative people to see that based on the recognition that we need to overcome division, and that many

ideologies reinforce or define divisions, we must take a new look at the thought systems we have.

> Gabriel Archangel, our planet so pure,
> in our bright new future we do feel secure,
> with your band of light encircling the earth,
> Saint Germain's Golden Age is now given birth.

> **Gabriel Archangel, of this we are sure,**
> **Gabriel Archangel, Christ light is the cure.**
> **Gabriel Archangel, intentions so pure,**
> **Gabriel Archangel, in you we're secure.**

Sealing

In the name of the I AM THAT I AM, I accept that Archangel Michael, Astrea and Shiva form an impenetrable shield around myself and all constructive people, sealing us from all fear-based energies in all four octaves. I accept that the Light of God is consuming and transforming all fear-based energies that make up the dark forces working against ending the era of ideology on earth!

23 INVOKING AWARENESS OF HOW IDEOLOGY LIMITS PROGRESS (PART 2)

In the name of the I AM THAT I AM, Jesus Christ, I use the authority that I have as a being in embodiment on earth to call upon Gautama Buddha to reinforce my calls and use my chakras to project the statements in this invocation into the collective consciousness and awaken people to the need to free ourselves from the ideological mindset. Awaken people to the reality that we are spiritual beings and that we can co-create a new future by working with the ascended masters. I especially call for …

[Make your own calls here.]

Part 1

1. Gautama Buddha, awaken the most creative people to see that there are many different thought systems that are not normally seen as ideologies, but they still reinforce divisions. Help people begin to question these unrecognized ideologies.

Raphael Archangel, your light so intense,
raise us beyond all human pretense.
Mother Mary and you have a vision so bold,
to see that our highest potential unfold.

Raphael Archangel, for vision we pray,
Raphael Archangel, show us the way,
Raphael Archangel, your emerald ray,
Raphael Archangel, our lives a new day.

2. Gautama Buddha, awaken the most creative people to see that there is a need to broaden people's understanding of what is an ideology or at least what is a thought system that creates division.

Raphael Archangel, in emerald sphere,
to immaculate vision we always adhere.
Mother Mary enfolds us in her Sacred Heart,
from Mother's true love, we're never apart.

Raphael Archangel, for vision we pray,
Raphael Archangel, show us the way,
Raphael Archangel, your emerald ray,
Raphael Archangel, our lives a new day.

3. Gautama Buddha, awaken the most creative people to see that many thought systems function exactly the same as an ideology, but people would never consider them to be ideologies. They do not even think that they are thought systems that have been defined by anybody. They are simply beliefs that people take for granted and never question.

Raphael Archangel, all ailments you heal,
each cell in our bodies in light now you seal.
Mother Mary's immaculate concept we see,
perfection of health our new reality.

Raphael Archangel, for vision we pray,
Raphael Archangel, show us the way,
Raphael Archangel, your emerald ray,
Raphael Archangel, our lives a new day.

4. Gautama Buddha, awaken the most creative people to see that there has been this veil over humankind for a very long time. In every historical period, in every generation, people have had certain ideas and beliefs that they took for granted and could not question.

Raphael Archangel, your light is so real,
the vision of Christ in us you reveal.
Mother Mary now helps us to truly transcend,
in emerald light with you we ascend.

**Raphael Archangel, for vision we pray,
Raphael Archangel, show us the way,
Raphael Archangel, your emerald ray,
Raphael Archangel, our lives a new day.**

5. Gautama Buddha, awaken the most creative people to see that they did not see them as ideas that had been defined by some source. They thought this is just the way life is. It is self-evident, it is obvious and there is no reason to question it.

Raphael Archangel, diseases are done,
as you help us see that all life is One,
we no longer do your true love reject,
immaculate vision on all we project.

**Raphael Archangel, for vision we pray,
Raphael Archangel, show us the way,
Raphael Archangel, your emerald ray,
Raphael Archangel, our lives a new day.**

6. Gautama Buddha, awaken the most creative people to see that in the past, people did not see a thought system as an ideology that could be opposed by an opposing ideology. There was nothing in people's minds that prompted them to challenge these beliefs.

Raphael Archangel, we're healing the earth,
in immaculate vision we give her rebirth,
a new era has on this day begun,
your emerald light now shines like a sun.

Raphael Archangel, for vision we pray,
Raphael Archangel, show us the way,
Raphael Archangel, your emerald ray,
Raphael Archangel, our lives a new day.

7. Gautama Buddha, awaken the most creative people to see that there are no beliefs on earth that just happened to appear. They were all engineered by the power elite beings for the specific purpose of controlling us, trapping our minds in blind alleys. They are all ideologies because they are defined specifically to control us.

Raphael Archangel, the fall is behind,
as all of earth's people the Christ path do find,
we call now to you all people to heal,
as four lower bodies in love you do seal.

Raphael Archangel, for vision we pray,
Raphael Archangel, show us the way,
Raphael Archangel, your emerald ray,
Raphael Archangel, our lives a new day.

8. Gautama Buddha, awaken the most creative people to see that the most effective way to imprison people is when we do not even realize we are imprisoned. We do not realize we are limited. We do not realize how limited we are. We might even think we are free because we do not recognize that our chains limit us.

Raphael Archangel, as you bring the light,
the forces of darkness swiftly take flight,
their day is now done as we claim the earth,
spreading to all an innocent mirth.

Raphael Archangel, for vision we pray,
Raphael Archangel, show us the way,
Raphael Archangel, your emerald ray,
Raphael Archangel, our lives a new day.

9. Gautama Buddha, awaken the most creative people to see that the belief that the earth was flat is an example of how we can use an idea, which

everybody today realizes was unrealistic, to imprison people without them realizing they were imprisoned. Many past civilizations have been imprisoned by ideas that people in the modern world can clearly see were out of touch with reality.

> Raphael Archangel, our vision set free,
> as we can now see God's reality,
> as Saint Germain's vision is manifest here,
> the earth is now sealed in immaculate sphere.

> **Raphael Archangel, for vision we pray,**
> **Raphael Archangel, show us the way,**
> **Raphael Archangel, your emerald ray,**
> **Raphael Archangel, our lives a new day.**

Part 2

1. Gautama Buddha, awaken the most creative people to see that we need to stand in front of the mirror and say: "Okay, do we in our civilization have some ideas, some beliefs, that we take for granted but they are in reality illusions? Is it possible that people in the future will look back at our civilization and think that some of our beliefs were just as primitive as what we think about the belief in a flat earth?"

> Uriel Archangel, immense is the power,
> of angels of peace, all war to devour.
> The demons of war, no match for your light,
> consuming them all, with radiance so bright.

> **Uriel Archangel, use your great sword,**
> **Uriel Archangel, consume all discord,**
> **Uriel Archangel, we're of one accord,**
> **Uriel Archangel, we walk with the Lord.**

2. Gautama Buddha, awaken the most creative people to make this shift in their awareness and start looking at today's world and see how many of the things that are not clearly defined as ideologies, as religions, as thought

systems, are floating around in the collective consciousness. It is difficult to pin down exactly where they came from, whether anybody has defined them or not, but very few people have questioned them.

Uriel Archangel, intense is the sound,
when millions of angels, their voices compound.
They build a crescendo, piercing the night,
life's glorious oneness revealed to our sight.

Uriel Archangel, use your great sword,
Uriel Archangel, consume all discord,
Uriel Archangel, we're of one accord,
Uriel Archangel, we walk with the Lord.

3. Gautama Buddha, awaken the most creative people to start this movement of questioning the unquestionable, questioning what has not been questioned before.

Uriel Archangel, from out the Great Throne,
your millions of trumpets, sound the One Tone.
Consuming all discord with your harmony,
the sound of all sounds will set all life free.

Uriel Archangel, use your great sword,
Uriel Archangel, consume all discord,
Uriel Archangel, we're of one accord,
Uriel Archangel, we walk with the Lord.

4. Gautama Buddha, awaken the most creative people to say: "Do we have ideologies? Do we have beliefs that are functioning as ideologies in terms of limiting us and creating conflict and division but we do not see it? We have not seen it as an idea that can be questioned just like any other idea. We take it for granted, we think it is a fact, something that should never be questioned."

Uriel Archangel, all war is now done,
for you bring a message, from heart of the One.
The hearts of all men, now singing in peace,
the spirals of love, forever increase.

Uriel Archangel, use your great sword,
Uriel Archangel, consume all discord,
Uriel Archangel, we're of one accord,
Uriel Archangel, we walk with the Lord.

5. Gautama Buddha, awaken the most creative people to see that this can open up for major progress in society. For example, one of the fundamental divisions we see in all democratic societies is the division between men and women. Many democratic societies have made considerable progress towards giving equality, but no society has fully questioned where the division between men and women comes from.

Uriel Archangel, your infinite peace,
from all warring beings our planet release,
war is a prison from which we are free,
embracing the peace of true unity.

Uriel Archangel, use your great sword,
Uriel Archangel, consume all discord,
Uriel Archangel, we're of one accord,
Uriel Archangel, we walk with the Lord.

6. Gautama Buddha, awaken the most creative people to see that the division between men and women was inflated and was turned into an ideology by the power elite beings for specific purposes. Men are more prone to go to war than women and that is why the elite decided to make men the superior sex and women the inferior sex.

Uriel Archangel, we send forth the call,
reveal now the oneness that unifies all,
help us the vision of peace now to see,
so we from all conflicts and struggles are free.

Uriel Archangel, use your great sword,
Uriel Archangel, consume all discord,
Uriel Archangel, we're of one accord,
Uriel Archangel, we walk with the Lord.

7. Gautama Buddha, awaken the most creative people to see that the division between men and women needs to be questioned. The idea that there is some fundamental difference between men and women needs to be questioned.

> Uriel Archangel, in service to life,
> you give us release from struggle and strife,
> forgetting the self is truly the key,
> to living a life in true harmony.

> **Uriel Archangel, use your great sword,**
> **Uriel Archangel, consume all discord,**
> **Uriel Archangel, we're of one accord,**
> **Uriel Archangel, we walk with the Lord.**

8. Gautama Buddha, awaken the most creative people to see that a difference in the physical body does not mean that there is a difference in the minds of men and women in the sense that women are inferior in their minds, incapable of understanding politics, science or other topics.

> Uriel Archangel, the earth now you raise,
> out of duality's death-bringing haze,
> we call now upon your great Flame of Peace,
> commanding that all petty squabbles do cease.

> **Uriel Archangel, use your great sword,**
> **Uriel Archangel, consume all discord,**
> **Uriel Archangel, we're of one accord,**
> **Uriel Archangel, we walk with the Lord.**

9. Gautama Buddha, awaken the most creative people to see that we are not men or women. We are spiritual beings, souls. There cannot be complete equality until reincarnation is recognized because then we see that all people have incarnated in both male and female bodies.

> Uriel Archangel, as peace is the norm,
> to your higher vision the earth does conform,
> as people have found your peace from within,
> a Golden Age is the prize that we win.

Uriel Archangel, use your great sword,
Uriel Archangel, consume all discord,
Uriel Archangel, we're of one accord,
Uriel Archangel, we walk with the Lord.

Part 3

1. Gautama Buddha, awaken the most creative people to see that as beings, as souls, we are not male or female, we are androgynous, we can embody in both bodies and we have the same level of intelligence, the same level of understanding, whether we are in a male or female body. There is no fundamental difference between the ability of men and women to grasp even the most complicated topics.

Zadkiel Archangel, your flow is so swift,
in your violet light, we instantly shift,
into a vibration in which we are free,
from all limitations of the lesser me.

Zadkiel Archangel, encircle the earth,
Zadkiel Archangel, with your violet girth,
Zadkiel Archangel, unstoppable mirth,
Zadkiel Archangel, our planet's rebirth.

2. Gautama Buddha, awaken the most creative people to see that there may be a certain cultural difference that has been imposed upon men and women where some women come to accept that: "Oh, I cannot understand math" and they give up before they have even tried.

Zadkiel Archangel, we truly aspire,
to being the master of your violet fire,
wielding the power, of your alchemy,
we use Sacred Word, to set all life free.

Zadkiel Archangel, encircle the earth,
Zadkiel Archangel, with your violet girth,

Zadkiel Archangel, unstoppable mirth,
Zadkiel Archangel, our planet's rebirth.

3. Gautama Buddha, awaken the most creative people to see that there is no fundamental difference in our ability to grasp these topics and this means that there is no validity to the idea that men are more suited to doing politics or science than women.

Zadkiel Archangel, your violet light,
transforming the earth, with unstoppable might,
so swiftly our planet, beginning to spin,
with legions of angels, our victory we win.

Zadkiel Archangel, encircle the earth,
Zadkiel Archangel, with your violet girth,
Zadkiel Archangel, unstoppable mirth,
Zadkiel Archangel, our planet's rebirth.

4. Gautama Buddha, awaken the most creative people to see that this is something that needs to be questioned and done away with. Many modern democracies are in the process, but there is still much more work to be done, especially by questioning the mentality behind it all.

Zadkiel Archangel, the earth is now free,
from burdens put on her by humanity,
all people are free from their inner strife,
embracing the freedom to start a new life.

Zadkiel Archangel, encircle the earth,
Zadkiel Archangel, with your violet girth,
Zadkiel Archangel, unstoppable mirth,
Zadkiel Archangel, our planet's rebirth.

5. Gautama Buddha, awaken the most creative people to see that when it comes to ending the era of ideology, it is more likely that men will have to take a back seat and that women be the forerunners.

Zadkiel Archangel, the earth will now spin,
much faster as we Christ victory win,

for in Christ the captives are truly set free,
bathed in Christ Light the earth now will be.

Zadkiel Archangel, encircle the earth,
Zadkiel Archangel, with your violet girth,
Zadkiel Archangel, unstoppable mirth,
Zadkiel Archangel, our planet's rebirth.

6. Gautama Buddha, awaken the most creative people to see that this is because women have been suppressed for so long that it is time for them to step forward and overcome the suppression and demonstrate that they have the ability to take society in a direction that men currently cannot do because of the programming of men.

Zadkiel Archangel, the forces of night,
are bound by your penetrating Freedom Light,
the earth is now cleared from forces so dark,
as your Violet Light provides a new spark.

Zadkiel Archangel, encircle the earth,
Zadkiel Archangel, with your violet girth,
Zadkiel Archangel, unstoppable mirth,
Zadkiel Archangel, our planet's rebirth.

7. Gautama Buddha, awaken the most creative people to see that when we look realistically at many societies, there is a difference between the minds of men and women, but there is no *inherent* division, they were not created with a division.

Zadkiel Archangel, we truly love you,
and to Saint Germain we will always be true,
help us now see our plans so Divine,
so we on this planet our full light can shine.

Zadkiel Archangel, encircle the earth,
Zadkiel Archangel, with your violet girth,
Zadkiel Archangel, unstoppable mirth,
Zadkiel Archangel, our planet's rebirth.

8. Gautama Buddha, awaken the most creative people to see that there may be a cultural division that has been imposed upon people over many generations, but all societies have young people that have incarnated who did not come from that civilization in past lifetimes and who are therefore not programmed by these divisions.

Zadkiel Archangel, there is no more night,
a new day is born from your great Violet Light,
transforming all manifestations of fear,
we know that the Golden Age is now here.

Zadkiel Archangel, encircle the earth,
Zadkiel Archangel, with your violet girth,
Zadkiel Archangel, unstoppable mirth,
Zadkiel Archangel, our planet's rebirth.

9. Gautama Buddha, awaken the most creative people to see that in every society there are men who are not trapped in the same mindset as most men in that society and we can find women who are not trapped in the mindset of most women. There is a possibility in every society that there are people who can give an alternative, give a frame of reference, that there is something outside of this cultural programming.

Zadkiel Archangel, your violet flame,
the earth and humanity, never the same,
Saint Germain's Golden Age, is a reality,
what glorious wonder, we joyously see.

Zadkiel Archangel, encircle the earth,
Zadkiel Archangel, with your violet girth,
Zadkiel Archangel, unstoppable mirth,
Zadkiel Archangel, our planet's rebirth.

Part 4

1. Gautama Buddha, awaken the most creative people to see that on a planetary scale it is far more likely that women can step up and challenge

these subtle ideologies, beginning with the idea that there is a difference between men and women and their abilities and therefore they should have different positions in society.

O Hercules Blue, we're one with your will,
all space in our beings with Blue Flame you fill,
a beacon that radiates light to the earth,
bringing about our planet's rebirth.

O Hercules Blue, all life you defend,
giving us power to always transcend,
in you the expansion of self has no end,
as we in God's infinite spirals ascend.

2. Gautama Buddha, awaken the most creative people to see that racism is normally not considered an ideology, but it *is* an ideology based on defining a fundamental division in humanity depending on artificial criteria that we call racial characteristics.

O Hercules Blue, your wisdom so great,
within us a sense of knowing create,
a new frame of reference we suddenly gain,
for going beyond duality's pain.

O Hercules Blue, all life you defend,
giving us power to always transcend,
in you the expansion of self has no end,
as we in God's infinite spirals ascend.

3. Gautama Buddha, awaken the most creative people to see that this is an ideology that divides people, and we need to question where it comes from.

O Hercules Blue, we lovingly raise,
our voices in giving God infinite praise,
in feeling your flame, so clearly we see,
transcending the self is the true alchemy.

O Hercules Blue, all life you defend,
giving us power to always transcend,
in you the expansion of self has no end,
as we in God's infinite spirals ascend.

4. Gautama Buddha, awaken the most creative people to see that many people are concerned about not appearing to be racist, but they still wonder: "Why do we have these differences? Why do people have different skin color? Why do they have these different characteristics? Could there be something to it?"

O Hercules Blue, all life now you heal,
enveloping all in your Blue-flame Seal,
we're grateful for playing a personal part,
In God's infinitely intricate work of art.

O Hercules Blue, all life you defend,
giving us power to always transcend,
in you the expansion of self has no end,
as we in God's infinite spirals ascend.

5. Gautama Buddha, awaken the most creative people to see that some people in the democratic world will be the first to say that society must not discriminate based on race, but in their minds they are still wondering where the concept of race came from.

O Hercules Blue, your Temple of Light,
revealed to us all through our inner sight,
your power allows us to forge on until,
we pierce every veil and climb every hill.

O Hercules Blue, all life you defend,
giving us power to always transcend,
in you the expansion of self has no end,
as we in God's infinite spirals ascend.

6. Gautama Buddha, awaken the most creative people to see that when we go to the very core of something, we see that there is no reality there,

there is only layers of illusion. Race is an artificial construct and there is no biological basis for dividing human beings into different races.

> O Hercules Blue, I pledge now my life,
> in helping this planet transcend human strife,
> duality's lies are pierced by your light,
> restoring the fullness of our inner sight.

> **O Hercules Blue, all life you defend,**
> **giving us power to always transcend,**
> **in you the expansion of self has no end,**
> **as we in God's infinite spirals ascend.**

7. Gautama Buddha, awaken the most creative people to see that for one dualistic polarity to exist, there must be another. In America there is a growing racism and white supremacy. This can only exist because there is the opposite polarity of those who have reformed their actions, but who have not truly freed themselves from the racist mindset.

> O Hercules Blue, we set all life free,
> from the subtlest lies of duality,
> the prince of this world no more has a bond,
> for with you we go completely beyond.

> **O Hercules Blue, all life you defend,**
> **giving us power to always transcend,**
> **in you the expansion of self has no end,**
> **as we in God's infinite spirals ascend.**

8. Gautama Buddha, awaken the most creative people to see that it is possible for some people in China to maintain the illusion that Marxism is a valid ideology because there is still a group of people in the democratic world who are believing in capitalism as a valid economic system, as an ideology.

> O Hercules Blue, in oneness with thee,
> we open our hearts to your reality,
> your electric-blue fire within us reveal,
> our innermost longing for all that is real.

O Hercules Blue, all life you defend,
giving us power to always transcend,
in you the expansion of self has no end,
as we in God's infinite spirals ascend.

9. Gautama Buddha, awaken the most creative people to see that there is always this pairing and the key to overcoming it is that some people in one of the polarities must begin to question the mindset behind it.

O Hercules Blue, you fill every space,
with infinite Power and infinite Grace,
you embody the key to creativity,
the will to transcend into Infinity.

O Hercules Blue, all life you defend,
giving us power to always transcend,
in you the expansion of self has no end,
as we in God's infinite spirals ascend.

Part 5

1. Gautama Buddha, awaken the most creative people to see that another camouflaged ideology is scientific Materialism. It attempts to give an explanation of how the world works and it is claimed that this explanation is infallible in its basic premise that there is nothing beyond the material universe and that everything that happens on earth has a materialistic explanation.

Beloved Apollo, with your second ray,
you open our eyes to see a new day,
We see through duality's lies and deceit,
transcending the mindset producing defeat.

Beloved Apollo, thou Elohim Gold,
your radiant light our eyes now behold,
as pages of wisdom you gently unfold,
our planet is free from all that is old.

2. Gautama Buddha, awaken the most creative people to see that Materialism has a program for change of society, namely to create a society where religion has been eradicated and where everybody is basing their worldview on the materialist interpretation of science, the materialist ideology that has been superimposed upon science.

Beloved Apollo, in your flame we know,
that your living wisdom is always a flow,
in your light we see our own highest will,
immersed in the stream that never stands still.

Beloved Apollo, thou Elohim Gold,
your radiant light our eyes now behold,
as pages of wisdom you gently unfold,
our planet is free from all that is old.

3. Gautama Buddha, awaken the most creative people to see that materialists will not see this as an ideology. They think it is based on scientific fact, and that they have a right to force society and force other people, they have a right to go out and undermine religion.

Beloved Apollo, your light makes it clear,
why we have taken embodiment here,
exposing all lies causing the fall,
you help us reclaim the oneness of all.

Beloved Apollo, thou Elohim Gold,
your radiant light our eyes now behold,
as pages of wisdom you gently unfold,
our planet is free from all that is old.

4. Gautama Buddha, awaken the most creative people to see that Materialism has the concept of a struggle. Materialists are portraying that implementing their program requires a struggle to overcome the resistance from religion because religious people will not voluntarily give up their religion and therefore there must be a struggle.

Beloved Apollo, exposing all lies,
we hereby surrender all ego-based ties,

we know our perception is truly the key,
to transcending the serpentine duality.

**Beloved Apollo, thou Elohim Gold,
your radiant light our eyes now behold,
as pages of wisdom you gently unfold,
our planet is free from all that is old.**

5. Gautama Buddha, awaken the most creative people to see that the question is how far this will go. A materialistic view was incorporated in Marxist ideology, it was found in the Soviet Union and there was violence used to eradicate religion in many of the countries in the Soviet Union. The same in China. Some materialists are indeed violent.

Beloved Apollo, we heed now your call,
drawing us into Wisdom's Great Hall,
working to raise our own cosmic sphere,
together we form the tip of the spear.

**Beloved Apollo, thou Elohim Gold,
your radiant light our eyes now behold,
as pages of wisdom you gently unfold,
our planet is free from all that is old.**

6. Gautama Buddha, awaken the most creative people to see that Materialism seeks to convert the broad population, but it also seeks to create a more committed elite. The rise in militant atheism is driven by a small elite that are committed to spreading this ideology of materialism.

Beloved Apollo, your wisdom so clear,
in oneness with you, no serpent we fear,
the beam in our eye we willingly see,
we're free from the serpent's own duality.

**Beloved Apollo, thou Elohim Gold,
your radiant light our eyes now behold,
as pages of wisdom you gently unfold,
our planet is free from all that is old.**

7. Gautama Buddha, awaken the most creative people to see that materialism defines that there is a certain elite that are the only ones capable of grasping the ideology and implementing it. There is also a tendency to think that it is intellectuals who can drive this because it is primarily the rational, intellectual, analytical people who can see the fallacies of religion.

> Beloved Apollo, you help us to see
> through your knowing eyes we truly are free,
> we willingly stand in your piercing gaze,
> empowered, we exit duality's maze.

> **Beloved Apollo, thou Elohim Gold,**
> **your radiant light our eyes now behold,**
> **as pages of wisdom you gently unfold,**
> **our planet is free from all that is old.**

8. Gautama Buddha, awaken the most creative people to see that Materialism in all respects functions as an ideology and therefore it has the same dynamic as other ideologies. One of the primary dynamics is that it limits human thought.

> Beloved Apollo, our vision we raise,
> we see that the earth is in a new phase,
> for nothing can stop the knowledge you bring,
> exposing that there's no separate thing.

> **Beloved Apollo, thou Elohim Gold,**
> **your radiant light our eyes now behold,**
> **as pages of wisdom you gently unfold,**
> **our planet is free from all that is old.**

9. Gautama Buddha, awaken the most creative people to see that the essence of the scientific method is that our current worldview is a starting point for formulating experiments that can be performed. As we observe how the world works and observe the results of our experiments, we are meant to refine our worldview. Therefore, we never have a final worldview.

> Beloved Apollo, in wisdom's great mirth,
> we all are together uplifting the earth,

as you now the true Flame of Wisdom reveal,
all of earth's people can see what is real.

**Beloved Apollo, thou Elohim Gold,
your radiant light our eyes now behold,
as pages of wisdom you gently unfold,
our planet is free from all that is old.**

Sealing

In the name of the I AM THAT I AM, I accept that Archangel Michael, Astrea and Shiva form an impenetrable shield around myself and all constructive people, sealing us from all fear-based energies in all four octaves. I accept that the Light of God is consuming and transforming all fear-based energies that make up the dark forces working against ending the era of ideology on earth!

24 INVOKING AWARENESS OF HOW IDEOLOGY LIMITS PROGRESS (PART 3)

In the name of the I AM THAT I AM, Jesus Christ, I use the authority that I have as a being in embodiment on earth to call upon Gautama Buddha to reinforce my calls and use my chakras to project the statements in this invocation into the collective consciousness and awaken people to the need to free ourselves from the ideological mindset. Awaken people to the reality that we are spiritual beings and that we can co-create a new future by working with the ascended masters. I especially call for …

[Make your own calls here.]

Part 1

1. Gautama Buddha, awaken the most creative people to see that any worldview is falsifiable, it is not complete, it is not infallible. There is always more to understand and when we understand that more, we might see that our current worldview is incomplete, perhaps even out of touch with reality.

O Heros-Amora, in your love so pink,
we care not what others about us may think,
in oneness with you, we claim a new day,
as innocent children, we frolic and play.

**O Heros-Amora, we reap what we sow,
yet this is Plan B for helping us grow,
for truly, Plan A is that we join the flow,
immersed in the Infinite Love you bestow.**

2. Gautama Buddha, awaken the most creative people to see that even though materialists are constantly referring to science as the ultimate authority, they are out of touch with this basic principle of science. They are not seeing the materialist philosophy as just a starting point for further observation and inquiry. They are seeing it as the final truth.

O Heros-Amora, a new life begun,
we laugh at the devil, the serious one,
the serpent is stuck in his duality,
but we are set free by Love's reality.

**O Heros-Amora, we reap what we sow,
yet this is Plan B for helping us grow,
for truly, Plan A is that we join the flow,
immersed in the Infinite Love you bestow.**

3. Gautama Buddha, awaken the most creative people to see that if we take the idea that a scientific theory should be falsifiable and apply that to Materialism, it is not falsifiable. We cannot demonstrate the claim that there is nothing beyond the material universe through the materialistic approach.

O Heros-Amora, awakened we see,
in true love is no conditionality,
we bathe in your glorious Ruby-Pink Sun,
knowing our God allows life to be fun.

**O Heros-Amora, we reap what we sow,
yet this is Plan B for helping us grow,**

**for truly, Plan A is that we join the flow,
immersed in the Infinite Love you bestow.**

4. Gautama Buddha, awaken the most creative people to see that there is no way in Materialism that we could prove the existence of something beyond the material universe. It is defined out of existence, there is no possibility of doing this.

O Heros-Amora, life is such a joy,
we see that the world is like a great toy,
whatever the mind into it projects,
the mirror of life exactly reflects.

**O Heros-Amora, we reap what we sow,
yet this is Plan B for helping us grow,
for truly, Plan A is that we join the flow,
immersed in the Infinite Love you bestow.**

5. Gautama Buddha, awaken the most creative people to see that materialists have violated the principle of falsifiability by defining the materialist ideology in such a way that within the ideology itself, there is no possibility of proving that the ideology is wrong. This is similar to many other ideologies, such as the Christian religion, the Muslim religion and Marxism.

O Heros-Amora, conditions you burn,
we know we are free to take a new turn,
Immersed in the stream of infinite Love,
we know that the Spirit came from Above.

**O Heros-Amora, we reap what we sow,
yet this is Plan B for helping us grow,
for truly, Plan A is that we join the flow,
immersed in the Infinite Love you bestow.**

6. Gautama Buddha, awaken the most creative people to see that many people in past lifetimes believed in the Christian promise that they would go to heaven after that lifetime. After they passed from the physical body, they realized they are not going to go to heaven, and after several lifetimes they no longer trust the Christian religion and its promises.

O Heros-Amora, we feel that at last,
we've risen above the trap of the past,
in true love we claim our freedom to grow,
forever we're one with Love's Infinite Flow.

O Heros-Amora, we reap what we sow,
yet this is Plan B for helping us grow,
for truly, Plan A is that we join the flow,
immersed in the Infinite Love you bestow.

7. Gautama Buddha, awaken the most creative people to see that some people gave up on the Christian religion, but became pulled into the materialist ideology. They have lived several lifetimes believing in the claim that there would be nothing after they died, but then they have experienced that there is, and they are ready to question the materialist claim.

O Heros-Amora, conditions are ties,
forming a net of serpentine lies,
but you have the antidote setting us free,
you take us beyond conditionality.

O Heros-Amora, we reap what we sow,
yet this is Plan B for helping us grow,
for truly, Plan A is that we join the flow,
immersed in the Infinite Love you bestow.

8. Gautama Buddha, awaken the most creative people to question the materialist claim, and say: "What if there really is something beyond the material universe?"

O Heros-Amora, your love is no bond,
for love only wants to take us beyond,
your love has no bounds, forever it flies,
raising all life into Ruby-Pink skies.

O Heros-Amora, we reap what we sow,
yet this is Plan B for helping us grow,
for truly, Plan A is that we join the flow,
immersed in the Infinite Love you bestow.

9. Gautama Buddha, awaken the most creative people to see that Materialism has defined the doctrine that the human mind can and must be explained as a material phenomenon. Everything that goes on in the mind is the result of material, physical, chemical, electromagnetic processes in the physical brain. There is nothing to us, our minds, our personalities, that does not come from the brain.

> O Heros-Amora, love bathing the earth,
> filling all people with infinite mirth,
> for fear and despair there is no more room,
> as all are awakened by love's sonic boom.

> **O Heros-Amora, we reap what we sow,**
> **yet this is Plan B for helping us grow,**
> **for truly, Plan A is that we join the flow,**
> **immersed in the Infinite Love you bestow.**

Part 2

1. Gautama Buddha, awaken the most creative people to see that this is currently the one factor that more than anything else is holding back scientific progress. It is also holding back the development in society because a democratic nation cannot fully overcome division until we see a connection between different people, and this connection is not physical.

> Beloved Astrea, your heart is so true,
> your Circle and Sword of white and blue,
> cut all life free from dramas unwise,
> on wings of Purity our planet will rise.

> **Beloved Astrea, in oneness with you,**
> **your circle and sword of electric blue,**
> **with Purity's Light cutting right through,**
> **raising the earth into all that is true.**

2. Gautama Buddha, awaken the most creative people to see that our bodies are separate. We cannot create a sense of oneness and equality between

people through physical means. If there is a connection between people, it must be a connection at the level of the mind.

> Beloved Astrea, in God Purity,
> accelerate all of our life energy,
> we're rising beyond every impurity,
> as Purity's Light forever we see.

> **Beloved Astrea, in oneness with you,**
> **your circle and sword of electric blue,**
> **with Purity's Light cutting right through,**
> **raising the earth into all that is true.**

3. Gautama Buddha, awaken the most creative people to see that human minds can be connected even though the bodies are separated by distance. If democracy is to be taken to a higher level, if scientific inquiry is to be taken to a higher level, we need to challenge the materialist ideology that says that the mind is a material phenomenon, the mind is produced by the body.

> Beloved Astrea, from Purity's Ray,
> send forth deliverance to all life today,
> acceleration to Purity, we are now free
> from all that is less than love's Purity.

> **Beloved Astrea, in oneness with you,**
> **your circle and sword of electric blue,**
> **with Purity's Light cutting right through,**
> **raising the earth into all that is true.**

4. Gautama Buddha, awaken the most creative people to see that when we overcome this, an entirely new plethora of opportunities open up for explaining the connection between people, overcoming the divisions and conflicts between people, realizing that all life is connected, that what we do to others really does affect ourselves.

> Beloved Astrea, accelerate us all,
> as for your deliverance we fervently call,

set all life free from vision impure
beyond fear and doubt, we're rising for sure.

**Beloved Astrea, in oneness with you,
your circle and sword of electric blue,
with Purity's Light cutting right through,
raising the earth into all that is true.**

5. Gautama Buddha, awaken the most creative people to see that politically, we can take society to a higher level, we can overcome the division between the rich and the poor world where the rich nations realize that it is their opportunity and their responsibility to use their affluence to help those in other nations.

Beloved Astrea, we're willing to see,
all of the lies that keep us unfree,
we surrender all lies causing the fall,
forever affirming the oneness of All.

**Beloved Astrea, in oneness with you,
your circle and sword of electric blue,
with Purity's Light cutting right through,
raising the earth into all that is true.**

6. Gautama Buddha, awaken the most creative people to see that we can open up for new scientific fields of inquiry where we start using scientific tools to investigate consciousness.

Beloved Astrea, accelerate life
beyond all duality's struggle and strife,
consume all division between God and man,
accelerate fulfillment of God's perfect plan.

**Beloved Astrea, in oneness with you,
your circle and sword of electric blue,
with Purity's Light cutting right through,
raising the earth into all that is true.**

7. Gautama Buddha, awaken the most creative people to see that the mind can have an influence on physical matter and on the health of our physical bodies, which has already been proven for anyone who is not trapped in the materialist ideological mindset.

Beloved Astrea, we lovingly call,
break down separation's invisible wall,
raising our minds into true unity
with the Masters of love in Infinity.

Beloved Astrea, in oneness with you,
your circle and sword of electric blue,
with Purity's Light cutting right through,
raising the earth into all that is true.

8. Gautama Buddha, awaken the most creative people to see that new inquiries for physical healing open up, but also new inquiries for psychological healing. The next logical step for the modern democracies is to go beyond *material* welfare to creating *psychological* welfare.

Beloved Astrea, help all of us find,
the secret that we create with the mind,
and thus what in ignorance we decreate,
in knowledge we easily can recreate.

Beloved Astrea, in oneness with you,
your circle and sword of electric blue,
with Purity's Light cutting right through,
raising the earth into all that is true.

9. Gautama Buddha, awaken the most creative people to see that we cannot do this if we do not understand how the psyche works. We cannot understand how the psyche works if we are not using scientific tools to investigate the mind.

Beloved Astrea, we all do aspire,
to learning to use your purity's fire,
to raise every form in infamy sown,
as Saint Germain makes this planet his own.

Beloved Astrea, in oneness with you,
your circle and sword of electric blue,
with Purity's Light cutting right through,
raising the earth into all that is true.

Part 3

1. Gautama Buddha, awaken the most creative people to see that by questioning Materialism, we open up a new field of philosophical inquiry. Western philosophers have based their philosophy on the rational mind. They have assumed that the rational mind is the ultimate tool for philosophical inquiry, and that the rational mind only works at the analytical, linear level.

Cyclopea so dear, the truth you reveal,
the truth that duality's ailments will heal,
your Emerald Light is like a great balm,
our emotional bodies are perfectly calm.

Cyclopea so dear, in Emerald Sphere,
in raising perception we shall persevere,
as deep in our hearts your truth we revere,
to immaculate vision the earth does adhere.

2. Gautama Buddha, awaken the most creative people to see that philosophers have generally assumed that they have the state of mind, the capacity of mind, to rationally understand all that is possible to understand about the universe.

Cyclopea so dear, with you we unwind,
all negative spirals clouding the mind,
we know pure awareness is truly our core,
the key to becoming the wide-open door.

Cyclopea so dear, in Emerald Sphere,
in raising perception we shall persevere,
as deep in our hearts your truth we revere,
to immaculate vision the earth does adhere.

3. Gautama Buddha, awaken the most creative people to see that what is missing from Western philosophy is the concept that there are different states of consciousness, higher states of consciousness, and that most human beings today are at a certain level of consciousness where they can see within a certain horizon, but they cannot see beyond that horizon.

> Cyclopea so dear, clear our inner sight,
> empowered, we pierce the soul's fearful night,
> we now see our life through your single eye,
> beyond all disease we're ready to fly.

> **Cyclopea so dear, in Emerald Sphere,**
> **in raising perception we shall persevere,**
> **as deep in our hearts your truth we revere,**
> **to immaculate vision the earth does adhere.**

4. Gautama Buddha, awaken the most creative people to see that it is possible for human beings to follow a systematic process of raising our consciousness, expanding our awareness, so that we can see beyond our observation horizon. We can come to see what people cannot see today and this is what has caused human progress.

> Cyclopea so dear, life can only reflect,
> the images that the mind does project,
> the key to our healing is clearing the mind,
> from the images the ego is hiding behind.

> **Cyclopea so dear, in Emerald Sphere,**
> **in raising perception we shall persevere,**
> **as deep in our hearts your truth we revere,**
> **to immaculate vision the earth does adhere.**

5. Gautama Buddha, awaken the most creative people to see that the expansion of knowledge really means an expansion of the observation horizon, how far we can see.

> Cyclopea so dear, we want to aim high,
> to your healing flame we ever draw nigh,

through veils of duality we now take flight,
bathed in your penetrating Emerald Light.

**Cyclopea so dear, in Emerald Sphere,
in raising perception we shall persevere,
as deep in our hearts your truth we revere,
to immaculate vision the earth does adhere.**

6. Gautama Buddha, awaken the most creative people to see that we have not discovered the ultimate limits for knowledge. By raising consciousness, we can expand the observation horizon and come to see things that we cannot see today. The key to doing this is to understand how the mind works and apply these universal principles for how we can expand our consciousness.

Cyclopea so dear, your Emerald Flame,
exposes every subtle, dualistic power game,
including the game of wanting to say,
that truth is defined in only one way.

**Cyclopea so dear, in Emerald Sphere,
in raising perception we shall persevere,
as deep in our hearts your truth we revere,
to immaculate vision the earth does adhere.**

7. Gautama Buddha, awaken the most creative people to see that all human beings have the potential to understand how life works, all of us have the capacity to raise our consciousness and fathom fundamental principles that guide life and how life works.

Cyclopea so dear, we're feeling the flow,
as your Living Truth upon us you bestow,
from all dual vision we are now set free,
planet earth in immaculate matrix will be.

**Cyclopea so dear, in Emerald Sphere,
in raising perception we shall persevere,
as deep in our hearts your truth we revere,
to immaculate vision the earth does adhere.**

8. Gautama Buddha, awaken the most creative people to see that ideology has always been profoundly elitist. Ideology is created by one person or a few people. It attracts a few adherents that think they are the superior elite who can understand and implement the ideology.

> Cyclopea so dear, the truth is now clear,
> we see higher purpose for which we are here
> we know truth transcends all systems below,
> immersed in your light, we continue to grow.

> **Cyclopea so dear, in Emerald Sphere,**
> **in raising perception we shall persevere,**
> **as deep in our hearts your truth we revere,**
> **to immaculate vision the earth does adhere.**

9. Gautama Buddha, awaken the most creative people to see that even though an ideology may appeal to a broader range of intellectuals, members of the elite define that there are some people who can grasp the ideology, but the broad population cannot. That is why the elite needs to force the ideology on society "for the greater good."

> Cyclopea so dear, we're feeling your joy,
> as creative vision we now do employ,
> in lifting earth out of serpentine cage,
> to manifest Saint Germain's Golden Age.

> **Cyclopea so dear, in Emerald Sphere,**
> **in raising perception we shall persevere,**
> **as deep in our hearts your truth we revere,**
> **to immaculate vision the earth does adhere.**

Part 4

1. Gautama Buddha, awaken the most creative people to see that according to the elite, the majority of the people do not need to be educated into grasping the ideology, they need to be forced into compliance with the ideology because they are not capable of grasping what the elite can grasp.

O Elohim Peace, in Unity's Flame,
there is no more room for duality's game,
we know that all form is from the same source,
empowering us to plot a new course.

O Elohim Peace, through your tranquility,
we are free from the chaos of duality,
in oneness with God a new identity,
we are raising the earth into Infinity.

2. Gautama Buddha, awaken the most creative people to see that this is a division and it is an illusion. Democracy proves that all people have the capacity to understand certain principles, certain mechanics of how the world works.

O Elohim Peace, the bell now you ring,
causing all atoms to vibrate and sing,
we give up the sense of a separate "me,"
we're crossing Samsara's turbulent sea.

O Elohim Peace, through your tranquility,
we are free from the chaos of duality,
in oneness with God a new identity,
we are raising the earth into Infinity.

3. Gautama Buddha, awaken the most creative people to see that the vast majority of people in many democratic societies have risen beyond a certain level of consciousness. They are not violent, they would not even dream of committing violence against another human being.

O Elohim Peace, you help us to know,
that Jesus has come your Flame to bestow,
upon all who are ready to give up the strife,
by following Christ into infinite life.

O Elohim Peace, through your tranquility,
we are free from the chaos of duality,
in oneness with God a new identity,
we are raising the earth into Infinity.

4. Gautama Buddha, awaken the most creative people to see that many people have overcome the old mindset that is built into most ideologies, namely the epic mindset where the ends can justify the means.

O Elohim Peace, through your eyes we see,
that only in oneness will we ever be free,
we now see that there is no separate thing,
to the ego-based self we no longer cling.

**O Elohim Peace, through your tranquility,
we are free from the chaos of duality,
in oneness with God a new identity,
we are raising the earth into Infinity.**

5. Gautama Buddha, awaken the most creative people to consciously dismiss the idea that the ends can justify the means, and realize that regardless of what goals we may have defined, using violence is not justified in order to reach those goals.

O Elohim Peace, you show us the way,
for clearing the mind from duality's fray,
you pierce the illusions of both time and space,
separation consumed by your Infinite Grace.

**O Elohim Peace, through your tranquility,
we are free from the chaos of duality,
in oneness with God a new identity,
we are raising the earth into Infinity.**

6. Gautama Buddha, awaken the most creative people to see that this is one of the fundamental principles, one of the mechanics, of a democratic society because if a democratic society is using violence to force people to become democratic, then it is not a democracy.

O Elohim Peace, what beauty your name,
consuming within us duality's shame,
the earth is set free from burden of fear,
accepting your peace is now manifest here.

**O Elohim Peace, through your tranquility,
we are free from the chaos of duality,
in oneness with God a new identity,
we are raising the earth into Infinity.**

7. Gautama Buddha, awaken the most creative people to see that all human beings have the same potential. There is a range of what people understand, but the basic principle of democracy is that people were not created with different capacities of the mind.

O Elohim Peace, with Christ at our side,
no force of duality can evermore hide,
It was through the vibration of your Golden Flame,
that Christ the illusion of death overcame.

**O Elohim Peace, through your tranquility,
we are free from the chaos of duality,
in oneness with God a new identity,
we are raising the earth into Infinity.**

8. Gautama Buddha, awaken the most creative people to see that all people were created with the same potential to expand their awareness and come to understand even complex topics. It is just a matter of how willing they have been to apply it, and how they have been able to apply it based on the knowledge they were given of how the mind works.

O Elohim Peace, you bring now to earth,
the unstoppable flame of Cosmic Rebirth,
we give up the sense that something is "mine,"
allowing your Light through our beings to shine.

**O Elohim Peace, through your tranquility,
we are free from the chaos of duality,
in oneness with God a new identity,
we are raising the earth into Infinity.**

9. Gautama Buddha, awaken the most creative people to see that many democracies fail in educating their children about the basic mechanics of the human psyche. All have the potential to expand their awareness and

give up the hidden ideology that acquiring knowledge is reserved for an elite and not for the general population.

> O Elohim Peace, as peace now we feel,
> all records of war you totally heal,
> the earth is now free from forces of war,
> restoring her purity known from before.

> **O Elohim Peace, through your tranquility,**
> **we are free from the chaos of duality,**
> **in oneness with God a new identity,**
> **we are raising the earth into Infinity.**

Part 5

1. Gautama Buddha, awaken the most creative people to see that there are two distinct ways of acquiring knowledge. One is the horizontal way, where we use observations to deduce certain general principles. We can make observations of specifics and expand this to generalities and therefore discover natural laws.

> Beloved Arcturus, release now the flow,
> of Violet Flame to help all life grow,
> in ever-expanding circles of light,
> it pulses within every atom so bright.

> **Beloved Arcturus, your Violet Flame pure,**
> **is for every ailment the ultimate cure,**
> **against it no darkness could ever endure,**
> **earth's freedom it will forever ensure.**

2. Gautama Buddha, awaken the most creative people to see that there is also a vertical way of acquiring knowledge. The vertical way is the mystical religions or the mystical path that has been taught in many different societies.

Beloved Arcturus, thou Elohim Free,
we open our hearts to your reality,
we have no attachments to life here on earth,
we claim a new life in your Flame of Rebirth.

**Beloved Arcturus, your Violet Flame pure,
is for every ailment the ultimate cure,
against it no darkness could ever endure,
earth's freedom it will forever ensure.**

3. Gautama Buddha, awaken the most creative people to grasp in more universal terms that it is possible to expand the capacity of our minds to where we can intuitively receive certain insights, ideas, impressions that give us a greater understanding.

Beloved Arcturus, be with us alway,
reborn, we are ready to face a new day,
expanding our hearts into Infinity,
your flame is the key to our God-victory.

**Beloved Arcturus, your Violet Flame pure,
is for every ailment the ultimate cure,
against it no darkness could ever endure,
earth's freedom it will forever ensure.**

4. Gautama Buddha, awaken the most creative people to see that there is a realm that contains all knowledge about how the universe works. Human progress happened because some people received a new idea from this universal library of knowledge.

Beloved Arcturus, your bright violet fire,
now fills every atom, raising them higher,
the space in each atom all filled with your light,
as matter itself is shining so bright.

**Beloved Arcturus, your Violet Flame pure,
is for every ailment the ultimate cure,
against it no darkness could ever endure,
earth's freedom it will forever ensure.**

5. Gautama Buddha, awaken the most creative people to see that what Einstein did was to receive an idea from the universal library and everybody can do the same.

> Beloved Arcturus, your transforming Grace,
> empowers us now every challenge to face,
> with your Freedom's Song filling the ear,
> we know that to God we're ever so dear.

> **Beloved Arcturus, your Violet Flame pure,**
> **is for every ailment the ultimate cure,**
> **against it no darkness could ever endure,**
> **earth's freedom it will forever ensure.**

6. Gautama Buddha, awaken the most creative people to see that we don't need to be as smart as Einstein, but we need to be open to receiving an idea based on our practical knowledge of a particular field.

> Beloved Arcturus, we surrender all fear,
> we're feeling your Presence so tangibly near,
> as your violet light floods our inner space,
> towards the ascension we willingly race.

> **Beloved Arcturus, your Violet Flame pure,**
> **is for every ailment the ultimate cure,**
> **against it no darkness could ever endure,**
> **earth's freedom it will forever ensure.**

7. Gautama Buddha, awaken the most creative people to see that we can use the rational mind to educate our minds about what is already known, and based on that foundation we can use the intuitive mind to reach for a new idea in this field.

> Beloved Arcturus, bring in a new age,
> help earth and humanity turn a new page,
> your transforming light gives us certainty,
> Saint Germain's Golden Age is a reality.

**Beloved Arcturus, your Violet Flame pure,
is for every ailment the ultimate cure,
against it no darkness could ever endure,
earth's freedom it will forever ensure.**

8. Gautama Buddha, awaken the most creative people to overturn elitism by abandoning the idea that only the elite can receive new ideas. Often, members of the elite cannot receive new ideas because their hidden ideology, their elitist mindset of superiority, blocks them from receiving these ideas.

Beloved Arcturus, illusions you pierce,
no serpent can stand against angels so fierce,
no forces of darkness can stop Violet Flame,
all discord on earth it will instantly tame.

**Beloved Arcturus, your Violet Flame pure,
is for every ailment the ultimate cure,
against it no darkness could ever endure,
earth's freedom it will forever ensure.**

9. Gautama Buddha, awaken the most creative people to see that when we have this democratization of knowledge, we will see an acceleration of invention and new ideas that we have not yet seen on this planet, even in the last century.

Beloved Arcturus, we love Saint Germain,
and therefore we call forth again and again,
your Violet Flame to flood all the earth,
so Saint Germain's eyes are filling with mirth.

**Beloved Arcturus, your Violet Flame pure,
is for every ailment the ultimate cure,
against it no darkness could ever endure,
earth's freedom it will forever ensure.**

Sealing

In the name of the I AM THAT I AM, I accept that Archangel Michael, Astrea and Shiva form an impenetrable shield around myself and all constructive people, sealing us from all fear-based energies in all four octaves. I accept that the Light of God is consuming and transforming all fear-based energies that make up the dark forces working against ending the era of ideology on earth!

25 EVERYONE HAS A PERSONAL IDEOLOGY

I AM the Ascended Master Gautama Buddha. When we step back from the topic of ideology, look at it from a greater distance, we see that although there are many different ideologies, thought systems, belief systems that have been introduced on earth, and although we see that there are many thought systems that are not normally considered ideologies, we can actually see that there is one particular issue that is common amongst virtually all of them. I started out by saying that one of the things an ideology has to explain is why there is suffering on earth, why there is dissatisfaction on earth. If you consider a planet like earth, that for a very, very long time has been a dense planet (where the population has been in duality, has been manipulated by various power elites, and deceived by various ideologies), how can you explain the fact that people almost universally have a sense that they should *not* be suffering, that there should be a better way to live, a better society, that there should be a way to escape suffering?

If you go back to the teaching I gave 2,500 years ago and look at the society in which I gave that teaching, and compare it to the more advanced nations in today's world, you would see that the way people lived back then was so different from modern society that you almost cannot fathom the difference. You who have grown up in a modern society cannot even begin to imagine how people lived, how people looked at life, how people felt back then. You see that 2,500 years ago, I still gave a teaching based on the concept that there is suffering, but that there is a way out of suffering.

Why could I give that teaching if it had not been for the fact that there is a universal recognition in most people that they should not be suffering, that there should be an alternative to suffering.

The reason for this is of course that you are, as we have said, *experiential* beings. There is an aspect of experience that goes through all four levels of the material universe. You may say, you are having a physical experience in the physical realm because you are in physical embodiment. But there is an aspect of your experience that is in the emotional, one that is in the mental and one that is in the identity realm. When you look at humankind and the history of humankind, you see that, over this very long-time span (far longer than recorded history) where people have been in embodiment on earth, there are certain patterns, certain matrices, that have been created in the emotional, mental and identity bodies. We might, to use a different terminology, say that there is a certain collective memory that has been established.

This memory actually goes back to when the earth was a natural planet. For those who have come from other planets, well they have taken with them some of the memory from those planets. This memory is not a *theory*. You may as a young child have touched a hot stove and burned your finger. You know that the stove is hot and it hurts if you touch it, which means you are not going to do it again. This is not a *theory* you have. This is not some kind of *ideology* you have adopted about hot stoves. You are not thinking about this. This is an *experience,* an *experiential* memory that you have. Likewise, humankind has a certain experiential memory, in the emotional, mental and identity realms. In the identity realm, there is a collective memory that there is an alternative to suffering.

Fallen beings can only create suffering

Now, you look at the fallen beings and you realize that they do not have this memory. When you fall to a different sphere, your memory is erased. You still have certain things you bring with you from the previous sphere: a certain mindset, certain beliefs, certain separate selves, a certain ideology, a certain state of denial, but the experiential memory is not brought with you. You start all over again, building a new experiential memory in that sphere, and the next sphere, and so on. That is why you actually have some fallen beings that do not have this sense that there should be an alternative to their present state of mind. They think it is the ultimate state of mind.

Some fallen beings would not even admit that it is causing them suffering, even though it is causing them constant tension. They think there is no alternative to it.

The vast majority of human beings on the planet, they have this sense that there should be an alternative to suffering. As I said, the basic question, we might say, on earth is: "Why is there suffering when everybody knows it should not be here?" This of course is what most ideologies attempt to explain because this is the only way that the fallen beings can control people.

What you see is very simple. The fallen beings can only cause suffering. They are on earth, they have an agenda, it involves or necessitates controlling human beings by forcing them. When you force people into an unnatural state, it causes tension, it causes suffering. The fallen beings cannot exist on the planet without causing suffering. In order to convince people that a certain ideology is valid, superior, infallible, they have to attempt to explain why there is suffering. Of course, they do so, among other things, by pointing the finger at some other group of people and anointing them as the scapegoat who is the cause of suffering.

What I want to point out here is that if you step back from this, and you look at the fact that there is this collective memory that suffering is not inevitable, then you can see that all ideologies are based on a very particular viewpoint, namely: Something has gone wrong on earth, something has gone wrong in the world, something has gone wrong in the universe.

People experience they are suffering. They have the memory that it should not be there. What the fallen beings do is they create ideologies and belief systems that say that the reason why there is suffering, that people know should not be there, is because something has gone wrong.

The ideology that something has gone wrong

Now, of course when you look at earth, you will see that the fallen beings have been very good at keeping their own identity, existence and presence secret for the vast majority of people. Even though there is some concepts of a devil and dark forces and this and that, it is still a very rudimentary understanding of this that basically hides the existence of fallen beings on the planet. Therefore, of course it hides the real cause of suffering. It also hides the duality consciousness because an ideology that springs from the duality consciousness cannot expose the duality consciousness.

What you see is that you have this sense (that has been around for a long time on this planet) that something has gone wrong. Now, this sense that something has gone wrong is not based on experience. You have a previous experience that there was not always suffering so there is an alternative to suffering. Now, you have an experience that there is suffering. You do not actually have this collective experience or memory that something has gone wrong in the universe. You have a memory of the contrast between suffering and non-suffering, but even though you might say that there was a period of time where suffering started, people were not aware why suffering started. They experienced that it started but they did not experience the explanation, the reason why. There is no collective memory of why suffering started. That is why many people are vulnerable to the fallen beings creating an ideology that explains what has gone wrong with the universe, and what is the kind of program that is needed to fix it, what is the struggle that needs to suppress, force or eliminate the scapegoat that is the cause of the suffering.

Now, we have of course given many teachings that the real cause of suffering is that people have gone into the dualistic mindset that can only cause suffering because you act as if you are a separate being. Therefore, you are out of alignment with the basic design principles of the universe, you are resisting the universe, you are resisting what I have called this effortless co-creation, effortless manifestation. You think you have to manifest everything by force. This means that people do not have this deeper understanding that it is their own mindset, the mindset of duality, that causes suffering. As we have explained, the inhabitants of the earth had gone into duality before the fallen beings arrived. They experienced suffering before the fallen beings came, but it was milder than what they experienced after the fallen beings came.

In a sense, you could say that the ideologies that are being created by the fallen beings have the specific purpose of explaining away the very suffering created by the fallen beings. This is one of the purposes behind the ideologies created by the fallen beings: to hide their own existence, and to hide that they are the cause of suffering. They want to portray that the reason people are suffering is either because of another group of people, or because something has gone wrong with God's plan for the universe. Then, they furthermore try to portray that this select group of people, this special group of people, *they* have to do something to correct what has gone wrong with God's plan because God cannot do it himself. Therefore, this particular group of people on this little planet (that is a speck of dust in the universe), they have to compensate and correct what has gone wrong with God's plan. This of course is what the fallen beings believe: That it is their destiny to correct the mistakes of God and make the universe function the way it really should be functioning. They have projected this onto the people. In order to explain why there is suffering, they have created ideologies based on the mindset that something has gone wrong.

What is the effect of these ideologies? Well, when such an ideology becomes accepted by a large number of people, they are then beginning to allow this ideology to affect their identity, mental and emotional bodies, meaning that when the energy from the spiritual realm flows through these people's minds, it is colored by the ideology. This of course can only increase tension. It can only increase conflicts between groups of people, it often leads to war, which of course creates even more suffering.

Why ideologies cannot remove suffering

What I am seeking to point out here, which actually many people who do not know about fallen beings or ascended masters are ready to see from a purely pragmatic viewpoint, is that while most ideologies promise that they can take people out of suffering, it is a complete lie. It is a complete illusion. The very ideologies that are based on this idea that something has gone wrong, and that some people must correct it by forcing other people, they only increase suffering.

What you actually see is that you have ideologies that have been developed to explain the suffering created by previous ideologies. This is partly what the philosopher Hegel saw when he talked about the dialectic. There is a thesis, one ideology created out of duality. This ideology, because it is created out of duality, must have an antithesis. There is a struggle between the two and this creates a new state, which he called a synthesis between the two. This synthesis then becomes a new thesis, which attracts an antithesis, and the struggle starts all over again.

This is what has happened with the ideologies created by the fallen beings. They become often more and more complex, more and more unreasonable and illogical, in order to explain this suffering created by the previous ideologies. Many people are ready to see that this is actually an endless cycle where people can go on endlessly creating new ideologies that supposedly are the final, the absolute, the ultimate ideologies that can explain what the other ideologies could not explain. The alternative is to abandon ideologies, abandon the ideological mindset, and as I have described, use the scientific method to observe how the world works, and then also seek to use your intuitive faculties to receive some higher vision of how the world works.

We have given teachings previously about this concept that something has gone wrong. We have said that, in reality, nothing has really gone wrong on earth. The earth is a reality simulator. It is created to give people any experience you want. It is perfectly capable of giving you a positive uplifting experience, but if you decide you want a different experience and go into duality, it is capable of giving you any experience you want because it simply out-pictures the collective state of consciousness. Based on this, based on this view that the earth is a reality simulator, what could possibly have gone wrong?

In the reality simulator, the concept of right and wrong really have no meaning. When you consider free will, and people are allowed to experiment with their free will until they have had enough of whatever experience they are having, what could go wrong there? When you really understand free will, and the purpose of free will and the purpose of allowing people to have any experience they want until they have had enough of it, what could go wrong in God's universe? Well, nothing.

From an ascended master perspective, from the perspective of the Creator, you can look at the fallen beings and say: "Did anything go wrong when they fell?" No, because within the Law of Free Will, they are allowed to have that experience. Of course, the fallen beings in their mindset, they experienced that something had gone wrong because they were not allowed to continue to act as if they were the gods on a particular planet. They were humbled, they were confronted with the reality that there was a power greater than them. They consider this to be wrong. They are allowed to have that experience. It is a matter of how long do they need to struggle with this before they give up the struggle?

Has something really gone wrong? Well, in *their* minds only. I know very well that if you look at most religions on earth, if you look at previous ascended master teachings, you would look at these teachings and conclude that something had gone wrong because these beings fell and there is all this manipulation and suffering and so on. In reality, nothing has gone wrong.

The situation of avatars coming to earth

Now this, of course relates especially to those of you who are avatars and who lived on a natural planet, and then decided (when you had reached as far as you could reach on that planet) to come to earth. Before you came to earth, you looked down on this planet and you saw the immense suffering that is taking place here. You felt compassion for people suffering, you felt the desire to help them escape the suffering because you of course knew it was completely unnecessary. You came here with the desire to alleviate suffering because you knew it was not necessary. This does not mean that on a natural planet, you had the concept that suffering was wrong. On a natural planet, you do not have these concepts of right and wrong, but you did see that suffering was not natural, it was not necessary, it was not unavoidable.

You saw that people were suffering. You felt the compassion for them, and you formulated the desire to help them be free of suffering. You decided to descend to earth and take embodiment here, which means you have to descend to the 48th level of consciousness. You cannot descend with the level of consciousness you had on a natural planet, you have to start at the level where the original inhabitants of the earth started. This means you now inevitably become affected by the consciousness of earth. Then, you experienced the original cosmic birth trauma, as we have called it—you experienced that shock. This is when you directly, on your own body, came to feel that it was wrong that you were exposed to this equation. You came here with the best of intentions, you should not have been attacked by the fallen beings, you should not have been rejected by the original inhabitants. Something happened that should not have happened—this was *wrong*.

This is when you become open to being pulled into the fallen beings' mindset: the dualistic value judgment that something is *right,* something is *wrong*. This is when you begin to think that, well, something must have gone wrong on earth since there are these appalling conditions here. Nobody should have been exposed to what you have been exposed to, nobody should be exposed to what most human beings are exposed to on earth. Something must have gone wrong. Then, you create these selves based on this idea, this view, that something has gone wrong. As long as you have these selves, you cannot ascend from earth because you have other selves that project that it is your job, your very purpose for being on earth, to correct what has gone wrong here. Therefore, you cannot leave until this has been corrected. Given that this could take a very long time, this means that your ascension is postponed indefinitely.

What is actually the best way, as an avatar, that you can help raise the earth? It is that you take embodiment here, you become enveloped in the consciousness that is prevalent on this planet, then you gradually (over a long period of time) free yourself from this consciousness—and then you ascend. This creates an incredible pull on the collective consciousness and that is the best way you can actually help free the earth from suffering— not by correcting specific problems down here on earth.

What you need to see as an avatar in order to be free from earth is precisely this. There is a self that projects (as we have said many times) that there is a problem you must solve: remove suffering from earth. You might think that the key to being free is to fulfill your reason for being here by solving this problem, but it is *not* the case. Even if you could alleviate suffering, that would not automatically qualify you for your ascension. The only way to really ascend is to realize that the problem is not a real problem and that you need to let the self die that projects the problem. Then, when you have let all of the selves die, *then* you can ascend, and that is how you help raise the earth in the ultimate way.

You also help the earth by being here and gradually raising your consciousness, being an open door for the light, being an open door for ideas and teachings from the spiritual realm. You help the earth by being here, but the ultimate way to help the earth is to ascend from earth.

An ideal society cannot be created through violence

Now, of course I do not expect the general public to understand this, but there are many, many people on earth who are actually ready to take a look at this idea that something has gone wrong. They have over many, many lifetimes been pulled into these ideologies where they have made the commitment, they have fought for the cause, they have killed and been killed for the cause. Then, after that lifetime, they saw that it actually did not make a difference. It only made things worse. You will see that there are many people who have experienced this.

Now, as just one example, let us take the Nazi ideology. We have said that many people were pulled into this, even avatars were pulled into this, because it projected that there was a beneficent intention behind it, namely to create an ideal society. Many, many avatars can lock in to this. Many,

many of the original inhabitants can lock in to this desire to create a better society, an ideal society. What was also found in Nazi ideology is of course the typical elements of the struggle. Essentially, what Nazi ideology said was (of course not directly, but between the lines) that the only way to create this ideal society is through violence and force. If you look at the reality of the situation, can violence and force create anything but suffering? The obvious answer is of course: "No!" You look at history and you see that violence and force, killing other people, can *only* create suffering, has always only created suffering.

Now, when you talk about an ideal society, how do most people see this ideal society? It is a society where they are not exposed to violence and force. How can you create an ideal society through violence and force? It logically, rationally makes no sense. Many people have experienced, over several lifetimes, being pulled into an ideology, fighting for this cause of creating an ideal society, and then going out of embodiment, looking back and realizing they actually did not bring the world closer to this ideal society, they created only more suffering that kept it or pulled it further away from the ideal society. When people have seen this a number of times, they come back into embodiment, knowing this is a hollow promise.

You cannot create an ideal society through violence and force. Many, many people on earth, even beyond the top 10%, have experienced this enough that they come back with a certain memory that this does not work. What is the proof of this? That you have democracies in the world. Because what is a democracy? Well, it is also in a sense an attempt to create at least a better society if not an ideal society. It is based on the very idea that an ideal society is not based on violence and force, it is based on human rights that are respected by the leaders of society. A democracy is not based on violence and force. A democracy cannot be based on an ideology that says that a democracy can only be established through violence and force.

You see that many people are ready to understand this aspect of ideology and to do away with this idea that something has gone wrong and needs to be corrected. In a sense, we can say that a democracy is *not* based on the idea of something having gone wrong, which needs to be corrected, some problem that needs to be solved, some disease that needs to be eradicated. Instead, we need to transcend the former state into a higher state.

There is a fundamental difference here. In the ideological approach, you identify a problem, a cause of the problem, and the only way to solve the problem is to destroy the cause of the problem, which is why it is sometimes necessary to destroy certain groups of people. In the democratic approach, it is not necessary to destroy a problem. It is necessary to transcend it, which is what many democratic nations have done. They have transcended their former state, their former state of government, their former state of religion, their former economy, their former way of people interacting with each other. For every aspect of society, they have transcended something in order to get to where the modern democracies are today.

Some democratic nations have not yet transcended it. We have said before that the Founding Fathers of America clearly had the problem that they could only establish an independent nation through violence and force. That is why they precipitated the Revolutionary War. We have said that America could have been established without violence and force, even though it would have taken longer. We have also said that the American nation has not yet freed itself from this mindset, which is why you see that there is still so much violence and force in American society. Even the fact that they maintain the largest military, but also the violence and force you clearly saw in the last election and the aftermath of that election.

Not all democracies have completely transcended this, but many have made significant progress. Many of the people there are ready to see that the way to make even more progress is to let go of the entire mindset behind ideology that something has gone wrong. Of course, there are current conditions, or past conditions that were not ideal. But instead of destroying something that has gone wrong, you transcend it, you transcend it into a higher state. That is again the purpose, or the principle, behind the scientific method. You have a certain view of the world, you observe, you make experiments, and then you transcend the old view and adopt a higher view. Many, many people are ready to make this transition and it can have profound effects.

All people have a personal ideology

Now, I want to go in a slightly different direction here. Again, when you look at ideologies, you can step back, and you can see a clear tendency in the thought systems, belief systems, ideologies that are clearly defined as such. A tendency you see is that they are defined by somebody. There is always a single person or an elite of people who are defining an ideology, who are interpreting it, who are executing it. This means that the vast majority of the people on earth either accept it or resist it. They submit to it, they either buy into it, or they at least submit to it.

The dynamic is that for most people on earth, the ideology comes to them from outside their own minds. It is sort of an impersonal, non-personal ideology. However, what have we said about the reality simulator on earth? We have said that this is a quite ingeniously designed piece of machinery. The purpose of the machinery is to give those who are inside the reality simulator an experience that they want to have. Also, to give them the experience that this is a completely real experience. They live in a real world that has certain characteristics and so on. When you look at the earth, you see that the earth is a very diverse planet. People are very diverse, they are in different levels of consciousness, they have different looks, different features, different ideas, different beliefs, different desires. They are so diverse that it is hard to find these common denominators.

You see that people are having many different experiences on earth. Different groups of people can be said to have a certain collective experience, but the collective experience of one group, living in one of the modern democracies, is incredibly different from a group of people living an Aboriginal existence in the Australian outback or the Amazon rainforest. It is really amazing when you look at it, that there can be seven billion people on this planet and there are so many different experiences that these people are having, yet all of them are convinced that their experience is real. How is this possible?

Well, as we have explained, it is possible because each human being has four lower bodies, each human being has over many lifetimes put certain contents in those four lower bodies, they form a perception filter. It is this perception filter that first of all shapes the individual experience that people are having. Second of all, it makes them feel that their experience is entirely real. This, of course is partly what makes it so difficult for people to communicate and come to agreement about things. The sort of constructive aspect of this is that you do not have that many unnatural planets like earth. You have to make the best use of the ones that are there. If you can cram seven billion people onto one planet, and give them all an experience that they think is real, then that planet serves its maximum capacity, in terms of taking people to the point where they have had enough of the experience and want something more. What this actually leads to is the realization that there are some ideologies that come to people from the outside, ultimately from the fallen beings. They are taking in these ideologies from the outside.

Now you look at a particular ideology, say Christianity, or Marxism, and you will see that when people are exposed to this ideology, they have different reactions to it. Some people accept it, become converted by it, become convinced that it is real, that the description of life that the ideology gives is real. Other people have the opposite experience, find that the same description is completely unreal. Between those two extremes, there is a certain spectrum. What determines whether one person accepts Marxism, becomes a flaming Marxist or another person rejects it and becomes an anti-communist fighting the Marxist? Well, what determines people's reaction to the ideology coming from the *outside* is how that ideology resonates with the ideology they have *inside* their minds. We have called it a perception filter, but you could just as well say that over many lifetimes, all human beings on earth have created a personal ideology.

This personal ideology may have certain elements based on one of the collective ideologies. It may have many things in common with other people in the same group, where these people have grown up in this lifetime, which is why they got magnetized to this group in the first place. There may be certain common beliefs, but nevertheless, if you still look at a group of people, such as the over a billion Catholics on earth, you might say that they have been brought up many of them in a catholic environment, they have been indoctrinated with catholic doctrine. They should have the same inner ideology, inner worldview. The reality is that each of the billion plus Catholics have an individual personal ideology, an individual personal worldview, created over many lifetimes partly adapted to the situation they are facing in this lifetime. They came to accept the catholic ideology because it resonated with something in them.

Elements of a personal ideology

You realize here that everybody is having a personal ideology that forms the foundation for how they interact with the world. This ideology has the same basic components that we have talked about. It needs to explain why these people are suffering, why they have tension, why they are not fulfilled and satisfied. It needs to have some explanation of how the world works that to these people explains why they are suffering, why there are certain things they cannot achieve, why they are limited beings, why they have to accept their lot in life.

Most people on earth, even though some have given up and are completely powerless, most people on earth need to have the hope that there could be improvement to their situation. Their personal ideology also has some ideas for what changes could be brought about in society. Since they clearly observe that there are other people that disagree with them, well, there is also the concept of a struggle because there are other people who do not believe what they believe.

The next element of an ideology is this desire for the commitment. Some people go into this commitment. They dedicate their lives to fighting for a cause, however they conceive of it. Others are more balanced because over many lifetimes they have experienced fighting for these causes. Their desire for commitment is not as strong. Their sense of conflict is not as strong in the sense that they must destroy the opposition. This is also why these people do not go into feeling superior to others, whereas those who make the commitment feel they have the absolute cause, they often feel superior to those who do not agree with their cause.

You see that the personal ideology has many of the same elements as the collective ideologies, which of course is why people accept the ideologies that come from without. What this leads to is, first of all, that there are many, many people who have lived in this state of mind, the ideological mindset, for many lifetimes. There are many of these people who have now incarnated in the modern democracies because they are the societies that are the least based on this ideological approach. They do not have the violence that these people have seen, that they quite frankly have had enough of. There are many people in the world, even beyond the top 10%, who are ready to take a look at this and actually take a look at themselves. You could say that this is the culmination of the process that Jesus started 2,000 years ago and that I started 2,500 years ago of causing people to look at themselves.

Buddhism is, by many, not considered a religion but more a method or philosophy for getting people to look at their own psychology and doing something about it. Christianity was meant to be the same: "The kingdom of God is within you. Do not look at the splinter in your brother's eye, but look at the beam in your own eye," and other teachings given by Jesus. Again, you see that there are these teachings that are beyond ideologies because they seek to liberate people. What do they always tell people? Look at yourself because the key to your personal liberation is inside your own mind.

There are many people on earth, especially in the modern democracies, who are ready to make this switch where they realize that the key to changing my personal life experience is inside my mind. It is to work with my mind, work with my psyche, learn how the psyche works, find a way to free myself from what limits me. Many are therefore ready to come to see that what limits you is actually your personal ideology. Because that personal ideology was created in response to life on earth, on this very chaotic, disharmonious planet.

Over many, many lifetimes, you have been confronted with these very violent, very chaotic, very traumatic circumstances. In order to be able to deal with this psychologically, you have created this personal ideology. You are now at the point where you have had enough of this, you are ready to transcend the personal ideology. This requires you to look into your own mind, to come to see the ideology, see the beliefs that it is based on and start questioning those beliefs. This is the process we have given you with separate selves, but many people are ready to start this process at whatever level they can see it.

Many people are ready to question ideology

You see it in many of the modern democracies. There is a rising awareness of the importance of psychology, the importance of working with your mind, the importance of doing something with the mind, whether it is meditation, yoga, mindfulness, therapy, study a book, certain teachings, spiritual teachings, New Age teachings, whatever you have. Basically, behind all of this is this desire to improve my life experience by seeking to change myself and my own mind instead of seeking to change the conditions outside myself.

This, again is one of these shifts that has already started happening of course, but as it gains more and more momentum, it is one of these shifts that can have a tremendous impact on society. A tremendous impact. You can see yourselves how finding a spiritual teaching and following it has had a tremendous impact on your own life. When we take a look at ascended master students, we see that the people who have followed this dispensation, who have listened to our teachings about the inner path versus the outer path, who have been willing to look at yourselves, look at the ego, follow the Course of Self-Mastery, and take the teachings on the separate selves and work with these books, you have made tremendous progress.

We see that many of you have overcome so many of these selves that it has been a fundamental shift in your lives. We see that other people have not yet reached that stage. Some people have not even locked in to it because they are, as Mother Mary said: "Seeing without seeing, hearing without hearing." Many of you have made tremendous progress. Many people have found other ways to make progress in working on their psychology.

What you can do is of course to continue raising your own mind, but also make these calls that more and more people come to see the limitations of these ideologies, both the external and the internal, and the need to question them. The need to adopt this mindset that instead of having an idea of how the mind *should* work, we look for how the mind or the world actually *does* work.

How do we know this? Well, we know this through a process of experimentation and observation, but also by studying. Studying books about psychology, about various aspects of life, and also studying spiritual teachings. Many, many people are ready to acknowledge that there is a spiritual realm. There are spiritual beings who serve as the teachers of humankind, and they have given teachings. We may say that there is a horizontal way to gain knowledge, to expand knowledge. There is a vertical way and it is ultimately to receive some revelation from the spiritual realm, from the ascended masters.

Not every idea is an ideology

Such a revelation is also beyond ideology. I know very well that the fallen beings will use the analytical mind to say: "Given all you have said here about ideology, it is clear to us that anything that can be said on this planet is an ideology. Therefore, what you say is also an ideology. Anything that anybody says is an ideology, democracy is an ideology." This is what some will say, but it is not correct.

A teaching that is given to liberate people is not in itself an ideology. A teaching given by the fallen beings in order to deceive and manipulate and control people, that *is* in itself an ideology. It is defined as an ideology. However, even such an ideology does not become an ideology until people go into the ideological mindset and seek to force it upon others.

Of course, you can take a teaching, even a teaching given by the ascended masters or some teaching discovered through science, and you can turn it into an ideology—as I said the militant atheists have done with the discoveries of science. Even some ascended master students have done this with the teachings of the ascended masters. There is a fundamental difference. Even though anything can be turned into an ideology, that is not the same as saying that everything *is* an ideology. *It is not.*

There are truly teachings in the world that have the capacity to help people transcend themselves, and even to help them transcend the external ideologies. Fewer teachings have the capacity to help people transcend the internal ideologies. This is of course the highest purpose of any teaching that is given. The purpose is not to bring forth an ultimate truth but to bring forth something that can help people raise their consciousness to the next level where they can then receive a higher teaching.

The purpose of bringing forth the teaching in today's world is to help those people who are ready to transcend their present level of consciousness and to help societies who are ready to transcend their present level and come up higher. Then, when they have come up higher, Saint Germain will be able to release an even higher teaching that will take them further into the golden age mindset. This process can of course continue for the next 2,000-year period of Saint Germain's Golden Age.

Now, I am very happy to say that, as happens at most of these conferences, we have a certain goal for what we think is realistic to achieve with a conference. Then, depending on how many people tune in, how engaged they are, we can see whether that goal can be fulfilled, or perhaps even exceeded. As has happened many times, so many people have been taking part in this conference, this process, that you have actually exceeded the goal we have defined. This means that I have been able to bring forth some teachings on ideology that really have not been brought forth on this planet, in the physical octave, in known history. They are actually more profound than what I had originally planned.

This I am very grateful for—that so many of you have been willing to participate in this process because it is not something we can do as ascended masters. As the messenger realizes, it certainly is not something that *he* can do; it can only be done when enough people come together in that unity of purpose.

Even though, as I said, ideology is a very complex topic, and many things could be said about it, I am very happy to say that we have brought forth so many teachings during this conference that I really feel this is a very complete package for helping people, a critical mass of people, make the shift that will, within a reasonable period of time, effectively end the era of ideology on earth. I am not saying that it has ended as a result of this conference, but certainly, we have started the process that will, within the foreseeable future, lead to that end of ideology.

When I talk about the end of ideology, I am not saying that this will mean that it is completely ended, that ideology is completely eradicated, that the ideological mindset is completely eradicated. Of course, you will see that there are some nations where people are so trapped in the ideological mindset that it will take perhaps generations before they get out of it. What I am talking about is the planetary level, where we have told you before that there is a period where it gradually builds up, where people become aware of a certain problem and the need to overcome it, then there comes the critical mass that has been built—now the shift occurs.

We have taught as an example about slavery. There was a period of building up to this shift where a critical mass of people abandoned the ideology behind slavery, the mindset behind slavery. As you can see, there are still some forms of slavery existing in the world today. Still, the planet has ended the era of slavery, and it basically ended not so long after slavery was officially outlawed in 1815. You see that there can also come that point where the critical mass has been built where, effectively, the planet has moved beyond the era of ideology, even though there will still be some groups of people that are stuck in it, and will be allowed by the Law of Free Will to outplay it, at least for a time. Eventually, as we move further into the golden age, there will come a time where these people will be faced with the choice to either abandon the consciousness of ideology, or to be removed from the planet.

Again, I am very happy, very fulfilled, very grateful that so many of you have been willing to respond to this call of ours. It may seem like a fairly abstract topic. Nevertheless, as you can see, it is a wide-ranging topic with many practical, even many personal, even many spiritual ramifications. Certainly, those of you who have locked in to the inner path will be able to see that you can use this conference and the teachings we have given to make personal spiritual progress by looking for these remnants of the ideological consciousness and your ideological approach to spiritual teachings, and letting those selves die when you separate yourself from them. This will then give you another tool for enhancing your spiritual progress, pulling up on the collective, thereby fulfilling these aspects of your Divine plan.

With this, I simply want to seal this conference, seal this release of light and teachings from the Office of the Lord of the World. I very much look forward to coming to the point where I can say, as the Lord of the World: "There is no more space on earth for ideology, or the mindset of ideology." With this, I seal you in the joyful peace of the Buddha. Why am I joyful? Why am I at peace? Because I have long ago transcended the mindset of ideology.

26 INVOKING AWARENESS OF PERSONAL IDEOLOGY (PART 1)

In the name of the I AM THAT I AM, Jesus Christ, I use the authority that I have as a being in embodiment on earth to call upon Gautama Buddha to reinforce my calls and use my chakras to project the statements in this invocation into the collective consciousness and awaken people to the need to free ourselves from the ideological mindset. Awaken people to the reality that we are spiritual beings and that we can co-create a new future by working with the ascended masters. I especially call for …

[Make your own calls here.]

Part 1

1. Gautama Buddha, awaken the most creative people to see that one of the things an ideology has to explain is why there is suffering on earth, why there is dissatisfaction on earth.

O Jesus, blessed brother mine,
I walk the path that you outline,
a great example to us all,
I follow now your inner call.

O Jesus, let the Fire of Joy,
consume the devil's subtle ploy,
transfigured is our planet earth,
the golden age is given birth.

2. Gautama Buddha, awaken the most creative people to see that considering earth is a dense planet where the population has been in duality and has been manipulated by various power elites, how can we explain that people almost universally have a sense that they should not be suffering.

O Jesus, open inner sight,
the ego wants to prove it's right,
but this I will no longer do,
I want to be all one with you.

O Jesus, let the Fire of Joy,
consume the devil's subtle ploy,
transfigured is our planet earth,
the golden age is given birth.

3. Gautama Buddha, awaken the most creative people to see that the reason is that we are experiential beings and there is an aspect of experience that goes through all four levels of the material universe.

O Jesus, I now clearly see,
the Key of Knowledge given me,
my Christ self I hereby embrace,
as you fill up my inner space.

O Jesus, let the Fire of Joy,
consume the devil's subtle ploy,
transfigured is our planet earth,
the golden age is given birth.

4. Gautama Buddha, awaken the most creative people to see that we are having a physical experience in the physical realm, but there are aspects of our experience that are in the emotional, the mental and the identity realm.

O Jesus, show me serpent's lie,
expose the beam in my own eye,
as Christ discernment you me give,
in oneness I forever live.

O Jesus, let the Fire of Joy,
consume the devil's subtle ploy,
transfigured is our planet earth,
the golden age is given birth.

5. Gautama Buddha, awaken the most creative people to see that over the long history of humankind, certain patterns, certain matrices have been created in the emotional, mental and identity bodies. There is a collective memory that has been established.

O Jesus, I am truly meek,
and thus I turn the other cheek,
when the accuser attacks me,
I go within and merge with thee.

O Jesus, let the Fire of Joy,
consume the devil's subtle ploy,
transfigured is our planet earth,
the golden age is given birth.

6. Gautama Buddha, awaken the most creative people to see that this memory goes back to when the earth was a natural planet. For those who have come from other planets, they have taken with them some of the memory from those planets.

O Jesus, ego I let die,
surrender ev'ry earthly tie,
the dead can bury what is dead,
I choose to walk with you instead.

**O Jesus, let the Fire of Joy,
consume the devil's subtle ploy,
transfigured is our planet earth,
the golden age is given birth.**

7. Gautama Buddha, awaken the most creative people to see that this memory is not a theory; it is an *experiential* memory. Humankind has an experiential memory, in the emotional, mental and identity realms that there is an alternative to suffering.

O Jesus, help me rise above,
the devil's test through higher love,
show me separate self unreal,
my formless self you do reveal.

**O Jesus, let the Fire of Joy,
consume the devil's subtle ploy,
transfigured is our planet earth,
the golden age is given birth.**

8. Gautama Buddha, awaken the most creative people to see that the vast majority of human beings on the planet have this sense that there should be an alternative to suffering.

O Jesus, what is that to me,
I just let go and follow thee,
with this I do pass ev'ry test,
to find with you eternal rest.

**O Jesus, let the Fire of Joy,
consume the devil's subtle ploy,
transfigured is our planet earth,
the golden age is given birth.**

9. Gautama Buddha, awaken the most creative people to consider: Why is there suffering when everybody knows it should not be here? This is what most ideologies attempt to explain because this is the only way that the power elite beings can control people.

O Jesus, fiery master mine,
my heart now melting into thine,
I love with heart and mind and soul,
the God who is my highest goal.

**O Jesus, let the Fire of Joy,
consume the devil's subtle ploy,
transfigured is our planet earth,
the golden age is given birth.**

Part 2

1. Gautama Buddha, awaken the most creative people to see that power elite beings can only cause suffering. They are on earth, they have an agenda, it involves or necessitates controlling human beings by forcing them. When they force people into an unnatural state, it causes tension, it causes suffering.

Maitreya, I am truly meek,
your counsel wise I humbly seek,
your vision I so want to see,
with you in Eden I will be.

**Maitreya, kindness is the cure,
in fires of kindness I am pure.
Maitreya, now release the fire,
that raises me forever higher.**

2. Gautama Buddha, awaken the most creative people to see that the power elite beings cannot exist on the planet without causing suffering. In order to convince people that a certain ideology is valid, they have to attempt to explain why there is suffering. They often do so by pointing the finger at some other group of people and anointing them as the scapegoat who is the cause of suffering.

Maitreya, help me to return,
to learn from you, I truly yearn,

as oneness is all I desire
I feel initiation's fire.

Maitreya, kindness is the cure,
in fires of kindness I am pure.
Maitreya, now release the fire,
that raises me forever higher.

3. Gautama Buddha, awaken the most creative people to see that all ideologies are based on a particular viewpoint, namely: Something has gone wrong on earth, something has gone wrong in the world, something has gone wrong in the universe.

Maitreya, I hereby decide,
from you I will no longer hide,
expose to me the very lie
that caused edenic self to die.

Maitreya, kindness is the cure,
in fires of kindness I am pure.
Maitreya, now release the fire,
that raises me forever higher.

4. Gautama Buddha, awaken the most creative people to see that we experience that we are suffering. We have the memory that it should not be there. The power elite beings create ideologies and belief systems that say that the reason why there is suffering is because something has gone wrong.

Maitreya, blessed Guru mine,
my heart of hearts forever thine,
I vow that I will listen well,
so we can break the serpent's spell.

Maitreya, kindness is the cure,
in fires of kindness I am pure.
Maitreya, now release the fire,
that raises me forever higher.

5. Gautama Buddha, awaken the most creative people to see that the power elite beings have been very good at keeping their own identity, existence and presence secret for the vast majority of people.

> Maitreya, help me see the lie
> whereby the serpent broke the tie,
> the serpent now has naught in me,
> in oneness I am truly free.

> **Maitreya, kindness is the cure,**
> **in fires of kindness I am pure.**
> **Maitreya, now release the fire,**
> **that raises me forever higher.**

6. Gautama Buddha, awaken the most creative people to see that even though we have concepts of a devil and dark forces, it is a rudimentary understanding that basically hides the existence of power elite beings on the planet.

> Maitreya, truth does set me free
> from falsehoods of duality,
> the fruit of knowledge I let go,
> so your true spirit I do know.

> **Maitreya, kindness is the cure,**
> **in fires of kindness I am pure.**
> **Maitreya, now release the fire,**
> **that raises me forever higher.**

7. Gautama Buddha, awaken the most creative people to see that this hides the real cause of suffering, it hides the duality consciousness because an ideology that springs from the duality consciousness cannot expose the duality consciousness.

> Maitreya, I submit to you,
> intentions pure, my heart is true,
> from ego I am truly free,
> as I am now all one with thee.

**Maitreya, kindness is the cure,
in fires of kindness I am pure.
Maitreya, now release the fire,
that raises me forever higher.**

8. Gautama Buddha, awaken the most creative people to see that for a long time, there has been this idea that something has gone wrong, but this is not based on experience.

Maitreya, kindness is the key,
all shades of kindness teach to me,
for I am now the open door,
the Art of Kindness to restore.

**Maitreya, kindness is the cure,
in fires of kindness I am pure.
Maitreya, now release the fire,
that raises me forever higher.**

9. Gautama Buddha, awaken the most creative people to see that we have a previous experience that there was not always suffering, so there is an alternative to suffering. Now we have an experience that there is suffering, but we do not actually have this collective experience or memory that something has gone wrong in the universe.

Maitreya, oh sweet mystery,
immersed in your reality,
the myst'ry school will now return,
for this, my heart does truly burn.

**Maitreya, kindness is the cure,
in fires of kindness I am pure.
Maitreya, now release the fire,
that raises me forever higher.**

Part 3

1. Gautama Buddha, awaken the most creative people to see that we have a memory of the contrast between suffering and non-suffering, but people were not aware why suffering started. They experienced that it started but they did not experience the reason why.

> Gautama, show my mental state
> that does give rise to love and hate,
> your exposé I do endure,
> so my perception will be pure.

> **Gautama, Flame of Cosmic Peace,**
> **unruly thoughts do hereby cease,**
> **we radiate from you and me**
> **the peace to still Samsara's Sea.**

2. Gautama Buddha, awaken the most creative people to see that there is no collective memory of why suffering started. That is why many people are vulnerable to the power elite beings creating an ideology that explains what has gone wrong with the universe, and what is the kind of program that is needed to fix it, what is the struggle that needs to eliminate the scapegoat that is the cause of suffering.

> Gautama, in your Flame of Peace,
> the struggling self I now release,
> the Buddha Nature I now see,
> it is the core of you and me.

> **Gautama, Flame of Cosmic Peace,**
> **unruly thoughts do hereby cease,**
> **we radiate from you and me**
> **the peace to still Samsara's Sea.**

3. Gautama Buddha, awaken the most creative people to see that the real cause of suffering is that people have gone into the dualistic mindset that can only cause suffering because we think we are separate beings.

Gautama, I am one with thee,
Mara's demons do now flee,
your Presence like a soothing balm,
my mind and senses ever calm.

Gautama, Flame of Cosmic Peace,
unruly thoughts do hereby cease,
we radiate from you and me
the peace to still Samsara's Sea.

4. Gautama Buddha, awaken the most creative people to see that in duality, we are out of alignment with the basic design principles of the universe, we are resisting the universe, we are resisting effortless co-creation, effortless manifestation. We think we have to manifest everything by force.

Gautama, I now take the vow,
to live in the eternal now,
with you I do transcend all time,
to live in present so sublime.

Gautama, Flame of Cosmic Peace,
unruly thoughts do hereby cease,
we radiate from you and me
the peace to still Samsara's Sea.

5. Gautama Buddha, awaken the most creative people to see that it is our own mindset, the mindset of duality that causes suffering. The ideologies that are being created by the power elite have the specific purpose of explaining away the very suffering created by the power elite.

Gautama, I have no desire,
to nothing earthly I aspire,
in non-attachment I now rest,
passing Mara's subtle test.

Gautama, Flame of Cosmic Peace,
unruly thoughts do hereby cease,
we radiate from you and me
the peace to still Samsara's Sea.

6. Gautama Buddha, awaken the most creative people to see that one of the purposes behind the ideologies created by the power elite beings is to hide their own existence, and to hide that they are the cause of suffering.

Gautama, I melt into you,
my mind is one, no longer two,
immersed in your resplendent glow,
Nirvana is all that I know.

Gautama, Flame of Cosmic Peace,
unruly thoughts do hereby cease,
we radiate from you and me
the peace to still Samsara's Sea.

7. Gautama Buddha, awaken the most creative people to see that the power elite wants to portray that the reason people are suffering is either because of another group of people, or because something has gone wrong with God's plan for the universe.

Gautama, in your timeless space,
I am immersed in Cosmic Grace,
I know the God beyond all form,
to world I will no more conform.

Gautama, Flame of Cosmic Peace,
unruly thoughts do hereby cease,
we radiate from you and me
the peace to still Samsara's Sea.

8. Gautama Buddha, awaken the most creative people to see that the power elite will try to portray that this special group of people have to do something to correct what has gone wrong with God's plan because God cannot do it himself.

Gautama, I am now awake,
I clearly see what is at stake,
and thus I claim my sacred right
to be on earth the Buddhic Light.

**Gautama, Flame of Cosmic Peace,
unruly thoughts do hereby cease,
we radiate from you and me
the peace to still Samsara's Sea.**

9. Gautama Buddha, awaken the most creative people to see that the power elite will say that this particular group of people on this little planet have to compensate and correct what has gone wrong with God's plan.

Gautama, with your thunderbolt,
we give the earth a mighty jolt,
I know that some will understand,
and join the Buddha's timeless band.

**Gautama, Flame of Cosmic Peace,
unruly thoughts do hereby cease,
we radiate from you and me
the peace to still Samsara's Sea.**

Part 4

1. Gautama Buddha, awaken the most creative people to see that the power elite beings believe it is their destiny to correct the mistakes of God, and make the universe function the way it really should be functioning, but they have projected this onto the people.

Sanat Kumara, Ruby Fire,
I seek my place in love's own choir,
with open hearts we sing your praise,
together we the earth do raise.

**Sanat Kumara, Ruby Ray,
bring to earth a higher way,
light this planet with your fire,
clothe her in a new attire.**

2. Gautama Buddha, awaken the most creative people to see that in order to explain why there is suffering, the elite has created ideologies based on the mindset that something has gone wrong.

> Sanat Kumara, Ruby Fire,
> initiations I desire,
> I am for you an electrode,
> Shamballa is my true abode.

> **Sanat Kumara, Ruby Ray,**
> **bring to earth a higher way,**
> **light this planet with your fire,**
> **clothe her in a new attire.**

3. Gautama Buddha, awaken the most creative people to see that when such an ideology becomes accepted by a large number of people, who allow it to affect their identity, mental and emotional bodies, the energy flowing through these people's minds is colored by the ideology.

> Sanat Kumara, Ruby Fire,
> I follow path that you require,
> initiate me with your love,
> the open door for Holy Dove.

> **Sanat Kumara, Ruby Ray,**
> **bring to earth a higher way,**
> **light this planet with your fire,**
> **clothe her in a new attire.**

4. Gautama Buddha, awaken the most creative people to see that this can only increase tension. It can only increase conflicts between groups of people, it often leads to war, which creates even more suffering.

> Sanat Kumara, Ruby Fire,
> your great example all inspire,
> with non-attachment and great mirth,
> we give the earth a true rebirth.

Sanat Kumara, Ruby Ray,
bring to earth a higher way,
light this planet with your fire,
clothe her in a new attire.

5. Gautama Buddha, awaken the most creative people to see that while most ideologies promise that they can take people out of suffering, it is a complete lie. It is a complete illusion. The very ideologies that are based on the idea that something has gone wrong, and that some people must correct it by forcing other people, they only increase suffering.

Sanat Kumara, Ruby Fire,
you are this planet's purifier,
consume on earth all spirits dark,
reveal the inner Spirit Spark.

Sanat Kumara, Ruby Ray,
bring to earth a higher way,
light this planet with your fire,
clothe her in a new attire.

6. Gautama Buddha, awaken the most creative people to see that we have ideologies that have been developed to explain the suffering created by previous ideologies. This is what the philosopher Hegel called the dialectic.

Sanat Kumara, Ruby Fire,
you are a cosmic amplifier,
the lower forces can't withstand,
vibrations from Venusian band.

Sanat Kumara, Ruby Ray,
bring to earth a higher way,
light this planet with your fire,
clothe her in a new attire.

7. Gautama Buddha, awaken the most creative people to see that there is a thesis, one ideology created out of duality. This ideology, because it is created out of duality, must have an antithesis. There is a struggle between the two and this creates a new state, which is called a synthesis between the

two. This synthesis, then becomes a new thesis, which attracts an antithesis, and the struggle starts all over again.

Sanat Kumara, Ruby Fire,
I am on earth your magnifier,
the flow of love I do restore,
my chakras are your open door.

Sanat Kumara, Ruby Ray,
bring to earth a higher way,
light this planet with your fire,
clothe her in a new attire.

8. Gautama Buddha, awaken the most creative people to see that this is what has happened with the ideologies created by the power elite beings. They become more and more complex, more and more unreasonable and illogical, in order to explain the suffering created by previous ideologies.

Sanat Kumara, Ruby Fire,
Venusian song the multiplier,
as we your love reverberate,
the densest minds we penetrate.

Sanat Kumara, Ruby Ray,
bring to earth a higher way,
light this planet with your fire,
clothe her in a new attire.

9. Gautama Buddha, awaken the most creative people to see that this is an endless cycle where people can go on creating new ideologies that supposedly are the final, the absolute, the ultimate ideologies that can explain what the other ideologies could not explain.

Sanat Kumara, Ruby Fire,
you are for all the sanctifier,
the earth is now a holy place,
purified by cosmic grace.

**Sanat Kumara, Ruby Ray,
bring to earth a higher way,
light this planet with your fire,
clothe her in a new attire.**

Sealing

In the name of the I AM THAT I AM, I accept that Archangel Michael, Astrea and Shiva form an impenetrable shield around myself and all constructive people, sealing us from all fear-based energies in all four octaves. I accept that the Light of God is consuming and transforming all fear-based energies that make up the dark forces working against ending the era of ideology on earth!

27 INVOKING AWARENESS OF PERSONAL IDEOLOGY (PART 2)

In the name of the I AM THAT I AM, Jesus Christ, I use the authority that I have as a being in embodiment on earth to call upon Gautama Buddha to reinforce my calls and use my chakras to project the statements in this invocation into the collective consciousness and awaken people to the need to free ourselves from the ideological mindset. Awaken people to the reality that we are spiritual beings and that we can co-create a new future by working with the ascended masters. I especially call for …

[Make your own calls here.]

Part 1

1. Gautama Buddha, awaken the most creative people to see that the alternative is to abandon ideologies, abandon the ideological mindset, and use the scientific method to observe how the world works, and use our intuitive faculties to receive a higher vision.

O Saint Germain, you do inspire,
my vision raised forever higher,
with you I form a figure-eight,
your Golden Age I co-create.

O Saint Germain, what love you bring,
it truly makes all matter sing,
your violet flame does all restore,
with you we are becoming more.

2. Gautama Buddha, awaken the most creative people to see that in reality, nothing has gone wrong on earth. The earth is a reality simulator. It is created to give people any experience we want. It is capable of giving us a positive uplifting experience, but if we decide we want a different experience and go into duality, it is capable of giving us any experience we want.

O Saint Germain, what Freedom Flame,
released when we recite your name,
acceleration is your gift,
our planet it will surely lift.

O Saint Germain, what love you bring,
it truly makes all matter sing,
your violet flame does all restore,
with you we are becoming more.

3. Gautama Buddha, awaken the most creative people to see that the earth simply out-pictures the collective state of consciousness. Based on this view that the earth is a reality simulator, what could possibly have gone wrong?

O Saint Germain, in love we claim,
our right to bring your violet flame,
from you Above, to us below,
it is an all-transforming flow.

O Saint Germain, what love you bring,
it truly makes all matter sing,

**your violet flame does all restore,
with you we are becoming more.**

4. Gautama Buddha, awaken the most creative people to see that in the reality simulator, the concept of right and wrong have no meaning. People are allowed to experiment with their free will until they have had enough of whatever experience they are having, so what could go wrong?

O Saint Germain, I love you so,
my aura filled with violet glow,
my chakras filled with violet fire,
I am your cosmic amplifier.

**O Saint Germain, what love you bring,
it truly makes all matter sing,
your violet flame does all restore,
with you we are becoming more.**

5. Gautama Buddha, awaken the most creative people to understand free will, and the purpose of free will and the purpose of allowing people to have any experience we want until we have had enough of it. Therefore, what could go wrong in God's universe?

O Saint Germain, I am now free,
your violet flame is therapy,
transform all hang-ups in my mind,
as inner peace I surely find.

**O Saint Germain, what love you bring,
it truly makes all matter sing,
your violet flame does all restore,
with you we are becoming more.**

6. Gautama Buddha, awaken the most creative people to see that the power elite beings experienced that something had gone wrong because they were not allowed to continue to act as if they were the gods on a particular planet. They were humbled, they were confronted with the reality that there was a power greater than them.

O Saint Germain, my body pure,
your violet flame for all is cure,
consume the cause of all disease,
and therefore I am all at ease.

**O Saint Germain, what love you bring,
it truly makes all matter sing,
your violet flame does all restore,
with you we are becoming more.**

7. Gautama Buddha, awaken the most creative people to see that many of us came to earth because we felt compassion for people suffering, we felt the desire to help them escape the suffering because we knew it was unnecessary.

O Saint Germain, I'm karma-free,
the past no longer burdens me,
a brand new opportunity,
I am in Christic unity.

**O Saint Germain, what love you bring,
it truly makes all matter sing,
your violet flame does all restore,
with you we are becoming more.**

8. Gautama Buddha, awaken the most creative people to see that we felt compassion for people on earth, and we formulated the desire to help them be free of suffering. We decided to descend to earth and take embodiment here.

O Saint Germain, we are now one,
I am for you a violet sun,
as we transform this planet earth,
your Golden Age is given birth.

**O Saint Germain, what love you bring,
it truly makes all matter sing,
your violet flame does all restore,
with you we are becoming more.**

9. Gautama Buddha, awaken the most creative people to see that we could not descend with the level of consciousness we had on a natural planet, we had to start at the level where the original inhabitants of the earth started. This means we inevitably became affected by the consciousness of earth.

O Saint Germain, the earth is free,
from burden of duality,
in oneness we bring what is best,
your Golden Age is manifest.

O Saint Germain, what love you bring,
it truly makes all matter sing,
your violet flame does all restore,
with you we are becoming more.

Part 2

1. Gautama Buddha, awaken the most creative people to see that most of us experienced our birth trauma as a great shock, and we came to feel that it was wrong. We came here with the best of intentions, we should not have been attacked by the power elite beings, we should not have been rejected by the original inhabitants. Something happened that should not have happened—this was wrong.

Divine Director, I now see,
the world is unreality,
in my heart I now truly feel,
the Spirit is all that is real.

Divine Director, send the light,
from blindness clear my inner sight,
my vision free, my vision clear,
your guidance is forever here.

2. Gautama Buddha, awaken the most creative people to see that this is when we were pulled into the mindset of the power elite: the dualistic value judgment that something is right, something is wrong.

Divine Director, vision give,
in clarity I want to live,
I now behold my plan Divine,
the plan that is uniquely mine.

**Divine Director, send the light,
from blindness clear my inner sight,
my vision free, my vision clear,
your guidance is forever here.**

3. Gautama Buddha, awaken the most creative people to see that we came to think that something must have gone wrong on earth since there are these appalling conditions here.

Divine Director, show in me,
the ego games, and set me free,
help me escape the ego's cage,
to help bring in the golden age.

**Divine Director, send the light,
from blindness clear my inner sight,
my vision free, my vision clear,
your guidance is forever here.**

4. Gautama Buddha, awaken the most creative people to see that we think nobody should have been exposed to what we have been exposed to, nobody should be exposed to what most human beings are exposed to on earth. Something must have gone wrong.

Divine Director, I'm with you,
my vision one, no longer two,
as karma's veil you do disperse,
I see a whole new universe.

Divine Director, send the light,
from blindness clear my inner sight,
my vision free, my vision clear,
your guidance is forever here.

5. Gautama Buddha, awaken the most creative people to see that this causes us to create selves based on this idea that something has gone wrong. As long as we have these selves, we cannot ascend from earth because we have other selves that project that it is our purpose to correct what has gone wrong here. We cannot leave until this has been corrected.

Divine Director, I go up,
electric light now fills my cup,
consume in me all shadows old,
bestow on me a vision bold.

Divine Director, send the light,
from blindness clear my inner sight,
my vision free, my vision clear,
your guidance is forever here.

6. Gautama Buddha, awaken the most creative people to see that the best way we can help raise the earth is to take embodiment here, become enveloped in the consciousness that is prevalent on this planet, then we gradually free ourselves from this consciousness, and then we ascend.

Divine Director, heart of gold,
my sacred labor I unfold,
o blessed Guru, I now see,
where my own plan is taking me.

Divine Director, send the light,
from blindness clear my inner sight,
my vision free, my vision clear,
your guidance is forever here.

7. Gautama Buddha, awaken the most creative people to see that this creates an incredible pull on the collective consciousness, and that is the best

way we can help free the earth from suffering—not by correcting specific problems down here on earth.

> Divine Director, by your grace,
> in grander scheme I find my place,
> my individual flame I see,
> uniqueness God has given me.
>
> **Divine Director, send the light,**
> **from blindness clear my inner sight,**
> **my vision free, my vision clear,**
> **your guidance is forever here.**

8. Gautama Buddha, awaken the most creative people to see that there is a self that projects there is a problem we must solve: remove suffering from earth. We tend to think that the key to being free is to fulfill our reason for being here by solving this problem, but it is not the case. Even if we could alleviate suffering, that would not automatically qualify us for the ascension.

> Divine Director, vision one,
> I see that I AM God's own Sun,
> with your direction so Divine,
> I am now letting my light shine.
>
> **Divine Director, send the light,**
> **from blindness clear my inner sight,**
> **my vision free, my vision clear,**
> **your guidance is forever here.**

9. Gautama Buddha, awaken the most creative people to see that the only way to ascend is to realize that the problem is not a real problem and that we need to let the self die that projects the problem. When we have let all of the selves die, then we can ascend, and that is how we help raise the earth in the ultimate way.

> Divine Director, what a gift,
> to be a part of Spirit's lift,

to raise mankind out of the night,
to bask in Spirit's loving sight.

Divine Director, send the light,
from blindness clear my inner sight,
my vision free, my vision clear,
your guidance is forever here.

Part 3

1. Gautama Buddha, awaken the most creative people to see that we also help the earth by being here and gradually raising our consciousness, being open doors for the light, being open doors for ideas and teachings from the spiritual realm. We help the earth by being here, but the ultimate way to help the earth is to ascend from earth.

O Saint Germain, you do inspire,
my vision raised forever higher,
with you I form a figure-eight,
your Golden Age I co-create.

O Saint Germain, what love you bring,
it truly makes all matter sing,
your violet flame does all restore,
with you we are becoming more.

2. Gautama Buddha, awaken the most creative people to see that we have, over many lifetimes been pulled into ideologies where we have made the commitment, we have fought for the cause, we have killed and been killed for the cause. Then, after that lifetime, we saw that it did not make a difference. It only made things worse.

O Saint Germain, what Freedom Flame,
released when we recite your name,
acceleration is your gift,
our planet it will surely lift.

O Saint Germain, what love you bring,
it truly makes all matter sing,
your violet flame does all restore,
with you we are becoming more.

3. Gautama Buddha, awaken the most creative people to see that many people were pulled into Nazi ideology because it projected that there was a beneficent intention behind it, namely to create an ideal society. What was also found in Nazi ideology was the typical elements of the struggle.

O Saint Germain, in love we claim,
our right to bring your violet flame,
from you Above, to us below,
it is an all-transforming flow.

O Saint Germain, what love you bring,
it truly makes all matter sing,
your violet flame does all restore,
with you we are becoming more.

4. Gautama Buddha, awaken the most creative people to see that indirectly Nazi ideology said that the only way to create an ideal society is through violence and force. Yet in reality, violence and force can never create anything but suffering. Violence and force, killing other people, can *only* create suffering, has always only created suffering.

O Saint Germain, I love you so,
my aura filled with violet glow,
my chakras filled with violet fire,
I am your cosmic amplifier.

O Saint Germain, what love you bring,
it truly makes all matter sing,
your violet flame does all restore,
with you we are becoming more.

5. Gautama Buddha, awaken the most creative people to see that most of us see an ideal society as one where we are not exposed to violence and

force. How can we create an ideal society through violence and force? It logically, rationally makes no sense.

> O Saint Germain, I am now free,
> your violet flame is therapy,
> transform all hang-ups in my mind,
> as inner peace I surely find.

> **O Saint Germain, what love you bring,**
> **it truly makes all matter sing,**
> **your violet flame does all restore,**
> **with you we are becoming more.**

6. Gautama Buddha, awaken the most creative people to see that we have experienced, over several lifetimes, being pulled into an ideology, fighting for the cause of creating an ideal society, and then going out of embodiment, looking back and realizing we did not bring the world closer to this ideal society, we created more suffering that pulled it further away from the ideal society.

> O Saint Germain, my body pure,
> your violet flame for all is cure,
> consume the cause of all disease,
> and therefore I am all at ease.

> **O Saint Germain, what love you bring,**
> **it truly makes all matter sing,**
> **your violet flame does all restore,**
> **with you we are becoming more.**

7. Gautama Buddha, awaken the most creative people to see that we have a memory that violence and force does not work. The proof of this is that we have democracies, which is an attempt to create a society that is not based on violence and force, it is based on human rights that are respected by the leaders of society.

> O Saint Germain, I'm karma-free,
> the past no longer burdens me,

a brand new opportunity,
I am in Christic unity.

**O Saint Germain, what love you bring,
it truly makes all matter sing,
your violet flame does all restore,
with you we are becoming more.**

8. Gautama Buddha, awaken the most creative people to see that a democracy is not based on violence and force, and therefore it cannot be based on an ideology that says that a democracy can only be established through violence and force.

O Saint Germain, we are now one,
I am for you a violet sun,
as we transform this planet earth,
your Golden Age is given birth.

**O Saint Germain, what love you bring,
it truly makes all matter sing,
your violet flame does all restore,
with you we are becoming more.**

9. Gautama Buddha, awaken the most creative people to see that we need to do away with this idea that something has gone wrong and needs to be corrected. Democracy is *not* based on the idea of something having gone wrong, but that we need to transcend the former state into a higher state.

O Saint Germain, the earth is free,
from burden of duality,
in oneness we bring what is best,
your Golden Age is manifest.

**O Saint Germain, what love you bring,
it truly makes all matter sing,
your violet flame does all restore,
with you we are becoming more.**

Part 4

1. Gautama Buddha, awaken the most creative people to see that there is a fundamental difference. In the ideological approach, we identify a problem, a cause of the problem, and the only way to solve the problem is to destroy the cause of the problem, which is why it is sometimes necessary to destroy certain groups of people.

Divine Director, I now see,
the world is unreality,
in my heart I now truly feel,
the Spirit is all that is real.

**Divine Director, send the light,
from blindness clear my inner sight,
my vision free, my vision clear,
your guidance is forever here.**

2. Gautama Buddha, awaken the most creative people to see that in the democratic approach, it is not necessary to destroy a problem. It is necessary to transcend it, which is what many democratic nations have done. They have transcended their former state. Every aspect of society has been transcended in order to get to where the modern democracies are today.

Divine Director, vision give,
in clarity I want to live,
I now behold my plan Divine,
the plan that is uniquely mine.

**Divine Director, send the light,
from blindness clear my inner sight,
my vision free, my vision clear,
your guidance is forever here.**

3. Gautama Buddha, awaken the most creative people to see that some democratic nations have not yet transcended the idea of force. The

Founding Fathers of America thought they could only establish an independent nation through violence and force.

> Divine Director, show in me,
> the ego games, and set me free,
> help me escape the ego's cage,
> to help bring in the golden age.

> **Divine Director, send the light,**
> **from blindness clear my inner sight,**
> **my vision free, my vision clear,**
> **your guidance is forever here.**

4. Gautama Buddha, awaken the most creative people to see that the American nation has not yet freed itself from this mindset, which is why there is still so much violence and force in American society.

> Divine Director, I'm with you,
> my vision one, no longer two,
> as karma's veil you do disperse,
> I see a whole new universe.

> **Divine Director, send the light,**
> **from blindness clear my inner sight,**
> **my vision free, my vision clear,**
> **your guidance is forever here.**

5. Gautama Buddha, awaken the most creative people to see that the way to make more progress is to let go of the entire mindset behind ideology that something has gone wrong. Instead of destroying something that has gone wrong, we transcend it into a higher state.

> Divine Director, I go up,
> electric light now fills my cup,
> consume in me all shadows old,
> bestow on me a vision bold.

> **Divine Director, send the light,**
> **from blindness clear my inner sight,**

**my vision free, my vision clear,
your guidance is forever here.**

6. Gautama Buddha, awaken the most creative people to see that the principle behind the scientific method is that we have a certain view of the world, we observe, we make experiments, and then we transcend the old view and adopt a higher view.

Divine Director, heart of gold,
my sacred labor I unfold,
o blessed Guru, I now see,
where my own plan is taking me.

**Divine Director, send the light,
from blindness clear my inner sight,
my vision free, my vision clear,
your guidance is forever here.**

7. Gautama Buddha, awaken the most creative people to see that ideologies are defined by somebody. There is always a single person or an elite of people who are defining an ideology, who are interpreting it, who are executing it. The vast majority of the people either accept it and submit to it or they resist it.

Divine Director, by your grace,
in grander scheme I find my place,
my individual flame I see,
uniqueness God has given me.

**Divine Director, send the light,
from blindness clear my inner sight,
my vision free, my vision clear,
your guidance is forever here.**

8. Gautama Buddha, awaken the most creative people to see that for most people, the ideology comes to them from outside their own minds. It is an impersonal, non-personal ideology.

Divine Director, vision one,
I see that I AM God's own Sun,
with your direction so Divine,
I am now letting my light shine.

**Divine Director, send the light,
from blindness clear my inner sight,
my vision free, my vision clear,
your guidance is forever here.**

9. Gautama Buddha, awaken the most creative people to see that the reality simulator on earth is an ingeniously designed piece of machinery. The purpose of the machinery is to give those who are inside the reality simulator an experience that they want to have and that seems completely real to them.

Divine Director, what a gift,
to be a part of Spirit's lift,
to raise mankind out of the night,
to bask in Spirit's loving sight.

**Divine Director, send the light,
from blindness clear my inner sight,
my vision free, my vision clear,
your guidance is forever here.**

Sealing

In the name of the I AM THAT I AM, I accept that Archangel Michael, Astrea and Shiva form an impenetrable shield around myself and all constructive people, sealing us from all fear-based energies in all four octaves. I accept that the Light of God is consuming and transforming all fear-based energies that make up the dark forces working against ending the era of ideology on earth!

28 INVOKING AWARENESS OF PERSONAL IDEOLOGY (PART 3)

In the name of the I AM THAT I AM, Jesus Christ, I use the authority that I have as a being in embodiment on earth to call upon Gautama Buddha to reinforce my calls and use my chakras to project the statements in this invocation into the collective consciousness and awaken people to the need to free ourselves from the ideological mindset. Awaken people to the reality that we are spiritual beings and that we can co-create a new future by working with the ascended masters. I especially call for …

[Make your own calls here.]

Part 1

1. Gautama Buddha, awaken the most creative people to see that the earth is a very diverse planet. People are very diverse, they are at different levels of consciousness, they have different looks, features, ideas, beliefs and desires. They are so diverse that it is hard to find common denominators.

Gautama, show my mental state
that does give rise to love and hate,
your exposé I do endure,
so my perception will be pure.

Gautama, Flame of Cosmic Peace,
unruly thoughts do hereby cease,
we radiate from you and me
the peace to still Samsara's Sea.

2. Gautama Buddha, awaken the most creative people to see that people are having many different experiences on earth. Different groups of people have a certain collective experience, but the collective experience of one group is different from another group.

Gautama, in your Flame of Peace,
the struggling self I now release,
the Buddha Nature I now see,
it is the core of you and me.

Gautama, Flame of Cosmic Peace,
unruly thoughts do hereby cease,
we radiate from you and me
the peace to still Samsara's Sea.

3. Gautama Buddha, awaken the most creative people to see that it is amazing that there can be seven billion people on this planet and there are so many different experiences that these people are having, yet all of them are convinced that their experience is real.

Gautama, I am one with thee,
Mara's demons do now flee,
your Presence like a soothing balm,
my mind and senses ever calm.

Gautama, Flame of Cosmic Peace,
unruly thoughts do hereby cease,
we radiate from you and me
the peace to still Samsara's Sea.

4. Gautama Buddha, awaken the most creative people to see that this is possible because each human being has four lower bodies, each human being has over many lifetimes put certain contents in those four lower bodies, and they form a perception filter.

Gautama, I now take the vow,
to live in the eternal now,
with you I do transcend all time,
to live in present so sublime.

Gautama, Flame of Cosmic Peace,
unruly thoughts do hereby cease,
we radiate from you and me
the peace to still Samsara's Sea.

5. Gautama Buddha, awaken the most creative people to see that it is this perception filter that shapes the individual experience that people are having. It also makes them feel that their experience is entirely real.

Gautama, I have no desire,
to nothing earthly I aspire,
in non-attachment I now rest,
passing Mara's subtle test.

Gautama, Flame of Cosmic Peace,
unruly thoughts do hereby cease,
we radiate from you and me
the peace to still Samsara's Sea.

6. Gautama Buddha, awaken the most creative people to see that there are some ideologies that come to people from the outside, ultimately from the power elite beings. They are taking in these ideologies from the outside.

Gautama, I melt into you,
my mind is one, no longer two,
immersed in your resplendent glow,
Nirvana is all that I know.

Gautama, Flame of Cosmic Peace,
unruly thoughts do hereby cease,
we radiate from you and me
the peace to still Samsara's Sea.

7. Gautama Buddha, awaken the most creative people to see that what determines whether one person accepts or rejects a particular ideology is how that ideology resonates with the ideology they have inside their minds. Over many lifetimes, all human beings on earth have created a personal ideology and it is part of our perception filter.

Gautama, in your timeless space,
I am immersed in Cosmic Grace,
I know the God beyond all form,
to world I will no more conform.

Gautama, Flame of Cosmic Peace,
unruly thoughts do hereby cease,
we radiate from you and me
the peace to still Samsara's Sea.

8. Gautama Buddha, awaken the most creative people to see that this personal ideology may have certain elements based on one of the collective ideologies. It may have many things in common with other people in the same group.

Gautama, I am now awake,
I clearly see what is at stake,
and thus I claim my sacred right
to be on earth the Buddhic Light.

Gautama, Flame of Cosmic Peace,
unruly thoughts do hereby cease,
we radiate from you and me
the peace to still Samsara's Sea.

9. Gautama Buddha, awaken the most creative people to see that each person has an individual personal ideology, an individual personal worldview, created over many lifetimes partly adapted to the situation we are facing

in this lifetime. We came to accept a certain ideology because it resonated with something in us.

> Gautama, with your thunderbolt,
> we give the earth a mighty jolt,
> I know that some will understand,
> and join the Buddha's timeless band.

> **Gautama, Flame of Cosmic Peace,**
> **unruly thoughts do hereby cease,**
> **we radiate from you and me**
> **the peace to still Samsara's Sea.**

Part 2

1. Gautama Buddha, awaken the most creative people to see that everybody is having a personal ideology that forms the foundation for how we interact with the world. This ideology has the same basic components as impersonal ideologies, and it needs to explain why we are suffering.

> O Shiva, God of Sacred Fire,
> It's time to let the past expire,
> I want to rise above the old,
> a golden future to unfold.

> **O Shiva, clear the energy,**
> **O Shiva, bring the synergy,**
> **O Shiva, make all demons flee,**
> **O Shiva, bring back peace to me.**

2. Gautama Buddha, awaken the most creative people to see that a personal ideology needs to have some explanation of how the world works that to us explains why we are suffering, why there are certain things we cannot achieve, why we are limited beings, why we have to accept our lot in life.

O Shiva, come and set me free,
from forces that do limit me,
with fire consume all that is less,
paving way for my success.

O Shiva, clear the energy,
O Shiva, bring the synergy,
O Shiva, make all demons flee,
O Shiva, bring back peace to me.

3. Gautama Buddha, awaken the most creative people to see that we need to have hope that there could be improvement to our situation. Our personal ideology has some ideas for what changes could be brought about in society.

O Shiva, Maya's veil disperse,
clear my private universe,
dispel the consciousness of death,
consume it with your Sacred Breath.

O Shiva, clear the energy,
O Shiva, bring the synergy,
O Shiva, make all demons flee,
O Shiva, bring back peace to me.

4. Gautama Buddha, awaken the most creative people to see that since we clearly observe that there are other people that disagree with us, there is also the concept of a struggle because there are other people who do not believe what we believe.

O Shiva, I hereby let go,
of all attachments here below,
addictive entities consume,
the upward path I do resume.

O Shiva, clear the energy,
O Shiva, bring the synergy,
O Shiva, make all demons flee,
O Shiva, bring back peace to me.

5. Gautama Buddha, awaken the most creative people to see that the personal ideology also contains a desire for commitment. Some people dedicate their lives to fighting for a cause, however they conceive of it. Others are more balanced because over many lifetimes they have experienced fighting for these causes.

O Shiva, I recite your name,
come banish fear and doubt and shame,
with fire expose within my mind,
what ego seeks to hide behind.

O Shiva, clear the energy,
O Shiva, bring the synergy,
O Shiva, make all demons flee,
O Shiva, bring back peace to me.

6. Gautama Buddha, awaken the most creative people to see that those who make the commitment feel they have the absolute cause, and they often feel superior to those who do not agree with their cause.

O Shiva, I am not afraid,
my karmic debt hereby is paid,
the past no longer owns my choice,
in breath of Shiva I rejoice.

O Shiva, clear the energy,
O Shiva, bring the synergy,
O Shiva, make all demons flee,
O Shiva, bring back peace to me.

7. Gautama Buddha, awaken the most creative people to see that the personal ideology has the same elements as the collective ideologies, which is why people accept the ideologies that come from without.

O Shiva, show me spirit pairs,
that keep me trapped in their affairs,
I choose to see within my mind,
the spirits that you surely bind.

O Shiva, clear the energy,
O Shiva, bring the synergy,
O Shiva, make all demons flee,
O Shiva, bring back peace to me.

8. Gautama Buddha, awaken the most creative people to see that many people have lived in the ideological mindset for many lifetimes. Many have incarnated in the modern democracies because they are the societies that are the least based on the ideological approach. They do not have the violence that these people have seen.

O Shiva, naked I now stand,
my mind in freedom does expand,
as all my ghosts I do release,
surrender is the key to peace.

O Shiva, clear the energy,
O Shiva, bring the synergy,
O Shiva, make all demons flee,
O Shiva, bring back peace to me.

9. Gautama Buddha, awaken the most creative people to see that we need to take a look at this and take a look at ourselves. This is the culmination of the process that Jesus started 2,000 years ago and that the Buddha started 2,500 years ago of causing us to look at ourselves.

O Shiva, all-consuming fire,
with Parvati raise me higher,
when I am raised your light to see,
all men I will draw onto me.

O Shiva, clear the energy,
O Shiva, bring the synergy,
O Shiva, make all demons flee,
O Shiva, bring back peace to me.

Part 3

1. Gautama Buddha, awaken the most creative people to see that in their original forms, Buddhism and Christianity were teachings that are beyond ideologies because they seek to liberate us. They always tell us to look at ourselves because the key to our personal liberation is inside our own minds.

> Surya, cosmic being bright,
> your balance is my pure delight,
> I am in orbit round God Star,
> in perfect unity we are.
>
> **Surya, banish all extremes,**
> **Surya, shatter Serpent's schemes,**
> **Surya, balance to me bring,**
> **Surya, making my heart sing.**

2. Gautama Buddha, awaken the most creative people to realize that the key to changing our personal life experience is inside our minds. It is to work with the mind, learn how the psyche works, find a way to free ourselves from what limits us.

> Surya, there is more to life,
> than human conflict, war and strife,
> your balance gives me inner peace,
> all outer conflicts do now cease.
>
> **Surya, banish all extremes,**
> **Surya, shatter Serpent's schemes,**
> **Surya, balance to me bring,**
> **Surya, making my heart sing.**

3. Gautama Buddha, awaken the most creative people to see that what limits us is our personal ideology, because that personal ideology was created in response to life on earth, on this very chaotic, disharmonious planet.

Surya, what a wondrous sight,
from Sirius you send the light,
of one mind, I now call to thee,
for your apprentice I would be.

Surya, banish all extremes,
Surya, shatter Serpent's schemes,
Surya, balance to me bring,
Surya, making my heart sing.

4. Gautama Buddha, awaken the most creative people to see that over many lifetimes, we have been confronted with very violent, chaotic and traumatic circumstances. In order to be able to deal with this psychologically, we have created this personal ideology.

Surya, radiate your light,
with balance you set all things right,
consuming energetic dross,
my letting go is not a loss.

Surya, banish all extremes,
Surya, shatter Serpent's schemes,
Surya, balance to me bring,
Surya, making my heart sing.

5. Gautama Buddha, awaken the most creative people to see that we are now at the point where we have had enough of this, we are ready to transcend the personal ideology. This requires us to look into our own minds, to come to see the ideology, see the beliefs that it is based on and start questioning those beliefs.

Surya, your light is alive,
for inner balance I do strive,
the alchemy is now begun,
my heart transformed into a sun.

Surya, banish all extremes,
Surya, shatter Serpent's schemes,

Surya, balance to me bring,
Surya, making my heart sing.

6. Gautama Buddha, awaken the most creative people to see that in many of the modern democracies there is a rising awareness of the importance of psychology, the importance of working with the mind. Behind this is this desire to improve our life experience by seeking to change ourselves instead of seeking to change the conditions outside ourselves.

Surya, come enlighten me,
duality you help me see,
extremes they cannot pull me in,
on Middle Way I always win.

Surya, banish all extremes,
Surya, shatter Serpent's schemes,
Surya, balance to me bring,
Surya, making my heart sing.

7. Gautama Buddha, awaken the most creative people to come to see the limitations of these ideologies, both the external and the internal, and the need to question them. Help us adopt the mindset that instead of having an idea of how the mind *should* work, we look for how the mind or the world actually *does* work.

Surya, in your cosmic sphere,
with Cuzco I your light revere,
from your perspective o so grand,
life finally I understand.

Surya, banish all extremes,
Surya, shatter Serpent's schemes,
Surya, balance to me bring,
Surya, making my heart sing.

8. Gautama Buddha, awaken the most creative people to see that there is a spiritual realm. There are spiritual beings who serve as the teachers of humankind, and they have given teachings. The vertical way to gain

knowledge is ultimately to receive revelation from the spiritual realm, from the ascended masters.

Surya, show me God's design,
I see that God is all benign,
you calm my feeling body's storm,
I know the God beyond all form.

Surya, banish all extremes,
Surya, shatter Serpent's schemes,
Surya, balance to me bring,
Surya, making my heart sing.

9. Gautama Buddha, awaken the most creative people to see that such a revelation is beyond ideology. A teaching that is given to liberate people is not in itself an ideology.

Surya, I come from afar,
and as you show me my home star,
I see now my internal light,
a star I am in my own right.

Surya, banish all extremes,
Surya, shatter Serpent's schemes,
Surya, balance to me bring,
Surya, making my heart sing.

Part 4

1. Gautama Buddha, awaken the most creative people to see that a teaching given by the power elite beings in order to deceive, manipulate and control us, that *is* in itself an ideology. It is defined as an ideology. However, even such an ideology does not become an ideology until people go into the ideological mindset and seek to force it upon others.

Beloved Alpha, God's great plan,
in Central Sun it all began,

what wondrous vision of a world,
the cosmic spheres were then unfurled.

Beloved Alpha, in your light,
I now see God with inner sight,
as man I will no longer live,
my life to God I fully give.

2. Gautama Buddha, awaken the most creative people to see that there are teachings in the world that have the capacity to help people transcend themselves, and even to help them transcend the external ideologies. Some teachings have the capacity to help people transcend the internal ideologies.

Beloved Alpha, serve the All,
this is Creator's timeless call,
from out Creator's perfect whole,
sprang lifestreams with a sacred goal.

Beloved Alpha, in your light,
I now see God with inner sight,
as man I will no longer live,
my life to God I fully give.

3. Gautama Buddha, awaken the most creative people to see that the highest purpose of any teaching is not to bring forth an ultimate truth but to bring forth something that can help people raise their consciousness to the next level where they can then receive a higher teaching.

Beloved Alpha, all was one,
as we were sent from Central Sun,
to you we shall in time return,
for cosmic union we do yearn.

Beloved Alpha, in your light,
I now see God with inner sight,
as man I will no longer live,
my life to God I fully give.

4. Gautama Buddha, awaken the most creative people to see that the purpose of bringing forth a teaching in today's world is to help those people who are ready to transcend their present level of consciousness and to help societies who are ready to transcend their present level and come up higher.

Beloved Alpha, I now see,
you with Omega form the key,
it was from your polarity,
that I received identity.

Beloved Alpha, in your light,
I now see God with inner sight,
as man I will no longer live,
my life to God I fully give.

5. Gautama Buddha, awaken the most creative people to see that when we have come up higher, Saint Germain will be able to release an even higher teaching that will take us further into the golden age mindset. This process can continue for the next 2,000-year period of Saint Germain's Golden Age.

Beloved Alpha, cosmic gate,
the nexus of your figure-eight,
I sprang from Cosmic Cube so bright,
I am at heart a spark of light.

Beloved Alpha, in your light,
I now see God with inner sight,
as man I will no longer live,
my life to God I fully give.

6. Gautama Buddha, awaken the most creative people to make the shift that will effectively end the era of ideology on earth. The end of ideology does not mean that ideology is completely eradicated, that the ideological mindset is completely eradicated.

Beloved Alpha, from your womb,
I did descend to matter's tomb,

but buried I will be no more,
my inner vision you restore.

**Beloved Alpha, in your light,
I now see God with inner sight,
as man I will no longer live,
my life to God I fully give.**

7. Gautama Buddha, awaken the most creative people to see that we can help move the planet to a point where a critical mass has been built, and effectively the planet has moved beyond the era of ideology, even though there will still be some groups of people that are stuck in it.

Beloved Alpha, I now know,
the love you did on me bestow,
a co-creator, I will bring,
the light to make all matter sing.

**Beloved Alpha, in your light,
I now see God with inner sight,
as man I will no longer live,
my life to God I fully give.**

8. Gautama Buddha, awaken the most creative people to look for remnants of the ideological consciousness and our ideological approach to spiritual teachings, and letting those selves die when we separate ourselves from them.

Beloved Alpha, on this earth,
a new age we are giving birth,
for we are here to bring the love,
that you are sending from Above.

**Beloved Alpha, in your light,
I now see God with inner sight,
as man I will no longer live,
my life to God I fully give.**

9. Gautama Buddha, I say with you: **There is no more space on earth for ideology, or the mindset of ideology.** (3X or more)

> Beloved Alpha, you and me,
> we form a true polarity,
> as up Above, so here below,
> with life's own river I do flow.
>
> **Beloved Alpha, in your light,**
> **I now see God with inner sight,**
> **as man I will no longer live,**
> **my life to God I fully give.**

Sealing

In the name of the I AM THAT I AM, I accept that Archangel Michael, Astrea and Shiva form an impenetrable shield around myself and all constructive people, sealing us from all fear-based energies in all four octaves. I accept that the Light of God is consuming and transforming all fear-based energies that make up the dark forces working against ending the era of ideology on earth!

9 788879 329782 1